The Crisis in
Youth Mental Health

Recent Titles in Child Psychology and Mental Health

THE CRISIS IN YOUTH MENTAL HEALTH

Critical Issues and Effective Programs

Volume 1

Childhood Disorders

Hiram E. Fitzgerald, Barry M. Lester, and Barry Zuckerman

Volume Editors

Hiram E. Fitzgerald, Robert Zucker, and Kristine Freeark

Editors in Chief

Praeger Perspectives
Child Psychology and Mental Health

Hiram E. Fitzgerald and Susanne Ayres Denham, Series Editors

Westport, Connecticut
London

KH

Library of Congress Cataloging-in-Publication Data

The crisis in youth mental health : understanding the critical issues and effective programs / editors Hiram E. Fitzgerald, Robert Zucker, and Kristine Freeark.
    p. cm.—(Child psychology and mental health)
    Includes bibliographical references and index.
    ISBN 0-275-98480-X (set : alk. paper)—ISBN 0-275-98481-8 (v. 1 : alk. paper)—
    ISBN 0-275-98482-6 (v.2 : alk. paper)—ISBN 0-275-98483-4 (v.3 : alk. paper)—
    ISBN 0-275-98484-2 (v.4 : alk. paper) 1. Adolescent psychopathology. 2. Child psychotherapy. 3. Youth--Counseling of. 4. Community mental health services.
    I. Fitzgerald, Hiram E. II. Zucker, Robert A. III. Freeark, Kristine. IV. Series.

RJ503.C76 2006
618.92'8914—dc22   2005030767

British Library Cataloguing in Publication Data is available.

Library of Congress Catalog Card Number: 2005030767
ISBN: 0–275–98480–X (set)
      0–275–98481–8 (vol. 1)
      0–275–98482–6 (vol. 2)
      0–275–98483–4 (vol. 3)
      0–275–98484–2 (vol. 4)
ISSN: 1538–8883

First published in 2006

Praeger Publishers, 88 Post Road West, Westport, CT 06881
An imprint of Greenwood Publishing Group, Inc.
www.praeger.com

Printed in the United States of America

The paper used in this book complies with the Permanent Paper Standard issued by the National Information Standards Organization (Z39.48–1984).

10 9 8 7 6 5 4 3 2 1

2/8/07

CONTENTS

SERIES FOREWORD

The twentieth century closed with a decade devoted to the study of brain structure, function, and development that in parallel with studies of the human genome has revealed the extraordinary plasticity of biobehavioral organization and development. The twenty-first century opens with a decade focusing on behavior, but the linkages between brain and behavior are as dynamic as the linkages between parents and children, and children and environment.

The Child Psychology and Mental Health series is designed to capture much of this dynamic interplay by advocating for strengthening the science of child development and linking that science to issues related to mental health, child care, parenting and public policy.

The series consists of individual monographs, each dealing with a subject that advanced knowledge related to the interplay between normal developmental process and developmental psychopathology. The books are intended to reflect the diverse methodologies and content areas encompassed by an age period ranging from conception to late adolescence. Topics of contemporary interest include studies of socio-emotional development, behavioral undercontrol, aggression, attachment disorders and substance abuse.

Investigators involved with prospective longitudinal studies, large epidemiologic cross-sectional samples, intensely followed clinical cases or those wishing to report a systematic sequence of connected experiments are invited to submit manuscripts. Investigators from all fields in social and behavioral sciences, neurobiological sciences, medical and clinical sciences and education are invited to submit manuscripts with implications for child and adolescent mental health.

Hiram E. Fitzgerald
Susanne Ayres Denham
Series Editors

ACKNOWLEDGMENTS

This project began at a lunch meeting when Norman Watt, Robert Bradley, Catherine Ayoub, Jini Puma and Hi Fitzgerald concluded that there was a great need for a book that summarized the benefits of early intervention. Shortly after agreeing to pursue such a book, Deborah Carvalko, acquisitions editor at Greenwood Publishing Group, contacted Hi to inquire if he knew anyone who would be interested in editing a series on the Crisis in Youth Mental Health. Bingo! This four-volume set is the result and volume 4 is that original lunch time project. The volumes represent a product forged from the labor and energy of an editorial team composed of long-time and current research and professional colleagues: Catherine Ayoub, Robert Bradley, William Davidson, Hiram Fitzgerald, Kristine Freeark, Whitney LeBoeuf, Barry Lester, Tom Luster, Jini Puma, Francisco Villarruel, Norman Watt, Robert Zucker, and Barry Zuckerman. Each editorial team drafted an extraordinary set of researchers who collectively frame the parameters of the crisis in youth mental health, provide cogent analyses of effective evidence-based preventive-intervention programs, and draw attention to policy implications of their work. Volumes such as these are labors of professional and personal love because the rewards to be gained are only those realized by the impact that words and ideas have on current and future generations of scientists, parents, and policy makers. No one has more passion for bringing science to bear on the problems of society than Lou Anna K. Simon, President of Michigan State University. In her commentary, she eloquently and forcefully articulates the need to forge campus–community partnerships, using evidence-based practices to both understand and resolve community-based problems.

Editors and authors provide the grist for anthologies, but there are many millers that grind the grain and bake it into a final loaf. First to thank is Deborah Carvalko who provided the opportunity to even imagine the project. Lisa Pierce, senior development editor at Praeger Press made sure that this host of contributors met their deadlines. Apex Publishing, assisted by four extremely meticulous and energetic copy editors (Ellie Amico [vol. 1], Bruce Owens [vol. 2], Caryl Knutsen [vol. 3], and Carol Burwash [vol. 4]), moved everyone through a tight time frame for copy editing and page proofs, assured cross-volume uniformity in format and style, removed split infinitives, identified missing references, and translated academic language into a more common prose. Finally, at Michigan State University, Vasiliki Mousouli was the diligent project manager who maintained contact with more than 60 editors, authors, and publishers, organized and tracked all of the manuscript activity, and made final format corrections for APA style. In her spare time she managed to complete her doctoral program requirements in school psychology and successfully defend her doctoral dissertation.

What began as lunchtime table talk, resulted in four volumes that collectively summarize much about the crisis in youth mental health. All involved have our deepest respect and thanks for their contributions.

Hiram E. Fitzgerald
Kristine Freeark
Robert A. Zucker

SPECIAL COMMENTARY: UNIVERSITIES AND THE CRISIS IN YOUTH MENTAL HEALTH

Lou Anna Kimsey Simon
President, Michigan State University

There are at least two key reasons why universities are concerned about the Crisis in Youth Mental Health. First, increasing numbers of students matriculating at colleges and universities have mental health problems. Because social and emotional well-being is paramount to academic success and to the ability to negotiate the demands of the workplace, universities must be concerned about student social-emotional health. Second, understanding the causes and life course progression of mental health problems relates directly to the scholarship mission of the university, especially those with historical ties to the land grant system of higher education. Land grant universities, established by the Morrill Act of 1862, were founded to allow all citizens access to higher education and to bind together the scholarships of discovery and application. Thus, land grant universities are about values and beliefs regarding the social role and social responsibility of universities with respect to ameliorating the problems of society.

In 2005, Michigan State University celebrates its 150th anniversary as an academic institution, and in 2012 it will celebrate its 150th anniversary as the first land grant university. We have been actively engaged in a campus conversation concerning the role of land grant institutions in the twenty-first century, and much of that conversation has focused on renewing the covenant between higher education and the public that higher education serves. When land grant institutions were founded, the focus of that covenant was on agricultural production and the mechanical arts. Today, the covenant extends to the broad range of problems in contemporary society, not the least of which are those associated with the causes, treatments, and prevention of mental health problems.

Professional and public documents increasingly draw attention to the pervasive problems affecting children throughout the United States and the world. Considering all forms of mental illness, recent studies indicate that half of the population will experience a mental health problem sometime during the life course. In the United States, 1 in 10 children and adolescents suffer from mental illness severe enough to cause some level of impairment, but only 1 in 5 receive treatment. Most mental health problems are transitory and relatively easily resolved by brief interventions, including support from mental health professionals, friends, family members, or other individuals in one's social support network. Epidemiologists report that approximately six percent of the population experiences profound mental health problems and may require psychotrophic medications and intense psychotherapy to maintain manageable levels of adaptive behavior. However, there is an increasing number of individuals who deal with mental health problems at a level of severity that lies between the ordinary and the profound. The number of children with learning disabilities, speech and language handicaps, mental retardation, emotional disturbances, poor self-regulatory skills, aggressive behavior, substance abuse disorders, and poor school achievement is increasing at alarming rates. 17 percent of all children in the United States have one or more developmental disabilities; 20 percent of all school age children have attention problems; and the age of first onset of drug use, smoking, and sexual activity continues to spiral downward (Fitzgerald, Lester, & Zuckerman, 2000; Koger, Schettler, & Weiss, 2005).

Collectively, students enrolled in higher education represent the rich spectrum of America's ethnic, racial, political, gender, religious, and physical diversity. If higher education does its job well, students will be challenged to examine their personal beliefs and values against this diversity, arriving at deeper understanding of their own values as well as those of others, both of which are implicit to sustaining a free, democratic, and diverse society. For many students, such free-ranging discussion and debate is exciting, provocative, and enriching. Other students may encounter diversity that is beyond their prior experience, and public discourse and challenge to their personal beliefs may provoke anxiety and distress. The mental health crisis among America's youth directly translates to a mental health crisis on America's college and university campuses. Increasing numbers of students report suicide ideation, feelings of hopelessness, depression, and anxiety, and a sense of being overwhelmed (Kadison & DiGeronimo, 2004). Increasing numbers of these students come from broken families, and many come from stressful neighborhoods and communities. The crisis in youth mental health contributes to the crisis in college student mental health, and both challenge university capacity to provide the depth of support necessary to help students maintain psychological and behavioral health in the context of pressures for academic success.

The good news is that prevention specialists from many different disciplines have developed evidence-based programs that not only have positive impacts on child behavior, but also have positive impacts on families and communities. This four-volume set was designed to affirm principles underlying the importance of prevention and the view that individual development is best understood within the framework of systems theory. Systems theory begins with the premise that from the moment of conception, the organism is embedded within an increasingly complex array of systems (family, neighborhood, school, community, society) and that all components mutually transact to shape development over the life course. The contextual embeddedness of mental health problems, therefore, requires perspectives from a broad range of social, behavioral, economic, and biomedical sciences as well as the arts and humanities, in order to understand behavior-in-context. Thus, universities are uniquely positioned to make significant contributions to the understanding and remediation of mental health problems because universities are the repositories of all of the disciplines and can provide the means for interdisciplinary, systemic research and the development and assessment of prevention and treatment approaches. Moreover, from a land grant perspective, such research and development activities gain even greater authenticity when conducted within the context of campus-community partnerships for health and well being.

Resolving the crisis in youth mental health is essential for maintenance of a mentally healthy society, because youth comprise society's future policy and political leadership. Universities contribute to the resolution by providing a range of wrap-around supportive structures and services and by building stronger campus-community partnerships in health. Equally important for universities is a commitment to search for causal factors that shape developmental pathways that generate mental health problems, to develop biomedical and behavior treatments, and to discover successful ways to prevent or ameliorate mental health problems early in development. The chapters in *The Crisis in Youth Mental Health* focus attention to each of these objectives.

REFERENCES

Fitzgerald, H. E., Lester, B. M., & Zuckerman, B. (Eds.). (2000). *Children of addiction: Research, health, and policy issues.* New York: Garland.

Kadison, R. D., & DiGeronimo, T. F. (2004). *College of the overwhelmed: The campus mental health crisis and what to do about it.* Boston: Jossey-Bass.

Koger, S. M., Schettler, T., & Weiss, B. (2005). Environmental toxicants and developmental disabilities. *American Psychologist 60,* 243–255.

Chapter 1

PERSPECTIVES ON STRESS AND SELF-REGULATORY PROCESSES

Kevin Everhart and Robert N. Emde

Kevin Everhart was supported in part by a Ruth L. Kirshstein Individual National Research Service Award, Program for Early Developmental Studies, University of Colorado Health Sciences Center, Denver, Colorado, and an Institutional National Research Service Award, Developmental Psychobiology Research Training Program, University of Colorado Health Sciences Center, Denver, Colorado.

IT TAKES ALL THE RUNNING YOU CAN DO, TO KEEP IN THE SAME PLACE

The Red Queen's lament in Lewis Carroll's "Through the Looking Glass" aptly captures the stress of maintaining status and access to resources in contemporary Western society. This analogy has been explored in the field of evolutionary biology by van Valen (1973), and more recently by Heylighen (1999), who note that when competition for resources leads to the improved adaptation of one population within an ecosystem, concomitant adaptation is required by other populations to avoid decreased survival rate. From the standpoint of evolution, the example of trees in a forest competing for sunlight (van Valen, 1973) nicely illustrates this concept. Any tree that penetrates the forest canopy represents a barrier to sunlight for the trees below it. Thus, the growth of one tree necessitates the increased growth of those around it just simply to preserve the current level of access to sunlight.

As a corollary, recent research on socioeconomic status and health suggests that the stress of keeping pace in competitive societies represents a potent force in shaping health and developmental trajectories (Hertzman & Keating,

1999; Wilkinson, 2001). To answer the tree illustration with a human one, the investment of time and energy necessary to graduate from high school may remain relatively constant, even as the marketable value of a high school education precipitously declines. To avoid falling into poverty, the expenditure of additional resources, in the form of training and education, becomes necessary to acquire skills of a commensurate value to the former value of a high school diploma.

The term "socioeconomic gradient" has been used to denote relative status disparities within a given culture. Such gradients appear to be an emergent characteristic of animal and human social organization and are a property of all cultural and social achievement. Gradients reflect group structure, cooperation, and competition. Under steep gradient conditions, large disparities in wealth and status characterize the social landscape. Where gradients are less steep, populations are more homogeneous with regard to access to power and resources. Interestingly, gradient slope has emerged as a better predictor of health than variables such as education, access to medical services, and material wealth (Hertzman, 1999b; Wilkinson, 2001; Wilkinson, 1999). This suggests that the material benefits of wealth, as well as the ill effects of abject poverty, may be compounded or offset by the stress associated with acquiring and maintaining social position.

SOCIOECONOMIC GRADIENTS AND REGULATORY CAPACITIES: FIVE KEY IDEAS

This chapter draws upon five key ideas that relate socioeconomic gradients to self-regulatory capacities. The first key idea is that of the hospitable or optimal niche (Hertzman, 1999a). For each individual, a hypothetical, optimal social and physical environment exists. Within such an environment, genetic capacities for health and adaptation (i.e., protective factors) are optimized, while those for disease and maladaptation (i.e., risk factors) are minimized. The second key idea, drawn from general systems theory, is that *self and social regulation are integral, inseparable processes.* From both an actual and symbolic standpoint, the self is always relational. The third key idea is that *regulation occurs over time and involves dynamic transactions of the individual within the social environment* (Sameroff & Emde, 1992). The fourth key idea is that *transactional effects are cumulative and can lead to canalization* (Gottlieb, 1991), such that relatively small events can trigger cascades in development. These cascades in development, or *multiplier effects* (Dickens & Flynn, 2001), lead to the amplification or mitigation of environmental influences on the ontogeny of the self, both as a consequence of intrinsic factors (e.g. gene-environment correlations} and cumulative environmental factors. From this perspective, individual multipliers (e.g., gender, temperament, ethnicity, verbal fluency, eating habits, and safety) may interact with social multipliers (e.g. access to health care, unemployment, neighborhood crime rates, racism, and stereotype threat) to moderate the relative status of individuals in relation to a hospitable or optimal niche.

Finally, a fifth key idea is that *multiplier effects are germane not only to individuals,* but to cohorts and populations, within cultural, geographical, and historical contexts. These effects may span generations, as with changes in media technology reaching and influencing behavior from radio, to television, to the Internet. From this perspective, multiplier effects may alter the slope of socioeconomic gradients for entire populations.

These five key ideas are integrated in our discussion of regulatory processes, which progresses from cultural and economic contexts, to gene-environment interactions, to parenting and co-regulation, to the development of self-regulatory processes. Figure 1.1 provides an overview of our contextual discussion of self-regulatory processes. At the level of the developing child, we focus on the multiplier effects of cumulative stress and adversity as a precursor to the development of maladaptive regulatory processes. Finally, we revisit the cultural and economic contexts of self-regulation from a socio-historical perspective, to discuss cohort effects and the implications of gradients and multiplier effects for understanding, and addressing the current crisis in children's mental health.

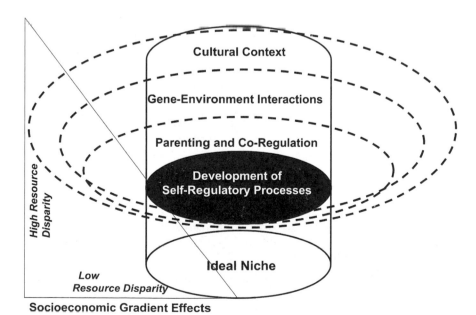

Figure 1.1 An overview of the social context of self-regulation in relation to socioeconomic gradient effects and the concept of the ideal niche

SOCIOECONOMIC GRADIENTS IN CULTURAL AND ECONOMIC CONTEXT

Numerous studies have established a clear link between gradient effects in industrialized countries and indices of population health and mortality. Central to this work has been work on the repercussions of economic disparities and relative poverty (Brooks-Gunn, Duncan, & Britto, 1999; Hertzman, 1999a; Lynch, Kaplan, & Shema, 1997; Wilkinson, 2001). The effects of socioeconomic gradients (Hertzman, 1999a) have been studied among states and provinces in North America, as well as among other nations. Level of income disparity has been associated with stability within the social milieu; the greater the level of income disparity, the greater the risk of gain or loss of wealth or status. Individuals who live in economies characterized by high levels of income disparity are likely to experience greater barriers, and higher risk of loss, in striving toward goals.

Research has linked gradient effects to community violence (Wilkinson, 1999; 2001; Wilkinson, Kawachi, & Kennedy, 1998). For example, it has been shown that state homicide rates closely correspond to rates of income inequality (Kaplan, Pamuk, Lynch, Cohen, & Balfour, 1996).Violence in communities with high income inequality occurs among those occupying the lowest strata of status and power. As Wilkinson has noted, competition for status is quite high under such conditions, and indications of slight or disrespect create heightened arousal (Wilkinson et al., 1998).

The apparent impact of socioeconomic gradients on the occurrence of violent behavior illustrates the manner in which gradient effects span both interpersonal and intrapersonal domains, linking social and self-regulation.

If we think of the steepness of socioeconomic gradients as being an index of competition for acquiring and maintaining access to power and resources, gradients can be conceptualized as a mechanism for regulating the extent to which individuals are able to access social and material capital. If the ontogeny of an individual represents a constructive, transactional process of interfacing genetic potentials and environmental press, gradients determine the probability of actualized potentials or averted vulnerabilities. For this reason, Hertzman (Hertzman, 1999a) has likened gradient effects as representing proximity to a hospitable or optimal niche. For any given individual, an optimal niche is a social context, reflected in status, in which resources are both abundant and can be protected without undue stress or threat of loss.

Resources that comprise an optimal niche may vary considerably in accordance with geopolitical, demographic, and economic characteristics. Nonetheless, it is proximity to an optimal niche, and the stress of maintaining proximity, that may have the most direct impact on the health and self-regulation. As proximity to an optimal niche increases, two things should occur. First, individual differences with regard to adaptive characteristics should become more evident, because access to power and resources should increase the agency with which individuals are able to construct hospitable environments. This is essentially a restatement of Bronfenbrenner and Ceci's (1994) hypothesis regarding proximal processes as mediating genetic expression within the ontogeny of the individual, such that, "when proximal processes are weak, genetically based potentials for effective psychological functioning remain relatively unrealized, but ... they become actualized to a progressively greater extent as proximal processes increase in magnitude" (p. 569). To this, we would add a second prediction, namely, that individual differences with regard to resiliency should become less evident, inasmuch as securing access to power and resources should decrease the stress of competition and cushion the impact of vulnerabilities and adversities. In other words, hospitable environments cover a multitude of risks.

Because socioeconomic gradients reflect both the social status and context of the developing individual, and an individual's access to material resources, it seems reasonable to suppose that gradients may mediate individual environmental interactions in development. This may be one way of interpreting Tremblay's (1999) report that similarity in levels of aggressive behavior among siblings varies as a function of socioeconomic status (SES). Tremblay found that among children living in low SES conditions, rates of aggressive behavior among siblings were significantly related. Conversely, siblings living in high SES conditions had dissimilar rates of aggressive behavior. Here the low SES environment appears to have a homogenizing effect on the expression of aggression among related individuals, suggesting that the adaptive value of aggressive behavior is likely to differ in accordance with proximity to the optimal niche. The idea that the relative adaptive value, and indeed purpose, of a given behavior may differ in association with gradient position and gradient steepness adds an additional layer of meaning to the complexity of individual-environment interactions. In other words, it becomes clear that parenting behaviors can be seen as mechanisms for the replication of regulatory strategies that are compatible with survival along a continuum of hostile to hospitable niches (Champagne & Meaney, 2001).

SOCIOECONOMIC GRADIENTS AND GENE-ENVIRONMENT INTERACTIONS

Attempts to statistically infer the relative contribution of genetics to the development of individual characteristics have relied on the analysis of identical, or monozygotic, and fraternal, or dizygotic, twins. Because dizygotic twins are as genetically dissimilar as other siblings, the contrast between the rate of similarities among dizygotic and those of identical twins provides a statistical basis for inferring the significance of environmental as well as heritable influences on development. Moreover, the study of twins makes it possible to assess gene-environment interactions, or instances in which genes are expressed only in particular environmental circumstances. Three recent twin studies illustrate gene-environment interactions for the circumstances of socioeconomic gradients. They illustrate the manner in which genes may interact with socioeconomic gradients to produce adaptive capacities or vulnerabilities. In a study of the physical health of a large sample of twins in relation to material wealth and perceived life control, Johnson and Krueger (2005) found an expected health advantage for those with greater material wealth. More interestingly, they identified a gene-environment interaction effect, in which higher socioeconomic status and higher perceived control were found to be associated with lower levels of health-related genetic variability. The reverse was also true, in that lower socioeconomic status and lower perceived life control were associated with higher levels in the expression of health-related genetic variability. In other words, wealth and status were shown in this study to have a homogenizing effect on health vulnerabilities, suggesting that wealth may reduce the risk for a myriad of potential health problems among individuals.

Recall that even as proximity to the optimal niche may dampen the vulnerability of individuals to health risks, such proximity should promulgate individual differences with regard to adaptation. This is precisely what Turkheimer and colleagues (2003) found in a twin study that examined the relative influence of heredity on the intelligence test performance of children as a function of socioeconomic status. These authors examined the extent to which performances on intelligence tests were similar among identical and fraternal twins, as a function of socioeconomic status. As might be expected from prior research, children from high SES families performed better than children from low SES families on a standardized intelligence test. However, of greater interest was the finding that the intelligence test scores for children from higher SES families were largely attributable to heredity, whereas the opposite was found among children from lower SES families.

The third, and perhaps most intriguing study was reported by Legrand, Iacono, and McGue (2005), in a discussion of unpublished results of a recent twin study that addressed the influence of heredity on the expression of externalizing behavior problems among individuals from urban, as opposed to rural communities. The authors report that although externalizing behavior problems appeared to be strongly influenced by hereditary among persons living in urban environments, almost no hereditary influence was evident among individuals from rural settings. Given that it is unlikely that significant genetic differences exist between these populations (McCord, 1999), the authors conclude that environmental factors mediate the expression of externalizing disorders. They suggest that the impetus for the observed difference between populations may be that urban environments provide a more complex array of environmental challenges capable of precipitating the expression of externalizing behavior problems.

While this interpretation seems plausible, particularly as an explanation for the multitude of different externalizing problems that may spring from a common diathesis, we suggest that socioeconomic gradients, in the context of urban poverty, may represent the primary impetus for a greater expression of externalizing behavior problems in urban populations. Support for the role of socioeconomic status in the expression of externalizing behavior is derived from a groundbreaking study by Costello, Compton, Keeler, and Angold (2003). The unique, quasi-experimental study occurred within the context of rapid economic change in a Native American community that opened a gambling casino during the time that Costello and colleagues were studying the prevalence of psychiatric disorders among children in the region. Examining the presence of both internalizing and externalizing behavior problems for four years prior to and after the opening of the casino, the researchers found that the mean number of externalizing symptoms decreased among children whose socioeconomic status increased as a result of shared casino earnings, dropping to a level consistent with that of children who had maintained a consistently high socioeconomic status. Conversely, children whose lower socioeconomic status did not improve (i.e., they remained at the low end of a steep gradient) continued to manifest higher rates of externalizing symptoms. Interestingly, the results were obtained only for externalizing symptoms; rates of anxiety and depressive symptoms were unaffected by improved socioeconomic status. Since the Costello et al. (2003) study was not conducted in an urban setting, its implications with regard to the twin data reported by Legrand, Iacono, and McGue (2005) are unclear. However, the findings of the Costello et al. (2003) study are consistent with those of studies conducted with urban populations that have linked the stress of poverty to antisociality (Eitle & Turner, 2002, 2003).

SOCIOECONOMIC GRADIENTS AND
PARENTING BEHAVIOR

Parents, as individuals, are lifetime participants in gradients. Several key studies of non-human primates illustrate possible mechanisms by which gradients may influence parenting and, in turn, the development of regulatory processes. Evidence from work with rhesus monkeys (Higley & Suomi, 1986; Suomi, 1999) suggests that low-ranking mothers are more restrictive of infant exploratory behavior than are high-ranking mothers, and that both low and high-ranking groups modify parenting to become more inhibiting in relation to increasing group instability (a corollary of degree of competition for status associated with gradient slope). Suomi (1999)has suggested that both instability and low-rank contribute to the probability of reprisals by higher-ranking group members against mothers of transgressing infants. Infants reared under these conditions evidence poorer social development and higher levels of hostility (Suomi, 1999). Research with baboon populations suggests that low-ranking individuals evidence elevated cortisol rates (found to be associated with aggression in humans) and are more likely to interpret ambiguous stimuli as threatening (Sapolsky, 2001). Thus, it would appear that low status may sensitize the stress-response system to be negatively biased to perceive threat, perpetuating the phenotypic expression of stress-responsive neurobiological systems, via caregiver behavior (Bremner & Vermetten, 2001; Bugental, Martorell, & Barraza, 2003; Franck, 2001; Gunnar & Vazquez, 2001) in order to foster aggressive adaptation in high stress environments. In considering the human interaction, Patterson (1995; 1999) echoes this position in emphasizing the transactional nature of coercive family dynamics, economic conditions, and juvenile delinquency. Ultimately, harsh parenting behavior among humans under conditions of chronic threat may reflect a toughening or coarsening process that prepares children for the realities of life in a violent community (Mead, 1935)

There is some evidence in support of this premise. Recent experimental research conducted with rats has established the existence of a positive feedback loop between brain mechanisms associated with hypothalamic pituitary adrenal axis (HPA) and neural mechanisms associated with aggression (Kruk, Halasz, Meelis, & Haller, 2004). The implication of this work is that frequent activation of the HPA axis in response to stress (discussed in detail below) increases the potential for aggressive responses. In her work with humans, Bugental (Bugental & Happaney, 2004) has suggested that heightened stress may create parental hyper-responsiveness to negative affect in children. Her research paradigm has been used to predict harsh parenting (Bugental & Happaney, 2004) and infant/child maltreatment (Bradley & Peters, 1991; Bugental, Blue, & Cruzcosa, 1989) in relation to a low maternal perceived balance of power in the dyadic relationship. In over a decade of research, Bugental and colleagues have linked "low perceived balance of power" to elevated cortisol levels (Lin, Bugental,

Turek, Martorell, & Olster, 2002), heightened negative affect (Bugental et al., 1993), sympathetic nervous system activation (Bugental et al., 1993; Bugental & Happaney, 2000), use of force (Bugental & Johnston, 2000), and the display of false positive affect (Bugental, Brown, & Reiss, 1996).

It is intriguing to speculate on the possible influences of gradient effects on the development of the mother/infant relationship. Maternal attributions of power dynamics in child-caregiver relationships may represent an analog of maternal self-efficacy in relation to subjective social status. In other words, the *income disparity,* or *gradient* effects documented by Hertzman (1999a, 1999b) and Wilkinson (1999; 2001; Wilkinson et al., 1998) may shape the perceived balance of power between mothers and young children living under adverse conditions. From this perspective, appraisals of personal efficacy may be adversely influenced by low social status, thus increasing the poignancy of child misbehavior as a threat to maternal control.

In summary, it can be postulated that as distance from the optimal niche increases, the expression of individual potential is compromised in the service of shorter-term survival benefits. Because of the stress of alienation from the optimal niche, one can speculate that a defensive formation ensues. This formation increases reliance on negative affectivity and restrictive parenting and constitutes a transgenerational regulatory process that serves to bolster the odds of surviving the chronic stress of hostile environments. To this point, our discussion has focused on the presence of hostility in the social environment and parenting practices that appear to develop as a response to a hostile environment. It is from this perspective that the mechanism through which environmental stress may precipitate antisociality, as discussed earlier (Costello et al., 2003; Legrand et al., 2005; Tremblay, 1999), comes into focus. Essentially, the competition, conflict, and deprivation that characterize daily life under steep-gradient conditions precipitate a trade-off, whereby aspects of an individual's long-term genetic potential for adaptation in a hospitable environment are circumvented in favor of short-term preservation strategies.

Short-term adaptations to stress, over time, extract a cost on living systems. The accumulation of stress effects has been referred to as allostatic load, that is, stress associated with how biological systems maintain or recover homeostasis in accommodating stressful events (McEwen, 1998, 2002; McEwen & Seeman, 1999; McEwen & Stellar, 1993; McEwen & Wingfield, 2003). This advance has opened the door to research on the developmental psychobiology of adversity-related stress, that is, how early experiences interact with the developing autonomic nervous system and hypothalamic-pituitary-adrenal (HPA) axis to shape the quality and intensity of subsequent stress responses through the life span.

GRADIENT EFFECTS AND THE DEVELOPMENT OF SELF-REGULATORY PROCESSES

Processes of regulation underlie the adaptive functioning of all biobehavioral systems. All physiological systems have evolved to operate within an optimal range, somewhere between having enough activation and not too much. Thus the functioning of systems can be described in terms of the well-known inverted U curve relating activation to performance. The mid-zone of optimal performance is between not enough activation in the system and too much activation.

Homeostasis is an adaptive regulatory concept and involves the idea of return to a set point after perturbation. It has its roots in Claude Bernard's (1863; 1949) "milieu interne" and continues through the work of Walter Cannon (1932) and in the relation of stress to adaptation in the work of Selye and Fortier (1950). In this tradition stress has been thought of as a "threat to homeostasis," with its adverse consequences for health and disorder often noted (for example, McEwen & Stellar, 1993; Weiner, 1992). More recent work on stress has continued this line of thinking by adding to our knowledge of the limbic hypothalamic pituitary adrenal (HPA) axis (Bremner & Vermetten, 2001; Gunnar, Morison, Chisholm, & Schuder, 2001; Gunnar & Vazquez, 2001; Walker, Walder, & Reynolds, 2001) and its connections with both regulatory and dysregulatory responses.

As stated earlier, McEwen and colleagues (McEwen, 1998; McEwen & Seeman, 1999; McEwen & Stellar, 1993) have concerned themselves with the accumulation of stress over time and, correspondingly, the additive cost of repeated stress conditions on regulatory systems. Over time, additive cost can lead to dysregulation and illness. Allostasis was a term introduced by Sterling and Eyer (1988) to refer to the physiological capacity of an individual to increase or decrease vital functions within an operating range in response to environmental challenge. The operating range of allostasis has been documented to be larger in health than in illness (Sterling & Eyer, 1988), and it has been noted that if one pushes beyond the operating range, a medical crisis can occur, such as when excessive exercise results in a myocardial infarction (Mittleman et al., 1993). It has also been noted that there is apt to be a narrowing of the adaptive operating range during aging in adults (Lipsitz & Goldberger, 1992). The concept of allostatic load was added to the concept of allostasis by McEwen and Stellar (1993) in order to refer to the strain on physiological systems or the adaptive cost that can be a consequence of repeated stress as experienced by an individual. Allostatic load takes account of external challenges to an individual that are repeated over time and that can induce new steady states of operation that decrease the range of adaptation. Ultimately, the effects of such increases or decreases in physiological responsiveness as well as the effects of elevated systems under challenge can result in metabolic and structural changes in tissues that predispose to or cause disease.

The models of allostasis and allostatic load are consistent with the dynamics of contemporary developmental systems theory (e.g. see Emde, 1980; 1988a, 1988b, 1994). What has been added? First, recognizing that developmental systems are not static and closed, but dynamic and open, and that set points are not fixed, allostasis is conceptualized as a process that involves change. It involves steady states that are evolving. Thus it deals with regulatory systems within individuals over spans of time and can include significant segments of a life span. Second, allostasis is conceptualized as an organismic process, such that "cost" in allostatic load can spill over from one physiological system to another (e.g., from the HPA system to the immune system), thereby leading to an organismic cost with expressions of distress, diminished capacity, and disease. Third, and most novel, McEwen and colleagues (McEwen, 1998; McEwen & Seeman, 1999; McEwen & Stellar, 1993) include a much broader class of environmental and other challenges as stressors that can increase allostatic load (and the likelihood of dysregulation) over time. Stressors that increase allostatic load can therefore include a variety of adversities (and, from our point of view a variety of risk factors). Disruptions of regulatory routines and health-related behaviors such as inadequate diet, lack of exercise, and smoking enter in, as well as what we usually think of as stressful events (such as child abuse, accidents, exposure to violence, loss, unemployment, and abrupt moves). These add to a variety of environmental and psychological adversities that are chronic and are considered to interact with individual difference factors that have to do with genetic and constitutional predispositions.

When we think of allostasis and allostatic load, we are considering such processes operating over time. As such it is useful to think of baselines or set points for activity wherein load may result in a restriction of the mid-zone range of optimal functioning. This can occur either via blunted or heightened responses. From this perspective, after perturbation of a given system, such as from external stimulation, there is a propensity to return to a baseline of activity. Repeated excessive perturbations in the form of stress experiences can cause a load or wear and tear not only because of simple additive accumulation but also because the return to baseline activity can be affected. Returns to activity within regulatory systems are dynamic events that can be described in terms of set points for steady states of inputs in relation to outputs for the system. Such set points can be influenced adversely by cumulative stress. In other words, what can happen in circumstances of repeated stressful inputs, according to the model, is an interference with an adaptive return to baseline with a restriction

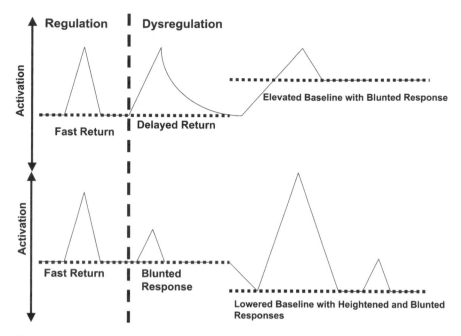

Figure 1.2   Examples of consequences of cumulative stress

of the optimal range of adaptive functioning. Thus subsequent responses may be blunted, elevated, or uneven. Additionally, because of altered steady states, systems may operate as if there were stress in the absence of challenging stimuli (McEwen & Seeman, 1999; Seeman, Singer, Rowe, Horwitz, & McEwen, 1997). We might represent some of these events in Figure 1.2, with allostasis on the left and a resetting of baseline following repeated stress on the right of the figure.

The model of allostatic load also includes a wide view of stressful life events, as noted earlier. It is both multisystem and life span in orientation, envisioning disease risks as a product of "... an individual's cumulative exposure to the wear and tear associated with elevations in physiologic activity across the body's multiple regulatory systems" (Seeman et al., 1997, p. 2264). The model was put to a test in the MacArthur studies of successful aging, using physiological assessments (Seeman et al., 1997). A cohort of 1189 high-functioning men and women between the ages of 70–79 years were followed for two to three years and a measure of allostatic load was constructed that included 10 variables reflecting levels of physiologic stress activity across a number of important regulatory systems. As reported by the authors these included the following:

systolic and diastolic blood pressure (indexes of cardiovascular activity); waist-hip ratio (an index of more long term levels of metabolism and adipose tissue deposition, thought to be influenced by increased glucocorticoid activity; serum high-density lipoprotein (HDL) and total cholesterol levels (indexes of long-term atherosclerotic risk); blood plasma levels of total glycosylated hemoglobin (an integrated measure of glucose metabolism during a period of several days); serum dehydroepiandrosterone sulfate (DHEA-S) (a functional HPA axis antagonist); 12-hour urinary cortisol excretion (an integrated measure of 12-hour HPA axis activity); 12-hour urinary norepinephrine and epinephrine excretion levels (integrated indexes of 12-hour sympathetic nervous system activity). (Seeman et al., 1997, p. 2260)

Results of this study indicated that higher allostatic load was predictive of decreased cognitive and physical functioning and an increased risk of cardiovascular disease. Two points are important to emphasize in addition to the initial success of the model's application. First, the model was applied to a group of individuals late in the life span who were selected as successfully adapting. Second, the model was assessed in a restricted fashion; that is, the general model includes wider behavioral and environmental stressors that were not included in the successful aging analysis.

Evans (2003, 2004; Evans & English, 2002) has pioneered in research addressing allostatic load as an index of the cumulative effects of poverty-induced stress in children. In a sample of predominantly white, school-age children living in rural communities, Evans (2003) demonstrated that, within this sample, cumulative risk factors associated with physical and psychosocial environmental characteristics were associated with several physiological indices of stress, including increased deposition of body fat, heightened neuroendocrine parameters (such as diurnal cortisol and epinephrine levels), and increased blood pressure.

Recently, we proposed an application of the allostatic load model to guide the longitudinal study of the effects of cumulative stress in children and families involved in an Early Head Start intervention, followed over time. Figure 1.3 presents a simple model of cumulative allostatic load as we have conceptualized it across five composite stress variables related to children raised in circumstances of extreme poverty. These included: (1) genetic and prenatal vulnerabilities; (2) disruption of regulatory routines; (3) parental distress and dysregulation; (4) family conflict; and (5) adverse economic/neighborhood ecology.

Although in its simplest form we may think of allostatic load as a linear progression, it is likely that the effects of stress increase sharply. In this sense, allostatic load may be analogous to Dickens and Flynn's (2001) description of the role of environment in perpetuating a steady increase in IQ over multiple generations. An upwards IQ drift, also termed the Flynn Effect, has posed a problem for traditional computational models of the heritability of intelligence test performance. Since increases in the

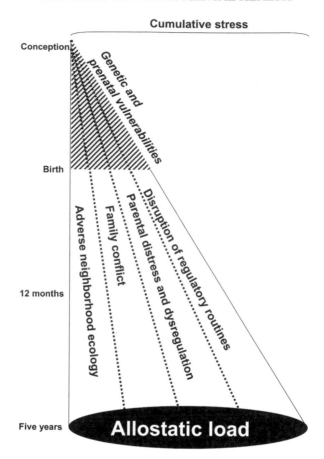

Figure 1.3   A simple model of cumulative allostatic
load across four composite stress variables

mean absolute IQ scores for industrialized populations have occurred too
rapidly for heritability to play a role, it has long been thought that environmental changes must, by default, be at work. However, gains in IQ
over generations are more precipitous than can be accounted for by environmental effects as estimated concurrently with genetic effects through
the study of twins. Dickens and Flynn (2001) suggest that relatively
small environmental changes may interact with phenotypic characteristics (including multiplier effects from gene-environment correlations) to
produce large-scale changes in population behavior. They illustrate this
effect by describing changes in the skills and physical characteristics of
professional basketball players, as a group, over the last several decades.
The authors suggest that a small environmental transformation, such as

the transmission of basketball games via television in the 1950s, could set in motion a cascade of individual multipliers (e.g., familiarity with the game, interest in competition, relative success due to height) and social multipliers (e.g. recreational centers building basketball courts, provision of college scholarships, increased salaries) that would ultimately lead to substantial improvements in the average ability of players over time.

If changes in IQ test performance can be so effected, why not other aspects of phenotypic expression, such those more closely linked to mental health and self-regulation? From a life-course perspective, an examination of potential interactions between different individuals and social multipliers may provide a useful way of examining the ontogeny of the individual. Later in this chapter, we revisit the concept of multiplier effects with regard to cohort and the socio-historical context of the current crisis in children's mental health.

Figure 1.3 illustrates the straightforward hypothesis that, as with the aforementioned studies with older age groups (Evans, 2003; Seeman et al., 1997), cumulative stress in early childhood should lead to adverse health outcomes in a child by five years of age. If, however, we consider stress at different points in development as exerting different degrees of influence in shaping self-regulatory processes, stressors can be seen having multiplier effects (Dickens & Flynn, 2001) Given our understanding of the development of the HPA system and our earlier review of socioeconomic gradients in cultural and economic context, there are several reasons to suspect that stressors occurring earlier in development should exact a higher toll on long-term adaptation. First, regulatory systems of an individual are most vulnerable to dysregulation early in life (Francis, Champagne, Liu, & Meaney, 1999; Champagne & Meaney, 2001). Second, early regulatory systems are more dependent on context (Francis et al., 1999). Third, early regulatory systems are likely to be strongly influenced by maternal stress and allostatic load (Champagne & Meaney, 2001).

We illustrate the developmental implications of early stress in Figure 1.4. The figure shows the predicted outcomes for regulatory difficulties for four temporally-related stress conditions during the period leading up to the pre-kindergarten assessment at five years. Risk for outcomes of regulatory difficulties would be predicted as greatest for continuous stress, and next for early remitting stress, with a lesser influence from later stress and the least influence for low stress during the period under consideration.

A recent study conducted by Essex, Klein, Cho, and Kalin (2002), with a similar sample of children, confirms these assumptions. In a prospective study, the researchers examined maternal reports of their own stress while caring for their infants at four time points (1, 4, and 12 months, and

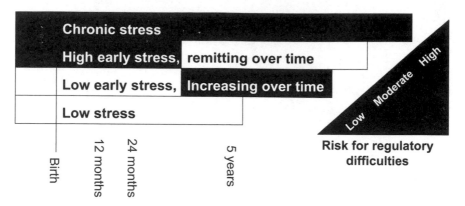

Figure 1.4   Four configurations of temporal distribution of stress in early childhood, with corresponding hypothesized risk for regulatory difficulties following school entry

4.5 years), in relation to child salivary cortisol levels at 4.5 years of age. They also examined child mental health symptoms when the children were enrolled in the first grade. The results closely match those hypothesized for our Early Head Start sample (shown in Figure 1.4.). Specifically, higher cortisol levels were associated with earlier versus later maternal stress, as well as cumulatively high stress (i.e., high maternal stress across infancy). Higher cortisol levels were also significantly associated with higher levels of child psychopathology.

SUMMARY AND CONCLUSIONS

To review, we have discussed how socioeconomic gradients have been seen as reflecting the degree of competition for access to an optimal or ideal niche. The flatter the gradient, the greater the access to social and material capital necessary for optimal development. Where steep gradients exist, those with less entrée to resources will experience greater levels of stress and aggression, as well as poorer physical health, than those with more access to resources. What is more, the level of competitiveness may drive the slope of the gradient, inflating the level of stress (allostatic load) generated through efforts to maintain status. Maternal allostatic load may influence the developing HTPA regulatory system, conditioning an infant or young child to adapt more continuously across life within a particular socioeconomic niche, and to cope with the level of threat and hostility present in the immediate social environment. This can occur because a child moves through life with a regulatory system that is highly sensitive to a first-generation environment, with an HTPA system that has been shaped largely by non-genomic influences (Champagne & Meaney, 2001).

To this point, we have emphasized the *presence* of stress as a mediating influence for the adverse effects of socioeconomic gradients. However, the adversity of steep socioeconomic gradients also comes about from the relative *absence* of social capital (i.e., socially supportive relationships) (Kawachi, 1999). Just as HPA activation and secretion of cortisol have been linked to the damaging effects of stress, affiliation behavior and social capital have been associated with the neuropeptide oxytocin, which appears to suppress HPA activation (DeVries, Glasper, & Detillion, 2003; Insel, 2000). Indeed, Champagne and Meaney (2001) have reviewed a growing body of evidence from research with rodents, non-human primates, and humans, that oxytocin plays a central role in the trans-generational transmission of parental behavior and stress responsivity. Oxytocin controls maternal nurturing behavior, which in turn shapes the stress response of the developing individual (Heinrichs, Baumgartner, Kirschbaum, & Ehlert, 2003; Insel, 2000; Liu et al., 1997). Given that oxytocin levels correspond to affiliative behavior, the social milieu of the mother is likely to influence her caregiving behavior.

Perhaps the most intriguing study to date on the effects of oxytocin on human affiliative behavior was conducted by Zak, Kurzban, and Matzner (2003). Using an experimental economics research paradigm, the researchers examined the formation of trust relationships in a monetary exchange exercise among paired strangers. In the study, the risk of trusting an unknown participant corresponded to greater potential loss or gain. After participation in the study, a measure of oxytocin blood level was taken. The researchers found that the experience of trust corresponded to increasing levels of oxytocin. In summary, emerging research on the role of oxytocin in regulating social behavior, from maternal-infant bonding to trust among strangers, has broad implications for understanding the mechanisms through which socioeconomic gradients exert influence over human regulatory processes.

MULTIPLIER EFFECTS OVER GENERATIONS

Just as an individual's capacity for self-regulation may be shaped via caregiver behavior within the context of gradient influences, the interplay between socioeconomic gradients and multiplier effects may be seen as molding the adaptive potential of successive generations and, in so doing, shaping the core social challenges of our age. Research on stereotype threat, that is, a cognitive and affective phenomenon characterized by unwitting conformity to pejorative stereotypes about one's group (Steele & Aronson, 1995), illustrates this process.

Examples of stereotype threat abound, across genders and ethnic/racial identities. Women have been found to perform better on GRE mathematics problems when not in the presence of men (Oswald & Harvey, 2000; Schmader, 2002). African Americans have been observed to perform significantly better on cognitive tasks when not in the presence of European Americans or reminded of negative stereotypes about their potential performance (Blascovich, Spencer, Quinn, & Steele, 2001; Steele, 1998; Steele & Aronson, 1998), and the performance of European Americans has been demonstratively compromised on mathematics tasks when stereotypes of Asian mathematics ability was evoked (Aronson et al., 1999).

When we consider the legacies of racism and sexism, the implications of stereotype threat for maintaining and perpetuating status inequalities appear as obvious as they are far-reaching. For our discussion, however, it bears highlighting that self-regulatory processes are implicated as a core mechanism through which stereotype threat may influence status differences. Specifically, the concept of regulatory focus (Higgins, 1997; 1999; Seibt & Förster, 2004) has been used to describe a cognitive and affective shift away from what Higgins (1997; 1999) has described as a self-regulatory process motivated toward creativity, accomplishment, and pleasure (i.e., a promotion focus) to one motivated by self-preservation and avoidance of pain (i.e., a prevention focus). When we consider that these concepts map onto the parenting strategies and processes we have described within the context of socioeconomic gradient effects, the social regulatory role of stereotype threat, over generations, becomes evident.

CONCLUSION

We began our discussion with an allusion to Lewis Carroll's Red Queen, and the analogy of trees competing for sunlight (Van Valen, 1973). In our discussion, we have challenged a static conceptualization of genetic and environmental influences on regulatory processes and have suggested instead a far more fluid, interactive process through which gradient and multiplier effects, in relation to time and place, may foster the development of self-regulatory processes within individuals and cohorts.

REFERENCES

Aronson, J., Lustina, M. J., Good, C., Keough, K., Steele, C. M., & Brown, J. (1999). When white men can't do math: Necessary and sufficient factors in stereotype threat. *Journal of Experimental Social Psychology, 35*(1), 29–46.

Bernard, C. (1863; 1949). *An introduction to the study of experimental medicine* (H. Copley Green, Trans.). New York: Abelard-Shuman, Inc.

Blascovich, J., Spencer, S. J., Quinn, D., & Steele, C. (2001). African Americans and high blood pressure: The role of stereotype threat. *Psychological Science, 12*(3), 225–229.

Bradley, E., & Peters, R. D. (1991). Physically abusive and nonabusive mothers' perceptions of parenting and child behavior. *American Journal of Orthopsychiatry, 61*(3), 455–460.

Bremner, J. D., & Vermetten, E. (2001). Stress and development: Behavioral and biological consequences. *Development & Psychopathology, 13*(3), 473–489.

Bronfenbrenner, U., & Ceci, S. J. (1994). Nature-nurture reconceptualized in developmental perspective: A bioecological model. *Psychological Review, 101*(4), 568–586.

Brooks-Gunn, J., Duncan, G. J., & Britto, P. R. (1999). Are socioeconomic gradients for children similar to those for adults?: Achievement and health of children in the United States. In D. P. Keating & C. Hertzman (Eds.), *Developmental health and the wealth of nations: Social, biological, and educational dynamics* (pp. 94–124). New York: The Guilford Press.

Bugental, D. B., Blue, J., Cortez, V., Fleck, K., Kopeikin, H., Lewis, J. C., & Lyon, J. (1993). Social cognitions as organizers of autonomic and affective responses to social challenge. *Journal of Personality and Social Psychology, 64*(1), 94–103.

Bugental, D. B., Blue, J., & Cruzcosa, M. (1989). Perceived control over caregiving outcomes—implications for child-abuse. *Developmental Psychology, 25*(4), 532–539.

Bugental, D. B., Brown, M., & Reiss, C. (1996). Cognitive representations of power in caregiving relationships: Biasing effects on interpersonal interaction and information processing. *Journal of Family Psychology, 10*(4), 397–407.

Bugental, D. B., & Happaney, K. (2000). Parent–child interaction as a power contest. *Journal of Applied Developmental Psychology, 21*(3), 267–282.

Bugental, D. B., & Happaney, K. (2004). Predicting infant maltreatment in low-income families: The interactive effects of maternal attributions and child status at birth. *Developmental Psychology, 40*(2), 234–243.

Bugental, D. B., & Johnston, C. (2000). Parental and child cognitions in the context of the family. *Annual Review of Psychology, 51,* 315–344.

Bugental, D. B., Martorell, G. A., & Barraza, V. (2003). The hormonal costs of subtle forms of infant maltreatment. *Hormones and Behavior, 43*(1), 237–244.

Cannon, W. B. (1932). *The wisdom of the body.* New York: W. W. Norton & Company, Inc.

Carroll, L. (1872). *Through the looking-glass, and what Alice found there.* London: Macmillan and Company.

Champagne, F., & Meaney, M. J. (2001). Like mother, like daughter: Evidence for non-genomic transmission of parental behavior and stress responsivity. *Progress in Brain Research, 133,* 287–302.

Costello, J. E., Compton, S. N., Keeler, G., & Angold, A. (2003). Relationships between poverty and psychopathology: A natural experiment. *JAMA— Journal of the American Medical Association, 290*(15), 2023–2029.

DeVries, A. C., Glasper, E. R., & Detillion, C. E. (2003). Social modulation of stress responses. *Physiology & Behavior, 79*(3), 399–407.

Dickens, W. T., & Flynn, J. R. (2001). Heritability estimates versus large environmental effects: The IQ paradox resolved. *Psychological Review, 108* 346–369.

Eitle, D., & Turner, R. J. (2002). Exposure to community violence and young adult crime: The effects of witnessing violence, traumatic victimization, and other stressful life events. *Journal of Research in Crime and Delinquency, 39*(2), 214–237.

Eitle, D., & Turner, R. J. (2003). Stress exposure, race, and young adult male crime. *Sociological Quarterly, 44*(2), 243–269.

Emde, R. N. (1980). Searching for perspectives: Systems sensitivity and opportunities in studying the infancy of the organizing child of the universe. In K. Bloom (Ed.), *Prospective issues in infancy research* (pp. 1–23). Hillsdale, NJ: Lawrence Erlbaum Associates.

Emde, R. N. (1988a). Development terminable and interminable: I. Innate and motivational factors from infancy. *International Journal of Psycho-Analysis, 69*(1), 23–42.

Emde, R. N. (1988b). Development terminable and interminable: II. Recent psychoanalytic theory and therapeutic considerations. *International Journal of Psycho-Analysis, 69*(2), 283–296.

Emde, R. N. (1994). Individuality, context, and the search for meaning. *Child Development, 65*(3), 719–737.

Essex, M., Klein, M., Cho, E., & Kalin, N. H. (2002). Maternal stress beginning in infancy may sensitize children to later stress exposure: Effects on cortisol and behavior. *Biological Psychiatry, 52*(8), 776–784.

Evans, G. W. (2003). A multimethodological analysis of cumulative risk and allostatic load among rural children. *Developmental Psychology, 39*(5), 924–933.

Evans, G. W. (2004). The environment of childhood poverty. *American Psychologist, 59*(2), 77–92.

Evans, G. W., & English, K. (2002). The environment of poverty: Multiple stressor exposure, psychophysiological stress, and socioemotional adjustment. *Child Development, 73*(4), 1238–1248.

Francis, A. D., Champagne, F. A., Liu, D., & Meaney, M. J. (1999). Maternal care, gene expression, and the development of individual differences in stress reactivity. *Annals of the New York Academy of Sciences, 896,* 66–84.

Franck, E. J. (2001). Outreach to birthfathers of children in out-of-home care. *Child Welfare, 80*(3).

Gottlieb, G. (1991). Experiential canalization of behavioral development: Theory. *Developmental Psychology, 27,* 4–13.

Gunnar, M. R., Morison, S. J., Chisholm, K., & Schuder, M. (2001). Salivary cortisol levels in children adopted from Romanian orphanages. *Development & Psychopathology, 13*(3), 611–628.

Gunnar, M. R., & Vazquez, D. M. (2001). Low cortisol and a flattening of expected daytime rhythm: Potential indices of risk in human development. *Development & Psychopathology, 13*(3), 515–538.

Heinrichs, M., Baumgartner, T., Kirschbaum, C., & Ehlert, U. (2003). Social support and oxytocin interact to suppress cortisol and subjective responses to psychosocial stress. *Biological Psychiatry, 54,* 1389–1398.

Hertzman, C. (1999a). The biological embedding of early experience and its effects on health in adulthood. In N. E. Adler, M. Marmot, B. S. McEwen, & J. Stewart (Eds.), *Socioeconomic status and health in industrial nations: Social, psychological, and biological pathways. Annals of the New York Academy of Sciences, Vol. 896* (pp. 85–95). New York: New York Academy of Sciences.

Hertzman, C. (1999b). Population health and human development. In D. P. Keating and C. Hertzman (Eds.), *Developmental health and the wealth of nations: Social, biological, and educational dynamics* (pp. 21–40). New York: The Guilford Press.

Hertzman, C., & Keating, D. R. (Eds.), (1999). *Developmental health and the wealth of nations: Social, biological, and educational dynamics.* New York: The Guilford Press.

Heylighen, F. (1999). The growth of structural and functional complexity during evolution. In F. Heylighen, J. Bollen, & A. Riegler (Eds.), *The evolution of complexity* (pp. 17–44). Dordrecht: Kluwer Academic.

Higgins, E. T. (1997). Beyond pleasure and pain. *American Psychologist, 52,* 1280–1300.

Higgins, E. T. (1999). Promotion and prevention as a motivational duality: Implications for evaluative processes. In S. Chaiken & Y. Trope (Eds.), *Dual-process theories in social psychology* (pp. 503–525). New York: Guilford Press.

Higley, J. D., & Suomi, S. J. (1986). Parental behavior in primates. In W. Sluckin & M. Herbert (Eds.), *Parental behavior* (pp. 152–207). Oxford, UK: Blackwell.

Insel, T. R. (2000). Toward a neurobiology of attachment. *Review of General Psychology, 4*(2), 176–185.

Johnson, W., & Krueger, R. (2005). Higher perceived life control decreases genetic variance in physical health: Evidence from a national twin study. *Journal of Personality & Social Psychology, 88*(1), 165–173.

Kaplan, G. A., Pamuk, E. R., Lynch, J. W., Cohen, R. D., & Balfour, J. L. (1996). Inequality in income and mortality in the United States: Analysis of mortality and potential pathways. *British Medical Journal, 312*(7037), 999–1003.

Kawachi, I. (1999). Social capital and community effects on population and individual health. In N. E. Adler, M. Marmot, B. S. McEwen, & J. Stewart (Eds.), *Socioeconomic status and health in industrial nations: Social, psychological, and biological pathways. Annals of the New York Academy of Sciences, Vol. 896* (pp. 120–130). New York: New York Academy of Sciences.

Kruk, M. R., Halasz, J., Meelis, W., & Haller, J. (2004). Fast positive feedback between the adrenocortical stress response and a brain mechanism involved in aggressive behavior. *Behavioral Neuroscience, 118*(5), 1062–1070.

Legrand, L. N., Iacono, W. G., & McGue, M. (2005). Predicting addiction. *American Scientist, 93*(2) 140–147.

Lin, E. K., Bugental, D. B., Turek, V., Martorell, G. A., & Olster, D. H. (2002). Children's vocal properties as mobilizers of stress-related physiological responses in adults. *Personality and Social Psychology Bulletin, 28*(3), 346–357.

Lipsitz, L. A., & Goldberger, A. L. (1992). Loss of "complexity" and aging. Potential applications of fractals and chaos theory to senescence. *JAMA, 267*(13), 1806–1809.

Liu, D., Diorio, J., Tannenbaum, B., Caldji, C., Francis, D., Freedman, A., Sharma, S., Pearson, D., Plotsky, P. M., & Meaney, M. J. (1997). Maternal care, hippocampal glucocorticoid receptors, and hypothalamic-pituitary-adrenal responses to stress. *Science, 277*(5332), 1659–1662.

Lynch, J. W., Kaplan, G. A., & Shema, S. J. (1997). Cumulative impact of sustained economic hardship on physical, cognitive, psychological, and social functioning. *New England Journal of Medicine, 337*(26), 1889–1895.

McCord, J. (1999). Crime: Taking an historical perspective. In P. Cohen, C. Slomkowski, & L. N. Robins (Eds.), *Historical and geographical influences on psychopathology* (pp. 17–35). Mahwah, NJ: Lawrence Erlbaum Associates.

McEwen, B. S. (1998). Protective and damaging effects of stress mediators. *New England Journal of Medicine, 338*(3), 171–179.

McEwen, B. S. (2002). Sex, stress and the hippocampus: Allostasis, allostatic load and the aging process. *Neurobiology of Aging, 23*(5), 921–939.

McEwen, B. S., & Seeman, T. (1999). Protective and damaging effects of mediators of stress: Elaborating and testing the concepts of allostasis and allostatic load. In N. E. Adler, M. Marmot, B. S. McEwen, & J. Stewart (Eds.), *Socioeconomic status and health in industrial nations: Social, psychological, and biological pathways. Annals of the New York Academy of Sciences, Vol. 896* (pp. 30–47). New York: New York Academy of Sciences.

McEwen, B. S., & Stellar, E. (1993). Stress and the individual. Mechanisms leading to disease. *Archives of Internal Medicine, 153*(18), 2093–2101.

McEwen, B. S., & Wingfield, J. C. (2003). The concept of allostasis in biology and biomedicine. *Hormones & Behavior, 43*(1), 2–15.

Mead, M. (1935). *Sex and temperament.* Oxford, UK: Morrow.

Mittleman, M. A., Maclure, M., Tofler, G. H., Sherwood, J. B., Goldberg, R. J., & Muller, J. E. (1993). Triggering of acute myocardial infarction by heavy physical exertion. Protection against triggering by regular exertion. Determinants of myocardial infarction onset study investigators. *New England Journal of Medicine, 329*(23), 1677–1683.

Oswald, D. L., & Harvey, R. D. (2000). Hostile environments, stereotype threat, and math performance among undergraduate women. *Current Psychology: Developmental, Learning, Personality, Social, 19*(4), 338–356.

Patterson, G. R. (1995). Coercion as a basis for early age of onset for arrest. In J. McCord (Ed.), *Coercion and punishment in long-term perspectives* (pp. 81–105). New York: Cambridge University Press.

Patterson, G. R. (1999). A proposal relating a theory of delinquency to societal rates of juvenile crime: Putting Humpty Dumpty together again. In M. J. Cox & J. Brooks-Gunn (Eds.), *Conflict and cohesion in families: Causes and consequences. The advances in family research series* (pp. 11–35). Mahwah, NJ: Lawrence Erlbaum.

Sameroff, A. J., & Emde, R. N. (Eds.). (1992). *Relationship disturbances in early childhood: A developmental approach*. New York: Basic Books.

Sapolsky, R. M. (2001). Physiological and pathophysiological implications of social stress in mammals. In B. S. McEwen & H. M. Goodman (Eds.), *Coping with the environment: Neural and endocrine mechanisms* (pp. 517–532). New York: Oxford University Press.

Schmader, T. (2002). Gender identification moderates stereotype threat effects on women's math performance. *Journal of Experimental Social Psychology, 38*(2), 194–201.

Seeman, T. E., Singer, B. H., Rowe, J. W., Horwitz, R. I., & McEwen, B. S. (1997). Price of adaptation—allostatic load and its health consequences. MacArthur studies of successful aging. *Archives of Internal Medicine, 157*(19), 2259–2268.

Seibt, B., & Förster, J. (2004). Stereotype threat and performance: How self-stereotypes influence processing by inducing regulatory foci. *Journal of Personality and Social Psychology, 87*(1), 38–56.

Selye, H., & Fortier, C. (1950). Adaptive reaction to stress. *Psychosomatic Medicine, 12*, 149–157.

Steele, C. M. (1998). Stereotyping and its threat are real. *American Psychologist, 53*(6), 680–681.

Steele, C. M., & Aronson, J. (1995). Stereotype threat and the intellectual test performance of African Americans. *Journal of Personality & Social Psychology, 69*(5), 791–811.

Steele, C. M., & Aronson, J. (1998). Stereotype threat and the test performance of academically successful African Americans. In C. Jencks & M. Phillips (Eds.), *The black-white test score gap* (pp. 401–427). Washington, DC: Brookings Institution.

Sterling, P., & Eyer, J. (1988). Allostasis: A new paradigm to explain arousal pathology. In S. Fisher & J. Reason (Eds.), *Handbook of life stress, cognition and health* (pp. 629–649). New York: John Wiley & Sons.

Suomi, S. J. (1999). Developmental trajectories, early experiences, and community consequences: Lessons from studies with rhesus monkeys. In D. P. Keating &

C. Hertzman (Eds.), *Developmental health and the wealth of nations: Social, biological, and educational dynamics* (pp. 185–200). New York: The Guilford Press.

Tremblay, R. E. (1999). When children's social development fails. In D. P. Keating & C. Hertzman (Eds.), *Developmental health and the wealth of nations: Social, biological, and educational dynamics* (pp. 55–71). New York: The Guilford Press.

Turkheimer, E., Haley, A., Waldron, M., D'Onofrio, B., & Gottesman, I. (2003) Socioeconomic status modifies heritability of IQ in young children. *Psychological Science, 14*(6), 623–628.

Van Valen, L. (1973). A new evolutionary law. *Evolutionary Theory, 1,* 1–30.

Walker, E. F., Walder, D. J., & Reynolds, F. (2001). Developmental changes in cortisol secretion in normal and at-risk youth. *Development & Psychopathology, 13*(3), 721–732.

Weiner, H. (1992). *Perturbing the organism: The biology of stressful experience.* Chicago: University of Chicago Press.

Wilkinson, R. (2001). *Mind the gap: Hierarchies, health and human evolution.* New Haven, CT: Yale University Press.

Wilkinson, R. G. (1999). Health, hierarchy, and social anxiety. In N. E. Adler & M. Marmot (Eds.), *Socioeconomic status and health in industrial nations: Social, psychological, and biological pathways. Annals of the New York Academy of Sciences, Vol. 896* (pp. 48–63). New York: New York Academy of Sciences.

Wilkinson, R. G., Kawachi, I., & Kennedy, B. P. (1998). Mortality, the social environment, crime and violence. *Sociology of Health & Illness, 20*(5), 578–597.

Zak, P. J., Kurzban, R. O., & Matzner, W. L. (2003). *The neurobiology of trust.* Paper presented at the Society for Neuroscience 33rd Annual Meeting, New Orleans, Louisiana.

Chapter 2

SUBSTANCE USE DURING PREGNANCY: RESEARCH AND SOCIAL POLICY

Barry M. Lester, Lynne Andreozzi, and Lindsey Appiah

A longer version of this manuscript was published in the *Harm Reduction Journal* (2004, I-5), and was supported by the Robert Wood Johnson Foundation Substance Abuse Policy Research Program.

OVERVIEW AND NATURE OF THE PROBLEM

The purpose of this review is to summarize policy research findings in the area of maternal prenatal substance abuse to (1) inform and advance this field, (2) identify future research needs, (3) inform policy making, and (4) identify implications for policy.

The issue of substance abuse is one that has perpetually plagued society. These complexities are even more defined in cases of substance abuse by pregnant women, an issue that has been pushed to the forefront of the public consciousness over the course of the past 20 years. Maternal prenatal substance abuse is defined as chronic use of alcohol and/or other drugs (Murphy & Rosenbaum, 1999). The acronym AOD is often used to describe the generic problem of alcohol and other drugs. However, AOD is not specific to mothers and includes both prenatal and postnatal use. This review will encompass the three main types of addictive substances used during pregnancy: alcohol, tobacco, and illegal drugs (ATID). Maternal Alcohol, Tobacco and Illegal Drugs (MATID) will be used to describe maternal use of these substances during pregnancy that threatens the well-being of the child.

Background

The sensationalistic coverage of the "crack epidemic" in the mid-1980s focused national attention on the relationship between drug use and the social and economic conditions that plagued our society. About 11 percent of the adult population of the United States suffers from a substance abuse problem (AOD) during the course of a year (Substance Abuse and Mental Health Services Administration [SAMHSA], 1999). That figure increases to 28 percent if we include substance abuse or mental health disorders, which are often inseparable. Of the 10 leading causes of disability worldwide in 1990, 5 were psychiatric conditions including AOD. The cost to society of drug use including crime, health care, and reduced work productivity was estimated at over $300 billion dollars annually (Califano, 1992). In 1997, the total expenditure for treatment of substance abuse was $11.9 billion in contrast to the social costs of $294 billion estimated for that year. In addition, substance abuse is a contributing factor in child abuse and neglect cases for 40 percent or more of the 1.2 million annual confirmed cases of child maltreatment families involved with the child welfare system. The presence of substance use disorders in parents increases the risk of child maltreatment three-fold or more. These children are also at substantial risk of placement in out-of-home care.

Maternal prenatal substance abuse became an issue for public health debate in the mid-1980s when the price of cocaine dropped, and a smokeable form, "crack," became widely available. The heightened attention came in response to the emergence of a perceived crack epidemic and their infants were labeled crack babies (Murphy & Rosenbaum, 1999). Cocaine is a special case because it riveted our attention to the problem of drug use by pregnant women. It became a moral as well as a public health issue and has forever changed the way we think about substance use by pregnant women.

Epidemiology and Prevalence Rates

Numerous attempts to answer the question of the prevalence of prenatal exposure have been made reflecting a variety of definitions, sampling procedures, and drug use detection procedures (Smeriglio & Wilcox, 1999). Drug use is typically detected by maternal report, history, or urine testing. The National Household Survey on Drug Abuse (NHSDA) contains 1999 national estimates based on interviews with 66,706 persons. The NHSDA estimated that among women 15 to 44 years old, rates of current use of alcohol, tobacco, and illicit drugs in 1999 were 47.8 percent, 31 percent, and 7.9 percent, respectively. Table 2.1 compares drug use between pregnant and non-pregnant women. Among pregnant women 15–44 years of age, 3.4 percent reported using illicit drugs. This was significantly lower than the rate among non-pregnant women age 15–44 years (8.1 %). For example, cocaine use is .2 percent for pregnant but .9 percent for non-pregnant women.

Table 2.1
Drug Use by Pregnant and Non-Pregnant Women in the United States (1999)

Drug	Non-Pregnant	Pregnant
Any illicit drug	8.1	3.4 (134,111)
Marijuana/Hashish	5.9	2.9 (114,389)
Cocaine	0.9	0.2 (7,889)
Heroin	0.1	*
Methamphetamine	0.2	0.2 (7,889)
Cigarettes	30.5	17.6 (694,223)
Alcohol	49.3	13.8 (544,334)
"Binge" alcohol	19.4	3.4 (134,111)
Heavy alcohol	4.0	0.5 (19,722)

Methamphetamine is scary because it is the only illicit drug that does not have a lower rate for pregnant (.2%) than for non-pregnant women (.2%). For pregnant women in the 15–44 age group, 3.4 percent, 17.6 percent, and 13.8 percent, respectively, used illicit drugs, tobacco and alcohol, indicating that a large number of women continued their substance use during pregnancy. In the United States in 1999, there were 3,944,450 births to women aged 15 to 44 years (Smeriglio & Wilcox, 1999). Using NHSDA estimates of substance use during pregnancy, the approximate numbers of births in 1999 complicated by maternal use of illicit drugs, tobacco, and alcohol were 134,110, 694,220, and 544,330, respectively. Thus, from the public health perspective, the impact of substance use during pregnancy extends far beyond maternal health to that of a large number of the unborn population.

There is also overlap between licit and illicit drugs. Approximately 32 percent of women who use illicit drugs during pregnancy also use alcohol and cigarettes (Wenzel, et al., 2001). From these estimates it has been suggested that approximately one million children each year are exposed to legal or illegal substances (i.e. MATID) during gestation. It is also important to point out that the NHSDA is based on self-report of drug use and therefore likely to underestimate the extent of prenatal drug exposure.

Research on Prenatal MATID Exposure and Child Outcome

MATID use during pregnancy is a major public health issue and social policy concern because of the possible adverse effect or harm to the developing child caused by the chemical effect of the drug, that is, the drug as a toxin. The best documentation of this effect is for alcohol. The teratogenic effects of alcohol are well established. One of the most widely chronicled problems attributed to alcohol use is fetal alcohol syndrome (FAS). FAS was first described in the literature in 1968 and refers to a constellation of physical abnormalities. FAS produces slow growth, damage to the nervous system, facial abnormalities, and mental retardation. It is most obvious in the features of the face and in the reduced size of the newborn and in problems of behavior and cognition in children born to mothers who drank heavily during pregnancy. Rates of FAS range from 0.5 to 3.0 cases per 1,000 births or from 2,000 to 12,000 per year in the United States.

In addition to FAS, there are children who do not show the facial dysmorphology of FAS but who do show deficits on a wide variety of neurobehavioral measures. Different labels have been used to describe this heterogeneous group including fetal alcohol effects (FAE) and alcohol-related neurodevelopmental disabilities (ARND). ARND/FAE may reflect more moderate levels of alcohol exposure as well as some degree of uncertainty about whether alcohol or other factors was the causal agent.

Tobacco is another legal drug that can have adverse effects on fetuses. Approximately 12.3 percent of all mothers report cigarette smoking while pregnant (Matthews, 2001). Cigarette smoke is a complex mixture of chemicals (U.S. Department of Health and Human Services [USDHHS], 1990), with approximately 4,000 compounds (Brunnemann & Hoffman, 1991), including carbon monoxide, which may also affect the fetus. Studies have shown that smoking is responsible for 20–30 percent of all infants of low birth weight, and that infants born to smoking mothers weigh an average 150–250 grams less than infants born to nonsmoking mothers (Andres & Day, 2000).

The nicotine in cigarette smoke acts as a neuroteratogen that interferes with fetal development, specifically the developing nervous system (Levin & Slotkin, 1998). Although the effects of cigarette smoking on fetal growth retardation have been known for many years, more recent work has linked prenatal nicotine exposure to sudden infant death syndrome as well as short and longer term behavioral and cognitive problems (Kahn et al., 1994), including effects on IQ (Fried, Watkinson, & Gray, 1998). In addition to these prenatal mechanisms there are postnatal mechanisms through which smoking can affect the child. These include research on the transmission of nicotine through breast milk and the consequences of second-hand smoke exposure on children (Bearer, Slavator, Buck, & Singer, 2001).

Illicit drugs are the most often targeted drugs in the fight against maternal substance abuse, by virtue of the fact they are perceived to produce the most harmful side effects in both the mothers and the children. Whether this is true or not is a topic that is certainly up for debate. For cocaine, we now know that early scientific reports were exaggerated and portrayed children who were exposed to cocaine in utero as irreparably doomed and damaged (Lester, LaGasse, Freier & Brunner, 1996; Lester & Tronick, 1994). Published studies on cocaine-exposed children suggest a pattern of small deficits in intelligence and moderate deficits in language (Lester, LaGasse & Seifer, 1998). Deficits have also been found in academic skills including poor sustained attention, more disorganization, and less abstract thinking.

We have seen how public understanding of the impact of prenatal exposure has lurched from an initial over-reaction in which drug-exposed children were characterized as irrevocably and irreversibly damaged to a perhaps equally premature excessive "sigh of relief" that drugs such as cocaine do not have lasting effects, especially if children are raised in appropriate environments. Exaggerated statements about the benign effects of cocaine as found in Frank, Augustyn, Knight, Pell, and Zuckerman (2001) can have negative policy implications. Infants exposed to drugs in utero may have a milder phenotype with appropriate environment input. We need to understand combinations of biological (including genetic) predispositions and environmental conditions that result in normal development and what specific factors might promote resilience. This will require changing some of our models for studying the effects of MATID.

Developmental Model

Most studies of MATID use and child developmental outcome follow the behavioral teratology model. The goal is to isolate the unique effects of the drug, typically by controlling other variables that could also explain child outcome (Lester, 1999; LaGasse, Seifer & Lester, 1999). The limitation of this approach is that it does not lend itself to study drug exposure as part of a developmental process in which the goal is to predict child outcome with ATID as one of many contributing factors. Developmental-ecological models have shown that many, if not most, child outcomes are due to multiple antecedent variables.

Developmental models also need to take into account the effects of polydrug exposure. Adverse MATID effects are thought to be due to mechanisms by which the drugs disrupt programs for brain development associated with alterations in brain structure and neuronal function that have unique behavioral consequences. Typically we think about the specific or individual effects of each drug. However, recent literature suggests a mechanism of action common to all drugs of abuse by increasing the levels of the neurotransmitter dopamine in the brain pathways that control pleasure (Malanga & Kosofsky, 1999). This model of a final common pathway for all drugs of abuse is critical because, as documented earlier, most prenatal drug use is polydrug use.

Theoretically, we can describe three types of consequences of MATID on child development: (1) immediate drug effects, (2) latent drug effects, and (3) postnatal environment effects as shown in Figure 2.1. Immediate drug effects are direct teratogenic consequences of MATID exposure and emerge during the first year before postnatal environmental effects become salient. These effects may be transient, such as catch-up in physical growth, or more long lasting, such as behavioral dysregulation that is observed in infancy and persists through school age. Latent drug effects are also direct teratogenic effects but reflect brain function that becomes relevant later in development. There are two kinds of latent effects. First, MATID can affect brain function that does not manifest until children are older, including cognitive processes, antisocial behavior, substance use onset, and psychopathology. Second, MATID affects the brain by causing a predisposition for dependence on drugs. These conditions would be activated during school age when opportunities to use drugs arise, leading to early substance use onset.

Postnatal environment effects include a general environmental that includes both risk and protective factors. MATID is associated with general psychosocial risk factors that compromise child outcome apart

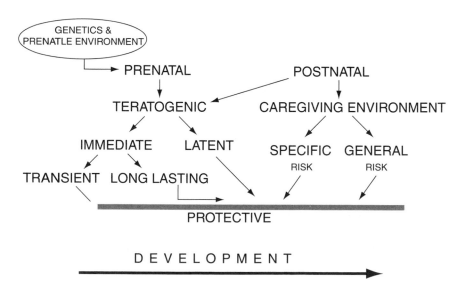

Figure 2.1 Developmental Model of the Effects of Maternal Alcohol, Tobacco, and Illegal Drug Use (MATID) during Pregnancy on Child Outcome

from substance abuse issues including poverty (National Institute Drug Abuse, N. I. H. [NIDA], 1996), chaotic and dangerous lifestyles (Finnegan, Oehlberg, Regan & Rudrauff, 1981; Hutchins & DePietro, 1997), symptoms of psychopathology, (Griffin et al., 1992; Ross, Glaser, & Stiasny, 1988; Rounsaville et al., 1991), history of childhood sexual abuse, (Miller, Downs, Condoli, & Keil, 1987; Wilsnack, Vogeltanz, Klassen, & Harris, 1997), and involvement in difficult or abusive relationships with male partners (Griffin, Weiss, Mirin & Lange, 1989; Hien & Scheier, 1996). There are also specific aspects of the caregiving environment unique to AOD using mothers analogous to the well-documented literature on "children of alcoholics" (COAs). Passive exposure to smoke is also a direct teratogenic effect that is also part of the environment (Fried et al., 1998).

The developmental model also includes protective or resiliency factors that buffer the child against adverse child outcome and the "development" arrow to indicate that development is a dynamic process.

POLICY OPTIONS

Views of Addiction

There is much societal debate on what should be the appropriate response to maternal substance abuse during pregnancy. One reason for the ongoing controversy is tied to the conflicting views of addiction. Society's approach to substance use has changed markedly over the decades from being viewed as an individual problem for which society has no responsibility to a major social problem that needs to be addressed by the mental health, medical, and criminal justice systems. Today this issue tends to get polarized, especially when it comes to pregnant women. There is the liberal perspective of drug abuse that calls on people to look at drug use as a public health problem that requires compassion and understanding. To deal with drug use during pregnancy in a harsh way would be unconstitutional, misogynistic, and ineffective (Brown et al., 1991). From this perspective, drug use during pregnancy must be treated in the same manner as depression or other mental illness. It has also been suggested that not only is it ineffective to treat drug and alcohol addiction as a criminal act, but it is also a punitive approach that is akin to criminalizing mental illness (Lester et al., 1996; Paltrow, 1998). The opposing conservative view of drug use during pregnancy is that it is a voluntary and illegal act that requires significant neglect of the rights of the fetus. From this view women who use drugs during their pregnancy are willfully committing a criminal act deserving of a legal response (Chasnoff, 1986).

Prosecution and State Statutes

There are many different reasons why state legislatures have taken an interest in addressing the problem of substance abuse by pregnant women. One reason is the basic notion that the state has an obligation to provide for the welfare of its citizens. It is also of financial importance to the state to address the issue (Chavkin, 1990). Immediate effects of MATID use include pregnancy complications as well as health issues for the newborn, driving up the amount of money that the state must spend on obstetrical and neonatal care. This is not where the cost of maternal drug use ends for the state. After birth, children born to mothers who used substances during pregnancy are at a higher risk of neglect, abuse, and abandonment, thus requiring the intervention of child protective services or juvenile courts at further cost to the states. First-year costs to states of births affected by maternal substance use can be as high as $50,000 each above the cost of "usual" births. State expenses for public assistance and foster care for each year after the first can be as high as $20,000 (Fein & Reynolds, 1990).

The costs to the state coupled with media attention as a result of the crack baby epidemic of the 1980s forced states to respond. Most often the response came in the form of legislation (Frohan, Lantz, & Pollack, 1999). Many different types of bills were introduced in an attempt to combat the problem on many different fronts and levels. Some bills addressed the roles of health professionals; specifically these bills often required doctors to report incidents of maternal substance abuse to the proper authorities; others required social service agencies to assess families affected by alcohol or drugs for abuse and neglect; and finally there were bills introduced requiring commercial vendors who sell alcohol and tobacco to post warnings about the effects of these substances on pregnant women (Gehshan & Steinberg, 2000).

State Approaches to Maternal Substance Use

States have employed a wide variety of strategies to combat maternal perinatal alcohol and drug use. Due to the public's outcry for an answer to the problem of crack babies and other drug-exposed infants, the courts implemented policies and practices that emphasized personal responsibility and punishment. User accountability was stated as the basis for most drug control policies. User accountability was based on the idea that if there were no drug users, there would be no drug problems and that users were responsible for creating the demand that made trafficking a lucrative criminal enterprise (Inciardi, Saum, & Surratt, 2000). Of course, our cultural penchant for punishment and criminalization may have played a role in justifying these policies.

Since there were not, and still are not, any statutes on the books specifically criminalizing drug use during pregnancy, women have been prosecuted under statutes that deal with child abuse, assault, murder, or drug dealing (Nelson, 1998). One of the newest attempts that have been used in prosecuting women is using statutes related to the delivery of drugs to a minor. However it is much more difficult to convince a judge and jury of prosecuting on these grounds because there is no explicit language in any of the statutes that delineates that a fetus can be considered a minor, entitled to all the rights and privileges afforded thereto (Anderson, 2000). Since 1985, approximately 240 women in 30 states have been criminally prosecuted in relation to their use of drugs during pregnancy (Marwick, 1998). State supreme courts have overturned nearly all of these convictions.

In formulating laws, whether criminal or civil, pertaining to perinatal substance abuse, there are certain general categories that are adhered to. There are laws dealing with the termination of parental rights and the removal of children from the home, testing/reporting/identifying drug-exposed infants, child abuse, and treatment for the mother and alcohol. Figure 2.2 shows the number of states with laws in each of these categories and Table 2.2 provides a summary of the specific laws.

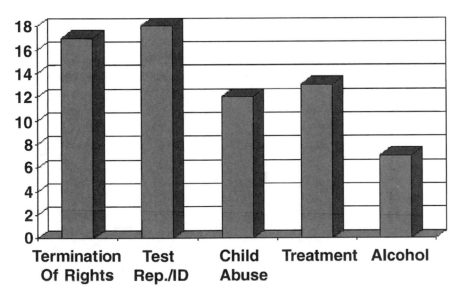

Figure 2.2 Number of states by type of substance abuse statute

Table 2.2
Type of Substance Abuse Statutes by State

STATE	Mandates Prenatal Testing/ Screening for Substance Use	Includes Maternal Substance Abuse or Infant Substance Exposure Under the Definition of Abuse	Mandates Neonatal Testing for Drugs	Mandates Reporting as Child Abuse or Neglect	Mandates Postnatal Reporting Assessment or Services	Mandates Priority Access to Treatment for Pregnant Women	Provides Treatment Program or Coordination of Services	Perinatal Substance Abuse Task Force Established by State Legislature	Mandates Posting of Dangers of Alcohol to Pregnant Women
AL									
AK									
AZ		Yes		Yes			Yes		
AR									
CA					Yes		Yes	Yes	
CO							Yes		
CT							Yes		
DE									
DC				Yes					Yes
FL		Yes		Yes					
GA						Yes			
HI									Yes
ID									

State								
IL								
IN		Yes		Yes				
IA		Yes		Yes		Yes		
KS	Yes				Yes	Yes	Yes	
KY						Yes	Yes	
LA								
ME								
MD		Yes		Yes	Yes	Yes		
MA		Yes		Yes				
MI		Yes		Yes			Yes	
MN	Yes	Yes	Yes			Yes		
MS								
MO								
MT								
NE								
NV				Yes				
NH							Yes	
NJ								Yes
NM								Yes
NY								Yes
NC						Yes		
ND								
OH						Yes		

(Continued)

Table 2.2
Type of Substance Abuse Statutes by State (Continued)

STATE	Mandates Prenatal Testing/Screening for Substance Use	Includes Maternal Substance Abuse or Infant Substance Exposure Under the Definition of Abuse	Mandates Neonatal Testing for Drugs	Mandates Reporting as Child Abuse or Neglect	Mandates Postnatal Reporting Assessment or Services	Mandates Priority Access to Treatment for Pregnant Women	Provides Treatment Program or Coordination of Services	Perinatal Substance Abuse Task Force Established by State Legislature	Mandates Posting of Dangers of Alcohol to Pregnant Women
OK				Yes				Yes	
OR									
PA							Yes		
RI									
SC		Yes		Yes					
SD		Yes		Yes			Yes		
TN									
TX									
UT				Yes					
VT									
VA	Yes	Yes		Yes			Yes	Yes	
WA									
WV							Yes		Yes
WI					Yes	Yes	Yes		
WY									

Barriers to Treatment

The overriding feeling among policy makers and social welfare agencies is that preserving the family is important where at all possible. This view has been reinforced by the Adoption and Safe Families Act (ASFA) passed in 1997, which requires permanent placement within 12 months of a child being removed from the biological mother. Substance use is not always a clear indicator of a parent's lack of commitment to his or her child. In fact many drug users are committed to being parents. One large barrier to seeking treatment is that the substance addict is afraid that if they seek help they will lose their children (Harrington, Heiser, & Howell, 1999). While the main goal of civil interventions is to protect children rather than punish mothers, many women view them as the state trying to take their children. Thus agencies have taken steps to make removing children from their homes the last resort. If this cannot be achieved, the next goal is family reunification, and often the success of a program is measured by how effectively the program preserves the family.

Thus in attempting to preserve the family, the preferred method of state intervention has become treatment and rehabilitation. There has been little consensus over the years on the best methods to employ in treating pregnant women with substance abuse problems. While treatment is recognized as the best method of addressing the issue, there exist serious barriers to treatment for pregnant substance users. Very few treatment programs have existed for women or have used treatment modalities designed specifically for women. Many programs have relied on male-based recovery models. This approach, focused on the individual and not the pregnant addict within the context of her family or environment, presents a challenge to women willing to access treatment. For instance, it is difficult for many users to be accepted into programs. Breibart, Chavkin, and Wise (1994), surveyed five U.S. cities as to the availability of treatment programs to pregnant women. Although the large majority of programs did accept pregnant women (80%), many did not accept women on Medicaid and did not provide or arrange for childcare. Addiction treatment is more effective when it is designed to account for women's needs. Addiction treatment counselors find that gender-specific treatment is much more effective than mixed-gender approaches. For seriously addicted women, the most effective treatments are long-term and residential. Also low-income women often have a variety of other service needs such as the need to learn parenting and career skills (Chavkin, 1990; Gehshan & Steinberg, 2000; Breibart et al., 1994; Milliken, 1999).

Another barrier to treatment is identification of the target population. Many pregnant substance users are reluctant to admit to drug use for fear of losing custody of their children, especially in states that legally require or practice mandatory reporting. Many of these women also fear criminal prosecution. The fear or threat of domestic violence is another serious concern.

The stigma against a pregnant user has been discussed in the literature. These women are frequently seen as weak-willed and negligent of their children and are often blamed for exposing their child to the drugs (Jessup & Green, 1987). This in turn has led to legal interventions such as criminal prosecution, mandatory treatment, and removal of custody. In addition, research has documented negative attitudes toward pregnant users by treatment providers (Finkelstein, 1993), which may make them reluctant to admit substance use.

Another barrier to treatment is the recognized lack of resources designed to help the pregnant addict and her children. Staffs often lack knowledge and training regarding issues of pregnancy and addiction. The first challenge is a concern over to how to medically manage these women. Addiction to alcohol and other drugs is a biochemical process. Many addicted women wish to quit using drugs or alcohol but are physically unable to stop. Detoxification is usually the first step in treatment. Usually this takes place is an inpatient setting and is a short-term way to eliminate chemical dependence, although it does not treat the enduring psychological and behavioral aspects of addiction. Since there is a fear of harming the unborn fetus with many of the medications used for detoxification, opiate-dependent women are especially susceptible to this barrier. Thus, their access is limited to most residential treatment programs. The concerns seem to be centered around the fact that detoxification can precipitate fetal withdrawal in utero, and that there is a high rate of recidivism among opiate-dependent individuals, which makes it harder to keep the unborn baby away from inconsistent levels of a drug and drug impurities. Many programs are ill-equipped to include infants and children in the program. There is also a fear of liability for negative birth outcomes and a lack of appropriate care for the infant and/or other children while the mother is in treatment. The lack of services for both the mother and the baby together leads to mothers being reluctant to obtain treatment due to the amount of time spent away from the child. All too often, it is a choice between treatment or caring for a new infant and other children. Even though programs do not include treatment services for children, they do not offer childcare as an alternative or incentive to treatment. Once again, the substance user must choose extended time away from the infant in order to obtain help. Such factors contribute to the low numbers of pregnant substance users receiving medical care. When women do receive prenatal care it provides an opportunity for intervention or access to support providers.

Another barrier is the lack of coordination between the resources needed by the pregnant substance user and lack of personnel who are sensitive to the issues and needs of this population. Also, many physicians are reluctant to identify the pregnant user for a variety of reasons. For instance, they may feel that they are ill-equipped to provide the pregnant women with support or they may have little confidence in social service agencies.

Finally, women may not seek treatment because they do not have transportation to and from programs and for economic reasons. They may not have insurance, money to pay for treatment, childcare, or treatment programs that are even available to them.

Historically, the approach for drug and alcohol treatment has been individually based, thus causing the pregnant addict to represent two avenues for intervention. Treatment professionals are often divided. First, there are those concerned with child welfare, and second, there are those concerned with the addiction, thus leaving a clear lack of coordinated, comprehensive, family-centered treatment (Finkelstein, 1993). Instead, a fragmented social service system stands in the wake of this division. Funding is usually not family centered so each service necessary in the treatment is in separate locations with unique regulations and procedures. Coordinating and accessing all of these services becomes a burden and thus services are not utilized. Clearly, barriers to treatment exist for pregnant women, and many programs are not providing the vital services needed for success.

Merely accessing treatment should be considered as a component for success. There is little definitive evidence in the treatment literature with regard to why a client interrupts or stops treatment. There may be differing rationales based on the type of user, that is, age, race, education, gender, and whether a woman is pregnant or parenting. Hser, Maglione, Polinsky, & Anglin (1998) examined factors affecting treatment entry. Characteristics that predicted treatment entry include legal pressure, lower levels of psychological distress and family or social problems, and prior successful treatment experiences. Perhaps treatment programs should identify such factors as part of their recruitment and service delivery and create individual, family-centered treatment services.

Research on Treatment Effectiveness

There is no clear empirical evidence as to what treatment modality is best for substance-using mothers, including inpatient or outpatient. The limited research on treatment programs is in part due to small sample sizes and the obvious lack of control or comparison groups. Amidst the descriptions of these programs exists a discussion of what is the most effective approach to treatment. In this question lies the debate over one-step expectation programs of immediate abstinence or programs that institute a stage process of recovery. The outcomes for these are usually retention in the treatment program and/or negative drug screens or abstinence from substances. Treatment retention has been related to successful program outcome (DeLeon & Jainchill, 1991).

Residential Treatment Programs

Camp and Finkelstein (1995) investigated 170 pregnant and parenting substance-dependent women who were placed in two residential treatment programs. Results suggest that participants improved considerably in their parenting knowledge and self-esteem. With regard to infant outcome, few infants exhibited poor birth outcomes such as low birth weight or early gestational ages. Completion of the program resulted in longer periods of abstinence.

The Salvation Army Treatment program in Honolulu is a long-term residential chemical dependency treatment facility. Women have been admitted to the program for approximately 6–18 months either with or without their children. Women admitted to the program with their children had better treatment retention and higher rates of successful treatment completion (treatment goals met) than women admitted without their children (Szuster, Rich, Chung, & Bisconer, 1996).

Amity Inc. in Arizona revised its program in 1981 to be more conducive to the female user. These changes significantly improved the treatment outcomes for both the men and women. The length of stay for the women increased over time; in fact, the length of stay for women with children in the program was highest overall. The authors suggest that another factor in addition to including children that contributed to the improved success was the creation of an environment in which female clients feel safe in disclosing and addressing treatment issues (Stevens, Arbiter, & Glider, 1989).

A Perinatal 20 project conducted by Hughes et al (1995), between April 1990 and October 1992, consisted of 53 women with children who were randomly assigned to either a standard residential treatment program or a demonstration residential program, in which the children were allowed to live with their mothers. Clients in the demonstration component of the program had significantly longer lengths of stay, suggesting that including children in the treatment program has implications for success. The authors also suggest that the inclusion of children could strengthen mother self-esteem and mother-child bonds while also improving post-treatment outcomes.

Outpatient programs

Haller, Knisely, Dawson, and Schnoll (1993) compared subjects randomly assigned to two outpatient treatment programs, a time-limited program of

5 months or a self-paced program for up to 18 months. Results showed that the women in the time-limited program had significant reductions in alcohol and drug use.

Another Perinatal 20 project was conducted in south central Los Angeles. This program was designed for the special treatment and support needs of drug-using women. It also sought to test the effectiveness of a modified relapse prevention approach. This project compared an intensive six-month treatment program with a traditional outpatient program. Results suggest that an intensive day treatment model is more effective than a standard outpatient treatment model for a variety of reasons. First, the staff at the day treatment program was made up mostly of women and the staff caseload was smaller that at the outpatient program. The study reports that if the day treatment clients retained custody of their infant, it was a predictor of length of stay in treatment; however, the more children the mother had at home was a negative predictor of length of stay. The authors suggest that it may have been harder for the mothers to secure childcare for more than one child, if they were in an intensive seven-day-a-week program (Strantz & Welch, 1995).

A New York City program, Pregnant Addicts and Addicted Mothers Program (PAAM), was created in 1975. PAAM is an outpatient program for pregnant women who are addicted to opiates or methadone. Women enrolled in the program must attend the program five times per week for methadone maintenance and attend prenatal visits, individual counseling sessions, and parent education classes. This is a comprehensive program that has demonstrated positive outcomes such as treatment compliance and favorable newborn outcomes (Suffet & Brotman, 1984).

California's Options for Recovery was created as an alternative to incarceration or relinquishment of custody of children by substance-dependent women. Options for Recovery offered specific residential and intensive day treatment services for dependence on alcohol and or other drugs, comprehensive case management, foster parent recruitment and training, and respite care for drug-exposed infants. Results have shown increased numbers of children reunited with their biological mothers after foster care placement. Children participating in Options programs displayed normal child development on standardized tests. Cost effectiveness was also assessed for Options for Recovery. Options for Recovery, as compared to the combined cost of incarceration and other drug and alcohol treatment, was significantly more cost effective (Brindis, Clayson, & Berkowitz, 1997).

The Parent and Child Enrichment Program (PACE) in Harlem began in 1990 and integrates the services of social workers, drug treatment counselors, parent educators, childcare workers, and medical personnel, including a pediatrician and a nurse midwife. PACE was set up to provide comprehensive, women-centered, and family-oriented services (Graham, Kan, Kerker, McMurtrie, & Rosenberg, 1999). The program reinforced the need to develop a female model of drug treatment. PACE showed that drug use does not happen in a vacuum. Including family members in the treatment process may help to establish a network of support for the women, both while they are in treatment and after. Quantitative results of the program have shown that the program has had a positive effect on its clients and thus the project is a useful model for drug treatment programs. Also the program helped to start a trend in the city of New York for providing treatment for pregnant and postpartum women.

Vital components for success

Most professionals agree that a comprehensive program is best for mothers. Services should be family-centered, community-based, multidisciplinary, and individually tailored, and it should promote competency of the individual. Finkelstein (1996) suggests a relational approach as a framework for the delivery of services to substance-dependent women. This model develops prevention and treatment in the context of a multigenerational and life-span perspective. A more family-centered model of care may improve treatment and post-treatment outcomes.

There is general agreement in the literature that programs need to include the following components: a cognitive/behavioral approach, parent role models and support, educational and vocational planning, transportation, mostly female staff, staff sensitive to issues of population, relapse considered part of treatment, outreach, case management, family support services such as child care, medical (including prenatal) care, mental health services, multi-method approaches to measure success, follow-up, parent training, child development services, family planning, legal services, crisis intervention, respite care, life skills management, pharmacological services, referral services, self help groups, and stress management.

Family Drug Court

Many states are establishing drug courts that deal with drug offenders. In drug courts the offender is given the opportunity to contract with the court to seek treatment instead of receiving a jail sentence. The most recent innovation in drug courts is family drug courts that deal specifically with maternal drug use during pregnancy. There are only a handful of these programs including our Vulnerable Infants Program of Rhode Island (VIP) (Lester, 2000). VIP is so named, in part, based on the research suggesting that drug exposed infants are vulnerable, not damaged, and that many of these infants can recover and develop normally given an appropriate environment. VIP works with Child Protective Services (CPS) and the Court to comply with ASFA and provide a program of coordinated care for drug-exposed infants and their families. VIP conducts a comprehensive and standardized assessment of the mother (maternal substance dependency, mental health, parenting and attachment, life skills, family support, and resources) and of the infant (medical and neurobehavioral status) as soon as the baby is identified as drug exposed in the hospital. The assessments are used to help CPS make recommendations to the court regarding placement of the infant with the biological mother or in foster care and to develop a treatment plan for use by the court. A special Family Treatment Drug Court for drug-exposed infants was established in 2003 based on the "treatment with teeth" concept. The program allows mothers the opportunity to get the appropriate treatment to be reunited with their infants and to provide the kinds of ancillary services including mental health, to make reunification effective and facilitate the development of the mother–infant attachment relationship. In this voluntary program, the VIP treatment plan is court ordered and sanctions are used for noncompliance, the ultimate sanction, of course, being loss of custody of the infant. This program has already shown success. We have been able to reduce by 60 percent the average length of stay of these infants in the hospital, and the number of infants reunified with their biological mother has doubled (which also means a 50% reduction in the number of infants placed in foster care).

POLICY ISSUES AND RECOMMENDATIONS

While it is widely acknowledged that there must be a societal response to the issue of maternal substance abuse, there is much controversy on just what this response should be. Much of this debate is linked to the complications and dilemmas that are present in the different policy responses that have arisen in attempts to address the issue.

Prevention

Most interventions to address the problem of maternal substance use during pregnancy have focused on preventing the problem in the first place. Yet, despite these efforts, drug use by pregnant women continues to be a significant public health problem. Thus, policy approaches for MATID must go beyond primary strategies to prevent drug use by pregnant women and include secondary and tertiary prevention strategies.

Primary prevention is aimed at preventing the initial occurrence of the problem, in this case, MATID abuse during pregnancy or avoiding pregnancy while using substances. This includes informing women of childbearing age about the dangers of prenatal drug exposure and education to abstain from drug use during pregnancy or to avoid pregnancy if using drugs. Providing treatment for drug-using women of childbearing age could help prevent drug use during pregnancy. Intervention to practice contraception is a way to prevent pregnancy in drug-using women and would also help reduce the spread of STDs and HIV. Use of fetal ultrasound to show mothers their fetus can increase attachment and lead to cessation of drug use during pregnancy.

Secondary prevention aimed at minimizing a problem when a risk factor exists would identify pregnant drug-using women and attempt to minimize their drug use through educational, treatment, research, and regulatory interventions (Wenzel et al., 2001). We mentioned earlier that many pregnant drug-using women receive little or no prenatal care, and it is known that fear of detection because of potential punitive actions against the women and the potential for removal of the child drive pregnant drug-using women away from the health care system. For prevention to be effective, the health care system needs to be perceived as friendly and supportive by drug-using pregnant women, not as punitive. They can be attracted to take advantage of prenatal care if they think it will help them and their child. Health care professionals can be better trained to detect substance abuse during pregnancy and to respond to comply with reporting requirements and in arranging services for the patient.

Tertiary prevention aims to minimize the adverse consequences of a problem, in this case the short-term or long-term harm to the child caused by drug exposure. This includes mental health, medical and social interventions, and treatment for the mother and family members as well as treatment for the infant and parenting and parent/child relationship therapy.

Prevention efforts should include education and treatment and target all drugs (i.e. licit and illicit) that have abuse potential during pregnancy including abuse of prescription drugs. Prevention efforts should be organized to enhance protective factors and to minimize risk factors. These efforts need to be developmentally and culturally appropriate, and capitalize on the mother's motivation to change and desire to keep or be reunited with her baby. They also need to deal with the complexity of these cases, including mental health co-morbidities, and should have a family and community focus.

Scientific Uncertainty

Policies have taken place in the context of uneven scientific knowledge about MATID use and developmental outcome. The literature is uneven with respect to type of drug (more is known about alcohol than other drugs), and in terms of drug effects there is uncertainty as to whether or not illegal drugs have more deleterious effects than legal drugs. Mostly we do not know the long-term developmental effects of prenatal drug exposure per se. It is remarkable that at a time when we acknowledge that most women who use drugs during pregnancy are polydrug users, studies have not examined the effects of polydrug exposure on developmental outcome. It is probably safe to say at this point that the scientific facts do not support the "quick fix" linear approach that focuses on the single-risk factor of prenatal drug exposure as the explanation for the outcomes of these children.

Public Awareness

A related issue is that the public needs to be aware of the scientific advances that have been made in the last 20 years. These advances include understanding of addiction as a chronic, relapsing medial/mental health problem, consequences of prenatal drug exposure for child development, and effectiveness of treatment. It does not appear as if this knowledge has reached (or been accepted by) the general public or has been applied in clinical programs or policy settings. This situation is exacerbated by the stigma surrounding drug use during pregnancy. Pregnant women are not extended the compassion normally displayed by the public toward individuals suffering from chronic diseases. The view that substance abuse should not be treated as another mental health and medical illness is at odds with established science.

Fetal rights

There have been several routes that the courts have taken in attempting to prosecute women for substance abuse during pregnancy. The most basic routes of societal response include the following: (1) use of the penal code to regulate all behavior of pregnant women that places the fetus at risk of harm; (2) use of the penal code to regulate all illegal behavior (particularly the use of controlled substances) that place the fetus at risk of harm; (3) use of family law and the power of the state to ensure that the best interests of the child are served, whether the behavior of the parent is legal or illegal; and (4) the use of no additional criminal or family law regulations specifically targeted at fetal abuse, relying instead on current language and policies to guide decision making (Madden, 1993; Janssen, 2000).

The filing of any charges against a substance-abusing mother hinges on the notion of fetal rights, namely that fetuses are human beings entitled to certain rights and privileges (Gosain, 1997). The question of what rights the fetus is entitled to is intrinsically tied to the argument of when life begins and when it is appropriate for society to regulate the current behavior of the mother in order to prevent potential future harm to the child (Lynch, 1996).

Fetal/maternal conflicts

It is important to acknowledge at the outset that policies for the pregnant woman/mother may be in conflict with policies for the fetus/infant. For example, high doses of methadone that are used for heroin-addicted pregnant women can produce withdrawal in the infant. Lower doses that would not produce withdrawal in the infant increase the risk that the methadone will be less effective and the pregnant woman return to street drugs. As another example, both managed care and welfare reform have resulted in sanctions that reduce services to drug-using mothers, such as when drug users are not eligible for benefits. The irony is that such policies are based on concern for the child and not only create a rift between advocates for women and advocates for children but also mean that mother and child face poverty without public assistance, or the child enters the foster care system.

Perinatal Drug Screening

One of the major issues that arise in trying to isolate a response to maternal drug use is related to screening for drug use in women and for exposure in newborns. It is difficult to determine who should be tested. Targeted testing, which leaves testing up to the discretion of the hospital and physicians, introduces the possibility of significant bias in decision making (Chasnoff, Landress, & Barrett, 1990). Universal testing of newborns has been suggested because it is the only way to employ testing that is devoid of social biases and also ensures that exposed infants who are detected will be able to receive all available services and treatment (Brestan, Ondersma, Simpson, & Ward, 2000).

However, the universal testing of infants places hospitals in a precarious position. If a newborn exhibits a positive toxicology screen and the state has a mandatory reporting law, the hospital has a responsibility to report to the necessary authorities, which can result in a conflict between the hospital's responsibility to protect the confidentiality of the mother and responsibility to protect the welfare of the infant (Marshall, 1998; Breibart, Chavkin, Elman, & Wise, 1998).

Another problem is that hospitals typically only screen for illegal drugs. Some have argued that the effects of nicotine are comparable if not worse than the effects of cocaine. Yet even though there are nicotine assays for urine and meconium. they are not used to identify exposed infants. And what would we do with this information? Would we really report up to 25 percent of new mothers to an already overburdened child welfare and criminal justice system because nicotine and cocaine have similar effects on the baby? If a mother is causing harm to her baby by using cocaine she is also causing similar harm to the baby by smoking cigarettes during pregnancy.

Another option for screening is to not test at all and simply rely on the self-report of the mother. The benefit of this option is that it greatly reduces the possibility of violating the civil liberties of the mother, treatment avoidance by the mother, and biased use of child welfare/criminal involvement. However there is also the risk that mothers will not disclose their drug use, rendering the physician unable to identify high-risk infants and thus unable to prevent negative outcomes (Brestan et al., 2000).

Finally, it might be possible to develop very specific criteria for drug testing that is based on specific medical indicators and avoids use of such open-ended criteria such as "clinical suspicion" that invite discriminatory testing. This solution would work with two caveats. First, all drugs would be included (legal, illegal, and prescription medication that can also be abused such as benzodiazepines, Percodan, or OxyContin). Second, the mother would not be automatically reported to CPS. Rather, the point of drug testing would be to provide hospital staff with the opportunity for intervention and the possibility of an additional standardized assessment if there is concern for the welfare of the child. Only if such an assessment indicated inadequate parenting would the mother be reported to CPS.

Who Gets Prosecuted

Another problem associated with criminalization is that of prejudicial reporting practices. Many fear that racial discrepancies in prosecutions are related to racial prejudices among people who report maternal substance abuse. Studies have shown that women of color are most likely to be prosecuted for perinatal substance use. This has led to the concern that criminalizing of perinatal substance abuse is in fact a process that is discriminatory against poor women of color (Marshall, 1998).

The government prosecutes more impoverished women than those in the middle class because middle-class women are more apt to use the services of private physicians (Chasnoff et al., 1990). Physicians are more likely to question poor minority women about their substance abuse and ultimately report their drug use (Anderson, 2000).

Constitutional Issues

There are many constitutional issues surrounding the prosecution of pregnant drug users. At the heart of the controversy are several Fourteenth Amendment entitlements, including due process, liberty, and equal protection. Based upon the criteria laid out by the due process clause of the Fourteenth Amendment, there have been several issues raised in relation to state intervention in the lives of drug-using mothers. First there is the issue of criminal prosecution itself. Is criminal prosecution really an effective intervention in deterring pregnant women from using drugs? There is much controversy over whether criminalization of the act really is an effective deterrent.

There is also the issue of physician disclosure of positive toxicology results to the authorities. The public disclosure of these results coupled with the use of the women's medical records are often used against the women in prosecutorial settings. This could be a violation of the women's right to privacy and freedom of association. Along the same lines it is often argued that by requiring physicians to report positive toxicology results the medical providers are forced into a situation where they are law enforcers and thus must obtain informed consent from their patients before performing any tests that may result in criminal prosecution (Inciardi, Surratt, & Saum, 1997). This is likened to law enforcement officials having to obtain a warrant before search and seizure. Often time drug screens are performed on the mothers without their knowledge let alone consent. This raises strong questions about violation of the mother's rights as related to their Fourth Amendment protection against illegal search and seizure.

Backlash Against Criminalization

There are other reasons beyond the constitutionality of prosecuting perinatal substance abusers that have come into play in the backlash against criminalization. Many professional health care and child welfare organizations have banded together against criminalization on the basis that it is antithetical to the best interests of both the mother and the child. They also argue that it puts health care providers in the inappropriate and uncomfortable position of having to police their patients. Reasons for the rejection of criminalization include that criminalization has no proven effect on improving infant health or deterring substance abuse by pregnant women. In fact criminalization may in fact deter the pregnant woman from seeking out necessary prenatal care for fear of losing her children or being arrested.

Criminalization of perinatal substance abuse creates untenable legal and ethical obligations for health care providers and other statutory mandatory reporters. It stretches the limits of what it means to be a caregiver. Finally, criminalization has been demonstrated to be applied with discrimination based on race and socioeconomic status (Marshall, 1998).

Conclusions

The issue of MATID use during pregnancy sits squarely at the intersection of behavioral teratology, jurisprudence, mental health, medicine, child protection, chemical dependency, civil rights, and women's issues perhaps in a way that no other controversy has. We learned a hard lesson from the cocaine controversy and saw the pendulum swing from an overestimation of risk associated with prenatal cocaine exposure to a more balanced view. That view includes the notion that, from a public health perspective, even subtle effects have significant societal impact and cost. The task at hand is to make sure that we view all drugs of abuse through a common lens, regardless of legal, social, or political considerations, so that their impact on child outcome can be adequately assessed, leading to appropriate policy making.

There is a substantial disconnect between our knowledge, policy, and practice regarding maternal drug use during pregnancy. For example, the drug control budget has more than doubled in the past decade. Yet the proportion of the budget devoted to treatment and prevention is unchanged, despite the gains made in science and in our understanding of the nature of addiction, based on research that has shown that treatment and prevention are effective. Arguably, the major barrier facing changes in policies for drug-using mothers is societal attitude. We have Supreme Court rulings that define drug use as a mental problem, we have modern evidence that treatment is effective and that there is no reason to consider drug use as different than any other mental/medical problem, there are treatment programs shown to be effective with drug using mothers, and there are treatment programs involving the courts. We have identified all of the other barriers, yet why has policy not changed? Is it because we are still angry and want to punish these mothers? That we will not forgive them for using drugs when they are pregnant? The great tragedy is that we are only harming the children. We harm them by denying services, by increasing the number of children in out-of-home placement, by undermining the ability of the children to form attachment relationships, and by labeling these children as damaged. We know the danger of self-fulfilling prophecies. If we expect these children to fail, they will fail. It is time to realize that getting angry and punishing the mother is not in the best interests of either the mother or the child. It is time that we develop a national consensus on how to deal with maternal prenatal drug use that does justice to the state-of-the-art knowledge in research and treatment and demonstrates a fair and unbiased attitude toward these women and their children.

REFERENCES

Anderson, M. (2000). *Criminal penalties for women engaging in substance abuse during pregnancy.* Newark, NJ: Women's Rights Law Reporter, Rutgers Law School.

Andres, R.L., & Day, M.C. (2000). Perinatal complications associated with maternal tobacco use. *Seminars in Neonatology, 5*(3), 231–241.

Bearer, C.F., Slavator, A.E., Buck, K., & Singer, L.T. (2001). *Fatty acid ethyl esters in meconium.* Paper presented at the RSA Satellite Workshop for the Detection of Prenatal Fetal Alcohol Exposure, Montreal, Canada.

Breibart, V., Chavkin, W., Elman, D., & Wise, P. (1998). National survey of the states: Policies and practices regarding drug-using pregnant women. *American Journal of Public Health, 88,* 117–119.

Breibart, V., Chavkin, W., & Wise, P. (1994). The accessibility of drug treatment for pregnant women: A survey of programs in five cities. *American Journal of Public Health, 84*(10), 1658–1661.

Brestan, E., Ondersma, S., Simpson, S., & Ward, M. (2000). Prenatal drug exposure and social policy: The search for an appropriate response. *Child Maltreatment, 5*(2), 93–109.

Brindis, C.D., Clayson, Z., & Berkowitz, G. (1997). Options for recovery: California's perinatal projects. *Journal of Psychoactive Drugs, 29*(1), 89–99.

Brown, S. (Ed.). (1990). *Children and prenatal illicit drug use: Research, clinical, and policy issues.* National Forum on the Future of Children and Families/National Research Council/Institute of Medicine. Washington, DC: National Academy Press.

Brunnemann, K., & Hoffman, D. (1991). Analytical studies on tobacco specific N nitrosamines in tobacco and tobacco smoke. *Critical Reviews in Toxicology, 21,* 235–240.

Califano, J.A. (1992). *Three-headed dog from hell: The staggering public health threat posed by AIDS, substance abuse and tuberculosis.* Washington Post, December 21, 1992.

Camp, J.M., & Finkelstein, N. (1995, February). *Fostering effective parenting skills and healthy child development within residential substance abuse treatment settings.* Center for Substance Abuse Prevention final report, Washington, DC.

Chasnoff, I. (Ed.). (1986). *Drug use in pregnancy: Mother and child.* Boston: MTP Press Limited.

Chasnoff, I. J., Landress, H. J., & Barrett, M. E. (1990). The prevalence of illicit drug or alcohol use during pregnancy and discrepancies in mandatory reporting in Pinellas County, Florida. *New England Journal of Medicine, 322,*1202–1206.

Chavkin, W. (1990). Drug addiction and pregnancy: Policy crossroads. *American Journal of Public Health, 80*(4), 483–487.

DeLeon, G., & Jainchill, N. (1991). Residential therapeutic communities for female substance abusers. *Bulletin of the New York Academy of Medicine, 67*(3), 277–290.

Fein, B., & Reynolds, W. (1990). Addicts, their babies, and their liability. *Legal Times 12*(50).

Finkelstein, N. (1993). Treatment programming for alcohol and drug-dependent pregnant women. Special Issue: Maternal drug use: Issues and implications for mother and child. *International Journal of the Addictions, 28*(13), 1275–1309.

Finkelstein, N. (1996). Using the relational model as a context for treating pregnant and parenting chemically dependent women. *Journal of Chemical Dependency Treatment, 6,* 23–44.

Finnegan, L. P., Oehlberg, S. M., Regan, D. O., & Rudrauff, M. E. (1981). Evaluation of parenting, depression, and violence profiles in methadone maintained women. *Child Abuse and Neglect, 5,* 267–273.

Frank, D. A., Augustyn, M., Knight, W. G., Pell, T., & Zuckerman, B. (2001). Growth, development, and behavior in early childhood following prenatal cocaine exposure: A systematic review. *Journal of the American Medical Association,* 285(12), 1613–1625.

Fried, P. A., Watkinson, B., & Gray, R. (1998). Differential effects on cognitive functioning in 9 to 12 year olds prenatally exposed to cigarettes and marijuana. *Neurotoxicology and Teratology, 20*(3), 293–306.

Frohan, J., Lantz, P., & Pollack, H. A. (1999). Maternal substance abuse and infant health: Policy options across the lifecourse. *Milbank Quarterly, 77*(4), 531–570.

Gehshan, S., & Steinberg, D. (2000, January). *State responses to maternal drug and alcohol use: An update.* Reported to The National Conference of State Legislatures, Washington, DC Supported by Robert Wood Johnson Foundation, Arlington, VA.

Gosain, C. (1997). Protective custody for fetuses: A solution to the problem of maternal drug use. *George Mason Law Review..*

Graham, E., Kan, J., Kerker, B., McMurtrie, C., & Rosenberg, K. (1999). A unique drug treatment program for pregnant and postpartum substance-using women in New York City: Results of a pilot project, 1990–1995. *American Journal of Drug and Alcohol Abuse, 25*(4), 701–713.

Griffin, M.L., Weiss, R.D., Mirin, S.M., & Lange, U. (1989). A comparison of male and female cocaine abusers. *Archives of General Psychiatry, 46,* 122–126.

Haller, D.L., Knisely, J.S., Dawson, K.S., & Schnoll, S.H. (1993). Perinatal substance abuse: Psychological and social characteristics. *The Journal of Nervous and Mental Disease, 18*(8), 509–513.

Harrington, M., Heiser, N., & Howell, E. (1999). A review of recent findings on substance abuse treatment for pregnant women. *Journal of Substance Abuse Treatment, 16*(3), 195–219.

Hien, D., & Scheier, J. (1996). Trauma and short-term outcome for women in detoxification. *Journal of Substance Abuse Treatment, 13,* 227–231.

Hser, Y.I., Maglione, M., Polinsky, M.L., & Anglin, M.D. (1998). Predicting drug treatment entry among treatment-seeking individuals. *Journal of Substance Abuse Treatment, 15*(3), 213–220.

Hughes, P.H., Coletti, S.D., Neri, R.L., Urmann, C.F., Stahl, S., Sicilian, D.M., & Anthony, J.C. (1995). Retaining cocaine-abusing women in a therapeutic community: The effect of a child live-in program. *American Journal of Public Health, 85*(8), 1149–1152.

Hutchins, E., & DiPietro, J. (1997). Psychosocial risk factors associated with cocaine use during pregnancy: A case-control study. *Obstetrics and Gynecology, 90,* 142–147.

Inciardi, J.A., Surratt, H.L., & Saum, C.A. (1997). Cocaine-exposed infants: Social, legal, and public health issues. Thousand Oaks, CA: Sage Publications.

Janssen, N. (2000). Fetal rights and the prosecution of women for using drugs during pregnancy. *Drake Law Review, 48*(4): 741–768.

Jessup, M., & Green, J.R. (1987). Treatment of the pregnant alcohol-dependent woman. *Journal of Psychoactive Drugs, 19*(2), 193–203.

Kahn, A., Groswasser, J., Sottiaux, M., Kelmanson, I., Rebuffat, E., Franco, P., Dramaix, M. & Wayenberg, J.L. (1994). Prenatal exposure to cigarettes in infants with obstructive sleep apneas. *Pediatrics, 93*(5), 778–783.

LaGasse, L.L., Seifer, R., & Lester, B.M. (1999). Interpreting research on pre-natal substance exposure in the context of multiple confounding factors. In B.M. Lester (Ed.), *Clinics in perinatology: Prenatal drug exposure and child outcome* (pp. 39–54). Philadelphia: W.B. Saunders Co.

Lester, B.M. (1999). To covary or not to covary: What is the question? *Journal of Drug Issues, 29*(2), 263–268.

Lester, B.M. (2003). What'll it be, legislators? For vulnerable infants, VIP works. *The Providence Journal Newspaper* (commentary) April 3, 2003.

Lester, B.M., Freier, C., Boukydis, C.F.Z., Affleck, P., & Boris, N. (1996). Keeping mothers and their infants together. *New York University Review of Law and Social Change, 22*(2), 371–396.

Lester, B.M., LaGasse, L., Freier, C., & Brunner, S. (1996). Human studies of cocaine exposed infants. 164th edition. Rockville, MD: Monograph Series for The National Institute of Drug Abuse.

Lester, B. M., LaGasse, L. L., & Seifer, R. (1998). Cocaine exposure and children: The meaning of subtle effects. *Science, 282,* 633–634.

Lester, B. M., & Tronick, E. Z. (1994). The effects of prenatal cocaine exposure and child outcome: Lessons from the past. *Infant Mental Health Journal, 15*(2), 107–120.

Levin, E. D., & Slotkin, T. A. (1998). Developmental neurotoxicity of nicotine. In W. Slikker & L. W. Chang (Eds.), *Handbook of Developmental Neurotoxicity* (pp. 587–615). St. Louis: Academic Press.

Lynch, T. (1996). Is the prosecution of "fetal endangerment" illegitimate? *American Bar Journal, 82*(72).

Madden, R. G. (1993). State actions to control fetal abuse: Ramifications for child welfare practice. *Child Welfare. 72*(2), 129–140.

Malanga, C. J., & Kosofsky, B. E. (1999). Mechanisms of action of drugs of abuse on the developing fetal brain. In B. M. Lester (Ed.), *Clinics in Perinatology: Prenatal drug exposure and child outcome* (pp. 17–38). Philadelphia: W. B. Saunders Co.

Marshall, M. (1998). An Ethical and Legal Analysis of State-compelled Loss of Liberty as an Intervention to Reduce the Harm of Perinatal Substance Abuse and Addiction. *Substance Abuse Policy Research Program.* http://www.saprp.org/grant_detail.cfm?AppID=1146.

Marwick, C. (1998). Challenging report on pregnancy and drug abuse. *Journal of the American Medical Association, 280*(12), 1039–1040.

Matthews, T. J. (2001). Smoking during pregnancy in the 1990s. *National Vital Statistics Reports, 49*(7), 4.

Miller, B. A., Downs, W. R., Gondoli, D. M., & Keil, A. (1987). The role of childhood sexual abuse in the development of alcoholism in women. *Violence and Victims, 2,* 157–172.

Milliken, J. R. (1999). Juvenile court county of San Diego: *The dependency court recovery project.* http://www.cffutures.org/Children_Family_Policy/CW/TAP/TAP_description.pdf.

Murphy, S., & Rosenbaum, M. (1999). *Pregnant women on drugs: Combating stereotypes and stigma.* New Brunswick, NJ: Rutgers University Press.

National Institute of Drug Abuse, N. I. H. (1996). National pregnancy and health survey: Drug use among women delivering live births. Washington, DC: U.S. Department of Health and Human Services.

Nelson, L. (1998). A legal analysis of state-compelled loss of liberty as an intervention to reduce the harm of perinatal substance abuse and drug addiction. In L. J. Nelson & M. F. Marshall (Eds.), *Ethical and legal analyses of three coercive policies aimed at substance abuse by pregnant women.* Charleston, SC: The Robert Wood Johnson Foundation.

Paltrow, L. M. (1998). Punishing women for their behavior during pregnancy: An approach that undermines the health of women and children. In C. L. Wetherington & B. Roman (Eds.), *Drug addiction research and the health of women* (pp. 467–501). Rockville, MD: U.S. Department of Health and Human Services/National Institute on Drug Abuse.

Ross, H.E., Glaser, F.B., & Stiasny, S. (1988). Sex differences in the prevalence of psychiatric disorders in patients with alcohol and drug problems. *British Journal of Addiction, 83,* 1179–1192.

Rounsaville, B.J., Anton, S.F., Carroll, K., Budde, D., Prusoff, B.A., & Gawin, F. (1991). Psychiatric diagnosis of treatment-seeking cocaine abusers. *Archives of General Psychiatry, 48,* 43–51.

Smeriglio, V.L., & Wilcox, H.C. (1999). Prenatal drug exposure and child outcome: Past, present, future. In B.M. Lester (Ed.), *Clinics in perinatology: Prenatal drug exposure and child outcome* (pp. 1–16). Philadelphia: W.B. Saunders Co.

Stevens, S., Arbiter, N., & Glider, P. (1989). Women residents: Expanding their role to increase treatment effectiveness in substance abuse programs. *International Journal of the Addictions, 24,* 425–434.

Strantz, I.H., & Welch, S.P. (1995). Postpartum women in outpatient drug abuse treatment: Correlates of retention/completion. *Journal of Psychoactive Drugs, 27*(4), 357–373.

Substance Abuse and Mental Health Services Administration. (2000). *National Household Survey on Drug Abuse.* Washington, DC.

Suffet, F., & Brotman, R. (1984). A comprehensive care program for pregnant addicts: Obstetrical, neonatal, and child development outcomes. *International Journal of the Addictions, 19*(2), 199–219.

Szuster, R.R., Rich, L.L., Chung, A., & Bisconer, S.W. (1996). Treatment retention in women's residential chemical dependency treatment: The effect of admission with children. *Substance Use and Misuse, 31*(8), 1001–1013.

U.S. Department of Health and Human Services. (1990). *The health benefits of smoking cessation: A report of the Surgeon General.* Rockville, MD.

Wenzel, S.L., Kosofsky, B.E., Harvey, J.A., Iguchi, M.Y., Steinberg, P., Watkins, K.E., & Shaikh, R. (2001). Prenatal cocaine exposure: Scientific considerations and policy implications: *Report from the New York Academy of Sciences and RAND.* http://www.rand.org/publications/MR/MR1347/index.html

Wilsnack, S.C., Vogeltanz, N.D., Klassen, A.D., & Harris, T.R. (1997). Childhood sexual abuse and women's substance abuse: National survey findings. *Journal of Studies on Alcohol, 58,* 264–271.

Chapter 3

DISORDERS OF ATTACHMENT

Brian S. Stafford

Although the concept of attachment disorders has entered mainstream culture as evidenced by its appearance in popular media, the concept continues to be a source of confusion for mental health professionals and social care workers. Some of the confusion about attachment disorders arises from the newness of the diagnostic category and the sparse amount of research in this area. In addition, psychiatric researchers may have a different concept of reactive attachment disorder (RAD) than practicing mental health clinicians and workers in the foster care system. Another factor contributing to confusion about this disorder is that the field of attachment theory (AT), a construct that is fundamental to the development and understanding of the attachment disorders concept, has only mild convergence with the study of attachment disorders.

In spite of this confusion, many agree that extremely adverse caregiving environments are associated with aberrant social behaviors in young children. It is also supposed that many psychiatric disturbances have their roots in disturbed or compromised caregiving. The psychiatric clinical disorder that attempts to describe distinctive patterns of disturbed social behavior in young children who were abused, neglected, or institutionalized is known as reactive attachment disorder (RAD). Fortunately, the study of clinical attachment disorders has developed beyond its own infancy and the research base on attachment disorders is rapidly expanding. The information obtained during this growth has led to an ongoing reevaluation of the validity of the attachment disorder construct, refinements in the clinical diagnostic criteria, and the development of suitable programs to assist these children and their caregivers. To best understand the manner in which professionals conceptualize, evaluate, and treat young children who have experienced extremely disturbed caregiving, we will review the following: development of attachment theory, history of the concept of reactive attachment disorder, current research about attachment disorders, alternative conceptualizations of attachment-disordered behavior, and appropriate and inappropriate interventions for children with disordered attachment behavior. Before that discussion, however, an explication of terms is warranted. Throughout this chapter, the term "attachment theory" refers to a theory describing the nature of the physical and emotional relationship between caregivers and infants. "Attachment classification" refers to specific categories of infant-to-caregiver behavior derived from a standardized laboratory procedure. "Attachment behavior" refers to the behaviors shown primarily by the infant toward the caregiver such as exploration or comfort-seeking. "Attachment disorder" or "reactive attachment disorder" is used to denote the psychiatric diagnostic label for children with "attachment disordered behavior."

ATTACHMENT THEORY

The standard theory to describe the infant's bond to its mother for most of the past century was proposed by Sigmund Freud. This "hunger-drive" theory posited that libido, aggression, and physical hunger were the primary forces in the child's relationship to his or her caregiver. John Bowlby (1982), a British psychoanalyst, developed his own theory of the mother-infant bond based on his observation that a high proportion of delinquent boys had suffered early separations from their mothers. Bowlby was influenced by the animal experiments of Lorenz and Harlow (Harlow, 1958) that seemed to suggest that the seeking of comfort by young offspring was an evolutionarily wired predisposition. Bowlby translated this to the human mother–infant relationship and proposed that the provision of comfort to an infant—not the provision of sustenance—was responsible for the relationship with the caregiver. Bowlby also drew upon the fields of control systems theory, cognitive science, and developmental psychology to formulate a model that explained the child's tie to its mother. He proposed that certain attachment behaviors were preferentially selected through evolution because they favored proximity between a caregiver and its dependent/defenseless offspring, thereby increasing the likelihood of that individual's and, therefore, the species' survival. The outcome of this evolutionary process is the presence of a biologically rooted motivational system in human infants. The attachment system that he proposed is one of several fundamental behavioral systems in the infant. Others include the exploratory system, the sociable system, and the wariness system.

Bowlby proposed that the most fundamental goal of the attachment system is to ensure survival of offspring by promoting mutual proximity of infants and their caregivers, thereby providing protection from predators. To ensure proximity-seeking behavior, infants must have the capacity to reference and respond to their caregivers' signals as well as signal their caregivers. The field of developmental psychology has confirmed these abilities. The attachment system also motivates young children to seek comfort, support, nurturance, and protection from discriminated attachment figures. Infants become attached to caregivers with whom they have had significant social interaction. Young children develop a preference for a caregiver and protest when separation is threatened. The caregiver also serves as a secure base from which to explore the environment and a safe haven to return to when distressed. Although the evolutionary goal of this motivational system is proximity-seeking, another function of this system is to regulate the infant's developing emotional states.

Based on their observations of infants in Uganda, Bowlby (1982) and his most important colleague, Mary Ainsworth (1967), described four main phases in the development of attachment during the first years of life:

Stage I: undiscriminating responsiveness (birth to 2 months)

Stage II: differential responsiveness (3 months to 6 months)

Stage III: proximity maintenance (7 months to 24 months)

Stage IV: goal corrected partnership (24 months to 60 months)

At birth the infant shows *undiscriminating responsiveness* to people through behavioral signaling (Stage 1). From age 2 to 3 months the infant demonstrates continuing responsiveness to other people but begins to show *differential responsiveness* to its mother and other primary caregivers (Stage II). Important changes in cognitive, emotional, communicative, and memory development occur at around 6 to 7 months. The onset of locomotion (crawling and walking) allows for new attachment behaviors to be displayed (following, secure base, refueling, *proximity maintenance* (Stage III), safe haven returns, and burying their face in the mother's lap, and, finally, differential clinging to mother when distressed (Ainsworth, 1967). Elaboration of the infant's cognitive skills and memory allow for the development of a rudimentary "internal working model" that allows the infant to achieve an end goal "i.e. proximity" and select behaviors that will help him or her accomplish this. Expansion of communicative skills allows for further visual and vocal engagement and signaling with others. Finally, in the preschool years, further cognitive, communicative, and emotional development allows for the formation of the goal-corrected partnership (Stage IV).

During the early phases of Stage II, the onset of other important behavioral systems occurs. These include the expansion of the *exploratory system,* the *sociable system,* and the *wariness system.* The *exploratory system,* fueled by the new-found skills of locomotion, enhances the infant's ability to learn and interact with the physical and social environment. The attachment and exploratory systems frequently act in concert. When the child feels comfortable with a caregiver's availability, that child will likely explore the immediate environment. However, if the attachment system is activated by fear or distress, exploration ceases and proximity-seeking to the caregiver becomes primary. The *sociable/affiliative system* during this period is one of initial wariness that may preclude exploration of the environment. If not intrusive, however, the infant is likely to interact socially with rapidly decreasing wariness. *Wariness* to novel situations has obvious survival value. The balance of the wariness system with the attachment and sociable systems accounts for much of the behavior observed in the strange situation procedure. The behaviors associated with these systems are coordinated in such a manner that they inhibit or potentiate one another.

What is observed between 6 and 12 months is that the infant begins to sharply define an attachment to its mother, with a striking decline in friendliness to others, and "maintenance of proximity to a discriminated figure by means of locomotion as well as signals" (Bowlby, 1982, 299). Protests at the mother's departure also develop. Ainsworth interpreted this as indicating that the infant had formed a "mental representation" of the mother. Exploratory behavior, the counterpart of attachment, takes place from the secure base provided by the attachment figure. In addition, from 12 to 14 months the infant begins to show developing attachments to figures other than the primary caregiver and may develop a hierarchy of attachment figures.

Mary Ainsworth, a developmental psychologist, and her numerous and productive students (Ainsworth & Marvin, 1995) have provided several major modifications and elaborations of Bowlby's original theory. These contributions include the elaboration of attachment behaviors, the development of a laboratory evaluation—the Strange Situation Procedure (SSP)—that elicits individual differences and allows formal classification of dyads, and the correlation between sensitive caregiving and attachment classifications. Ainsworth began this journey by conducting longitudinal naturalistic observations of Ugandan caregivers and their infants. The attachment behaviors she observed include: crying, smiling, and vocalizing differentially toward the caregiver; orientation and attention toward the caregiver; following the caregiver; clambering over and exploration of the caregiver; and happiness when reunited with the caregiver after a brief separation.

A few years later in a follow-up study conducted in Baltimore among middle-class American babies, she again observed these behaviors and also identified striking individual differences in the way that attachment behaviors are organized together and directed toward an attachment figure. On the basis of that study, Ainsworth and colleagues inferred the existence of an underlying dimension to the quality of the attachment relationship that was described as *secure* or *insecure*. She also designed a laboratory procedure, the Strange Situation Procedure, to assess the security-insecurity of the attachment relationship.

The Strange Situation Procedure (SSP) (Ainsworth, Blehar, Waters, & Wall, 1978) is a laboratory paradigm designed to heighten attachment stress and elicit attachment patterns in the infant. The SSP assesses the organization of the behavioral system behaviors and the security of the caregiver-infant attachment relationship between 9 and 12 months of age. It assesses these primarily through the infant's reactions toward the mother during a series of brief, controlled separations and reunions involving the caregiver, infant, and a female stranger. The scoring of infant behaviors is done on two levels. One level identifies and rates the occurrence of specific categories of infant behaviors, such as proximity-seeking, contact-seeking, and resistance. At the second level, the child's behavior is classified according to three categories of organized behavior: secure, insecure-avoidant or insecure-resistant.

Securely attached infants use the caregiver as a *secure base* from which to explore. They will experiment in an unfamiliar environment and with unfamiliar objects while the attachment figure is present. They move freely away from her but keep track of her location with an occasional checking glance back at her. They move back to the caregiver to make brief contact with her from time to time, and they respond positively when picked up. However, they do not want to be held for long and, as soon as they are put down, they move off to play happily. When the attachment figure is absent, there is little exploration and heightened attachment is expressed in calling and looking for the attachment figure. *Insecure-avoidant* infants seem to be preoccupied with exploration though aware of the caregiver. They are unlikely to be distressed by caregiver departure, they may be friendlier to the stranger than to the caregiver, and they conspicuously ignore or avoid the caregiver on her return. *Insecure-resistant* infants are reluctant to leave the caregiver to explore and may be fretful even before her departure. They are extremely distressed by her departure, but greet her return with a mixture of contact-seeking and rejection (resistance to comfort or contact). They seem unable to settle and return to play and may be either angry at the caregiver or extremely passive.

Attachment theory also attempts to answer the caregiving precursors to the unique strategies observed. Ainsworth's original Baltimore study was two-pronged, with the Strange Situation Procedure preceded by hours of home observations of caregiver-infant observations. She originally identified four dimensions of maternal behavior that appeared to be related to security of attachment: sensitivity, acceptance, cooperation, and acceptability (Meins, Fernyhough, Fradley, & Tuckey, 2001). Infants who demonstrated a secure attachment in the SSP had caregivers who were observed to be emotionally responsive to their infant's distress and bids for comfort. Infants with insecure-avoidant attachments had caregivers that were striking in their aversion to providing physical comfort and expressing little emotion to their infants. Finally, caregivers of insecure-resistant/ambivalent infants had caregivers that had responded inconsistently to their infant's bids. Group analysis of numerous studies confirms that maternal behavioral sensitivity is strongly associated with classification of attachment (De Wolff & van Ijzendoorn, 1997).

To Ainsworth, "sensitivity" meant behaviorally responding to the child "as a separate person" and being "capable of seeing things from the child's point of view." This goes beyond a basic ability to recognize and respond to the child's physical states such as hunger and distress, to a capacity to be able to "read" the baby's behavior and to intuit or infer the child's mental state. This behavioral response is informed by the caregivers' cognitive and emotional capacity to understand and respond to their infant as an individual with their own capacity for feelings and desires, as well as the means to send behavioral cues indicative of these states. This ability to intuit and respond to their infants appropriately is captured by terms such as "mind-mindedness," "mentalizing ability," or "reflective functioning" (Meins et al., 2001). This ability is demonstrated by a caregiver making statements to the child commenting on his or her feelings and intention: "I see you looking at that toy and I think you want me to help you reach it." "Mentalizing" requires awareness of the infant's signals, the capacity to accurately interpret the signals, and to appropriately and promptly respond to the infant's signals. At this point it appears as if the cognitive and emotional ability to see the child as a unique individual and the ability to appropriately respond leads to a secure attachment.

A decade later, other researchers described a fourth classification, a *disorganized/disoriented* attachment, characterized by atypical reunion behaviors such as dissociative or disoriented episodes, as well as a combination of secure, avoidant, and ambivalent behaviors that were poorly or bizarrely coordinated (Main & Solomon, 1986). Disorganized attachments are associated with high-risk environments and are supposed to be attachment sequelae of threatening, frightening, or dissociated caregiving

(Main & Hesse, 1990). This pattern is thought to represent the simultaneous activation of the attachment system and the fear/wariness system. This yoking presents the infant with an inherent conflict. Fear of the parent activates the attachment system and the drive for proximity; however, as proximity increases, the fear does as well, which may lead to contradictory approaches. In these scenarios, the attachment figure is both the *solution* and the *source* of the attachment alarm.

Secure, avoidant, and ambivalent attachments are called "organized" strategies, and avoidant and ambivalent are also known as insecure strategies, while a disorganized/disoriented attachment is considered "non-organized". A secure attachment demonstrates a comfortable balance in the infant between his attachment and exploratory systems. There is a great deal of evidence to support the substance of attachment theory, in particular for the stability of attachment classifications (Weinfield, Sroufe, & Egeland, 2000). Longitudinal studies of children within these classifications have demonstrated strikingly unique social outcomes. Infants assessed as secure at 18 months were enthusiastic and persistent in solving toy tasks at age two, while insecure infants tended to be more easily frustrated and whiny. Preschoolers who were secure infants were more flexible, curious, socially competent, and self-reliant than their anxious counterparts. These findings are expected to become more dramatic as they become teenagers. The patterns of attachment are "relationship-specific" rather than :within-the-child" traits and may be different with different caregivers.

Infants approaching one year of age can monitor the attachment figure's whereabouts, signal their needs, and follow their attachment figures. Preschool children, whose cognitive and linguistic skills are substantially more advanced, seek opportunities to communicate with their attachment figures regarding their mutual access to one another (Where are you going? Are you coming back?, etc.). Attachment behaviors do not cease as the child enters the toddler period. It is true that separation distress tends to decrease and refueling periods become briefer with age and, by age three, less physical contact is required. Toddlers increasingly organize their interactions with attachment figures on the basis of physical orientation, eye contact, nonverbal expressions, affect, and conversations about separations, reunions, feelings, shared activities, and plans. Toddlers' attachment behaviors can be coded according to behavior in the SSP with a different coding system that takes into account these further developed capacities.

Summary

To review, by 9–12 months, children in *normative* child-rearing environments demonstrate attachment relationships with caregivers that

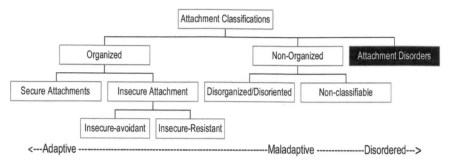

Figure 3.1   Spectrum of attachment disturbance

are organized (secure, insecure avoidant, insecure resistant). Infants in more *threatening* environments are more at risk to develop *disorganized* attachments. A caregiver with the capacity to see the child as a unique and intentional individual and the ability to respond to their child's cues with sensitivity will likely lead to secure attachments for their infants. Clearly, developmental research in attachment continues to grow exponentially. On the other hand, clinical disorders of attachment have only recently received attention. For example, in Cassidy and Shaver's encyclopedic *Handbook of Attachment* (1999), there are over 2,000 references cited about attachment theory, but not a single reference to attachment disorders (See figure 3.1.). This disparity is emblematic of the need for more attention to clinical disorders of attachment.

HISTORY OF REACTIVE ATTACHMENT DISORDER

Until recently, most studies of attachment classifications have been in standard or high-risk environments. Not all child-rearing environments, however, conform to what Bowlby called "*average expectable environments.*" Indeed, many infants who are abused, neglected, or institutionalized endure environments that are far from the average expectable environment. For example, institutionalized infants may not have the opportunity to develop selective attachments, based on lack of exposure to a consistent individual. Many institutions delegate shifts so that a child may encounter a different caregiver, not just every day, but for every shift of every day. This lack of opportunity creates an environmental impasse in the ability to form caregiver-child specific attachments. Other environments may also contribute to the development of abnormal attachment behaviors. Children in the foster care system have, by definition, a history of an abusive or neglectful relationship with a caregiver. These factors alone are likely to lead to insecurity or disorganization of the attachment. In addition, many of these young children experience numerous placements in the foster care system. These placements, with the associated disruptions, may also create a non-average expectable environment for attachment to develop.

Children observed in institutions and once removed from these environments demonstrate unusual social behaviors. Initial observations of these behaviors were described in formerly institutionalized children as "superficially affectionate," "indiscriminately exhibitionistic," and "socially disinhibited." A second form of disturbed social behavior has also been described in a small number of children with a history of severe maltreatment. These "inhibited" children were described as having "extreme fear" or "stranger terror." Observations of the disinhibited and inhibited social behaviors of these children led to the development of the pathological psychiatric condition known as reactive attachment disorder.

This disorder first appeared in the *Diagnostic and Statistic Manual of Mental Disorders*, 3rd Edition (DSM III) (American Psychiatric Association, 1980), in the descriptive list of psychiatric disorders and symptoms. Despite the potential importance of reactive attachment disorder (RAD), there have been very few published studies to validate the diagnosis in the past 25 years. In fact, virtually all of the studies relevant to the validity of the diagnosis have been published in the past 10 years. Not surprisingly, the criteria for RAD were not based on direct research evidence (Boris & Zeanah, 1999), but rather on indirect studies and case reports of maltreated and institutionalized young children described earlier (Zeanah & Emde, 1994). Nevertheless, there is a consensus that the disorder describes symptoms and signs not described by other disorders (Richters & Volkmar, 1994). A growing body of research supports the presence of the disorder if not the validity of the current criteria.

In DSM-III, reactive attachment disorder was initially confused with failure to thrive, a pediatric condition that involves infant withdrawal, feeding difficulties, and growth failure. The diagnostic criteria for RAD were substantially revised for DSM-IV (American Psychiatric Association, 2000), the current diagnostic manual, and will likely undergo further revision for the next version. Currently, the disorder is defined by aberrant social behaviors that appear in early childhood and are evident across social contexts. Two unique patterns are defined, an emotionally withdrawn pattern and an indiscriminately social pattern. DSM-IV defines RAD as a markedly disturbed and developmentally inappropriate social relatedness in most contexts, beginning before age five years, as evidenced by either restricted or indiscriminate social interaction. Developmental delay or autism cannot strictly account for the abnormal social relatedness. In addition, evidence of pathogenic care such as institutionalization, emotional or physical neglect, or multiple changes in primary caregivers must be evident.

In addition to revisions in the DSM diagnostic criteria for RAD, other diagnostic systems exist and also contribute to the confusion in this area of study. The ICD-10, the worldwide diagnostic manual created by the World Health Organization (2003), has slightly different criteria for the disorders. For example, ICD-10 labels them as inhibited attachment disorder and reactive attachment disorder. These diagnostic criteria are descriptive in nature and may be more helpful to clinicians and social care workers; however, narrative descriptions make research attempts at validation more difficult. A specialized manual for describing syndromes of infants and toddlers appeared with the arrival of the Diagnostic Criteria 0–3 (Zero To Three, 1994). This description brought alternative criteria but preserved the subtypes. These criteria, however, are more focused on deficiencies and risk factors in the caregiving environment rather than on the child's behavior. In addition, they do not include criteria or guidelines to define the two patterns, which makes it difficult to exclude other problems and to know what symptomatic threshold must be met to diagnose the disorder.

The DSM-IV criteria imply that the child's attachment relationships are impaired in reaction to "pathogenic caregiving." In addition, the socially aberrant behaviors are evident across social contexts. In keeping with the DSM-IV's view of psychopathology within an individual, RAD is not conceptualized as a disorder of the attachment relationship (as attachment theory would describe); rather it is a disorder of social relatedness within the child. This divergence from attachment theory accounts for much of the confusion in the use of the term "attachment disorder." A reactive attachment disorder, in current diagnostic systems, is a disorder of social relatedness within the child rather than a characteristic of that child's relationship with a specific caregiver. In attachment theory language, RAD more likely describes non-differentiation (disinhibition) or paucity (inhibition) of a child's social bids during the second phase of attachment development rather than a nonoptimal attachment pattern described in Phase III (i.e., disorganized type).

Summary

Although reactive attachment disorder has some foundation in attachment theory, they do not describe the same processes. Attachment theory and the SSP show unique aspects of a relationship between caregivers and infants while an attachment disorder describes deficits in the child's social behaviors both toward caregivers and toward strangers.

IS RAD A VALID PSYCHIATRIC DISORDER?

The process of determining the presence of a disorder in a population and the appropriate symptoms, known as diagnostic criteria, is the "validation" process. In adult psychiatric populations, this process has taken 40 years of intense description, observation, and research, with revisions occurring frequently. The validation process of psychiatric disorders in children lags far behind that of the adult populations, and the process in infants and toddlers is far behind all other populations. Validating any disorder requires a sophisticated and stepwise multistage process, beginning with the description of clinical phenomenology in the form of reports of case studies and series of cases (Cantwell, 1996). Clinical experience leaves little doubt that serious disturbances, if not disorders, of attachment exist (Hinshaw, Fuselier, Boris, & Zeanah, 1999; Richters & Volkmar, 1994). The next stages in validating a disorder focus on external validating factors such as associated psychosocial, family environment, demographic, biologic, genetic, natural course as well as response of the disordered child to treatment. A few longitudinal studies have been completed on these groups and document compromised long-term relationships and a high incidence of impairment and co-morbidity (Hodges & Tizard, 1989; Tizard & Hodges, 1978).

In spite of these successes, significant difficulties have also been found when attempting to validate the disorder. Researchers (Boris, Zeanah, Larrieu, Scheeringa, & Heller, 1998) found that experienced clinicians disagree when asked to apply current DSM-IV diagnostic criteria to case material from an abused/neglected sample. In addition, others also found difficulties in applying ICD-10, DSM-IV, DC: 0–3, and a proposed alternative research criteria to infants and toddlers in Romanian institutions (Smyke & Zeanah, personal communication, Sept., 2004). In spite of the difficulties of validating specific diagnostic criteria, there is ample evidence for the presence of both subtypes in a variety of settings of maltreatment, neglect, and institutionalization. Further refinements of the number of symptoms and the severity of impairment may lead clinicians and researchers to agreement.

Inhibited Social Pattern

The inhibited subtype of RAD is defined as emotional withdrawal, failure of social and emotional reciprocity, and lack of seeking or responding to comforting when distressed. There is an absence of an expected tendency to initiate or respond appropriately to social interactions. Instead excessively inhibited, hypervigilant (fearful), or highly ambivalent (contradictory) reactions are exhibited.

Attachment behaviors, such as seeking and accepting comfort, showing and responding to affection, relying on caregivers for help, and cooperating with caregivers are absent or markedly restricted. In addition, exploratory behavior is frequently limited due to the absence of a preferred attachment figure. These children may also demonstrate problems of emotion regulation that range from affective blunting, to withdrawal, to "frozen watchfulness." This subtype was initially described in institutionalized children (Tizard & Rees, 1975). Of note, however, is the apparent lack of persistence of these behaviors in ex-institutionalized toddlers. In regard to the aforementioned behavioral systems, inhibition of attachment behaviors could be related to hyper-arousal of the fear/wariness system, inhibition of the social and attachment systems, or a combination of the above.

Disinhibited/Indiscriminately Social Pattern

This pattern is characterized by more interaction with caregivers; however, there is a failure to demonstrate "selectivity" in interacting with others. These children often lack selectivity in seeking comfort, support, and nurturance. In addition, these children may seem overly friendly and only superficially attached. Stranger wariness, which normally appears as early as seven months of age and remains apparent for several years, is absent. Children with this subtype may approach strangers without expected social wariness; they may seek comfort or help from a stranger and may demonstrate a variety of social relatedness problems that depend upon accurately reading social cues and understanding interpersonal boundaries. This subtype has been demonstrated in children who do not experience average expectable environments during their early years. It is not known if environmental or child variables are responsible for who gets which type of disorder.

Of note and contrary to the DSM-IV's conceptualization of two distinct subtypes of the disorder, most infants and toddlers in these compromised caregiving circumstances demonstrate signs of both subtypes.

RAD DIVERGENCE FROM CLASSIFICATIONS OF ATTACHMENT

To address the question of how SSP classifications of attachment mapped onto clinical disorders of attachment, Boris and Zeanah (1999) proposed a spectrum of attachment, *including disorders of non-attachment, a disrupted attachment disorder, and secure-base distortions.* Disorders of non-attachment best correspond to the DSM-IV and ICD-10 conceptualizations of RAD. Secure-base distortions are attachment relationships that are characterized by extremely fearful, hypercompliant, self-endangering, or role-reversed behavior. A disrupted attachment consists of infant or toddler behaviors associated with acute grief after separation or loss from a caregiver. Until recently, there were few data from which to evaluate this proposal, and results from several different studies have failed to support the spectrum, suggesting instead that the situation is more complicated.

The results of several research studies of institutionalized infants found that infants adopted out of institutions could be "securely-attached" by an attachment theory measure and could still demonstrate indiscriminate social behaviors and be diagnosed with RAD. Institutionalized infants, however, are less likely to have "organized" attachments with their caregivers, and many had relationships that could not be classified or suggested "early stages" of attachment formation. These results suggest that clinical disturbances, as reflected in signs of RAD, are related to how fully developed and expressed attachment behaviors are, but not necessarily to any particular pattern of attachment.

Summary

In the past decade, systematic studies of children who do not reside in "average expectable environments" have enlightened our understanding of original observations. Inhibited and disinhibited attachment behaviors are found in both institutionalized and abused/neglected toddlers. Disinhibited attachment behaviors are known to persist for several years in children adopted out of institutions. Inhibited attachment behaviors are not known to persist after adoption out of institutions. In addition, disinhibited and inhibited attachment behaviors are observed in abused/neglected toddlers with their foster parents after three months in care. In addition, the two supposed DSM-IV subtypes do not appear to be discrete, as behaviors of both types appear to co-occur in both groups of extreme caregiving. Finally, socially-disordered attachment behaviors indicative of a reactive attachment disorder appear to diverge from measures of classifications prescribed by attachment theory.

ASSOCIATED FEATURES

Prevalence

The prevalence of RAD is unknown but it is believed to be rare; however, the rate of children at risk for the disorder based on "pathogenic care" is not low. In the United States, the prevalence of documented abused or neglected children being evaluated by child protection agencies approaches two million in one year. In one study in a single U.S. county, approximately 40 percent of children who had experienced abuse or neglect had attachment disordered behavior.

Longitudinal Course

As stated earlier, disinhibited social behaviors are known to persist for several years (Chisholm, 1998; O'Connor & Rutter, 2000) but may decrease as the child ages (Tizard & Rees, 1975), while inhibited behaviors rarely persist if the caregiving environment is improved. Longitudinal assessments of previously studied children will be extremely helpful in this matter.

Assessment

No established protocol exists for diagnosing RAD; however, there is promising support for structured observations and interviews. Since clinical observations of inhibited and disinhibited behavior are central to the diagnosis, they serve as a natural starting point (O'Connor & Zeanah, 2003). Observations of infants' responses toward caregivers and toward strangers are essential. In addition, structured episodes that activate the wariness system, as in the SSP separations, allow clinicians to observe attachment behaviors upon reunion. Unfortunately, at this point, there is no gold standard to define an inhibited approach to an attachment figure or an indiscriminate approach to a stranger. In addition, the role of temperament may also complicate our interpretations, as "bold-temperamented" infants may be more prone to disinhibition, while "shy" infants may be more prone to inhibited social behaviors.

Likewise, there is no gold standard interview, although several groups have demonstrated the adequacy of semi-structured clinical interviews in the identification of disordered attachment behaviors. The interview should cover all of the possible symptoms associated with all descriptions of RAD and explore the various environments and situations where the behaviors are observed, as well as the course of these behaviors.

The use of questionnaires brings many difficulties. Since clinicians have difficulty agreeing upon concepts and meanings, it is likely that parents will have more divergent understandings of the terms "attachment disorder," "indiscriminate sociability," and "inhibited bids." The use of such terms are not recommended at this time.

At present, most experts recommend detailed observations in naturalistic and clinical settings as well as multiple caregiver reports. This approach must suffice until further validity of the diagnosis is confirmed.

At this point, it is important to observe general social relatedness as well as specific attachment behaviors to determine the strengths of the child as well as the relationship.

Co-morbidity / Differential Diagnosis

The same environmental conditions associated with abuse, neglect, and institutionalization that may cause the socially disturbed behavior of RAD may also serve as a risk factor for the development of several other developmental disturbances. Indeed, clinicians frequently encounter several other behaviors or delays that may be more concerning to caregivers and may cause more impairment than the disturbed social behaviors.

Mental Retardation (MR)

Non-"average expectable" environments may also increase a child's risk for developmental delays and mental retardation (O'Connor, Bredenkamp, Rutter, & the English and Romanian Adoptees study team 1999, Zeanah, 2000). As noted above in the DSM-IV diagnostic criteria for RAD infants must have at least a nine-month cognitive capacity to form an attachment relationship, exemplified by the development of selectivity expressed as stranger wariness and separation anxiety. Some neglected or delayed infants and preschoolers with mental retardation may not develop attachments that are consistent with their age but are consistent with their developmental level. Thus, clinicians should assess the cognitive level of children who appear indiscriminate to be sure that they are not merely delayed. A developmental screen and adjusting for the child's overall mental age should suffice. Removal from the neglectful, abusive, or institutional setting and placement in a supportive and stimulating environment frequently lead to substantial improvements in the child's cognitive abilities.

Pervasive Developmental Disorders (PDD)

Both children diagnosed with autism-spectrum or pervasive developmental disorders and with RAD, inhibited subtype, demonstrate deficits in reciprocal social interaction. In autism these deficits are observed early in life and are at the core of the disorder. Children with PDD spectrum disorders do form selective attachments, although their attachments may be deviant (Capps, Sigman, & Mundy, 1994). Also complicating this picture is that children with autism spectrum disorders frequently have cognitive delay and stereotypies, conditions that are frequently associated with institutionalization or profound neglect. An evaluation of the social environment is required to help elucidate these cases. If there is no history of pathologic caregiving and the psychosocial and caregiving environment are deemed adequate, the social disturbance is most likely a social deficit in the child rather than reactive to, or a consequence of, the caregiving environment. In this case, PDD will be the most likely diagnosis. Changes in the caregiving environment are not likely to improve social or attachment behaviors; rather, it is most likely that changes in caregivers will worsen the child's condition due to loss of an attachment figure.

Conduct Disorder

There has been much confusion (Zeanah, 2000) about older children and adolescents regarding RAD and psychopathy. Psychopathy is described as traits of extreme egocentricity, aggression, deceitfulness, shallow affect, manipulativeness, selfishness, and lack of empathy, guilt, or remorse. Some of the confusion appears to derive from the ICD-10 (World Health Organization, 2003) description as well as the social care and lay conception of a child with RAD as a troubled adopted child with aggressive and murderous impulses toward his new caregivers and his siblings. In addition, many children who experienced early abuse and/or neglect may also develop disruptive behavior disorders. It is not uncommon for these children to have troubled relationships with their caregivers, thus leading to an assumption that symptoms and signs of aggression, oppositionality, and anger are, in fact, disorders of attachment (Levy & Orlans, 2000; Wolkind, 1974). In many cases, the emphasis on oppositionality, aggression, and lack of empathy suggests something other than RAD, perhaps a relationship disorder, a secure-base distortion, or a unique developmental pathway to oppositional defiant disorder, or early-onset conduct disorder, which is often a precursor to antisocial personality disorder. It is likely that shared risk factors may contribute to both disorders through unique pathways.

Attention Deficit Hyperactivity Disorder (ADHD)

Young children with RAD, disinhibited type, demonstrate a persistent pattern of socially impulsive behavior. These behaviors must be distinguished from the impulsivity that characterizes ADHD. A recent study demonstrates that inattention and overactivity (I/O) is directly correlated with duration of deprivation in a European orphanage and may constitute an institutional-deprivation syndrome that may or may not present a different clinical picture than ordinary varieties of ADHD (Kreppner et al., 2001).

If the child meets criteria for both disorders, both diagnoses should be assigned. It is unknown if this institutional impulsivity syndrome responds to typical medication used to treat the symptoms of ADHD.

Post-Traumatic Stress Disorder (PTSD)

Children who have been abused or witnessed violence may show fear, clinging, or withdrawal from caregivers (Hinshaw-Fuselier et al., 1999). These symptoms may be consistent with the hyperarousal and avoidant clusters of a preschooler's posttraumatic symptomatology (Scheeringa, Peebles, Cook, & Zeanah, 2001). These symptoms overlap with the inhibited, hypervigilant, or highly ambivalent and contradictory responses defined by DSM-IV criteria for RAD. To be certain, abuse and exposure to domestic violence is "pathogenic caregiving," but it is uncertain whether these symptoms should primarily be considered as PTSD or RAD, inhibited/emotionally withdrawn type. If in question, the clinician should inquire into and observe for other symptoms consistent with PTSD such as: reexperiencing (posttraumatic play, play reenactment, nightmares, dissociation, distress on exposure), and increased arousal (sleep disturbances, impaired concentration, hypervigilance, and exaggerated startle) (Scheeringa, Zeanah, Drell, & Larrieu, 1995). At the current time, however, if evidence for both exists suitable treatment should be provided for both conditions.

Summary

Abuse, neglect, and deprivation are significant risk factors for developing multiple emotional, behavioral, and developmental problems. These disorders or delays frequently cause more impairment for the child or the relationship between the child and caregiver than do attachment disordered symptoms. These other symptoms require their own unique therapeutic modalities.

INTERVENTION

By definition, attachment disorders are encountered in children who have not experienced an opportunity to form lasting and supportive relationships. Common scenarios include children raised in institutions, placed in multiple foster care homes, or who have experienced extremely disturbed experiences with caregivers. Intervention, therefore, should take into account the universal needs of toddlers and their caregivers as well as the totality of the child's prior experience, current placement, and other significant relationships. I will address intervention from three standpoints: (1) infants and their caregivers in international institutions, (2) infants and their biological caregivers in the American foster care system, and (3) infants and their adoptive and foster parents.

Institutional Intervention

Infants in international institutions frequently have little opportunity to form selective attachments due to changes in caregivers and extreme caregiver-to-child ratios. In an innovative program in Romania, researchers compared noninstitutionalized community infants to infants who were institutionalized either on a typical orphanage unit or on a pilot unit. Caregiver-to-child ratios on traditional units approach 30 children per caregiver, and caregivers are assigned randomly to work rotating shifts. The pilot unit was designed to provide more consistent caregiving by assigning routine shifts to a total of four caregivers serving groups of 10 to 12 children. Signs of disordered attachment behaviors were greatest in infants reared on the typical unit, were reduced in the pilot unit, and were not found in noninstitutionalized children. Hence, the opportunity to form selective attachment relationships through a structural institutional intervention decreased disordered social behavior in those infants. Ongoing systems intervention includes the development and support of a foster care system in Romania through training and education of social workers, therapists, and political leaders (Smyke, Dumitrescu, & Zeanah, 2002).

Intervention in the American Foster Care System

American children in the foster care system and their caregivers typically come from impoverished settings and require numerous social agencies to address their significant needs. These needs are best approached through a community system of care (Marx, Benoit, & Kamradt, 2003), which assesses strengths and weaknesses of the caregivers and provides "wrap-around" support to address the numerous factors that affect these families. A template of treatment typically includes referral and case management from social service and developmental agencies, education regarding the child's universal requirements and individual needs, and further assessments of the child and caregiving relationship to determine the appropriate therapeutic approach. More affluent families who foster or adopt infant and toddlers with attachment disturbances may not require the system of care approach, but they also benefit from educational, developmental, and therapeutic environs.

Once these issues of poor health care, ongoing surveillance, and developmental delays have been addressed, the nurturing environment should be evaluated and supported to help the current caregivers provide an appropriately attentive, nurturing, structured, and stimulating environment (Bradley & Caldwell, 1995). An assessment of parental fitness may be warranted if the child currently resides in a dangerous or destructive caregiving environment. If the child has sustained life-threatening injuries or is in imminent jeopardy, removal of the child is mandated. While the placement of the child in foster care necessarily disrupts the child's relationship with the primary caregiver, safety must be the first priority.

After placement in care, approaches to determining whether reunification is possible, or whether the child should be freed for adoption should be implemented expeditiously. Clinical approaches designed to minimize harm to the child in the context of a disrupted relationship have been advocated (Smyke, Wajda-Johnston, & Zeanah, 2004). These approaches emphasize building new attachment relationships and helping the child gradually transition from one setting to the next. Most families who have a child in foster care have multiple problems; therefore, treatment requires comprehensiveness as well as flexibility and long-term commitment to the child and caregivers. Successful treatment programs do exist, and most attempt to integrate the legal, social care, and health systems (Larrieu & Zeanah, 2004). Throughout the evaluation and treatment process, it is necessary to maintain a focus on the child's best interest while determining whether reunification or termination of parental rights and adoption is indicated. Intervention in these programs is also based on principles of "infant mental health"—a concept that focuses on the centrality of caregiving relationships for the child's current well-being and future developmental trajectory.

As in the case of institutionalized infants, the provision of a nurturing attachment figure is the next step in improving the child's experience and outcome. As stated earlier, an appropriate parental figure is one who can provide sustenance, stimulation, support, structure, and surveillance. In addition to these functions, clinicians and researchers have highlighted characteristics of caregivers that foster secure attachments. In their research on the development of attachment relationships in foster care children, Dozier, Stovall, Albus, and Bates (2001) found that foster parents who demonstrate an ability to show high "reflective functioning" about their experience of receiving care from their own parents during a semi-structured interview (called the Adult Attachment Interview—AAI) developed secure attachments with their foster children. Another interview, the Working Model of the Child Interview (WMCI), taps into the caregiver's "working model" or "psychological representation" of this child (Zeanah & Benoit, 1995). These are valuable assessment tools. What is common to both interviews is the ability to elicit the caregiver's psychological investment in close relationships in general (AAI), and to this child in particular (WMCI). The interviews assess the caregiver's ability to discuss and reflect upon caregiving experiences and their ability to "mentalize" about this child's experiences, circumstances, and personality, and their own relationship with the child.

Intervention with Foster and Adoptive Parents

Most foster and adoptive families do not have the multiple problems that most biological caregivers of children in foster care do. However, biological relatives who are awarded custody may also struggle with similar issues. Whereas clinicians commonly identify disordered attachment behaviors by the child as a barrier to a successful relationship, caregivers frequently highlight disordered sleep, feeding, and aggressive behaviors as barriers to mutually rewarding relationships. Other important aspects of treatment include assessment of the caregiving environment, education of caregivers about developmental delays and capacities, and the provision of appropriate behavioral, dyadic, individual, and group therapies.

Common Interventions

Although no specific psychotherapeutic modality has been shown to be effective for children with attachment disorders, a number of treatments have been proposed, and there is substantial interest in trying to meet the high level of needs of children with an attachment disorder and their biological, foster, and adoptive parents. A set of attachment-based interventions (see Lieberman & Zeanah for review, 1999) have been successfully applied and shown to be effective for parent-infant dyads at high risk for insecure attachments. These interventions are moderately effective, but the mechanisms underlying the treatment response are not clear, and very few studies compare attachment-based interventions with alternative interventions that may be more commonly used in the community. These interventions are based upon real-life interactions between the caregiver and child and focus on parental sensitivity to infant and toddler distress. Improving the parent's ability to act as a secure base is thought to increase the child's willingness to seek out the parent and loosen inhibition as well as focus indiscriminate attachment behaviors.

Child–parent psychotherapy is a multifaceted intervention that combines insight-oriented psychotherapy, unstructured developmental guidance, emotional support, and concrete assistance to caregivers and their toddlers (Lieberman , 2004). This method uses joint or "dyadic" work with the caregivers and toddlers, with the ultimate goal of improving parent-toddler relationships and the child's socioemotional functioning by providing a therapeutic relationship characterized by flexibility and receptiveness to the parent's and the child's needs. Interactions between dyads are observed and serve as a catalyst to the caregiver's affective experience as well as a link to his or her own relationship experiences in the past as well as the present. Enduring changes in the parent's and child's experiences of one another occurs through the corrective emotional experience with the therapist and with each other during sessions.

Interaction guidance (McDonough, 2004) is a dyadic therapy that was designed to meet the needs of families who had not previously been successfully engaged in treatment and may be overburdened by poverty, lack of education, large family size, substance abuse, inadequate housing, and lack of social support. The interaction guidance approach assists family members in gaining enjoyment from their relationships with their children and in developing an understanding of their children's behavior through an experience of interactive play. Through immediate and reflective viewing of videotaped play interactions, the caregiver is praised for appropriate interactive strengths. Parent-initiated discussions of more troublesome interactions may also become a focus of treatment.

Another treatment informed by attachment theory is the novel group therapy known as The Circle of Security (Marvin, Cooper, Hoffman, & Powell, 2002). The group intervention's protocol consists of a 20-week parent education and psychotherapy intervention designed to shift patterns of attachment-caregiving interactions in high-risk caregiver-child dyads to a more appropriate developmental pathway. Using edited videotapes of their interactions with their children, caregivers are encouraged to increase their sensitivity and appropriate responsiveness to their children's signals for exploration as well as comfort. They are also led into an opportunity to increase their ability to reflect on their child's and their own behavior, thoughts, and feelings regarding their attachment-caregiving interactions. Finally they are encouraged to reflect on experiences in their own histories that affect their current caregiving patterns.

Individual treatment with the parent may complement behavioral techniques. This psychotherapy focuses on factors that inhibit or impair the parent's ability to operate as a secure base from which the child can explore and a safe haven to which their distressed toddler may return. Frequently, individual psychopathology related to depression, PTSD, and substance use are encountered in biological caregivers. Individual psychotherapy and psychopharmacologic means are employed. Unfulfilled expectations, previous relationships, unresolved loss, and poor temperamental fit between child and caregiver are frequent themes in psychotherapy.

As previously mentioned, many toddlers have multiple co-morbid disorders that require attention. Frequently, disruptive behavior may cause more impairment than do inappropriate social or attachment behaviors. Individual play therapy with the toddler or preschool aged child helps by providing a consistent, supportive, positive, structured relationship experience as well as a developmentally appropriate play venue to help the child approach, process, and overcome extremely difficult experiences. Training caregivers in appropriate behavioral modification techniques is also warranted. Many extremely disruptive toddlers can then be integrated into a dyadic therapy with a caregiver.

ALTERNATIVE TREATMENTS TO BE AVOIDED

An alternative approach to therapy comes from social care circles and is known as holding therapy. Holding therapy is a derivative of "rage reduction" therapies that were used as alternative treatments for children with autism. Holding therapy consists of several core elements (Keck & Kupecky, 1995), with the main component being close physical contact. This might entail one or several therapists and include direct eye contact and positioning, or "holding" on the laps of the therapists. These treatments are to be practiced on a daily basis for considerable periods of time (greater than 45 minutes). Empirical evidence for these treatments is minimal, and the available evidence has been criticized (O'Connor & Zeanah, 2003; Mercer, 2002, 2003) on multiple conceptual and methodological flaws. Most importantly, six reported deaths of children in the United States have been attributed either directly to holding therapy or its variants (e.g., "rebirthing therapy" or "compression holding"). In these cases, practitioners or parents who were being advised by therapists practicing these methods attempt to "coerce," "thaw," or "release" the child's inability to attach. The Academies of Pediatrics, Psychiatry, Child Psychiatry, and Child Abuse have all published position statements about the inappropriate nature and dangerousness of these therapies. Clearly, these methods have no basis in attachment theory where sensitivity and consistency are valued.

CONCLUSION

There is little evidence that the current diagnostic descriptions of reactive attachment disorder are valid. In addition, there is even less consensus of opinion regarding methods of assessment or treatment. This implies extreme dissatisfaction with the current conceptualization of attachment disorders. Some of this dissatisfaction may be related to the fact that although apparent to clinicians and researchers, other concerns, such as emotional, behavioral, and developmental disturbance in the child may cause more impairment for the family. Lack of a consensus guideline has led to the formation of alternative treatments that are ill-conceived, misapplied, and dangerous. The increased interest in understanding the phenomena implied by the diagnosis means there is considerable space for further research into appropriate diagnostic descriptors, methods of assessment, and safe and effective therapies.

10 Things to Remember About Attachment Disorders:

1. The concept of attachment disorders has its roots in attachment theory but does not specifically describe relationships between caregivers and adults.

2. There are several different criteria for defining and diagnosing attachment disorders, and all are inadequate.

3. The two subtypes of attachment disorders, inhibited and disinhibited, are not likely to be discrete, and overlapping symptoms are more common.

4. Inhibited attachment behaviors are likely to improve when the caregiving environment is improved while disinhibited social behaviors are more likely to persist.

5. Assessment of a child who has been reared under nonoptimal circumstances should include multiple informants and objective observations of the child interacting with caregivers and with strangers.

6. As significant impairment from other behavioral and emotional disorders may co-occur, assessment for and treatment of these problems is frequently warranted.

7. No treatments have been shown to be effective for children with attachment disorders.

8. Holding therapies or other coercive treatments are not based on attachment theory principles and are considered dangerous.

9. Treatment of children with an attachment disorder should include the following: providing a stable caregiving environment, caregiver sensitivity to bids for autonomy and comfort, and treating other child and caregiver barriers to relationships.

10. Ample room exists to develop accurate definitional criteria, helpful methods of assessment, and suitable treatments.

REFERENCES

Ainsworth, M.D.S. (1967). *Infancy in Uganda: Infant care and the growth of love.* Baltimore, MD: Johns Hopkins University Press.

Ainsworth, M.D.S., Blehar, M., Waters, E., & Wall, S. (1978). *Patterns of attachment: A psychological study of the strange situation.* Hillside, NJ: Lawrence Erlbaum Associates.

Ainsworth, M.D.S. & Marvin, R.S. (1995). On the shaping of attachment theory and research: An interview with Mary D.S. Ainsworth (Fall 1994). *Monographs of the Society for Research in Child Development, 60*(2–3), 3–21.

American Psychiatric Association. (1980). *Diagnostic and statistic manual of mental disorders,* 3rd Edition Revision. Washington, DC: American Psychiatric Association.

American Psychiatric Association. (2000). *Diagnostic and statistic manual of mental disorders,* 4th Edition Revision. Washington, DC: American Psychiatric Association.

Boris, N.W., & Zeanah, C.H. (1999). Disturbances and disorders of attachment in infancy: An overview. *Infant Mental Health Journal, 20,* 1–9.

Boris, N.W., Zeanah, C.H., Larrieu, J., Scheeringa, M., & Heller, S. (1998). Attachment disorders in infancy and early childhood: A preliminary study of diagnostic criteria. *American Journal of Psychiatry, 155,* 295–297.

Bowlby, J. (1982). Attachment and loss: Retrospect and prospect. *American Journal of Orthopsychiatry, 52*(4), 664–678.

Bradley, R.H., & Caldwell, B.M. (1995). Caregiving and the regulation of child growth and development: Describing proximal aspects of caregiving systems. *Developmental Review, 15,* 28–85.

Cantwell, D.P. (1996). Classification of child and adolescent psychopathology. *Journal of Child Psychology, Psychiatry, and Allied Disciplines, 37,* 3–12.

Capps, L., Sigman, M, & Mundy, P. (1994). Attachment security in children with autism. *Development and Psychopathology, 6,* 249–262.

Cassidy, J., & Shaver, P. (Eds.). (1999). *Handbook of attachment.* New York: Guilford Press.

Chisholm, K. (1998). A three year follow-up of attachment and indiscriminate friendliness in children adopted from Romanian orphanages. *Child Development, 69*(4), 1092–1106.

DeWolff, M., & van Izjendoorn, M. (1997). Sensitivity and attachment: A meta-analysis on parental antecedents of infant attachment. *Child Development, 52,* 857–865.

Dozier, M, Stovall, K.C., Albus, K., & Bates, B. (2001). Attachment for infants in foster care: The role of caregiver state of mind. *Child Development, 72,* 1467–1477.

Harlow, H.F. (1958). The nature of love. *American Psychologist, 13,* 673–685.

Hinshaw-Fuselier, S., Boris, N., & Zeanah, C.H. (1999). Reactive attachment disorder in maltreated twins. *Infant Mental Health Journal, 20,* 42–59.

Hodges, J., & Tizard, B. (1989). Social and family relationships of ex-institutional adolescents. *Journal of Child Psychology, Psychiatry, and Allied Disciplines, 30,* 77–97.

Keck, G.C., & Kupecky, R. (1995). *Adopting the hurt child.* Colorado Springs, CO: Pinon Press.

Kreppner, J. M., O'Connor, T.T.G., Rutter, M., & the English and Romanian Adoptees Study Team (2003). Can inattention/overactivity be an institutional deprivation syndrome? *Journal of Abnormal Child Psychology, 29,* 513–528.

Larrieu, J., & Zeanah, C. H. (2004). Treating parent-infant relationships in the context of maltreatment: An integrated systems approach. In A. Sameroff, S. McDonough, & K. Rosenblum (Eds.), *Treatment of infant-parent relationship disturbances* (pp. 243–266). New York: Guilford Press.

Levy, T., & Orlans, M. (2000). Attachment disorders as an antecedent to violence and antisocial patterns in children. In T. Levy (Ed.), *Handbook of attachment interventions* (pp. 1–16). San Diego, CA: Academic Press.

Lieberman, A. (2004). Child–parent psychotherapy. In A. Sameroff, S. McDonough, & K. Rosenblum (Eds.), *Treatment of infant-parent relationship disturbances* (pp. 97–122). New York: Guilford Press.

Lieberman, A., & Zeanah, C. H. (1999). Contributions of attachment theory to infant-parent psychotherapy and other interventions with infants and young children. In J. Cassidy & P. Shaver (Eds.), *Handbook of attachment* (pp. 555–574). New York: Guilford Press.

Main, M., & Hesse, E. (1990). Parents' unresolved traumatic experiences are related to infant disorganized attachment status: Is frightened and/or frightening parental behaviour the linking mechanism? In M. T. Greenberg, D. Cicchetti, & E. M. Cummings (Eds.), *Attachment in the preschool years. Theory, research, and intervention* (pp. 161–182). Chicago: University of Chicago Press.

Main, M., & Solomon, J. (1986). Discovery of an insecure-disorganized/ disoriented attachment pattern. In T. B. Brazelton & M. W. Yogman (Eds.), *Affective development in infancy* (pp. 95–124). Norwood, NJ: Abler.

Marvin, R, Cooper, G., Hoffman, K., & Powell, B. (2002). The circle of security project: Attachment-based intervention with caregiver-preschool child dyads. *Attachment and Human Development, 4,* 107–124.

Marx, L., Benoit, M., & Kamradt, B. (2003). Foster children in the child welfare system. In A.J. Pumariega & N. C. Winters (Eds.), *The handbook of child and adolescent systems of care* (pp.332–352). San Francisco: Jossey-Bass.

McDonough, S. (2004). Interaction guidance. In A. Sameroff, S. McDonough, & K. Rosenblum (Eds.), *Treatment of infant-parent relationship disturbances* (pp. 79–96). New York: Guilford Press.

Meins, E., Fernyhough, C., Fradley, E., & Tuckey, M. (2001). Rethinking maternal sensitivity: Mental processes predict security of attachment at 12 months. *Journal of Child Psychology and Psychiatry, 42,* 637–648.

Mercer, J. (2002). Attachment therapy: A treatment without empirical support. *The Scientific Review of Medical Practice, 2,* 105–112.

Mercer, J. (2003). Violent therapies: The rationale behind a potentially harmful child psychotherapy. *The Scientific Review of Medical Practice, 3,* 27–37.

O'Connor, T. G., Bredenkamp, D., Rutter, M., and the English and Romanian Adoptees study team. (1999). Attachment disturbances and disorders in children exposed to early severe deprivation. *Infant Mental Health Journal, 20,* 10–29.

O'Connor, T.G., & Rutter, M. (2000). Attachment disorder behavior following early severe deprivation: Extension and longitudinal follow-up. *Journal of the American Academy of Child and Adolescent Psychiatry, 39,* 703–712.

O'Connor, T.G., & Zeanah, C.H. (2003). Attachment disorders: Assessment strategies and treatment approaches. *Attachment and Human Development 5,* 223–244.

Richters, M.M., & Volkmar, F. (1994). Reactive attachment disorder: Case reports. *Journal of the American Academy of Child and Adolescent Psychiatry, 33,* 328–332.

Scheeringa, M., Peebles, C., Cook, C., & Zeanah, C.H. (2001). Towards establishing the procedural, criterion, and discriminant validity of PTSD in early childhood. *Journal of the American Academy of Child and Adolescent Psychiatry, 40,* 52–60.

Scheeringa, M., Zeanah, C.H., Drell, M., & Larrieu, J. (1995). Two approaches to the diagnosis of post-traumatic stress disorder in infancy and early childhood. *Journal of the American Academy of Child and Adolescent Psychiatry, 34,* 191–200.

Smyke, A.T., Dumitrescu, A., & Zeanah, C.H. (2002). Disturbances of attachment in young children: I. The continuum of caretaking casualty. *Journal of the American Academy of Child and Adolescent Psychiatry, 41,* 972–982.

Smyke, A.T., Wajda-Johnston, V., & Zeanah, C.H. (2004). Working with young children in foster care. In J.D. Osofsky (Ed.), *Traumatized children* (pp. 260–284). New York: Wiley.

Tizard, B., & Hodges, J. (1978). The effect of early institutional rearing on the development of eight-year old children. *Journal of Child Psychology and Psychiatry, 19,* 99–118.

Tizard, B., & Rees. J. (1975). The effect of early institutional rearing on the behavioral problems and affectional relationships of four-year-old children. *Journal of Child Psychology and Psychiatry, 27,* 61–73.

Weinfield, N., Sroufe, L. A., & Egeland, B. (2000). Attachment from infancy to early adulthood in a high-risk sample: Continuity, discontinuity, and their correlates. *Child Development,* 71, 695-702.

Wolkind, S. (1974). The components of affectionless psychopathy in institutionalized children. *Journal of Child Psychology and Psychiatry, 15,* 215–220.

World Health Organization. (2003). *The ICD-10 Classification of Mental and Behavioral Syndromes: Clinical descriptions and diagnostic guidelines.* Geneva: World Health Organization.

Zeanah, C.H. (2000). Disturbances of attachment in young children adopted from institutions. *Journal of Developmental and Behavioral Pediatrics, 21,* 230–236.

Zeanah, C.H., & Benoit, D. (1995). Clinical applications of a parent perception interview in infant mental health. In K. Minde (Ed.), *Child and adolescent psychiatry clinics of North America: Infant psychiatry. Vol. 4* (3) (pp. 539–554). Philadelphia: Saunders.

Zeanah C.H., & Emde, R.N. (1994). Attachment disorders in infancy. In M. Rutter, L. Hersov, & E. Taylor (Eds.), *Child and adolescent psychiatry: Modern approaches* (pp. 490–504). Oxford: Blackwell.

Zeanah, C.H., Smyke, A.T., & Dumitrescu, A. (2002). Disturbances of attachment in young children: II. Indiscriminate behavior and institutional care. *Journal of the American Academy of Child and Adolescent Psychiatry, 41,* 983–989.

Zero to Three, National Center for Clinical Infant Programs. (1994). *Diagnostic classification of mental health and developmental disorders of infancy and early childhood.* Washington, DC: Author.

Chapter 4

LEARNING DISABILITIES AND MENTAL HEALTH ISSUES: PREDICTIONS FROM NEONATAL REGULATION, ATTENTION, AND NEUROBEHAVIORAL ASSESSMENTS

Bernard Z. Karmel and Judith M. Gardner

This research was supported in part by funds from the New York State Office of Mental Retardation and Developmental Disabilities and by a National Institute of Child Health and Human Development Grant R01-HD-21784 awarded to Judith M. Gardner, and a National Institute of Drug Abuse Grant R01-DA-06644 awarded to Bernard Z. Karmel The authors wish to express their sincere thanks to the Infant Development Staff at the IBR, to the Medical and Nursing Staff of the Neonatal Intensive Care Unit and Newborn Nursery at SVCMC, St. Vincent's Hospital, Staten Island, and to our participating infants and their families.

INTRODUCTION

Public policy directed toward the early identification of disability has a long history. From Binet's addressing needs of the French egalitarian school system, to the U.S. Army's need to recruit trainable inductees, to the varying laws seeking public resources for the learning disabled and the mentally and physically challenged, disability issues in public policy have been debated from various theoretical and practical views. Thus, accuracy of assessment and efficacy of intervention are debated with respect to whether anything can be done to prevent or ameliorate disabilities and, if so, what the cost/benefit ratio would be. From the current view, many of us involved in the field take the perspective that public policy should reinforce societal requirements to administer to, habilitate, or rehabilitate the developmentally disabled because: (a) early detection is indeed possible, and (b) intervening earlier rather than later, for example, in infancy rather than at school age, is most therapeutic and cost effective. We assume that disability emanates from some insult or perturbance to normal growth and development and can best be understood in terms of a developmental neurofunctional analysis of early brain-behavior relationships. If we are smart enough and devise the appropriate ways of studying and interpreting our findings, we should be able to accurately detect atypical behavior or its antecedents from the earliest points in development. This in turn should lead to reliable and valid methods of intervention directed toward the specific neurofunctional problems detected. This chapter will show how assessment of normal and atypical neurofunctional organization can be accomplished as early as the neonatal period and subsequently over the first years of life.

Defining the consequences of chronic and acute central nervous system (CNS) injury in neonates is important for predicting both short-term recovery and long-term outcome. Advances in reproductive medicine have produced a dramatic increase in infants born at risk due to chronic insults to the CNS (e.g., intrauterine growth retardation or restriction [IUGR], multiple gestation), and advances in perinatal and neonatal medicine have increased the survival rate of these infants and of those with acute CNS injury due to hypoxic-ischemic events. But these advances are not without risk for later developmental problems. Newborns chronically stressed *in utero* tend to be born early with signs of IUGR. They frequently are hypertonic, although this typically does not reach clinical pathological criteria (Amiel-Tison & Pettigrew, 1991; Gardner, Karmel, & Freedland, 2001). The consequences of such increased tone may be associated with the deficits in coordination and visual-motor performance reported in others' longitudinal studies of IUGR (Leitner et al., 2000) and in our own (Gardner et al., 2001). This is in contrast to the hypotonicity seen in newborns with acute CNS injury at birth that is more typically associated with later general cognitive and motor deficits, such as mental retardation and cerebral palsy (Volpe, 2001).

Whether from an economically advantaged region where the benefits of advances in reproductive, perinatal, and neonatal care have enhanced survival of the infant, or an economically disadvantaged region where malnutrition and lack of medical services may exist, the effects of chronic stress or acute CNS injury on the developing fetus are similar. Thus, independent of etiology, once there is survival, the newborn with chronic stress may already be showing signs of subsequent coordination and visual-motor integration problems, and the newborn with acute CNS injury may be showing early manifestations of later overt cognitive and motor deficits. And, as in the case of our most recent surviving cohort of micropremies (born weighing <750 g and/or <27 weeks gestation), they may be showing the effects of both.

WHY STUDY AROUSAL AND ATTENTION
OVER DEVELOPMENT?

Our studies indicate that in neonates arousal and attention to stimulation are inseparable interdependent processes. Exogenous (external) effects of stimuli mutually interact with other exogenous effects and, as a set, interact with endogenous (internal) effects such as feeding. These endogenous and exogenous effects combine to reflect an optimal level of arousal maintained in a self-regulating homeostatic manner. This can be conceptualized as an inverted U-shaped function with the optimal level at the peak. The contributions of internal and external stimulation are balanced so that, for example, if internal levels are high, the infant will seek lower levels of external stimulation to achieve the same overall optimal level (i.e., homeostasis), or if internal levels are low, the infant will seek higher levels of external stimulation to achieve the same overall optimal level. We interpret these effects to be sensory nonspecific, most likely reflecting general central arousal and attention mechanisms rather than peripheral receptor or sensory-specific effects. Stimuli are attended relative to context and not relative to specific attributes. Thus, any activation that produces orienting to specific stimuli also will include input from the nonspecific arousal system. Arousal influences not only tonic activity, but also gates specific sensory processing when internal or external factors are manipulated through feeding or stimulation (Gardner & Karmel, 1983; Gardner, Karmel, & Flory, 2003; Karmel, Gardner, & Magnano, 1991). This self-limiting homeostatic behavioral system helps neonates maintain their arousal at the same overall level and maintains equilibrium, with distinctions between internal and external changes in environmental energy probably arbitrary and artificial for the neonate (also see Porges, 1996 for a detailed description of homeostatic regulation of physiological systems in neonates).

The Role of Arousal and Attention in Regulatory Behavior

Early information about infants' arousal, attention, autoregulation, and motor behavior can be used to assess current neurofunctional status and predict future outcome. Based on our and others studies, these processes have been shown to be fundamental to the mechanisms involved with learning disabilities and other mental health problems, especially those involving self-regulation. The integration of arousal and attention and its transformation throughout development plays an important role in the transaction between an infant or child and his/her environment for both typically developing children and for those at risk for poor outcome.

High-risk infants also are more likely to have autoregulatory problems that affect their ability to attend to and interact with their environment. Infants who are disorganized, overaroused, and/or irritable tend to have fewer or less efficient autoregulatory strategies. They are less able to handle increased amounts of stimulation and so turn away from both persons and objects. In contrast, infants who are underaroused tend to need more stimulation to attend to their environment. It is important to note that these conditions not only can exist, but they can be identified early during the neonatal period. Thus, we propose that adequate neurofunctional development involving arousal, attention, and motor behavior underlies normal autoregulatory development, and deficits in autoregulation will have far-reaching effects, producing problems in perceptual, cognitive, social/emotional, executive function, language, and motor organization (Gardner et al., 2003; see also Cicchetti, 1993; Greenspan, 1992; Porges, 1996) that contribute to later specific learning disabilities and other mental health problems.

CNS Effects on Development of Autoregulatory Processes

It has long been recognized that damage to the CNS can compromise arousal, attention, motor, and state modulating capacities in the developing infant and child (see Brazelton, Nugent, & Lester, 1987; Field, 1981; Karmel, Kaye, & John, 1978; Korner, 1972; Lester & Tronick, 2004). In addition, disturbed arousal and attention, especially as precursors to later motivation and temperament characteristics, have been suggested to underlie certain deficits in performance in more specific populations, such as infants prenatally exposed to cocaine (Lester et al., 1991; Mayes, Grillon, Granger, & Schottenfeld, 1998). We determine the specific characteristics of early brain function associated with adverse outcomes due to problems in autoregulation by experimentally manipulating arousal and evaluating effects on ongoing behavior (Gardner & Karmel, 1983; Gardner et al., 2003; Karmel et al., 1991). We have extended the concepts of homeostatic regulation and spontaneous behavior to ones involving challenge and elicited behavior. Rather than viewing state as a confounding variable, we find that challenging the infant by controlled manipulation of arousal within the active awake state provides a wealth of information about the infant's regulatory abilities. Understanding these autoregulatory mechanisms is important for studying the developmental course that atypical arousal and attention processes impact on the subsequent regulation of different types of behavior, and the extent to which disorganization of the CNS distorts this regulatory ability when there is chronic as well as acute injury.

Why Study Potential Disruptors to Autoregulatory Development

Our goal has been to identify and study at least two major disruptors, acute CNS injury and chronic stress in utero, and show how these perturbances affect neurofunctional development, especially those involving arousal, attention, and motor processes. Indeed, much evidence, including our own work, demonstrates that in early infancy these processes, as mediated by neural regulation of physiologic systems, depend on the maturation and integrity of the CNS. That is, if early arousal, attention, and motor processes form the substrate for emerging autoregulatory functioning underlying later perceptual, cognitive, motor, social/emotional, executive function, and language behavior, injury to CNS structure and function should disrupt or alter development through damage to mechanisms controlling them. We further argue that arousal, attention, and motor development will differ in diverse risk populations, depending on the type of CNS structural or neurofunctional perturbance that has occurred. Thus, we have chosen to study both typically and atypically-developing populations, the latter emphasizing high-risk infants assigned to the neonatal intensive care unit (NICU) who are likely to have experienced acute and/or chronic stress to their developing CNS. Using this strategy, we not only expand the range of potential responses that can be measured, but at the same time try to provide some practical insight into why certain risk populations develop as they do.

How and when these CNS disruptions take place, and how plasticity affects recovery, have implications for development well beyond early infancy. For instance, acute stress during labor and delivery (e.g., birth asphyxia, neurological events) may have the same or different consequences as chronic stress (e.g., placental insufficiency, infection, multiple gestation, intrauterine growth retardation), environmental toxins (e.g., cocaine or alcohol exposure), and numerous other factors (e.g., gender, cleft palate, renal hypoplasia, dopaminergic dysfunction, Down syndrome) depending on the nature, timing, and duration of the influence. Studying processes involving arousal, attention, motor, and autoregulation, and how these processes are affected by different pre- and postnatal risk conditions, becomes both fundamental to understanding a broad array of biobehavioral processes and their development, and of major theoretical and practical importance to multiple disciplines.

Shifts in Cohorts: Chronic Stress Infants

Advances in medical care have produced changes in cohorts. Younger and sicker infants are surviving and there are increased numbers of very-low-birth-weight infants coming from multiple gestation pregnancies due to in vitro fertilization. Furthermore, women of childbearing age are conceiving at older ages, resulting in a decrease in the efficacy of germinal material as well as in the placental environment. Beneficial effects known to improve developmental outcome that are associated with increased maternal age such as greater maturity of caregivers, higher educational and socioeconomic levels, and better home environments (Bradley et al., 1995; Casey, Bradley, Nelson, & Whaley, 1988) may be valid when little or no CNS injury has occurred, but whether such effects can overcome the deficits associated with early CNS injury that can result remains to be demonstrated (see Wallace, Rose, McCarton, Kurtzberg, & Vaughan, 1995). At present, any study of maternal education, caregiver interactions, and environmental rearing conditions must take into consideration the large increase in at-risk infants born to this segment of the population. Indeed, our initial data using the PROCESS Inventory (Casey et al., 1988) appear to indicate that better caregiving environments are associated only with better outcomes in the population of infants with less CNS injury and even then only with mental, not motor, functioning.

It has long been known that chronic stress conditions during pregnancy can affect the developing fetus. In most cases, growth is likely disturbed so that infants are born prematurely or weighing too little for their gestational age and are considered IUGR, small for gestational age, or deemed dysmature by clinical evaluation. A number of chronic conditions may be responsible for such effects, frequently related to poor oxygen transport or uptake (e.g., poor placental perfusion, placental or chorionic infection, multiple gestation). In addition, the number of multiple gestation births has increased from approximately one percent of all births to from five to six percent or higher, most of whom are born prematurely with low birth weight. In a number of these multiple births, one infant is much smaller, less than 15–20 percent of the other(s) weight, producing an even greater risk condition for this discordant infant. We now have the situation that medical advances have increased the fertility of women who may have a number of risk conditions due to advanced maternal age or multiple gestation, and have increased the survival of these risk infants. It can only be assumed that these infants will have problems at the brain stem level, due to the age and stage of CNS development when born.

One example is that the auditory brain stem responses (ABRs) of neonates with chronic stress conditions in utero appear to have a different, but equally aberrant pattern compared to neonates with known structural pathology such as intraventricular hemorrhage. Depending on the degree of chronic stress and when in fetal development it occurred, the neonate may appear as if more mature. Thus, in our data and in that reported by others (Amiel-Tison & Pettigrew, 1991), the ABRs of these infants tend to have shorter than normal component latencies so long as there is no concomitant acute CNS injury that will produce the opposite effects by lengthening component latencies (Karmel, Gardner, Zappulla, Magnano, & Brown, 1988). And we have convincing evidence that gender may play a significant role in that being a girl may be more protective, reducing the number and severity of CNS effects. Why NICU boys tend to have more medical problems and be less mature than girls, despite being heavier at birth, may relate to differential brain stem function as evidenced by their being more likely to have slower or abnormal neuronal transmission speeds in ABRs. How such atypical brain stem functioning translates into behavior could be important for understanding later effects on specific learning disabilities, especially as concerns language and self-regulation and especially as concerns the greater likelihood of males being found among the developmentally disabled populations. The role of glial cell loss and recovery in the face of chronic and acute CNS effects is suspected to underlie these ABR findings and may relate to later gender differences, but this idea remains speculative. Regardless, the fact that arousal and attention are mediated by brain stem mechanisms, such as the reticular activating system, is important to note.

Along with progress in survival and fertility, there has been better detection of conditions compromising the CNS of the fetus, including better specification of the developmental consequences of IUGR. Although not specifically recruited for suspicion of chronic stress in utero, preliminary analyses of our data have produced interesting findings, particularly with respect to motor systems. In addition, we have studied infants and children exposed to cocaine prenatally who tend to be born small for gestation and to have smaller head circumference. These children are presumed chronically stressed in utero not only from the cocaine exposure but from the poor nutrition and high level of cigarette smoking by their mothers when pregnant. They also have an interesting pattern of behavior, especially with respect to arousal, attention, and autoregulatory processes. They frequently appear precocial or more mature, especially in their stimulus-seeking behavior during infancy that is related to later deficits in inhibitory control. This precocial maturity early on may lead to atypical patterns of behavior later. Classic studies by Shapiro (1967) on the effects of maternal thyroid levels during gestation in human infants or chemically manipulated in rat pups indicated that there probably is an optimal rate of development such that if it is too fast or too slow there will be adverse effects later on.

Although initially it was thought that the important factor in pregnancy was the timing of when the IUGR effect occurred, with earlier IUGR producing greater deficits, it may actually be the degree of chronic stress rather than the timing that may determine whether adverse effects are seen. Amiel-Tison and Pettigrew (1991) suggested that some degree of chronic stress producing more maturity was protective on the developing fetus; but too much stress would damage the developing nervous system, producing behavioral deficits. IUGR more typically has been associated with abnormal outcome. Harel and colleagues (Harel, 2002; Leitner et al., 2000) found deficits in performance associated with IUGR at 3 and 6–7 years related to coordination and fine and gross motor control, and at 9–10 years on a wide variety of tasks, especially those assessing neural development. Deficits in visual-motor integration and in fine motor skills also have been found at early school age in a large proportion of apparently normal very low birth weight infants, especially those born weighing less than 750 gm (Goyen & Lui, 2002). This higher proportion of deficits recently has been reported in a large sample of six-year-olds born at 25 weeks or less gestation, with more than 75 percent showing some form of disability (Marlow, Wolke, Bracewell, & Samara, 2005). Such extreme low birth weight and prematurity typically are assumed to be related to some chronic stress condition. In our preliminary studies, in addition to more extensive findings with respect to acute brain injury, there appear to be direct effects on neonatal arousal and attention and neurobehavioral performance as well as indications of long-term sequelae from various types of chronic stress. Thus, infants in our population having birth weights less than 750 gm or gestational ages less than 27 weeks have lower performance on standard assessments that cannot be explained by acute CNS injury alone.

NEONATAL EVALUATIONS USING NEUROFUNCTIONAL TECHNIQUES

Newborn assessment procedures are designed to evaluate early behavioral capabilities and dysfunctions in attention, state regulation, and motor system organization, areas frequently disrupted by CNS injury secondary to hypoxia, IUGR, or exposure to neurotoxic agents. In neurobehaviorally assessing high-risk infants, at least four important goals should be noted. The assessments should (1) provide valid estimates of the infant's behavior and neurofunctional status; (2) reflect recovery from the effects of CNS injury; (3) predict subsequent outcome and potential areas of deficits; and (4) point to specific intervention strategies for any problems noted. We currently assess infants during the newborn period using a protocol that includes cranial ultrasound, auditory brain stem responses, arousal-modulated attention (AMA), and neurobehavioral (NB) evaluation just prior to hospital discharge and at one month, followed by behavioral testing every three months. More than 3,500 infants have been assessed with AMA and NB during the newborn period. Although findings from the evaluations are related to each other, each also contributes unique information. We will limit this chapter to the behavioral procedures and the relations to attention and autoregulation at older ages.

Arousal-Modulated Attention (AMA) and Motor Activity

We have found that autoregulatory control of attention is a basic characteristic of behavior during the first months of life, can be disrupted by CNS pathology, and predicts later developmental outcome (Gardner et al., 2003). We have operationally differentiated AMA in a series of studies. Using converging evidence from both two-choice visual preference and visual recognition memory techniques, systematic differences in neonatal attention can be obtained with controlled manipulations of arousal due to changes in internal (endogenous) and external (exogenous) sources of stimulation. Normal newborns and one-month-olds are excellent modulators, preferring (looking longer at) more stimulating and novel events when less aroused after feeding, and preferring less stimulating and more familiar events when more aroused before feeding or with additional stimulation. By four months, they show specific preferences independent of the arousal manipulations, and prefer more stimulation or novelty across all conditions (Gardner & Karmel, 1995; Geva, Gardner, & Karmel, 1999). Thus, normal neonates maintain equilibrium of their optimal level in their arousal and attention.

In contrast, CNS pathology adversely affects the homeostatic regulatory mechanism that maintains this equilibrium, thereby undermining the ability to control arousal and attention. The greater the CNS involvement, the less the shift in attention toward higher stimulation or novelty when less aroused, resulting in attention to less stimulation or familiarity in general (Gardner, Karmel, & Magnano, 1992). Thus, infants with CNS injury are poor modulators, avoiding high levels of stimulation even after feeding. We call these infants stimulus or novelty avoiders. Neurotoxicity due to cocaine exposure also produces deficits in AMA, but in the opposite direction, toward being stimulus or novelty seekers. Thus, infants with intrauterine cocaine exposure also are poor modulators but in the opposite direction, seeking high levels of stimulation or novelty even before feeding or with additional stimulation. By four months, only infants with functional (ABR) but not structural (cranial ultrasound) abnormalities or with the most severe CNS pathology still show arousal modulation effects by preferring lower levels of stimulation when more aroused or by preferring novelty after but not before feeding, thereby failing to mature from patterns more typical of neonates. This is a two-fold process. Infants with CNS pathology appear to have a shift downward in their optimal level on the inverted U-shaped function, with both a lowered threshold for withdrawal from stimulation and a narrower bandwidth or range within which to respond (Als, Lester, & Brazelton, 1979; Field, 1981; Gardner & Karmel, 1983; Karmel et al., 1991). The lowered threshold is seen by not looking at more stimulation or novel events, even when in an optimal arousal state. The narrower bandwidth is measured by decreased differences in behavior between more and less aroused conditions. Thus, visual processing in young infants appears to be simple but actually is affected by a variety of factors. Both visual preferences to greater stimulation and to novelty are decreased by higher arousal, increasing CNS injury, and decreasing age. Such documentation of autoregulatory behavior provides information about the infant's ability to handle stimulation as well as strategies for intervention.

We recently extended this paradigm of arousal influences on attention to arousal influences on spontaneous movements. By decreasing the ambient room light by turning off an overhead examination light, we observe an increase in spontaneous motor activity in healthy NICU infants just prior to hospital discharge. This modulation of motor activity by exogenous stimulation appears analogous to that observed for attention, but its sensitivity and specificity in relation to acute and chronic CNS injury and later outcome requires further study.

Neurobehavioral Evaluation (NB)

We (Gardner, Karmel, Magnano, Norton, & Brown, 1990; Gardner et al., 2001; Karmel & Gardner, 2005) have developed and standardized a neonatal NB that uses a combination of two procedures containing behaviors (elicited and spontaneous) assumed important for development or that were likely affected by adverse pre- and perinatal events.

(1) Rapid Neonatal Neurobehavioral Assessment Procedure (RNNAP). Our categorical clinical evaluation of sensory and motor systems, developed over the past 20 years, assesses visual, auditory, state control, feeding, and passive and elicited motor behaviors, the latter designed to challenge the infant and also used for designing intervention (after Katona, 1988; Gardner et al., 1990, 2001; Karmel & Gardner, 2005). It is efficient (<10 min to administer) and nonstressful (appropriate for use with small, sick, fragile neonates). It yields a behavioral profile of the infant's patterns of deficits that is useful for formulating interventions emphasizing self-produced movements and is designed to assess those neurofunctional behaviors that differentiate brain injury in neonates.

For example, the infant is placed prone head down on an incline so that crawling-like responses while righting to gravity can be observed. Such self-produced motor responses typically can be elicited and assessed even if the infant is hyperreflexive or hypertonic, such as may be found with IUGR or drug exposure. These nonreflex-type movements are similar to those seen in subsequent voluntary motor activity presumed to be mediated by non-cortical centers such as the basal ganglia, although other regions such as the cerebellum and vestibular system might be involved. The basal ganglia are especially susceptible to periventricular CNS damage that leads to deficits such as cerebral palsy (Katona, 1988; Volpe, 2001). The RNNAP has both concurrent and predictive validity. Based on specific criteria, categories involving visual and auditory attention, sensory symmetry, head/neck control, extremity movement and tone, motor symmetry, jitteriness, feeding, and state control are judged by a trained examiner on a 3-point scale from normal to very abnormal. The more severe the CNS injury, the greater the number and degree of abnormal judgments. As recovery progresses (from newborn to one-month post-term age), abnormalities decrease, approaching those of normal infants. Restricting decision possibilities allows for immediate feedback to parents and other professionals and helps with concurrent diagnosis of potential abnormalities. Infants with different types and degrees of CNS pathology have different patterns and amounts of abnormalities, as well as lower standardized scores at later ages on the Bayley Scales of Infant Development (BSID; Bayley, 1993) and the Griffiths Mental Development Scales (Griffiths, 1984). Moreover, the immediate behavioral profile of the infant's patterns of deficits is useful for formulating intervention strategies in specific areas of functioning.

(2) Qualitative Assessment of General Movements (GMs, after Prechtl, 1997; Einspieler, Prechtl, Ferrari, Cioni, & Bos, 1997). The quality of spontaneous movements and the changes that occur during the first four months have been shown by Prechtl and colleagues to relate to poor outcome if less than optimal. Predictable changes occur in GMs during the first four months post term that are assumed to reflect underlying normal CNS development. During the neonatal period (term ± 8 weeks), normal GMs are characterized by having a writhing quality, typically flowing through the whole body, involving a complex and varied sequence of arm, leg, neck, and trunk movements. After 6–9 weeks, a new pattern emerges, characterized as fidgety movements, which are defined in awake infants as small continuous movements of the neck, hands, and feet. They peak at 10–12 weeks but are still evident until 20 weeks, after which voluntary, goal-directed movements begin to dominate. According to specific criteria, GMs are judged as normal or abnormal from videotaped recordings

by trained observers. Consistently abnormal GMs through four months are reliable predictors of later deficits.

Comparisons among Early Evaluations

In a subsample of our highest risk neonates, we evaluated the relations and predictablility of AMA with RNNAP and GMs. We found that perinatal CNS injury and early performance are related, but information about structural CNS injury alone is not sufficient to identify the range of neurofunctional abnormalities that can be encountered and is not adequate enough to design strategies for specific intervention needs or to predict later outcome. Behavioral evaluation in the neonatal period is indispensable. Early regulation of attention, and elicited and spontaneous motor performance all show a tendency toward normalization, with each having different strengths and time courses (as also is the case for nonbehavioral effects). In this high-risk population, infants who behave normally during the neonatal period, as well as those with moderate abnormalities in autoregulation and elicited motor performance, appear to have normal development into the second year. In contrast, infants with early transient abnormalities in spontaneous motor performance who appear to normalize by four months show deficits in mental and motor behavior in the second year. For all measures, increased degree or duration of abnormal behavior in early infancy predicts the worst outcome in the second year. In infants with the most abnormal early behavior, deficits appear first in motor function. Effects on mental function become most apparent after one year of age. This could reflect shortcomings in the selection of outcome measures used in early infancy (in this case, the BSID) or genuine recovery at younger ages when neurofunction is reacquired as the CNS heals. More likely, the higher-level mental function that develops at older ages is more affected than earlier mental function and thus appears more strongly predicted by atypical early behavior.

Our findings highlight the importance of autoregulation and attention in combination with elicited and spontaneous motor performance in the context of extended longitudinal follow-up. Multiple measures in the neonatal period (presumably assessing different CNS systems) provide converging information. Multiple assessments over time provide additional information to meet the goals of more comprehensive and valid measures of behavior and neurological status, better tracking of recovery from acute effects, and more accurate prediction to later outcome.

Despite the fact that each procedure has concurrent and predictive validity, and that the procedures complement each other but also provide independent information so that the information obtained from the combined set yields the most information, the feasibility of using each technique to (1) establish widespread use, such as in other countries, (2) obtain information in a timely fashion to give feedback to physicians, therapists, parents, and others, and/or (3) devise intervention programs based on information obtained, differs across procedures. All three procedures offer both theoretical and practical significance to varying degrees. For instance, the information obtained from AMA is immediate and available to give caregivers advice on intervention when the infant is too easily overstimulated and therefore gaze-averts and turns away. This type of deficit in autoregulation is a setup for poor caregiver-infant interactions and allows the infant only to be exposed to a narrow range of environmental information. The AMA visual preference procedure has been technically more difficult to expand to multiple sites compared to visual recognition memory, but collaborators in Israel and Hungary have established their use for clinical and research purposes. Observers in numerous countries are being trained to interpret the information obtained from GMs. However, GMs are scored off-line from videotapes and therefore do not offer immediate feedback. On the other hand, evaluation of GMs allows for assessment and information beyond the neonatal period to four to five months, which offers a distinct advantage. The RNNAP is easy to learn by anyone trained to handle young infants, such as nurses, occupational and physical therapists, early development specialists, psychologists, and physicians. It can be used by any culture in any circumstance and offers immediate on-line feedback with respect to areas of deficit and potential intervention strategies. But it is most appropriate for the neonatal period unless the infant is extremely premature or severely CNS-involved.

AUTOREGULATORY DEVELOPMENT: THE FIRST THREE YEARS

Development of Arousal and Attention after the Neonatal Period through the First Year

What are the developmental consequences of a unitary early homeostatic system for later development? Theories about brain-behavior relations in infants and children have been put forth with respect to visual attention (e.g., Johnson, 1996; Karmel & Maisel, 1975; Richards, 2001), physiological regulation (Porges, 1996), emotional regulation (Fox, 1994), and inhibitory control and cognition (Diamond, Prevor, Callender, & Druin, 1997). Likewise, there has been a long tradition of theories to explain both the development of arousal and attention systems in the first few years of life and their interaction in adults (Berlyne, 1960). But with the exception of Porges's hierarchical model of neural regulation of autonomic state as an antecedent substrate for later emotional, cognitive, and behavioral regulation, these theories tend to start after the neonatal period and do not deal with the earliest modes of behavior.

A number of changes occur after the neonatal period during the first year that are linked to underlying neural systems. Different forms of attention (possibly under inhibitory control, such as inhibition of return and object habituation) undergo substantial development and are influenced by collicular function and the development of the posterior attention system (Posner, 1988). The posterior attention system is involved with orienting/investigative functions that we refer to as the sensory-specific period of attention, since many studies show a concomitant developmental shift in behaviors as well as cortical localization of stimulus modality.

During this sensory-specific period, the coordination of vigilance and distress is important for normal development, with orienting attention necessary for modulating distress and vigilance necessary for attention to relevant stimuli (Rothbart, Ziaie, & O'Boyle, 1992). Evidence for autoregulation (Fox, 1994; Porges, 1996) suggests that deficits in the ability to inhibit and regulate intensity of arousal may be more likely in high-risk than in healthy term infants. In Fox's studies, these deficits emerged in the context of a social interaction, as well as during tasks involving perceptual/cognitive processing. Field (1982) showed differences in physiological and attention responses to animate and inanimate stimuli differing in arousal content. Eckerman, Hsu, Molitor, Leung, and Goldstein (1999) also reported differences in arousal control and distress while attending arousal-producing stimuli during a social interaction. Our preliminary findings using social interaction in the form of a peek-a-boo paradigm (adapted from Eckerman et al., 1999) with four-month-olds indicated effects were complex and not straightforward. Most infants (independent of CNS injury) showed the ability to regulate with more positive than negative affect, very good attention with little gaze aversion, and greater inhibition of movement while attending an increasingly arousal-producing stimulus (by increasing the number of modalities involved in the presentation of a puppet in the peek-a-boo procedure). Contrary to expectations, more normal infants showed less positive affect. Regulation was positively correlated to the degree of IUGR and negatively correlated to the ability to handle stimulation as neonates. Although there are a number of developmental and procedural explanations, the cognitive load required for the strategy used to process the information rather than just responding to the amount of stimulation may influence the age-appropriate ability to regulate in any particular situation. More studies are needed to clarify these effects.

The Transition to Autoregulatory Behaviors
in One- to Two-Year-Olds

Development of higher levels of attention control requires greater inhibitory control that emerges during the latter part of the first year (Diamond, 1990; Ruff & Rothbart, 1996). High-risk infants frequently have deficits in focused attention (Lawson & Ruff, 2005), which we find is related to early AMA deficiencies. Indeed, the inability to shift attention appropriately between stimuli, sustain attention, and resist distraction represents cognitive control over external events and impacts on subsequent learning and social relations. In the Focused Attention task, infants sit at a table on their parents'/caregivers' laps playing with a series of toys while cartoons (distractors) appear briefly at random intervals on a monitor to their right. The amount of time spent focused on the toy, and the frequency of turns to the distractor when focused or not, is measured. We find that as infants with CNS pathology develop, their early difficulties regulating arousal may be manifested by attention regulation problems in distracting environments, one of the hallmark behaviors exhibited by ADHD children. The period from 10 to 16 months is especially interesting, as focused attention and distractibility change from a sensory-specific system of attention to one under greater frontal cortical control. At 16 months infants with early CNS involvement take longer to organize focused attention, and show more distractibility and less time in focused attention. They do not show higher-level organization, acting more like infants in the sensory-specific period. Moreover, for all infants, neonatal AMA predicts focused attention behavior after one year of age.

We find relationships of early AMA to a number of other measures as well. For example, in our Open Field procedure, children (between 13 and 25 months) have free play with toys with their mothers/caregivers present in a novel environment when they are more and less aroused due to a stranger being present or absent. Not only do the toddlers at 13 and 16 months explore less and stay closer to their mothers with the stranger present, but their pattern of behavior is differentially related to AMA as neonates, that is, how well they handled stimulation when less aroused and their degree of modulation across arousal conditions, as a function of their CNS involvement. Normal toddlers were the best neonatal modulators and were best able to handle the stress of the arousing stranger (by using their mothers/caregivers as a safe base). CNS-injured toddlers showed a range of behavior. Those who were the best neonatal modulators were most reactive and those who were the worst neonatal modulators were least reactive. However, by 19 months, the effect of the stranger was diminished. So, we made the situation more arousing at the older ages by adding a two-foot-tall mechanical robot controlled by the stranger. Although we have not yet analyzed the relationship to neonatal AMA, preliminary findings at 25 months indicate that the introduction of the robot extended our effects, relating the ability to regulate in this highly arousing situation and CNS involvement. Consistent with the less positive affect at four months in the peek-a-boo paradigm, normal toddlers showed more negative emotion to the robot. Again, there are a number of developmental and procedural explanations for the findings, but the underlying age-appropriate ability to regulate was more apparent in the normal than in the CNS-involved children at both ages. As both activation and inhibition are necessary components of these behaviors, the question is which aspects of early autoregulatory precursors are involved and how are they related to other areas and ages that are likely affected by early autoregulatory mechanisms, such as motor and social communication, as well as later executive function.

Executive Function and Higher Levels of Control after Two Years

CNS-involved infants have an increased likelihood of later school-related learning and attention problems. Although the global adverse effects of severe brain insult have been documented, less is known about "the lesser degrees of brain damage ... thought to be responsible for fine motor impairments, visuoperceptual and math difficulties, and hyperactivity" (Hack, Klein, & Taylor, 1995). Moreover, the specific neonatal problems that are predictive of poor outcome in selected areas of later functioning are not well understood.

Direct linkages between subcortical arousal systems and cortical frontal inhibitory control systems support our position on the importance of normal homeostatic functioning of neural regulation in the neonatal period, such as in AMA, as a precursor to later executive function. From the second year on, higher-level controls develop into regulatory mechanisms mediated by continued maturation of the frontal cortex (Diamond, 1990). Both early acute CNS injury and chronic stress in utero can alter, modify, or deviate the course of normal neurofunctional and neurostructural development, affecting arousal and attention systems, at a minimum through disruption of developing neurotransmitter systems, mainly of monoaminergic pathways. Dopaminergic and serotonergic projections play a dynamic interacting role in development, especially in higher-level frontal cortical areas. The prefrontal cortex, involved in inhibitory control in adults, becomes richly connected with the upper parts of the brain stem and thalamus and with other cortical zones, as well as with subcortical arousal systems.

Inhibitory control is necessary for planning and organizing as well as maintaining and shifting behavioral actions or mental sets. Deficits in inhibitory control are reflected in difficulties making mental or behavioral shifts, which may result in perseverative, impulsive, or distractible behavior. Investigators have long suspected insufficient inhibitory control as the underlying cause of ADHD symptoms. We find that infants with certain CNS problems show deficits in inhibitory control in the early preschool years in regulating both verbal and motor output, and these deficits also are related to neonatal AMA. Other studies have found that children with ADHD are slower and have more errors reflecting disinhibition (consistent with deficiencies in the frontal cortical inhibitory system) on reaction time tasks requiring visual sustained attention. Thus, we contend that the relationship of early CNS injury to later educational problems may be better understood by studying disruptions in early autoregulatory systems, hypothesizing that poorer executive function at older ages relates to less optimal regulation at younger ages. Support for this position comes from research relating early deficits in regulation to later behavioral and psychological problems (Cicchetti, 1993; Greenspan, 1992; Porges, 1996), and from the relation of attention processes with autoregulation, particularly with respect to the role of temperament in the development of executive function (Rothbart & Posner, 2001). The issue of genetic influences has been raised by some, but a number of other factors, such as CNS injury due to acute or chronic stress, spontaneous attention versus attention under challenge, and changes in stimulation coming from internal states as well as external sources must be ruled out before a genetic explanation can be accepted.

Predicting Later Behavior Using Arousal and Attention Measures

Our findings at three years are interesting in relation to early AMA and subsequent autoregulation with respect to executive function at school age. We find a relationship between AMA and inhibitory control of response output in preschoolers using a Rapid Sequential Automated Naming Task and a Grapho-Motor Task adapted for these young children. Interestingly, we also have found a relationship between neonatal AMA and social fear at three years (using the Toddler Behavior Assessment Questionnaire, Goldsmith), which may be associated with other findings, such as between neonatal AMA and language inhibition at four to seven years of age. Strong developmental links among temperament, emotion regulation, and developing autoregulatory systems suggest that, in addition to the effect of CNS injury on these developing systems, the ability to handle stimulation in early infancy may reflect underlying biological systems that are involved in individual temperament and emotion regulation independent of their being a consequence of CNS injury.

We also have found that neonatal AMA predicts later performance on standard assessments. The better the ability to handle increased levels of stimulation when less aroused, and the greater the modulation between more and less aroused conditions, the higher the scores on the BSID Mental and Psychomotor Development Indices (MDI and PDI; Bayley, 1993), independent of CNS injury. The utility of AMA also is seen by its predictive validity to the GMDS (Griffiths, 1984) at 28, 34, and 42 months.

We have used the PROCESS Inventory (Casey et al., 1988) to try to understand how the predictive relationship between AMA and later cognitive scores may be affected by the caregiving environment. This is possible if the ability to handle stimulation as a newborn affects the development of autoregulatory skills that, in turn, influence the caregiving environment. Interestingly, we have found a complex relationship of the PROCESS to AMA in interaction with CNS injury on cognitive performance, that is, its effect is limited to normal (not CNS-injured) infants and only for the Bayley Mental Development Index (not the Psychomotor Development Index). Thus, better quality caregiving environments appear to promote better autoregulation so long as the infant is typically developing, but if the infant has had significant CNS injury, it is more difficult to offset deficits in autoregulation and cognitive development even in the best of environments. It is possible that more specific intervention strategies directed toward detected abnormalities need to be employed. Such findings are consistent with those of Wallace et al. (1995) with the effects of education on normal and CNS-injured preterm infants.

SUMMARY AND CONCLUSIONS

Arousal and attention form an inseparable dynamically transacting process during the neonatal period. Normal neonates have an intact homeostatic regulatory system that may form the substrate for their ability to modulate their attention according to their arousal. Thus, they prefer more stimulation when less aroused and less stimulation when more aroused. Brain injury is differentiated by specific disruptions of this process, with infants having different types and severity of CNS problems modulating their attention differently. Infants with functional brain stem problems and those with more severe intraventricular hemorrhage or seizures are poor modulators and tend to avoid higher levels of stimulation and prefer lower levels of stimulation even when less aroused. Infants prenatally exposed to cocaine also are poor modulators, but in the opposite direction. They tend to seek higher amounts of stimulation even when more aroused. Such different modes of early response to stimulation appear to have repercussions for information processing and social interactions not only during the neonatal period but also later in development. During the neonatal period, information is attended based on the amount of input from all sources, both internal and external. For normal neonates, who are excellent modulators, the range of information to which they are exposed would be very large. They would attend to and potentially process all types and amounts of information from all modalities, and they would experience the differences in the amount of stimulation in the information when in different states. Such experience would result in their learning to integrate their unique internal and external stimulation experience. For infants with CNS involvement, cocaine exposure, or potentially chronic stress, who are poor modulators, the range of total information processed would be restricted and the infant would learn to modulate or control information only in a more limited way. This restriction would result in almost always attending to reduced stimulation if CNS injured and increased stimulation if cocaine exposed or with chronic stress, thereby producing less variable information about the world and perhaps greater individual stereopathy and less ability to regulate.

During the first year, information processing becomes much more investigative and sensory specific. The infant who has experience with a whole range of input can now differentiate information coming from different sensory pathways at levels above the brain stem and midbrain areas. The infant is using this period to process enormous amounts of specific information about his/her world. For example, visual perception of forms, shapes, and complex patterns are all integrated at this time for use in skills such as visual recognition memory that then can be integrated into higher-level cortical categorization and cognition. Tasks that tap into the organization of the arousal and self-regulatory components of attention may be better discriminators of CNS pathology than simple attention tasks alone. Thus, visual attention or discrimination tasks may be better for studying normal perceptual processes, but arousal-modulating tasks may be better for differentiating individual differences if they indeed underlie the mechanisms for transitions in development.

Information processing skills that emerge toward the end of the first year, such as those measured by focused attention and distractibility tasks, have a large self-regulatory component. The ability to modulate arousal and attention as a neonate appears to form an important substrate for these higher-level self-regulatory visual information processing skills. These higher-level skills relate to lack of modulation of early attention and are associated with early CNS insult. The infant who has poor modulation as a neonate tends to have poor autoregulation of information processing on higher-level tasks at older ages. Whether this is due to the restricted range of information attended or the lack of experience with integrating internal and external amounts of stimulation with state transitions, or some combination of both, is not known. But we do propose that it is not the initial brain injury that solely determines outcome after the first year of life, but rather the transaction between the consequences of the brain injury and the degree of recovery, and its changing effect on the infant's ability to attend to, control, or respond to his/her environment. Thus, shifts in perceptual, cognitive, and self-regulatory development are found to be differentially related to early arousal/attention interactions as influenced by severity of CNS problems, with the degree of modulation of attention during the newborn period a major predictor of later functioning. More specifically, infants who have had early mid- and lower brain stem dysfunction as neonates (even if transient) that is manifest in deficits in homeostatic autoregulatory control, may have difficulty in their ability to control, plan, and execute intentional acts as older children. Since such inhibitory control and executive function appear to be necessary for specific areas of functioning underlying adequate performance in multiple areas, including cognitive, motor, social/emotional, and language skills, we would expect both individual differences and reductions in levels of specific areas as well as in general intellectual functioning associated with autoregulatory control deficits.

In conclusion, in conjunction with the underlying behavioral relationships, the importance of early CNS injury to later learning disabilities and mental health issues cannot be ignored. Nor is it sufficient to recognize that some injury has occurred without explicitly identifying the neurofunctional consequences, both immediate and long-term, that can arise. Further, the dynamic changing nature of the recovery process from such injury should be the expected norm unless the injury is so massive as to prevent any recovery of function. Since this degree of severity fortunately is rare, there is a substantial need for multidisciplinary infant health care providers who not only are expert with neurofunctional techniques, but also are trained to select and guide the best program of intervention strategies targeting specific individual requirements as early as possible. Specific interventions can be instituted very early based on valid diagnostic criteria derived from appropriate behavioral evaluation procedures and should not wait for a lag in development to be demonstrated.

Although we find perinatal CNS injury and early performance are strongly related, a one-to-one relationship does not exist. That is, our data indicate that information about CNS injury alone is not enough to predict later outcome. Behavioral evaluation in the neonatal period is just as important. This is a positive finding for economically disadvantaged regions that do not have technological resources and must rely on the accuracy and validity of behavioral techniques.

There are unfortunate negative similarities between economically advantaged and economically challenged regions with respect to provision of intervention to high-risk infants to prevent or ameliorate developmental disabilities. Even in economically advantaged countries with intervention on a fee-for-service basis, the infant gets into programs late and there is a tendency to exclude the parents from providing intervention to their child except in terms of parenting techniques. This is in contradiction to findings that early abnormalities can be habilitated to a major extent if appropriate intervention is implemented earlier and more intensely than is currently the general practice. The efficacy of this approach has been shown in this country with autistic children and in Hungary with CNS-injured neonates who have motor problems. Moreover, it is not cost effective to assess and diagnose later in infancy and childhood when problems are more difficult to ameliorate or reverse, and the costs for taking care of or providing resources for disabled populations of children are very expensive. In a time with decreasing funds allocated for intervention services, it is important to include the parent in the plan for providing intervention, and use the resources of the professional to teach and monitor the progress of the parent and infant. Similarly, in economically challenged regions, it is essential to empower the caregiver with the knowledge and ability to provide intervention, again using the professional to teach and monitor progress. Thus, in both situations, resources have to be used economically and efficiently, with the outcome of the child of primary importance.

REFERENCES

Als, H., Lester, B.M., & Brazelton, T.B. (1979). Dynamics of the behavioral organization of the premature infant: A theoretical perspective. In T. Field, A. Sostek, S. Goldberg, & H.H. Shuman (Eds.), *Infants born at risk: Behavior and development.* New York: Spectrum.

Amiel-Tison, C., & Pettigrew, A.G. (1991). Adaptive changes in the developing brain during intrauterine stress. *Brain Development, 13,* 67–76.

Bayley, N. (1993). *Bayley scales of infant development* (2nd ed.). San Antonio, TX: Psychological Corporation.

Berlyne, D.E. (1960). *Conflict, arousal, and curiosity.* London: McGraw-Hill.

Bradley R.H., Whiteside, L., Mundfrom, D.J., Blevins-Knabe, B., Casey, P.H., Caldwell, B.M., Kelleher, K.H., Pope, S., & Barrett, K. (1995). Home environment and adaptive social behavior among premature, low birth weight children: Alternative models of environmental action. *Journal of Pediatric Psychology, 20,* 347–362.

Brazelton, T. B., Nugent, J. K., & Lester, B. M. (1987). Neonatal behavioral as assessment scale. In J. Osofsy (Ed.), *Handbook of infant development* (2nd ed.) (pp. 780–818). New York: Wiley.

Casey, P. H., Bradley, R. H., Nelson, J. Y. & Whaley, S. A. (1988). The clinical assessment of a child's social and physical environment during health visits. *Developmental and Behavioral Pediatrics, 9,* 333–338.

Cicchetti, D. (1993). Developmental psychopathology: Reactions, reflections, projections. *Developmental Review, 13,* 471–502.

Diamond, A. (1990).The development and neural bases of memory functions as indexed by the AB and delayed response tasks in human infants and infant monkeys. In A. Diamond (Ed.), *The development and neural bases of higher cognitive functions.* Annals of the New York Academy of Sciences (Vol. 608) (pp. 267–317). New York: New York Academy of Sciences.

Diamond, A., Prevor, M. B., Callender, G., & Druin, D. P. (1997). Prefrontal cortex cognitive deficits in children treated early and continuously for PKU. *Monographs of the Society for Research in Child Development, 62,* (4, Serial No. 252).

Eckerman, C. O., Hsu, H., Molitor, A., Leung, E.H.L., & Goldstein, R. F. (1999). Infant arousal in an en-face exchange with a new partner: Effects of prematurity and perinatal biological risk. *Developmental Psychology, 35,* 282–293.

Einspieler, C., Prechtl, H.F.R., Ferrari, F., Cioni, G., & Bos, A. F. (1997). The qualitative assessment of general movements in preterm, term, and young infants—review of the methodology. *Early Human Development, 50* (Special Issue).

Field, T. M. (1981). Infant arousal, attention, and affect during early interactions. In L. P. Lippsitt & C. Rovee-Collier (Eds.), *Advances in infancy research,* Vol. 1 (pp. 51–100). Norwood, NJ: Ablex.

Field, T. M. (1982). Affective displays of high-risk infants during early interactions. In T. Field & A. Fogel (Eds.), *Emotion and early interaction* (pp. 101–125). Hillsdale, NJ: Erlbaum.

Fox, N. (1994). The development of emotion regulation: Biological and behavioral considerations. *Monographs of the Society for Research in Child Development,* Serial No. 240.

Gardner, J. M., & Karmel, B. Z. (1983). Attention and arousal in preterm and full-term neonates. In T. Field & A. Sostek (Eds.), *Infants born at risk: Behavior and development* (pp. 69–98). New York: Grune & Stratton.

Gardner, J. M., & Karmel, B. Z. (1995). Development of arousal-modulated visual preferences in early infancy. *Developmental Psychology, 31,* 473–482.

Gardner, J. M., Karmel, B. Z., & Flory, M. J. (2003). Arousal modulation of neonatal visual attention: Implications for development. In S. Soraci, Jr. & K. Murata-Soraci (Eds.), *Visual information processing* (pp. 125–154). Westport, CT: Praeger Publishers.

Gardner, J. M., Karmel, B. Z., & Freedland, R. L. (2001). Determining functional integrity in neonates: A rapid neurobehavior assessment tool. In L. T. Singer & P. S. Zeskind (Eds.), *Biobehavioral assessment of the infant* (pp. 398–422). New York: Guilford Publications.

Gardner, J. M., Karmel, B. Z., & Magnano, C. L. (1992). Arousal/visual preference interactions in high-risk neonates. *Developmental Psychology, 28,* 821–830.

Gardner, J. M., Karmel, B. Z., Magnano, C. L., Norton, K. I., & Brown, E. G. (1990). Neurobehavioral indicators of early brain insult in high-risk neonates. *Developmental Psychology, 26,* 563–575.

Geva, R., Gardner, J. M., & Karmel, B. Z. (1999). Feeding-based arousal effects on visual recognition memory in early infancy. *Developmental Psychology, 35,* 640–650.

Goyen, T. A., & Lui, K. (2002). Longitudinal motor development of "apparently normal" high-risk infants at 18 months, 3 and 5 years. *Early Human Development, 70,* 103–115.

Griffiths, R. (1984). *The Abilities of Young Children. A comprehensive system of mental measurement for the first eight years of life.* Bucks, UK: The Test Agency LTD.

Greenspan, S. I. (1992). *Infancy and early childhood: The practice of clinical assessment and intervention with emotional developmental challenges.* Madison, CT: International Universities Press.

Hack, M., Klein, N. K., & Taylor, H. G. (1995). Long-term developmental outcomes of low birth weight infants. *The Future of Children: Low Birth Weight, 5,* 176–196.

Harel, S. (2002, May). *Comparison between IUGR and control children.* Conference on Social and Cognitive Issues in Development, Bar Ilan University, Tel Aviv, Israel.

Johnson, M. H. (1996). From cortex to cognition: Cognitive neuroscience studies of infant attention and perception. In C. Rovee-Collier & L. P. Lipsitt (Eds.), *Advances in infancy research,* Vol. 10 (pp. 161–217). Norwood, NJ: Ablex.

Karmel, B. Z., & Gardner, J. M. (2005). Neurobehavioral assessment in the neonatal period: The impact of Ferenc Katona. *Clinical Neuroscience/ Ideggyógyászati Szemle, 58,* 315–323.

Karmel, B. Z., Gardner, J. M., & Magnano, C. L. (1991). Attention and arousal in early infancy. In M. J. Weiss and P. R. Zelazo (Eds.), *Newborn attention: Biological constraints and the influence of experience* (pp. 339–376). Norwood, N.J.: Ablex.

Karmel, B. Z., Gardner, J. M., Zappulla, R. A., Magnano, C. L., & Brown, E. G. (1988). Brain stem auditory evoked responses as indicators of early brain insult. *EEG and Clinical Neurophysiology, 71,* 429–442.

Karmel, B. Z., Kaye, H., & John, E. R. (1978). Developmental neurometrics: The use of quantitative analysis of brain electrical activity to probe mental function throughout the life span. In A. Collins (Ed.), *XII Annual*

Minnesota Symposium in child psychology (pp. 141–198). Minneapolis: University of Minnesota Press.

Karmel, B. Z., & Maisel, E. B. (1975). A neuronal activity model for infant visual attention. In L. Cohen & P. Salapatek (Eds.), *Infant perception: From sensation to cognition,* Vol. 1 (pp. 77–131). New York: Academic.

Katona, F. (1988). Developmental clinical neurology and neurorehabilitation in the secondary prevention of pre- and perinatal injuries of the brain. In P. M. Vietze & H. G. Vaughan (Eds.), *Early identification of infants with developmental disabilities* (pp. 121–146). Philadelphia: Grune and Stratton.

Korner, A. F. (1972). State as variable, as obstacle, and as mediator of stimulation in infant research. *Merrill-Palmer Quarterly, 18,* 77–94.

Lawson, K. R., & Ruff, H. A. (2005). Early focused attention predicts outcome for children born prematurely. *Developmental and Behavioral Pediatrics, 25,* 399–406.

Leitner, Y., Fattal-Valevski, A., Geva, R., Bassan, H., Posner, E., Kutai, M., Many, A., Yaffa, A. J., & Harel, S. (2000). A six year follow-up of children with intrauterine growth retardation: A long-term prospective study. *Journal of Child Neurology, 15,* 781–786.

Lester, B. M., Corwin, M. J., Sepkoski, C., Seifer, R., Peucker, M., McLaughlin, S., & Golub, H. L. (1991). Neurobehavioral syndromes in cocaine-exposed newborn infants. *Child Development, 62,* 694–705.

Lester, B. M., & Tronick, E. Z. (2004). *The NICU Network Neurobehavioral Scale (NNNS).* Baltimore, MD: Brooks.

Marlow, N., Wolke, D., Bracewell, M. A., & Samara, M. (2005). Neurologic and developmental disability at six years of age after extremely preterm birth. *The New England Journal of Medicine, 352,* 9–19.

Mayes, L. C., Grillon, C., Granger, R., & Schottenfeld, R. (1998). Regulation of arousal and attention in preschool children exposed to cocaine prenatally. In J. A. Harvey & B. E. Kosofsky (Eds.), *Cocaine: Effects on the developing brain.* Annals of the New York Academy of Science (Vol.846) (pp. 126–143). New York: New York Academy of Sciences.

Porges, S. W. (1996). Psychological regulation in high-risk infants: A model for assessment and potential intervention. *Development and Psychopathology, 8,* 43–58.

Posner, M. I. (1988). Structures and functions of selective attention. In T. Boll & T. Bryant (Eds.), *Master lectures in clinical neuropsychology and brain function research, measurement, and practice* (pp. 171–202). Washington, DC: APA.

Prechtl, H. F. R. (1997). Spontaneous motor activity as a diagnostic tool. Functional assessment of the young nervous system. *Early Human Development, 50*(Special Issue): 148.

Richards, J. E. (2001). Attention in young infants: A developmental psychophysiological perspective. In C. A. Nelson & M. Luciana (Eds.), *Handbook of Developmental Cognitive Neuroscience* (pp. 321–338). Cambridge, MA: Bradford.

Rothbart, M. K., & Posner, M. I. (2001). Mechanism and variation in the development of attentional networks. In C. A. Nelson & M. Luciana (Eds.), *Handbook of Developmental Cognitive Neuroscience.* Cambridge, MA: MIT Press.

Rothbart, M. K., Ziaie, H., & O'Boyle, C. G. (1992). Self-regulation and emotion in infancy. In N. Eisenberg & R. A. Fabes (Eds.), *Emotion and its regulation in early development* (New Directions in Child Development, No. 55, pp.7–24). San Francisco: Jossey-Bass.

Ruff, H. A., & Rothbart, M. K. (1996). *Attention in early development. Themes and variations.* New York: Oxford University Press.

Shapiro, S. (1967, April). *Animal studies in development.* Los Angeles: Society for Research in Child Development.

Volpe, J. J. (2001). *Neurology of the newborn* (4th ed.). Philadelphia: WB Saunders Company.

Wallace, I. F., Rose, S. A., McCarton, C. M., Kurtzberg, D., & Vaughan, H. G. (1995). Relations between infant neurobehavioral performance and cognitive outcome in very low birth weight preterm infants. *Journal of Developmental and Behavioral Pediatrics, 16,* 309–317.

Chapter 5

EARLY INTERVENTION PROGRAMS AND POLICIES FOR CHILDREN WITH AUTISTIC SPECTRUM DISORDERS

Natacha A. Akshoomoff and Aubyn Stahmer

Supported by NIMH grants 1K23MH71796 (N.A.) and 5K01MH065325 (A.S.)

Autistic Spectrum Disorder (ASD) is characterized by impairments in social interaction and communication along with restricted, repetitive, and stereotyped patterns of behavior. Social deficits manifest in avoidance of eye contact, failure to develop peer relationships, resistance of affection, high levels of isolated play, and limited play skills. The preference for being alone may persist as the child grows older. Approximately 30 percent of children with autism do not develop language. Children who do acquire speech often develop noncommunicative speech patterns, use language sparingly, and the language they do develop is often quite rote in nature. Speaking children with autism often exhibit a specific speech anomaly called *echolalia,* the repetition of words or phrases spoken by others. Disturbances of behavior may include a demand for sameness in the environment, ritualistic preoccupations (e.g., memorizing bus schedules; closing doors), or self-stimulatory behavior (e.g., hand flapping; spinning objects). Finally, these children may exhibit anomalies in their sensory responding including over- or under-response to sound, pain, touch, or light. While the severity of these symptoms varies across children and changes with development, they affect almost every aspect of social and psychological development. Children with autism face many of the same challenges at home, in school, and in the community as other children with mental health problems.

Most children with autism (as many as 75%) have impaired cognitive development such that their level of functioning falls into the mentally retarded range. While higher-functioning individuals with autism can have average to above average abilities in several domains, they typically experience difficulty in some academic areas. A child with autism may be able to recite the dialogue from a movie, complete with voices and expression, yet rarely vary his voice when speaking with others. She may have no interest in playing with other children, instead choosing to engage in repetitive behaviors or playing with toys in unusual ways. As he gets older, he may seek attention from others but only to talk about his own interests. A young child with autism may show the remarkable ability to identify letters and numbers and "read" words but have delayed language abilities. An older child with autism may be able to perform well on standardized academic tests and yet have difficulty making it through school without special accommodations, and will often have difficulty holding a job.

These symptoms are pervasive and often severe, which can cause significant challenges to families. Families of children with autism exhibit higher levels of stress than parents of children with other disabilities (Holroyd & McArthur, 1976). Many parents report feeling their child is not emotionally attached to them. In some cases, children may have some social attachment to their parents, which often manifests as extreme clinging to parents in new situations, or the affection may be odd, such as hugging parents backwards or enjoying physical contact only in the context of rough-and-tumble play. Difficulties with communication often cause frustration. This frustration, along with sensory sensitivities, can lead to issues such as severe tantrum behavior, nutrition issues (from limited food preferences), and dental problems (from refusal to brush teeth). Some children have difficulty with crowded places and therefore cannot go to the grocery store or a restaurant. This can severely limit family mobility. Parents struggle with their child's inability to engage with peers or play appropriately. Children with autism often need constant supervision, have difficulty sleeping, and because they do not use their parents as a secure base, may run off easily. As we will see, families also struggle with obtaining an appropriate diagnosis as well as adequate treatment for their children, often paying out-of-pocket for many essential services. Autism is a disorder that affects the entire family for a lifetime.

Autism is now more commonly seen as a spectrum of disorders (Lord & Bailey, 2002). This includes Autistic Disorder, children with more "classic" symptoms of autism; Asperger's Disorder, children with average to above average cognitive abilities and less severe communication problems; and Pervasive Developmental Disorder-Not Otherwise Specified (PDD-NOS), children who have many of the symptoms associated with Autistic Disorder but do not meet the full diagnostic criteria (American Psychiatric Association, 2000). The prevalence of ASD is approximately

60 per 10,000 (Fombonne, 2003), which makes them more common than previously thought but lower in incidence than other child mental health problems. It appears that better identification, broader categorization, and the growth of available services have contributed to the increased number of children being identified with ASD and requiring specific educational interventions.

The specific causes for autism are not clear. Data from family and twin studies suggest that there is a genetic component in autism. Studies have found a variety of genetic abnormalities associated with autism; the genetic underpinnings are complex and related to a variety of factors. A number of studies are currently being conducted to determine the genes that appear to be most commonly affected in children with autism. Across a number of brain imaging and postmortem studies, a range of structural and functional abnormalities in the brain have been identified in children and adults with autism (for review, see Akshoomoff, Pierce, & Courchesne, 2002). More recent findings suggest that brain growth abnormalities occur early in postnatal development, before the behavioral symptoms become apparent, and may vary with the functional outcome of the child (Akshoomoff et al., 2004; Courchesne, Carper, & Akshoomoff, 2003).

The authors of a report about a group of 12 children with pervasive developmental disorders raised the possibility that there was a link between the gastrointestinal problems observed in the children, the development of autism, and the measles, mumps, and rubella (MMR) vaccine. Although this suggestion has led to a great deal of concern about the safety of the MMR vaccine (Horton, 2004), epidemiological studies have not supported the relationship between prevalence of autism and the MMR vaccine (Institute of Medicine, 2001; Madsen et al., 2002; Taylor et al., 2002). Ten of the authors of the original study that suggested this possibility published a retraction of that interpretation of their data (Murch et al., 2004). Others have raised concerns that perhaps it is the mercury-based preservative in the vaccines, thimerosal, that is linked to the development of ASD. A review of 10 epidemiologic studies and 2 pharmacokinetic studies of ethylmercury concludes that there is not sufficient evidence to demonstrate a link between thimerosal-containing vaccines and ASD (Parker, Schwartz, Todd, & Pickering, 2004). The pharmacokinetics of ethylmercury also appear to make such an association less likely.

EARLY IDENTIFICATION AND DIAGNOSIS

Recent progress has been made in the early identification of children with autism, and most children are now identified in the early preschool ages (Charman & Baird, 2002). Primary healthcare providers and other professionals who interact with very young children have more information available to them about the early features of autism, and screening tools have become more readily available.

Not all parents may be aware that their child is showing delays in their development or exhibiting unusual behaviors. However, parental concerns have been shown to be an important early indicator for children later diagnosed with autism. Screening questionnaires were never intended to be a diagnostic "gold standard," particularly for low-base-rate disorders. When the parent or the primary care provider raises concerns about a young child, the child should then be referred for a comprehensive evaluation. While parents may be concerned about labeling, and primary care providers may be concerned about incorrect diagnosis or alarming the parent unnecessarily, the referral should be viewed as a standard follow-up practice to a failed screening and the potential for early intervention, if deemed necessary. A general medical examination and a hearing test should be part of the initial screening process.

Diagnostic accuracy has been a critical area of investigation for autism researchers for a number of years due to the increasing number of studies aimed at uncovering the underlying biological causes and concern about increased prevalence rates. Diagnostic precision is perhaps less of a concern among community professionals responsible for identifying children with ASD who may benefit from early intervention programs. However, children under the age of four who appear to have an ASD should be considered to have a "provisional diagnosis" for a number of reasons (Lord & Risi, 1998; National Research Council, 2001). In very young children, it may be difficult to differentiate the symptoms of autism from language delay or global developmental delays. A proportion of children identified with "possible autism" before age three may not meet criteria for DSM-IV Autistic Disorder at later follow-up but are highly likely to meet criteria for PDD-NOS, a less severe form of autism. Alternatively, children under age four may not show significant evidence of repetitive and stereotyped behaviors and restricted patterns of interest as required to meet the DSM-IV criteria. The use of a standardized observation of social and communicative behavior and play, such as the Autism Diagnostic Observation Schedule (ADOS; Lord, Rutter, DiLavore, & Risi, 2001), is critical for determining how the young child's behavior fits within the developmental context and may warrant a diagnosis. The ADOS may be more sensitive and stable over time than the use of a standardized parent report measure (such as the Autism Diagnostic Interview-Revised [ADI-R]; Lord, Rutter, & Le Couteur, 1994) alone. As the child gets older and receives intervention, repeated assessment, including the use of a tool such as the ADI-R, is necessary for diagnostic clarification and to assist in treatment planning.

The ADI-R and the ADOS are complementary diagnostic instruments originally created for research that are now available for clinical purposes. It is not known how useful they will be in community settings or schools, where the mix of developmental problems is wide compared to specialty clinics or research studies targeted towards children with ASD. Research indicates that experienced clinical judgment using information from a variety of sources is more reliable for determination of diagnosis in very young children than the use of standard assessment instruments alone.

Given the increasing population of children with autism in the community, earlier diagnosis for this population, and the cost of intensive services provided by many agencies, the effectiveness of assessment is increasingly important. Several reports have concluded that the proper assessment should consist of a formal multidisciplinary evaluation of social behavior, language and nonverbal communication, adaptive behavior, motor skills, atypical behaviors, and cognitive status by a team of professionals experienced with autistic spectrum disorders (Charman & Baird, 2002; National Research Council, 2001). This will typically include an experienced clinical psychologist or school psychologist, a speech/language pathologist, and an occupational therapist. Many children with ASD experience difficulties with fine motor coordination, low muscle tone, behavior control and aggression, and/or the presence of a seizure disorder, warranting a consultation with an experienced pediatric neurologist or child psychiatrist. While experts agree that experienced professionals are needed for proper assessment, a formal definition of "experience" is lacking.

Two "best practices" guidelines from California present a list of instruments for diagnostic assessment, developmental assessment, adaptive assessment, communication assessment, standardized tests of intelligence and nonverbal intelligence, and behavior assessment (California Department of Developmental Services, 2002; California Departments of Education and Developmental Services, 1997). Limited specific information is provided about reliability, validity, and training requirements for each instrument. Limited information about the utility of these instruments in educational settings is available. This type of "best practices" guide therefore has limited practical value for professionals responsible for assessment in the schools or for clinicians who are asked to provide assessment information and recommendations for the child that will be utilized by the school.

SERVICE SYSTEMS FOR CHILDREN WITH ASD

During the past 25 years, the United States has developed systems for providing early intervention services for children with developmental disabilities, including autism. In 1990, when Congress updated Public Law

94–142 and changed the title to the "Individuals with Disabilities Education Act" (IDEA; P.L. 101–476), the term "autism" and its definition was added to the previous list of disability terms and definitions. Many schools and early intervention programs did not have services specific to the disorder before that time. A number of amendments followed (IDEA'97; P.L. 105–117), which include provisions for full, individualized, and appropriate evaluations and educational services to be provided by the local schools.

Under IDEA, Congress made funds available to help states and territories provide additional services for children with special needs, including school-age children as well as infants, toddlers, and preschoolers. A majority of states have chosen to provide one set of services for children ages birth to three and a different set of services (usually provided by the school district) from three to five years of age. States are following federal break-downs of services in doing this, as the government has provided different guidelines for children in each of these age categories. For children under age three, services (educational and otherwise) can be provided by the education system, the mental health system, the Department of Health and Human Services, and/or the developmental disabilities agency. Infants and toddlers with autism or at-risk for an autistic spectrum disorder are served under the category "other health impaired." Services for children ages three to five follow the same regulations as those for school-age children with autism and are primarily provided by the school district, which provides educational services. Other agencies may be responsible for behavioral intervention, parent support, and so on. Service intensity, type and amount of family support, service quality, and the agency responsible for service coordination vary greatly state by state and even city by city. Only a few states provide comprehensive services in a single system from birth through five (e.g., Oregon).

Some states (e.g., Delaware, North Carolina, Florida) have service agencies that provide services to children with autism specifically. However, the majority of states serve children with autism using the same service providers as children with other disabilities. Other states, such as California, provide differential services for children with autism (e.g., different intervention techniques, increased intensity), but use the same service pathways as are used for other children with disabilities. All states are required to provide an Individual Family Service Plan (IFSP) for each child under the age of three, which outlines goals and services needed to reach those goals, including family-centered services. At age three, the school district provides an Individual Education Plan (IEP) that focuses solely on the needs of the child who qualifies under Special Education law. IDEA also requires that states use treatments that have an evidence base and that a fair and appropriate public education (FAPE) is provided.

The diagnosis of autism typically occurs between 24 and 36 months of age, at which time the early intervention system develops an IFSP for the family. As a part of this process, service providers develop a relationship with the family and set up an initial intervention program based on the needs of the child and the policies of the area in which the child lives. Unfortunately for children with autism, very soon after early intervention begins (when the child reaches 36 months of age), many families must transition to a new system with different eligibility criteria, service provision, and standards for family participation. Additionally, the services provided are not typically coordinated across agencies such that families may not receive the same level or type of services once their child turns three. The lack of coordination and planning between these systems can lead to conflict, confusion, and litigation for families of children with autism and the school system (Schreibman & Anderson, 2001).

In general, federal guidelines for the administration of early intervention programs provide individual states with a large amount of decision-making authority in order to make programming appropriate for families in their own area. This has led to many different methods of administering services for children with or at risk for developmental disabilities. The federal regulations do not offer any specific guidelines for administering programs for specific disabilities such as autistic spectrum disorders. Systematic studies of the effect of service systems are imperative for the development of appropriate programming and service delivery for this population. Additionally, a cursory examination of state policies did not lead to an understanding of the actual services children and families receive. States appear to have very similar services on the surface; however, further investigation indicates that services may differ for children in the same city, and even in the same school district.

Numerous litigation cases over the appropriate identification of and the development of educational services for children with ASD have occurred over the past decade (Yell, Katsiyannis, Drasgow, & Herbst, 2003). Many more disputes are resolved through mediation or due process hearings. While these processes ensure that school districts and early intervention agencies comply with regulations, they are often associated with high costs and controversy. Disputes and procedural violations are often associated with a failure to evaluate all areas of the student's need, having evaluations conducted by school personnel with no knowledge of autism or appropriate evaluation procedures to assess students with autism, developing inadequate IEPs or IFSPs, not adequately involving parents in the IEP of IFSP process or informing parents of their procedural rights, and not having qualified personnel needed to work with students with autism.

PROVISION OF DIAGNOSTIC SERVICES

Who is responsible for providing a comprehensive multidisciplinary evaluation? Although nationwide data are not readily available, medical professionals through their healthcare plan probably most commonly evaluate children diagnosed with autism when they are young and then they are reevaluated by state services agencies and/or their local school districts. These agencies also follow the children to assess continued need for and effectiveness of services. The National Research Council's Committee on Educational Interventions for Children with Autism (NRCA) recommended that if the school system cannot carry out a formal multidisciplinary assessment, the local education authority should fund the assessment through external sources (National Research Council, 2001). However, the provision of such services may not necessarily be the responsibility of the local school district, depending on the child's age, location, and the extent of the evaluation. For children over the age of three, the California Department of Developmental Services stated, "The educational system is not responsible for providing concomitant medical or other diagnostic evaluation services that may be necessary for a comprehensive interdisciplinary evaluation. Thus, while it is necessary to refer families of children with ASD and other developmental disabilities to the school district for special education services, referral to a comprehensive diagnostic team is usually necessary for a full diagnostic evaluation" (California Department of Developmental Services, 2002).

Colorado has interpreted IDEA'97 such that trained school personnel can be involved in making the *educational diagnosis* rather than requiring a differential *medical diagnosis* to determine eligibility for special education services (Noland & Gabriels, 2004). They acknowledge that it is important for school personnel to know when to refer an identified child to a physician. It is thus clear that differences across states with regard to the IDEA definition of the autism category make it difficult to use prevalence estimates based on students enrolled in the autism category, which may be limited to their interpretations of the educational diagnosis rather than the more specific medical diagnosis required for epidemiological studies (Noland & Gabriels, 2004).

Experts agree that school districts should have professionals with expertise in the area of autism conduct comprehensive and individualized evaluations of referred students. This again raises the question of how to define "expertise." If a school district's personnel do not have the necessary expertise, the school district must either train their personnel or hire outside consultants to conduct the evaluations (Yell et al., 2003). This is an issue that is not easily resolved.

Using funds provided to the state through Part B of IDEA'97, a multi-disciplinary evaluation team was developed in two rural school districts in Colorado (Noland & Gabriels, 2004). Implementation of the project involved training, purchase of instruments associated with best practices for screening and assessing ASD, and supervision from an outside consultant with extensive experience in the assessment and treatment of children with ASD. This model is appealing because it utilizes evidence-based practices, includes provision for both assessment and intervention services, uses a team approach, and provides necessary training for school personnel rather than relying on a more expensive outside consultant approach. Further research is needed to determine how well this program can be maintained without additional funding, and the degree to which this program improves identification and service delivery compared to standard practice. Before such a program is implemented in other school districts, consideration needs to be given to whether any modifications may have an impact on reliability and validity and cost effectiveness.

TREATMENT

Although we continue to have a poor understanding of the etiology of autism and early development of the disorder, recent research in the field of autism has heavily emphasized the importance of early intervention (i.e., treatment before the age of four years). This emphasis may be attributed in part to results of treatment studies suggesting substantial gains may be achieved when treatment is provided at a very early age (National Research Council, 2001). Treating children with autism at an early age is the best hope we currently have for "preventing" the most severe cases of the disorder. Gains made by children with autism in early intervention programs may result in a cost savings of nearly one million dollars by the time a person with autism reaches 55 years of age (Columbia Pacific Consulting, 1999).

Although children with ASD may face significant limitations (i.e., mental retardation, severe autistic symptoms), and the initial causes of the disorder are believed to be biological, it is important to remember that the environment has a significant influence on the outcome of the child, including the development of the brain. Although early intervention is critical for optimizing outcome, intervention should not end after age five. It is also important to note that if a child is not diagnosed until a later point in development or did not receive early intervention services, behavioral and educational intervention services can still have a major impact on promoting development and the best possible outcome.

Currently, no treatment method completely ameliorates the symptoms of ASD and no specific treatment has emerged as the established standard of care for all children with ASD. Several methods have been demonstrated to be efficacious with some children in research settings. The most well-researched programs are based on the principles of applied behavior analysis. Treatments based on behavioral principles represent a wide range of early intervention strategies for children with autism. These range from highly structured programs that are conducted in a one-on-one treatment setting to behaviorally based inclusion programs that include typically developing children as models.

The first types of treatment programs researchers developed and examined were highly structured, very intensive, one-on-one programs, which were shown to be highly effective for as many as half of children enrolled (Lovaas, 1987; McEachin, Smith, & Lovaas, 1993). However these intensive programs were very expensive and children often had difficulty generalizing the information they learned into group and community settings. To remedy this issue, researchers began using less structured, more naturalistic, behavioral programming in both individual and school settings (e.g., Schreibman & Koegel, 1996). Children had greater generalization of skills, and these programs were more easily adapted for use in parent education and training programs (Schreibman, Kaneko, & Koegel, 1991). Again, approximately half of the children have good outcomes in these types of programs. Studies of inclusion models (educating children with autism alongside typically developing peers) using naturalistic behavioral techniques also report positive results for children with autism. As with studies of in-home programs, inclusion programs lead to as many as 50 percent of children being mainstreamed into regular education programs (McGee, Morrier, & Daly, 2000). Other behavioral techniques are also reporting promising results. Some techniques involve comprehensive educational programs, while others focus on one area of difficulty, such as communication or problem behaviors.

A few techniques that are not behavioral in nature are beginning to demonstrate effectiveness as well. Some of these are functional techniques that use structured environments, visual cueing, and other strategies to assist children with autism in navigating their environments. Case studies and studies of components of these techniques are supportive of treatment efficacy (e.g., Panerai, Farrante, & Zingale, 2002). Developmental models have also shown some promising results and, again, indicate that about half of the children do very well (Greenspan & Weider, 1997). In addition, many model programs for early intervention have shown success using the techniques described above or a combination of techniques (for a complete description of several model programs see Handleman & Harris, 2001).

Some researchers believe that combining treatments in a systematic way may be most appropriate (e.g., Rogers, 1996; Siegel, 1996), as the exclusive use of one treatment method may ignore important aspects of social, emotional, communicative, or preacademic development. Early studies indicate that combining methods is a promising avenue to pursue (e.g., Stahmer & Ingersoll, 2004); however, some researchers feel it may actually be detrimental to learning, confuse the children, and reduce the fidelity with which any one treatment is administered (e.g., McGee, Morrier, & Daly, 1999). Community programs typically report using more than one method; therefore, continued research on the efficacy of treatment combinations is imperative.

The medications most commonly used in the treatment of individuals with ASD are directed toward improving the associated symptoms of the disorder, such as hyperactivity, aggression, irritability, and agitation, to increase the likelihood that the child will benefit from behavioral and educational programs. While improvement in core symptoms is unlikely to result from medication use, some aspects of social behavior may improve as a result of the reduction in associated symptoms.

Recent, well-controlled studies have focused on the atypical antipsychotic medications, most notably risperidone. In the largest controlled drug treatment study in autistic disorder to date, the RUPP Autism Network completed a randomized controlled trial of risperidone in 101 children with autistic disorder (McCracken et al., 2002). Treatment for eight weeks was effective in reducing tantrums, aggression, or self-injurious behavior in children with autistic disorder. Side effects included weight gain, increased appetite, fatigue, drowsiness, dizziness, and drooling. In an open-label, naturalistic study of 53 preschoolers with ASD, low-dose risperidone was associated with reducing behavior problems and affect dysregulation (Masi, Cosenza, Mucci, & Brovedani, 2003). Few controlled studies of selective serotonin reuptake inhibitors have been completed (McDougle & Posey, 2003). Studies of fluvoxamine (Luvox) suggest that it may be less efficacious and less tolerated in children and adolescents with ASD than adults (McDougle et al., 1996). Studies of fluoxetine (Prozac) indicate favorable results, although possible side effects include hyperactivity, agitation, decreased appetite, and aggression (Cook, Rowlett, Jaselskis, & Leventhal, 1992). The use of psychostimulants (e.g., Ritalin) has generally resulted in mixed results (McDougle & Posey, 2002). While motor hyperactivity and poor attention may improve in some children with autism, adverse side effects of aggression and irritability have been noted. There is some interest in the use of clonidine and guanfacine, particularly for those children and adolescents with ASD who are nonresponders to psychostimulants. All medications should be prescribed by an experienced specialist with regular monitoring.

There has also been a proliferation of treatments that do not have an evidence base. Perhaps due to the limited understanding of the disorder, the heterogeneity of the children, or the splinter skills often seen in this population, hope for a miracle treatment among parents and some professionals has been extremely high. Promoters of specific treatments often report dramatic results in a few children but do not have scientific data to support their claims. Often extensive media coverage and the enthusiasm of families looking for a cure provide an avenue for dissemination of unproven methods. While some of these methods may be effective for some children, there is currently no evidence to support them. Therefore, clinicians and families are advised to proceed with caution when examining methods that promise a cure for all children on the autism spectrum.

EXAMINING EVIDENCE-BASED PRACTICES FOR AUTISM

Thus far, direct comparison of specific behavioral treatment methods has not been conducted. Therefore, no one program can claim to be more effective than another, nor are we able to predict efficacy of individual treatment methods for specific children (Feinberg & Vacca, 2000; Lord et al., in press). Researchers are beginning to compare methods directly; however, this has proved difficult due to differences in assessment procedures and populations served. Additionally, parents are hesitant to allow their child to be randomly assigned to a specific treatment method at such a critical stage in development. Therefore, choosing a specific treatment for use with a particular child can be difficult for families and community providers.

Recently, there have been several movements to deal with the proliferation of multiple treatment methods for children with autism. The first involves the development of best practice guidelines, which either list common practices used with children with autism, or include a critical assessment of available practices. Some best practice guidelines list the majority of treatments available for children with autism, without regard for whether or not research has shown these treatments to be effective (California Departments of Education and Developmental Services, 1997). Others consider the limited experimental evidence for treatment efficacy when defining best practice (New York State Department of Health Early Intervention Program, 1999). However, these guidelines still offer no recommendations for specific strategies to be used or how to choose a strategy for a specific case.

Secondly, in order to address the multiple treatments that appear to be effective, as well as the possibility that a combination of treatments may be necessary, researchers have delineated some elements common to various treatments. Several researchers have reviewed programs and techniques with both published descriptions and intake and outcome data (Dawson & Osterling, 1997; Hurth, Shaw, Izeman, Whaley, & Rogers, 1999; National Research Council, 2001). Iovannone, Dunlap, Huber, & Kincaid (2003) examined those reviews and expanded them to include not only early intervention, but also recommendations for school-age children as well. Table 5.1 depicts common elements found across reviews of effective practices. These critical elements are common across many of the techniques listed in best practice guidelines and may be more important to child outcome than the use of individual programs or philosophies.

The heterogeneity and developmental nature of the disorder make it unlikely that one specific treatment will be best for all children, or will work for any one child throughout his or her educational career. Because there is always a subset of children who do not respond favorably to each of the studied treatment methods, many researchers recognize the need for the individualization of treatment based on specific characteristics of the individual child and family (Anderson & Romanczyk, 1999). The goal, then, is not to find the perfect treatment, but to identify the important variables that influence the effectiveness of specific interventions for each child. Research that furthers our understanding of how to match clients with efficacious treatments will enable consumers to make better choices between procedures, decrease the outcome variability that characterizes early intervention research at present, and provide for the most efficient allocation of resources during the critical early intervention time-period. This type of research is in its infancy but is imperative if we are to determine a priori which treatment method will be most effective for a specific child.

This line of research may lead to guidelines similar to those available for other mental health disorders, such as childhood depression, in which practice guidelines have been developed for both adults and children with the disorder (American Academy of Child and Adolescent Psychiatry, 1998; Karasu, Gelenberg, Merriam, & Wang, 2002). Treatment recommendations vary based of many individual case factors, such as the severity of the disorder, age/developmental level of the individual, family involvement, motivation for treatment, and comorbid features. These factors are considered when choosing the first route of treatment as well as in treatment adjustment and maintenance. Like autism, this disorder is being recognized at younger and younger ages, and the development of new treatments and assessment methods for this age is essential. As is the case with all childhood disorders, numerous child and environmental factors that must be examined in order to obtain appropriate guidelines that

Table 5.1
Comparison of Commonality Studies. (Adapted from Iovannone et al., 2003.)

Component	Powers (1992)	Dawson and Osterling (1997)	Hurth et al. (1999)	National Research Council (1999)	Ivannone et al. (2003)
Supportive/structured learning environment	X	X	X		X
Family involvement	X	X	X	X	X
Early intervention	X		X	X	
Specialized curricula focusing on communication and social interaction	X	X	X	X	X
Integration with typical peers	X				
Predictability and routine		X			
Functional approach to problem behaviors		X		X	X
Planned transitions between preschool and kindergarten/ first grade		X			
Individualization of supports and services			X	X	X
Systematic, carefully planned instruction			X	X	X
Intensity of engagement			X	X	
Developmentally appropriate practices				X	

have a research base but are also flexible enough to manage complex cases complicate assessment and treatment.

In summary, while positive results have been reported for many treatment methods, there are no autism treatments that currently meet criteria for well-established or probably efficacious, empirically-supported treatment (Lonigan, Elbert, & Johnson, 1998). Additionally, due to the heterogeneity of the disorder and the changing needs of children with autism as they develop, it is unlikely that one specific treatment will emerge as the treatment of choice for all children. Currently, researchers and clinicians must use their judgment and training to choose the most suitable methodology for a specific child. Critical elements have been defined that can assist in the development of treatment programs. Eventually, a prescriptive method of choosing treatment based on child and family characteristics may be developed.

TRANSLATION OF EVIDENCE-BASED PRACTICE TO COMMUNITY SETTINGS

Research in other areas of child psychotherapy indicates the importance of examining outcomes of children when translating research-based treatments into systems settings. There is a large body of work that shows that psychotherapeutic treatments delivered in highly controlled studies can produce improved clinical and functional outcomes for children. In contrast, research comparing children receiving treatment in a community setting with those receiving no treatment found that there were no differences between treatment and no-treatment groups in terms of outcomes (Weisz, Weiss, Han, Granger, & Morton, 1995). This highlights the need to examine the use of efficacious programs for children within a system setting.

The outcome data for the treatment methods designed for children with autism comes from highly controlled research programs. Research examining the effectiveness of any of these techniques in the context of service systems, such as early intervention programs, community clinics, and schools is lacking (National Research Council, 2001). There are many potential differences between the research intervention programs and community settings. Schools that attempt to replicate research models often do not have the funding to replicate all aspects of the research program. For example, it is likely that very few early intervention programs in community service systems are currently providing the same intensity of services as the research programs, which often schedule 20 to 40 hours per week of programming (e.g., Handleman & Harris, 2001). In addition, research programs have rigorous fidelity of implementation standards to ensure appropriate application of the treatment. These standards have not been translated to community settings due to limited training, limited time for measurement, and complexity of fidelity measures. Quality control in community programs (both public and private) is extremely variable and staff turnover is high. These factors may greatly alter the effectiveness of research-based treatment strategies and may result in poorer outcomes for children with autism.

Legislators and researchers are currently emphasizing the delivery of research-based practices in many areas of child mental health, including disruptive disorders, attention deficit disorders, childhood depression, and autism services (National Research Council, 2001). Therefore it is critically important to examine the attitudes and experiences of treatment providers in community-based settings as we attempt to move these practices into service settings. A recent paper asked early intervention providers about specific treatment use in autism programs (Stahmer, Collings, & Palinkas, 2005). Although many treatment providers were supportive of the use of evidence-based techniques, most did not have a good understanding of the research. While most of the providers reported using at least one evidence-based technique, these same providers were just as likely to report techniques with no published research reports. Additionally, all of the providers stated that they modified existing methods to fit the needs of their specific program and therefore were not using the methods as they were researched.

These findings provide insight into recommendations for successful translation of research-based practices into intervention programs for children with autism and highlight the need for effectiveness trials. Pragmatic issues regarding the use of the techniques in classroom and group settings must be addressed. Validity concerns when techniques are combined or modified should also be examined.

FUTURE DIRECTIONS

Although the autistic spectrum disorders are relatively less common than other child mental health problems, they have become more commonly identified in recent years, particularly with the establishment of autism as a category for special education and early intervention services under IDEA. These disorders are complex in their presentation and service needs, causing confusion and concern among parents wanting the best for their children and service providers who must determine need and allocate resources for services.

Some of the major service issues for children with autism and their families that need to be addressed include the inconsistency of services in various areas of the country, individualization of services, and eligibility for services. Families in different states, and even districts in the same county, may receive very different services in terms of type, intensity, and quality. Additionally, the transition from the earliest intervention (birth to three) to the preschool programming needs to be examined. This transition comes at a period when children with autism are first receiving a diagnosis, and this sometimes difficult transition may affect treatment efficacy.

Additionally, very few of the research programs described have taken family variables into consideration, even though it is clear that family variables play a role in the type of services a child receives. Family structure, culture, resources, and support may be very important to the intensity and types of services children are receiving (Dunlap, 1999). Research in the area of special needs indicates that parents with more limited skills and/or resources are less likely to receive intensive services for their children. The most intensive services are received by children whose parents have time and resources to negotiate effectively for those services (Mahoney & Filer, 1996). Families with increased financial resources also often supplement services with privately funded therapies, thereby increasing the intensity of programming. Families with higher educational levels and/or access to information regarding the possibility of legal action may take an agency to fair hearing in order to obtain appropriate programming for their child. Many agencies that now use research-based treatments do so because they have been ordered to do so by the courts. Consequently, an abundance of active families in an area may lead to an increased use of research-based programs in community early intervention and school-based programs. A lack of such families, or an increase in families with high stress and low resources, may lead to a shortage of evidence-based services for these children.

As in other areas of mental health, few efficacy studies have included sufficient numbers of ethnic minority children to permit generalization across cultures. Efficacy studies in autism have rarely examined efficacy for ethnic minority groups separately, and most do not even provide information about the race/ethnicity of the subjects. This lack of research is a concern given the widespread recognition that culture has a powerful impact on service utilization, treatment attendance, parenting, and other service-related factors (e.g., McCabe, Clark, & Barnett, 1999). Available data suggest that children from ethnic minority backgrounds are more likely to be diagnosed and receive treatment at a later age than white children, for reasons that do not appear to be due to race alone (Croen, Grether, & Selvin, 2002). Parental immigrant status, language barriers, access to quality health care, level of parental education, and social support are among the factors that have been hypothesized to lead to suboptimal identification, diagnostic accuracy, and access to early intervention services for these children.

Early intervention research looking at the system of services provided to young children clearly indicates that early intervention is highly effective for children who are at-risk for, or have a developmental disability. Guralnick (1993) suggests that it is time for a second generation of early intervention research that looks more specifically at child characteristics, family characteristics, and program features that can better enhance outcomes. One way to assess programming is by looking at the specific needs of a particular population of children, such as children with ASD. Because of the pervasive nature of this disorder, and the severe difficulties these children have with learning from their environment, it appears that a higher-intensity treatment with relative specificity to the needs of the child and family at each stage of the disorder is necessary. No research to date has looked at how our system of early intervention provision affects this disorder, or how specific family and child characteristics may affect the system.

State agencies across the country are working to determine the best way to provide services to children and families dealing with this very difficult and pervasive diagnosis. However, empirical data regarding accuracy of diagnostic and functional assessment for children being served by public agencies are lacking. Improvement in diagnostic and assessment practices through public schools was identified by the NRCA as one of the highest priorities in developing and disseminating services for children with ASD (National Research Council, 2001).

There is a large gap between the diagnostic and treatment methods used for controlled research studies and the practices employed in community and school settings for children with ASD. This is an area that we are currently investigating in our research studies. The first step is to determine what standard practices are currently employed in community and school settings and the rationale behind these practices. When conducting services research, it is essential to determine the constraints of the system, issues related to service provider experience and background, and willingness for change. Models of assessment and treatment derived from research studies may need to be modified before they can be implemented within individual community settings. However, these modifications need to be limited so as to not compromise the effectiveness, reliability, and validity demonstrated in controlled studies. We hope to find effective ways to bring more evidence-based practices into community and school settings to improve the delivery of services for children with ASD.

REFERENCES

Akshoomoff, N., Lord, C., Lincoln, A. J., Courchesne, R. Y., Carper, R. A., Townsend, J., & Courchesne, E. (2004). Outcome classification of preschoolers with autism spectrum disorders using MRI brain measures. *Journal of the American Academy of Child and Adolescent Psychiatry, 43,* 349–357.

Akshoomoff, N., Pierce, K., & Courchesne, E. (2002). The neurobiological basis of autism from a developmental perspective. *Development and Psychopathology, 14,* 613–634.

American Academy of Child and Adolescent Psychiatry. (1998). Practice parameters for the assessment and treatment of children and adolescents with depressive disorders. AACAP, *Journal of the American Academy of Child and Adolescent Psychiatry, 37*(10 Suppl.), 63S-83S.

American Psychiatric Association. (2000). *Diagnostic and Statistical Manual of Mental Disorders* (4th rev. ed.). Washington, DC: American Psychiatric Association.

Anderson, S.R., & Romanczyk, R.G. (1999). Early intervention for young children with autism: Continuum-based behavioral models. *Journal of the Association for Persons with Severe Handicaps, 24*(3), 162–173.

California Department of Developmental Services. (2002). *Autistic spectrum disorders: Best practice guidelines for screening, diagnosis, and assessment.* Sacramento: Author.

California Departments of Education and Developmental Services. (1997). *Best practices for designing and delivering effective programs for individuals with autistic spectrum disorders.* Sacramento: Author.

Charman, T., & Baird, G. (2002). Practitioner review: Diagnosis of autism spectrum disorder in 2- and 3-year-old children. *Journal of Child Psychology & Psychiatry, 43*(3), 289–305.

Columbia Pacific Consulting. (1999). *Preliminary report: Cost-benefit analysis of Lovaas treatment for autism and autism spectrum disorders (ASD).* Vancouver, BC: Harper Grey Easton Barristor and Soliciters.

Cook, E., Rowlett, R., Jaselskis, C., & Leventhal, B. (1992). Fluoxetine treatment of patients with autism and mental retardation. *Journal of the American Academy of Child and Adolescent Psychiatry, 31,* 739–745.

Courchesne, E., Carper, R., & Akshoomoff, N. (2003). Evidence of brain overgrowth in the first year of life in autism. *Journal of the American Medical Association, 290,* 337–344.

Croen, L.A., Grether, J.K., & Selvin, S. (2002). Descriptive epidemiology of autism in a California population: Who is at risk? *Journal of Autism and Developmental Disorders, 32*(3), 217–224.

Dawson, G., & Osterling, J. (1997). Early intervention in autism: Effectiveness and common elements of current approaches. In M.J. Guar nick (Ed.), *The effectiveness of early intervention: Second generation research* (pp. 307–326). Baltimore, MD: Paul H. Brooks.

Dunlap, G. (1999). Consensus, engagement and family involvement for young children with autism. *Journal of the Association for Persons with Severe Handicaps, 24,* 222–226.

Feinberg, E., & Vacca, J. (2000). The drama and trauma of creating policies on autism: Critical issues to consider in the new millennium. *Focus on Autism and Other Developmental Disabilities, 15*(3), 130–137.

Fombonne, E. (2003). The prevalence of autism. *Journal of the American Medical Association, 289*(1), 87–89.

Greenspan, S.I., & Weider, S. (1997). Developmental patterns and outcomes in infants and children with disorders in relating and communicating: A chart review of 200 cases of children with autistic spectrum diagnosis. *The Journal of Developmental and Learning Disorders, 1,* 87–141.

Guralnick, M.J. (1993). Second generation research on the effectiveness of early intervention. *Early Education and Development, 4,* 366–378.

Handleman, J.S., & Harris, S.L. (2001). *Preschool education programs for children with autism* (2nd ed.). Austin, TX: PRO-ED, Inc.

Holroyd, J., & McArthur, D. (1976). Mental retardation and stress on the parents: A contrast between Down's syndrome and childhood autism. *American Journal of Mental Deficiency, 80*(4), 431–436.

Horton, R. (2004). The lessons of MMR. *Lancet, 363,* 747–749.

Hurth, J., Shaw, E., Izeman, S.G., Whaley, K., & Rogers, S.J. (1999). Areas of agreement about effective practices among programs serving young children with autism spectrum disorders. *Infants and Young Children, 12,* 17–26.

Institute of Medicine. (2001). *Immunization safety review: Measles-mumps-rubella vaccine and autism.* Washington, DC: National Academy Press.

Iovannone, R., Dunlap, G., Huber, H., & Kincaid, D. (2003). Effective educational practices for students with autism spectrum disorders. *Focus on Autism & Other Developmental Disabilities, 18,* 150–165.

Karasu, T.B., Gelenberg, A., Merriam, A., & Wang, P. (2002). American Psychiatric Association practice guidelines for the treatment of psychiatric disorders: Compendium 2002. In *American Psychiatric Association practice guidelines for the treatment of psychiatric disorders: Compendium 2002* (2nd ed., pp. 463–545). Washington, DC: American Psychiatric Press.

Lonigan, C.J., Elbert, J.C., & Johnson, S.B. (1998). Empirically supported psychosocial interventions for children: An overview. *Journal of Child Clinical Psychology. Special Issue: Empirically Supported Psychosocial Interventions for Children, 27*(2), 138–145.

Lord, C., & Bailey, A. (2002). Autism spectrum disorders. In M. Rutter & E. Taylor (Eds.), *Child and adolescent psychiatry: Modern approaches* (4th ed., pp. 636–663). Oxford: Blackwell Publications.

Lord, C., & Risi, S. (1998). Frameworks and methods in diagnosing autism spectrum disorders. *Mental Retardation and Developmental Disabilities Research Reviews, 4,* 90–96.

Lord, C., Rutter, M., DiLavore, P.C., & Risi, S. (2001). *Autism diagnostic observation schedule.* Los Angeles: Western Psychological Services.

Lord, C., Rutter, M., & Le Couteur, A. (1994). Autism Diagnostic Interview-Revised: A revised version of a diagnostic interview for caregivers of individuals with possible pervasive developmental disorders. *Journal of Autism and Developmental Disorders, 24*(5), 659–685.

Lord, C., Wagner, A., Rogers, S., Szatmari, P., Aman, M.G., & Charman, T. (in press). Challenges in evaluating psychosocial interventions for autistic spectrum disorders. *Journal of Autism and Developmental Disorders.*

Lovaas, O.I. (1987). Behavioral treatment and normal educational and intellectual functioning in young autistic children. *Journal of Consulting and Clinical Psychology, 55*(1), 3–9.

Madsen, K., Hviid, A., Vestergaard, M., Schendel, D., Wohlfahrt, J., Thorsen, P., Olsen, J., & Melbye, M. (2002). A population-based study of measles, mumps, and rubella vaccination and autism. *New England Journal of Medicine, 347,* 1477–1482.

Mahoney, G., & Filer, J. (1996). How responsive is early intervention to the priorities and needs of families? *Topics in Early Childhood Special Education, 16*(4), 437–457.

Masi, G., Cosenza, A., Mucci, M., & Brovedani, P. (2003). A 3-year naturalistic study of 53 preschool children with pervasive developmental disorders treated with risperidone. *Journal of Clinical Psychiatry, 64,* 1039–1047.

McCabe, K. M., Clark, R., & Barnett, D. (1999). Family protective factors among urban African American youths. *Journal of Clinical Child Psychology, 28*(2), 137–150.

McCracken, J. T., McGough, J., Shah, B., Cronin, P., Hong, D., Aman, M. G., Arnold, E., Lindsay, R., Nash, P., Hollway, J., McDougle, C. J., Posey, D., Swiezy, N., Kohn, A., Scahill, L., Martin, A., Koenig, K., Volkmar, F., Carroll, D., Lancor, A., Tierney, E., Ghuman, J., Gonzalez, N. M., Grados, M., Vitiello, B., Ritz, L., Davies, M., Robinson, J., McMahon, D. J., & the Research Units on Pediatric Psychopharmacology Autism Network. (2002). Risperidone in children with autism and serious behavioral problems. *New England Journal of Medicine, 347,* 314–321.

McDougle, C. J., Naylor, S. T., Cohen, D. J., Volkmar, F. R., Heninger, G. R., & Price, L. H. (1996). A double-blind, placebo-controlled study of fluvoxamine in adults with autistic disorder [see comments]. *Archives of General Psychiatry, 53*(11), 1001–1008.

McDougle, C. J., & Posey, D. (2002). Genetics of childhood disorders: XLIV. Autism, part 3: Psychopharmacology of autism. *Journal of the American Academy of Child and Adolescent Psychiatry, 41,* 1380–1383.

McDougle, C. J., & Posey, D. J. (2003). Autistic and other pervasive developmental disorders. In A. Martin, L. Scahill, D. S. Charney, & J. F. Leckman (Eds.), *Pediatric psychopharmacology* (pp. 563–579). New York: Oxford University Press.

McEachin, J. J., Smith, T., & Lovaas, O. I. (1993). Long-term outcome for children with autism who received early intensive behavioral treatment. *American Journal of Mental Retardation, 97*(4), 359–372; discussion, 373–391.

McGee, G. G., Morrier, M., & Daly, T. (1999). An incidental teaching approach to early intervention for toddlers with autism. *Journal of the Association for Persons with Severe Handicaps, 24,* 133–146.

McGee, G. G., Morrier, M., & Daly, T. (2000). The Walden preschool. In J. S. Handleman & S. L. Harris (Eds.), *Preschool education programs for children with autism* (2nd ed.). Austin, TX: PRO-ED, Inc.

Murch, S. H., Anthony, A., Casson, D. H., Malik, M., Berelowitz, M., Dhillon, A. P., Thomson, M. A., Valentine, A., Davies, S. E., & Walker-Smith, J. A. (2004). Retraction of an interpretation. *Lancet, 363,* 750.

National Research Council. (2001). *Educating children with autism. Committee on Educational Interventions for Children with Autism. Division of Behavioral and Social Sciences and Education.* Washington, DC: National Academy Press.

New York State Department of Health Early Intervention Program. (1999). *Clinical practice guidelines: Report of recommendations, autism/pervasive developmental disorders.* New York: Author.

Noland, R.M., & Gabriels, R.L. (2004). Screening and identifying children with autism spectrum disorders in the public school system: The development of a model process. *Journal of Autism and Developmental Disorders, 34,* 265–277.

Panerai, S., Farrante, L., & Zingale, M. (2002). Benefits of the Treatment and Education of Autistic and Communication Handicapped Children (TEACCH) programme as compared with a non-specific approach. *Journal of Intellectual Disability Research, 46*(4), 318–327.

Parker, S.K., Schwartz, B., Todd, J., & Pickering, L.K. (2004). Thimerosal-containing vaccines and autistic spectrum disorder: A critical review of published original data. *Pediatrics, 114,* 793–804.

Rogers, S.J. (1996). Brief report: Early intervention in autism. *Journal of Autism and Developmental Disorders, 26*(2), 243–246.

Schreibman, L., & Anderson, A. (2001). Focus on integration: The future of the behavioral treatment of autism. *Behavior Therapy, 32*(4), 619–632.

Schreibman, L., Kaneko, W.M., & Koegel, R.L. (1991). Positive affect of parents of autistic children: A comparison across two teaching techniques. *Behavior Therapy, 22,* 479–490.

Schreibman, L., & Koegel, R.L. (1996). Fostering self-management: Parent-delivered pivotal response training for children with autistic disorder. In E.D. Hibbs & P.S. Jensen (Eds.), *Psychosocial treatments for child and adolescent disorders: Empirically based strategies for clinical practice.* Washington DC: American Psychological Association.

Siegel, B. (1996). *The world of the autistic child.* New York: Oxford University Press.

Stahmer, A.C., Collings, N.M., & Palinkas, L.A. (2005). Early intervention practices for children with autism: Descriptions from community providers. *Focus on Autism and Other Developmental Disabilities, 20,* 66–79.

Stahmer, A.C., & Ingersoll, B. (2004). Inclusive programming for toddlers with autistic spectrum disorders: Outcomes from the Children's Toddler School. *Journal of Positive Behavioral Interventions, 6*(67–82).

Taylor, B., Miller, E., Lingam, R., Andrews, N., Simmons, A., & Stowe, J. (2002). Measles, mumps, and rubella vaccination and bowel problems or developmental regression in children with autism: Population study. *British Medical Journal, 324,* 393–396.

Weisz, J.R., Weiss, B., Han, S.S., Granger, D.A., & Morton, T. (1995). Effects of psychotherapy with children and adolescents revisited:

A meta-analysis of treatment outcome studies. *Psychological Bulletin, 117,* 450–468.

Yell, M.L., Katsiyannis, A., Drasgow, E., & Herbst, M. (2003). Developing legally correct and educationally appropriate programs for students with autism spectrum disorders. *Focus on Autism and Other Developmental Disabilities, 18,* 182–191.

Chapter 6

EMOTION-RELATED REGULATION

Nancy Eisenberg

Work on this chapter was supported by grants from the National Institutes of Mental Health (Nancy Eisenberg & Tracy Spinrad, PIs) and the National Institute of Drug Abuse (Laurie Chassin & Nancy Eisenberg, PIs). The authors thank the participants in our longitudinal sample who provided data, and their teachers.

INTRODUCTION

A key capacity for healthy psychological and behavioral development is children's self-regulation, especially as it relates to the regulation of the experience and expression of emotion. Indeed, a 2000 National Academy of Science committee report, *From Neurons to Neighborhoods,* concluded, "The growth of self-regulation is a cornerstone of early childhood development that cuts across all domains of behavior" (Shonkoff & Phillips, 2000, p. 3). Similarly, in a recent National Institute of Health report concerning risk factors for academic and behavioral problems at the beginning of school, Huffman, Mehlinger, and Kerivan (2000) concluded, "Children's competency also seems to depend on social skills and emotion regulation capacities" (p. 4). In accordance with the Hoffman et al. (2000) report, regulation can be conceptualized as a "casual risk factor," that is, one that can be changed and, when changed, alters the risk of an outcome (e.g., problems with adjustment, the development of social competence, or academic achievement) for children.

In this chapter, we discuss conceptions of emotion-related regulation and its relation to children's adjustment and social competence. Relevant literature is reviewed, with an emphasis on work from our laboratory. The goal is to demonstrate that regulation is very important for children's adjustment and likely plays a causal role in healthy development. In addition, I argue that socialization in the family likely affects children's adjustment.

CONCEPTUAL ISSUES

Emotion-related regulation can be defined "as the process of initiating, avoiding, inhibiting, maintaining, or modulating the occurrence, form, intensity, or duration of internal feeling states, emotion-related physiological, attentional processes, motivational states, and/or the behavioral concomitants of emotion in the service of accomplishing affect-related biological or social adaptation or achieving individual goals" (Eisenberg & Spinrad, 2004). More concisely, it refers to processes used to manage and change if, when, and how (e.g., how intensely) one experiences emotions and emotion-related motivational and physiological states, and how emotions are expressed behaviorally.

Regulation and Control

Emotion-related regulation overlaps considerably with Mary Rothbart's construct of effortful control. Effortful control is central to the process of self-regulation, be it emotion-related or not, and is defined as "the ability to inhibit a dominant response to perform a subdominant response" (Rothbart & Bates, 1998, p. 137) or the "efficiency of executive attention, including the ability to inhibit a dominant response and/or to activate a subdominant response, to plan, and to detect errors" (Rothbart & Bates, in press). Effortful control pertains to the ability to willfully or voluntarily inhibit, activate, or change (modulate) attention and behavior as needed to adapt. Effortful control is viewed by Rothbart as one of the three primary dimensions of temperament (Rothbart, Ahadi, Hershey, & Fisher, 2001), with temperament being defined as "constitutionally based individual differences in emotional, motor, and attentional reactivity and self-regulation" (Rothbart & Bates, 1998, p. 109) that are relatively stable across situations and over time, and affected by biological factors as well as the environment.

More concretely, measures of effortful control in the temperament literature typically include indices of attentional regulation and/or behavioral regulation. Attentional regulation includes the abilities to voluntarily focus or shift attention as needed (i.e., *attention shifting* and *attention focusing*); for example, to focus on a task when there are distractions in the room and to shift attention from one task to another as needed. The behavioral aspect of effortful control includes both (a) the ability to effortfully inhibit behavior as appropriate (e.g., to sit still in church), called *inhibitory control,* and (b) the ability to activate behavior when needed, especially when someone does not feel like doing so (e.g., making oneself study rather than go out with friends), called *activation control.* Parents' or teachers' reports on questionnaires often are used to assess these capacities (e.g., Eisenberg et al., 2004; Rothbart et al., 2001). In addition, researchers have devised numerous behavioral tasks to assess effortful control. An example of attentional effortful control is a situation in which children must direct their attention to one stimulus (despite distracting cues) or measures of attentional persistence on a boring task (e.g., Eisenberg, Fabes, Guthrie, & Reiser, 2000). Inhibitory and activational control sometimes are measured using tasks that involve "Simon Says" type games. For example, children may be asked to do what the nice bird says (e.g., "touch your head") but not to do what the mean dragon says (Kochanska, Murray, & Harlan, 2000). Or children may be instructed to tap twice with a wooden dowel when the experimenter taps once, and once when the experimenter taps twice. This task requires children to inhibit a natural tendency to mimic the action of the experimenter while remembering the rule for the correct response. A task that likely taps both attentional and inhibitory control is the "Day and Night" task, a task designed to measure executive functioning. In this task, children are instructed to say "day" when shown a black card with a moon and to say "night" when shown a white card with a sun.

Effortful control is viewed as involving higher-level executive attention skills and, thus, is involved in the awareness of one's planned behavior (Posner & DiGirolamo, 2000) and subjective feelings of voluntary control of thoughts and feelings. Accordingly, it is believed to come into play when resolving conflict (e.g., in regard to discrepant information), correcting errors, and planning new actions. It is believed that effortful control is seated primarily in the anterior cingulate gyrus (in the paleocortex or midfrontal lobe; Posner & DiGirolamo, 2000)—a fairly advanced part of the brain—with numerous links to the prefrontal cortex (another advanced part of the brain; Rothbart & Bates, in press). Effortful control is believed to play a very important role in both the regulation of the experience of emotion (e.g., through shifting attention away from upsetting events or actively reducing anxiety by managing the situation one is in) and in the ways in which emotion is expressed (e.g., by hiding or faking facial expressions or by inhibiting aggression when a person is angered).

We explicitly differentiate between the terms "control" and "regulation," although regulation includes some level of control. Control can be defined as inhibition. Like a number of other investigators (Cole, Michel, & Teti, 1994), we believe that well-regulated people are not overly controlled or undercontrolled; rather, they can respond flexibly to the varying demands of experience with a range of responses that are socially acceptable but also allow for spontaneity. Regulated individuals should be able to respond in a spontaneous manner when in contexts where such reactions are socially acceptable and also rein in their overt behavior when the situations calls for regulated behavior (Cole et al., 1994). Thus, well-regulated people usually should be relatively high in effortful control because it can be used at will and is flexible, although there may be times when people willfully over-regulate themselves. To achieve appropriate regulation, one has to allow emotional expression when appropriate and curb it when such expression is not appropriate.

Because of the vital role of flexibility in adaptation, it is useful to try to differentiate between effortful control and less voluntary over- or under-control processes, or what we have labeled reactive overcontrol and undercontrol (Eisenberg & Morris, 2002; Eisenberg & Spinrad, 2004). Sometimes children may appear to be regulated, but their inhibition is relatively involuntary or automatic. An example would be children who are behaviorally inhibited—who are wary and overly constrained in novel or stressful situations and seem to have difficulty modulating (e.g., relaxing) their inhibition (Kagan, 1998). Similarly, the impulse to approach people or inanimate objects in the environment (sometimes called surgency; Rothbart et al., 2001) often may be relatively involuntary. For example, people may be "pulled" toward rewarding or positive situations or stimuli with little ability to inhibit themselves. People who tend to approach situations without effortfully regulating themselves generally are viewed as impulsive. Several investigators have argued that approach/avoidance tendencies of these sorts (that seem be less willfully controlled) are anchored in relatively less advanced subcortical systems in the brain rather than in cortical areas, although there are many connections between subcortical and cortical parts of the brain (Pickering & Gray, 1999).

Theoretical Expectations

To reiterate, our view is that high levels of inhibition or constraint are not always adaptive for a child. Rather, inhibition is likely to be adaptive if it can be turned on and off in a voluntary manner through the use of effortful control.

Based on the aforementioned differentiation between voluntary effortful control and less voluntary, reactive over/undercontrol processes, we initially hypothesized that different aspects of effortful control and reactive over/undercontrol are associated with three distinct (albeit heuristic) styles of social functioning: overcontrolled, undercontrolled, and optimally controlled (Eisenberg & Morris, 2002). Specifically, we predicted that highly inhibited or overcontrolled individuals are high in involuntary reactive control, for example, behavioral inhibition (i.e., rigid inhibition in novel situations); low to average in the ability to effortfully inhibit behavior as needed (inhibitory control); low in effortful attentional regulation (the ability to willfully shift and focus attention); and low in the ability to activate behavior as needed (activational control). These individuals are seen as somewhat low in effortful attentional (but not inhibitory) effortful regulation (because shifting or focusing attention can be used to reduce negative emotions) and high in involuntary, reactive overcontrol. Such individuals are expected to be prone to internalizing problems (e.g., depression, anxiety, social withdrawal), especially if they are also predisposed to experience negative emotions. Children who fall into this group are likely to be wary and cautious in novel situations and with unfamiliar people and lack the ability to be loose and spontaneous in all but very familiar settings.

In contrast, undercontrolled individuals are predicted to be low in all types of effortful control, including inhibitory, attentional, and activation control. They also are hypothesized to be high in reactive approach tendencies and low in reactive overcontrol—that is, they are expected to be impulsive and low in behavioral inhibition. In general, individuals with this style of control are predicted to be relatively low in social competence and prone to externalizing behavior problems (e.g., aggression, defiance, stealing, lying, delinquent actions). They include children who tend to be out of control and aggressive, and who tend to approach social interactions and potentially dangerous situations without stopping to think or to control what they say or do.

Finally, optimally regulated individuals are hypothesized to be fairly high in various modes of effortful control (i.e., attention, inhibitory, and activation control), and in regard to reactive control, neither overcontrolled nor undercontrolled. These individuals are expected to be well adjusted, socially competent, and resilient when stressed. In other words, they typically regulate their behavior as is socially appropriate in a given context but also can be spontaneous and unconstrained. In addition, they deal relatively well with adversity and bounce back when stressed.

To summarize, if we are correct in our theorizing, one would expect children with externalizing problem behaviors such as aggression, defiance, and antisocial behavior to be low in effortful control and high in impulsivity. In contrast, internalizing problems such as social withdrawal and anxiety would be expected to correlate with moderate to low attentional effortful control, low levels of impulsivity, and a tendency toward rigid, overcontrolled behavior. Thus, the difference between effortful control and reactive over/undercontrol is believed to be important because it is high levels of effortful control, not reactive overcontrol, that predict better adjustment in children. As we now discuss, we have obtained support for these predictions, although a relation between low attentional control and internalizing problems seems to hold only in young children.

LINKS OF REGULATION/CONTROL WITH SOCIOEMOTIONAL FUNCTIONING

Until about a decade ago, there was relatively little research on the role of regulation in children's social functioning. However, in recent years, there is growing evidence that children who are low in regulation (often assessed as effortful control) are prone to exhibit externalizing behavior problems, and are relatively low (compared to peers) in social competence (see Eisenberg, Fabes, et al., 2000; Rothbart & Bates, 1998), compliance with their mothers, and the development of a conscience (Kochanska, Murray, & Coy, 1997; Kochanska, Tjebkes, & Forman, 1998). For example, according to both adults' reports and performance on laboratory tasks, children who can effortfully regulate their attention, in contrast to children who are distractible and lack persistence, are socially skilled (Eisenberg et al., 1993, 1995; NICHD Early Childcare Research Network, 2003), and low in externalizing and internalizing problem behaviors (Brody & Ge, 2001) and antisocial behavior and risk at school (Tremblay, Pihl, Vitaro, & Dobkin, 1994). Further, there is initial evidence that overcontrolled children are prone to internalizing problems (Kagan, Snidman, Zentner, & Person, 1999), whereas impulsive, undercontrolled children are relatively likely to exhibit externalizing problems (Eisenberg, Valiente, Fabes, et al., 2003). Moreover, the ability to delay gratification (e.g., delay eating a treat for a period of time in order to obtain a larger reward) has been found to predict a host of positive outcomes up to two decades later, including academic and social competence and the ability to cope with frustration and stress (e.g., Mischel & Ayduk, 2004).

Findings from Laboratory Studies

We have conducted three longitudinal studies examining the relations of children's regulation to their adjustment and social competence. In the two more recent studies, we also have tried to differentiate effortful control from reactive over/undercontrol in order to see if they related differently to adjustment. I now report some of the findings to illustrate that individual differences in children's regulation (i.e., effortful control) predict how well children are developing not only at the present time, but also into the future.

An Initial Longitudinal Study

In an early study with four- to six-year-olds (Eisenberg et al., 1993), children's socially appropriate behavior was rated by undergraduates who observed the children's naturally occurring interactions with peers and teachers at school for extended periods of time. For example, the observers rated whether the children had good social skills, tended to get into trouble because of their actions, and acted appropriately. Moreover, peer evaluations of sociometric status (popularity) were obtained by asking children to sort pictures of their classmates into piles that indicated how much they liked to play with each peer. Teachers and parents (usually mothers) also rated children on the intensity of their expressions of negative emotion (negative emotional intensity), frequency of experiencing and/or expressing negative emotion, attentional regulation (the abilities to shift and focus attention), constructive coping (instrumental coping or trying to take care of the problem by fixing the problem and seeking support), and nonconstructive coping (aggression and venting emotion versus avoidance). (We view coping behaviors as partly reflecting regulatory capacities.) Those boys who were reported to act in socially appropriate ways by observers and who were popular with their peers, in comparison to less socially skilled boys, were viewed by adults (especially their teachers) as able to regulate their attention, as high in constructive coping and low nonconstructive coping, and as low in the frequency and intensity of experiencing negative emotions. Fewer findings were obtained for girls, although those rated by observers as socially appropriate were low in nonconstructive coping and in negative emotionality intensity. Many of the findings were fairly strong. In addition, children who were both low in attentional regulation and high in negative emotional intensity were particularly likely to be low in socially appropriate behavior and popularity.

Further, individual differences in children's regulation and emotionality predicted their actual behavior when they were angered in their social interactions at school (Eisenberg, Fabes, Nyman, Bernzweig, & Pinuelas, 1994). Naturally occurring events involving anger and frustration were observed across the school year. Children who were more likely than their peers to use nonabusive verbalizations to deal with anger (e.g., "stop that!" or "I don't like that")—a constructive strategy—were viewed by their teachers as constructive copers, attentionally controlled, and low in nonconstructive coping and negative emotional intensity. In addition, such children were viewed by their mothers as high in constructive modes of coping, and low in aggressive coping and in the tendency to experience intense negative emotions.

The children were followed up two, four, and six years later, when they were age 6 to 8 years, 8 to 10 years, and 10 to 12 years old. At the 2-year follow-up (when the children were age 6 to 8), children who were viewed by teachers as socially appropriate/nonaggressive and prosocial/sociable tended to be viewed (at the same follow-up) as relatively high in regulation and constructive coping and/or low in nonconstructive coping and negative emotionality. Thus, as when the children were younger, teachers' ratings of children's social functioning were related to their ratings of emotionality and regulation (including ways of coping). Of particular interest, children reported to be high in attentional regulation and constructive coping, low in nonconstructive coping, and low in emotional intensity at age 4–6 years were rated by different teachers two years later as socially skilled and adjusted. Parental reports of regulation (including low impulsivity and high effortful control at this and later assessments) and emotionality were infrequently related to teachers' reports of social functioning at age 6–8 in the school context. However, parents who reported that their children were unregulated and prone to negative emotions at this age also reported high levels of externalizing problem behaviors in the home concurrently (at age 6–8). Moreover, children who were viewed by their parents as low in attentional regulation and prone to negative emotion at age 4 to 6 years were viewed as having externalizing problem behaviors two years later, albeit primarily for boys.

At the four-year follow-up, when the children were aged 8 to 10, a composite index of socially competent behavior was computed (see Eisenberg et al., 1997). Included in this measure were teachers' reports of children's socially appropriate behavior, popularity, prosocial behavior, and aggressive and disruptive behavior. Also included were ratings of how friendly versus hostile children were when they acted out with puppets what they would do in five hypothetical situations involving the potential for conflict with peers (e.g., when the child is excluded from activities or called a "baby"). Children high in this aggregate measure of social functioning generally were viewed by their teachers and parents as being well regulated and low in negative emotionality, particularly the latter, both contemporaneously (at age 8–10), as well as two and four years earlier. Moreover, children who had externalizing problem behaviors at age 8 to 10 years were viewed by their teachers and parents as high in nonconstructive coping; parents also viewed these youth as low in regulation at age 8–10, as well as two or four years earlier (Eisenberg et al.,1997).

At the six-year follow-up, when the children in this study were 10 to 12 years old, teachers' reports of children's social competence and adjustment at school generally continued to be related with teachers' and parents' reports of children's regulation, concurrently as well as two, four, and sometimes six years earlier, as well as with adults' (parents' and/or teachers') reports of children's low negative emotionality years earlier. Moreover, parents' reports of children's problem behaviors were related to their reports of children's low regulation and high negative emotionality up to four years earlier (Murphy, Shepard, Eisenberg, & Fabes, 2004). Thus, in general, high regulation and low intensity and frequency of negative emotionality predicted socially competent behavior and low levels of problem behavior contemporaneously and across time. A number of the aforementioned relations held even at age 10 to 12 when the level of children's problem behaviors at younger ages was controlled in the analyses—that is, when one took into account the degree to which children exhibited externalizing problems at a younger age (Murphy et al., 2004).

As expected, we frequently found that the effects of emotionality and regulation were additive as well as overlapping when predicting social functioning within a given setting (i.e., home or school), even over time (see Eisenberg et al., 1995; Eisenberg et al., 1997). In other words, both accounted for some prediction of child outcomes that was independent of one another.

We also obtained evidence that children's emotional intensity and regulation interacted when predicting social competence. In general, children's regulation was positively related to their social competence, but this association was strongest for children prone to intense emotions (negative emotions or emotions in general). Thus, regulation generally was a positive predictor of social competence, but especially for children prone to intense emotion, perhaps because emotional children had more need to regulate themselves.

In summary, in this initial longitudinal study, we found that children's regulation, as well as their emotionality, predicted their social competence and adjustment, often across a number of years. However, the number of children in this study was relatively small, the sample was not diverse in terms of social class or ethnicity/race, and we did not include many behavioral measures after the first assessment. Thus, we felt it was important to replicate and extend the findings from this initial study with new longitudinal samples.

Later Studies: A Focus on Effortful Control (Regulation) and Reactive Control

Despite the growing number of excellent studies on emotion-related regulation, many of them are not designed to answer certain questions. For example, with very few exceptions investigators have not statistically controlled for earlier levels of externalizing problems when predicting adjustment at an older age from other variables such as regulation. Thus, it is difficult to draw even tentative conclusions about causality from most data. Moreover, few researchers have attempted to differentiate between effortful control (EC) and reactive over/undercontrol when predicting developmental outcomes. Yet this differentiation may be critical if the two constructs relate differently to adjustment and social competence.

In recent years we have been examining the differential prediction of different aspects of EC and reactive control to children's social competence and adjustment in two longitudinal samples. Both studies are still underway, so findings are not yet available from all assessments.

Prediction of Adjustment

In one of our longitudinal studies, we have oversampled children at risk for problem behavior. We did this for two reasons: (1) because we were interested in the prediction of externalizing and internalizing problems, and (2) we believed that it would be useful for the testing of our heuristic model to include children who were likely to vary not only in effortful control, but also in their reactive over- and undercontrol.

In this study, we selected a sample of school children using primary caregivers' reports on the Child Behavior Check List (CBCL; Eisenberg, Cumberland et al., 2001). Children ages 4.5 through 7 years were recruited from preschools, elementary schools, after-school programs, and a newspaper ad. Out of a pool of 315, we selected all children with CBCL scores that are considered at least borderline risk, in contrast to scores that clearly reflect clinical problems. We matched these children (considering them as either externalizing or internalizing, depending on which score was higher) with control children of the same sex and race, similar social class, and about the same age. Control children were those with CBCL scores of less than 60 on both internalizing and externalizing scales. However, we did not exclude a child who had a *t* score of 60 or above if we could not match him or her with other children on all criteria. The final sample included 214 children (median age = 73 months). There was considerable variability in socioeconomic status in the sample (median income = $35,000), and about 26 percent were from various minority racial or ethnic groups.

In one set of studies we have examined whether children categorized as having at least borderline levels of externalizing or internalizing problem behaviors (or both) varied from one another and from well-adjusted children in various aspects of regulation/control. Thus, at the first assessment (T1), we examined the relations of specific modes of effortful control, as well as reactive undercontrol (in this case, impulsivity), to children's classification as an internalizer (e.g., prone to social withdrawal, anxiety, and depression), externalizer (e.g., aggressive, delinquent), comorbid, or nondisordered control child. We obtained teachers' and a parent's reports of children's effortful attention shifting, attention focusing, and inhibitory control, as well as impulsivity. Mothers, fathers, and teachers reported on children's internalizing and externalizing problems, and we administered several laboratory (observed) measures of children's effortful regulation. The tasks assessed children's abilities to persist rather than cheating on a puzzle when working for a prize, to sit still when requested to do so prior to being left alone with physiological equipment attached to their bodies, and to exhibit positive versus negative facial or verbal reactions to a disappointing prize.

As might be expected, externalizing children or comorbid children (these two groups were combined in the analyses), in comparison to control (i.e., nondisordered) children, were low in all types of control, effortful or involuntary, and findings generally were obtained across reporters. Thus, they were low in teachers' and parents' reports of their abilities to shift and focus attention as needed, as well as in their ability to inhibit behavior. They were quite high in adult-rated impulsivity and also had more difficulty than control (nondisordered) children in sitting still when asked to do so and in persisting rather than cheating on the puzzle task. As might also be expected, these children were prone to anger and, to some degree, to sadness.

Internalizing children were compared with both externalizers and non-disordered children. Like externalizing children, internalizers were rated by adults as somewhat lower than control children in the ability to regulate their attention, although internalizers were higher than externalizers in the ability to effortfully shift and focus attention. Internalizers were higher than externalizers in adult-rated inhibitory control, but usually did not differ from control children in this aspect of effortful regulation. Internalizers were only very slightly lower than control children in effortful control on the observed behavioral regulation tasks (e.g., marginally lower for one sex or the other on some tasks), but were higher than externalizers on some of the behavioral measures of regulation. For example, internalizers showed less negative emotion than externalizers in response to a disappointing gift and internalizing boys exhibited more persistence on the puzzle task than did externalizing boys. Moreover, internalizers were quite low in impulsivity, generally even lower than nondisordered control children (and much lower than externalizing children). Of interest because of the relation between regulation and negative emotionality, internalizing children were prone to sadness, but not especially prone to anger.

Thus, internalizers were relatively high on involuntarily reactive control (as tapped with low impulsivity) and were somewhat deficient in attentional effortful control, but not in the ability to inhibit their behavior. In contrast, externalizers were quite low on both effortful control and reactive control. It was notable that both externalizers and internalizers were low in attentional modes of effortful control—the types of regulation that would be expected to help modulate the experience of negative emotions such as anxiety, fear, or anger. Because externalizers, but not internalizers, were low in the ability to willfully inhibit their overt behavior, they would be expected to have more problems than internalizers in regard to displays of inappropriate behavior.

In the two-year follow-up of this sample, the findings were very similar for children classified as externalizers at the follow-up assessment. However, unlike two years earlier, children with pure internalizing problems were similar in attentional control to nondisordered children (Eisenberg et al., 2005). As at the younger age, children with adjustment problems were prone to experience negative emotion; at this age, internalizers were somewhat higher than nondisordered children in both sadness and anger.

Moreover, change in children's adjustment status over the two years (e.g., change from an externalizer [or internalizer] to a nondisordered child or vice versa) was predicted by levels of children's regulation and impulsivity at the follow-up, even when controlling for levels of those variables two years earlier. Change in (or out) of an externalizing status was related to the degree of problems in the children's regulation and impulsivity, as well as their tendencies to experience negative emotions. Change in negative emotionality (assessed with adults' reports) over the two years, but in neither effortful control nor impulsivity, was consistently associated with change in internalizing status. Perhaps anger and sadness change more markedly for some children than does regulation (and perhaps impulsivity) due to either neurological development or socialization (Belsky, Fish, & Isabella, 1991; Posner & Rothbart, 1998), which could account for the greater prediction from negative emotionality (especially anger). Consistent with this idea, children's regulation and impulsivity were more stable over the two years than were their sadness and anger. Moreover, because negative emotionality likely is closely linked to specific experiences in social settings, discontinuities in experiences with parents, peers, teachers, and other individuals might result in less stability in negative emotion than in aspects of regulation/control (Eisenberg et al., 2005).

Additive, Unique, and Multiplicative (Moderational) Prediction of Socioemotional Functioning from Effortful Control and Reactive Over/Undercontrol

In the at-risk sample and another longitudinal sample of typical school children, we have examined several other issues pertaining to the prediction of children's adjustment from their regulation or control. First, we have examined the additive contributions of emotionality and regulation to the prediction of developmental outcomes—that is, whether better prediction of developmental outcomes (such as adjustment) is obtained when measures of both effortful and reactive control are used to predict social and emotional functioning (rather than either one by itself). In addition, as already discussed in regard to our initial longitudinal study, we have examined whether dispositional negative emotionality often moderates the relations of effortful control—and sometimes reactive control—to developmental outcomes. (A moderator is a variable such as sex, race/ethnicity, or dispositional characteristics that affects the direction or strength of the relation between an independent or predictor variable and a dependent or criterion variable.) In addition, we hypothesized that personality resiliency—the ability to cope adaptively with, and rebound from, stress—mediates some relations between effortful control and socioemotional functioning (especially relations with internalizing problem behaviors and social competence).

In the same at-risk longitudinal study just discussed, we used structural equation modeling (SEM) to predict adjustment at the initial assessment (T1—age 4.5 to 7) and two years later (T2). In this analysis, effortful control was assessed with adults' reports of inhibitory control and attentional regulation and a behavioral measure of regulation (persistence on our puzzle task). Impulsivity, resiliency, externalizing, and internalizing were indicated by reports from teachers and primary caregiving parents, and fathers also provided data on adjustment. Experts' ratings were used to drop items on the regulation, emotion, and adjustment questionnaire scales that were confounded with one another (e.g., adjustment items rated by experts as more indicative of temperament than of adjustment were dropped from externalizing or internalizing scales). In initial measurement models, we found support for the conclusion that effortful control and reactive control were separate constructs.

Next we predicted both externalizing and internalizing problems from effortful control and impulsivity so we could assess their unique prediction—with relations to adjustment being mediated by resiliency. We computed models within the Time 1 (T1) and Time 2 (T2) assessments, as well as across time. Because they were similar, only the longitudinal findings are discussed. At both the initial assessment and T2 (see Figure 6.1), we found that high levels of children's effortful control and impulsivity predicted children's resiliency, and that resiliency in turn significantly mediated their relations to internalizing. In addition, externalizing problems were predicted directly by low effortful control and high impulsivity, although at T1 (in the longitudinal but not contemporaneous model), there was mediation through resiliency from EC

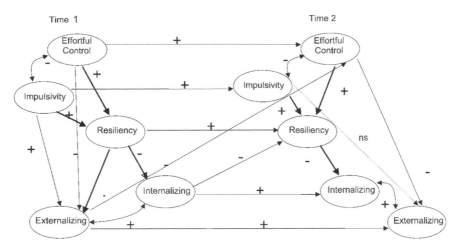

Figure 6.1 Longitudinal panel model with unstandardized measurement and parameter estimates. (Adapted from Eisenberg et al., 2004).

and impulsivity to externalizing problems. These relations held at T2 even when controlling for levels of the various constructs at T1 with one exception: the path from impulsivity to externalizing problems became nonsignificant. Thus, with the exception of that one path, relations at T2 were not due merely to the consistency of relations and variables at T1 over time. One possible explanation of the fact that impulsivity was a weaker predictor of externalizing problems at T2 is that, with the development of better regulatory capabilities, children with higher effortful control can better minimize outer manifestations of impulsivity.

In addition, in the longitudinal model there was evidence that T1 adjustment predicted T2 effortful control and resiliency; thus, the relation between adjustment and effortful control or resiliency appeared to be bidirectional. Moreover, when we conducted additional analyses with only cross-lagged paths (paths going in both directions across time), effortful control and resiliency at T1 affected adjustment at T2, and vice versa. Thus, again there was evidence of bidirectionality of relations among these variables (Eisenberg, Spinrad et al., 2004).

Recall that resiliency was positively related to impulsivity, as well as effortful control. One would expect children high in effortful control to be resilient because they can adjust their level of control as needed to adapt successfully. However, it might initially seem counterintuitive that impulsivity was also *positively* related to personality resiliency. Recall, however, the argument that rigid overcontrol (an aspect of reactive control) is not adaptive. Consistent with this idea, Block and Kremen (1996) asserted that "the human goal is to be as undercontrolled as possible and as overcontrolled as necessary. When one is more undercontrolled than is adaptively effective or more overcontrolled than is adaptively required, one is not resilient" (p. 351). If they are correct, children who are not only high in effortful control but also moderate to moderately high in reactive undercontrol, who are relatively spontaneous and impulsive, are more likely than overcontrolled children to deal well with stress. In fact, we have found positive linear relations between reactive undercontrol (or impulsivity) and resiliency in three samples of younger children, as well as quadratic relations in two samples (Eisenberg & Morris, 2002). More concretely, school-aged children who were moderate or sometimes high on impulsivity tended to be more resilient than those who were high in reactive overcontrol (or very low in impulsivity; Eisenberg, Spinrad, & Morris, 2002). In early to mid-childhood, when many children are wary and overcontrolled, some spontaneity, as reflected in impulsivity, may contribute to children's ability to be flexible and rebound from stress. However, by early adolescence, impulsivity tends to be modestly negatively related to resiliency (unless the overlapping relation of effortful control to resiliency is controlled, and then the relation becomes positive in structural equation models; Eisenberg, Valiente, Fabes et al., 2003). Thus, reactive impulsivity appears to be decreasingly related to high resiliency with age.

We also examined the hypothesis that negative emotionality moderates the relations of effortful control or reactive control to adjustment. Consistent with the results found for the initial longitudinal study, we found that effortful regulation was negatively related to externalizing problems for children; however, this relation was strongest for children who were higher in teacher-reported anger. Similarly, there was a positive relation between impulsivity and externalizing problems for all levels of teacher-reported anger, but this relation was stronger for children who were high in anger (Eisenberg et al., 2004).

We have obtained similar findings to those just described in our second ongoing longitudinal study of elementary school children who were not selected on the basis of risk status. In this sample, we have found that effortful and reactive control are different constructs that sometimes provide some unique prediction of outcomes such as social competence and adjustment. With age, reactive control (over- vs. under-control) appeared to be a weaker unique predictor of externalizing problems than was effortful control. Resiliency did not mediate relations to externalizing; however, resiliency sometimes mediated the relations of high effortful control and/or low reactive control to children's socially appropriate behavior (Eisenberg, Guthrie et al., 2000; Eisenberg, Valiente Fabes et al., 2003). Thus, although both low effortful control and high reactive control provided some unique prediction of externalizing problems at T1, only effortful control uniquely predicted externalizing problems at the third assessment (four years after the first assessment; T3; Valiente et al., 2003). In addition, the results suggested that prediction of externalizing problems at T3 was not due solely to the stability of externalizing problems over time. Moreover, as in the other sample, the negative relation between effortful control and problem behaviors was strongest at high levels of negative emotionality.

In brief, findings in the two longitudinal samples were quite similar in indicating the following: (a) for school children, we can predict children's adjustment (and social competence) better from the combination of effortful control and reactive control than from either by itself (although effortful control and reactive undercontrol are negatively related), (b) with age, effortful control generally becomes the stronger unique predictor of developmental outcomes, (c) resiliency often mediates or partially accounts for the relations between effortful control or impulsivity and internalizing problems or social competence, and (d) relations between children's regulation and adjustment and social competence tend to be most evident for those children prone to negative emotions.

PROMOTION OF EMOTION-RELATED REGULATION

Overall, our findings support the assumption that children's emerging regulation plays a pivotal—albeit complex—role in their emerging social skills and adjustment. Thus, efforts to promote children's emotion-related regulation would seem to be an important avenue for intervention, especially with high-risk children. Is there reason to believe that children's regulation can be systematically fostered?

Effortful control—an aspect of emotion-related regulation—clearly has a temperamental and genetic basis. Nonetheless, there is reason to believe that environmental factors contribute to its development and change. Investigators have found that children's regulation of emotion is related to socializers' warmth and sensitivity, sometimes across time (Eisenberg, Gershoff, et al., 2001, Eisenberg, Valiente, Morris, et al., 2003). Thus, interventions that change teachers' sensitivity/support and teaching practices with young children are likely to influence students' regulation, as well as their social competence and perhaps their understanding of emotion, which in turn may affect academic motivation and skills.

Interactions with Socializers

There are numerous reasons that supportive relations with socializers might promote children's regulation, social competence, and adjustment.

In the first months of life, it is the caregiver who provides most of the exogenous stimulation (holding, blanketing, swaddling, etc.) that serves to regulate the infant. With age, the caregiver (as external regulator) and infant (as self-regulating system) organize themselves into a dynamic relationship. Children who have higher-quality relationships with socializers are likely to be emotionally attached to them and to believe that their socializers are concerned with their welfare; consequently, they are likely to be motivated by feelings of trust and reciprocity and to comply with and internalize supportive socializers' standards for appropriate behavior, including demands for self-regulation. Moreover, sensitive, responsive socializers model positive ways of responding to others and to events, whereas negative ones model hostile, uncontrolled approaches to dealing with emotions. Investigators have also suggested that negative, nonsupportive behavior by socializers is associated with children's heightened emotional reactivity and dysregulation (Eisenberg, Cumberland, & Spinrad, 1998; Gottman, Katz, & Hooven, 1997), which can undermine their learning of socially appropriate behavior (Hoffman, 2000).

Considerable research with parents supports the association of sensitive, warm parenting with children's social competence, emotional understanding, and regulation (see Denham & Kochanoff, 2002; Eisenberg et al., 1998, Eisenberg, Gershoff, et al., 2001; Landry, Smith, Miller-Loncar, & Swank, 1998; Landry, Smith, Swank, Assel, & Vellet, 2001; Rubin, Bukowski, & Parker, 1998). Moreover, high-quality child-teacher relationships and interactions (which affect children's attachments to teachers) have been linked to children's social competence and adjustment, even across years (e.g., NICHD Early Childcare Research Network, 2001; Hamre & Pianta, 2001). Further, there is initial support for the mediation by children's regulation of the relation between quality of parenting (e.g., warmth and/or positive affectivity) and children's social competence or adjustment (Eisenberg, Valiente, Fabes et al., 2003). Similar mediated relations might be expected for interventions that promote teachers' sensitivity and foster emotional competence.

In addition, socializers' open discussion of emotions, their expression, and their regulation appear to be related to children's understanding of emotion and low levels of problem behavior (Eisenberg, Losoya et al., 2001; see Eisenberg et al. 1998). For example, Denham, Zoller, and Couchoud (1994) found that socializers' explanations about emotions, positive responsiveness to emotions, and low negative responsiveness to emotions were related to high levels of preschoolers' emotion understanding. These relations held even when controlling for age and cognitive abilities. Thus, attempts to teach children about emotion and its regulation would be expected to foster emotion understanding, adjustment, and social competence, and this expectation is supported by research on interventions (see the following).

The relations of parents' sensitivity and emotion-related practices to developmental outcomes sometimes are moderated by child characteristics (Rothbart & Bates, in press). In addition, children's temperament can moderate relations between teacher sensitivity and children's behavior problems. For example, Rimm-Kaufman et al. (2002) found that socially bold 15-month-olds with more sensitive teachers showed more self-reliant behavior, fewer negative behaviors, and less time off-task compared to socially bold children with less sensitive teachers. There was no relation between teachers' sensitivity and child behavior for socially wary children. It is likely that children's adjustment and EC also moderate the relations of teachers' sensitivity to children's socioemotional functioning.

Programmatic Interventions

Finally, preventative intervention research suggests that procedures that foster emotion understanding and children's regulation of emotion lessen the incidence of children's problem behaviors. For example, Greenberg, Kusche, Cook, & Quamma (1995) implemented the PATHS (Promoting Alternative Thinking Strategies) program with second- and third-grade elementary students in regular education and first- to third-grade students in special education. Students with this training, in comparison to control students, improved in their emotional vocabularies and the number of examples provided of feelings relating to their own lives, as well as in their understanding of feelings and the ability to recognize emotions in others. Special needs students increased in their understanding of how others manage, hide, and change their feelings. A year later, intervention children were higher on emotion understanding and interpersonal problem solving, less aggressive, more nonconfrontational (indicating higher self-control), and more prosocial in their solutions to problems than the control group children; special needs students showed similar patterns of results but did not maintain their gains in emotional understanding. PATHS also has been found to reduce the rate of growth of internalizing and externalizing symptoms two years after the intervention for school-aged special needs children (Kam, Greenberg, & Kusche, 2004) and has been found to be effective in improving the emotional competence and reducing aggression for at-risk first graders in those inner-city schools that effectively supported the intervention (i.e., where there was adequate support from school principals and a high degree of classroom implementation by teachers; Kam, Greenberg, & Walls, 2003). Finally, in a study of preschoolers in 20 Head Start classes, those trained with PATHS, in comparison to the controls, were higher in emotion understanding and social competence and lower in internalizing (but not externalizing) behavior (Domitrovich, Cortes, & Greenberg, 2002).

In future studies, it would be important to test the role of children's regulation, as well as other skills such as emotion understanding, in the effectiveness of intervention programs such as PATHS. Experimental interventions are one of the best ways to test both causal relations and processes that might mediate relations of intervention components to developmental outcomes such as children's socioemotional development.

REFERENCES

Belsky, J., Fish, M., & Isabella, R. (1991). Continuity and discontinuity in infant negative and positive emotionality: Family antecedents and attachment consequences. *Developmental Psychology, 27*, 421–431.

Block, J., & Kremen, A. M. (1996). IQ and ego-resiliency: Conceptual and empirical connections and separateness. *Journal of Personality and Social Psychology, 70*, 349–360.

Brody, G. H., & Ge, X. (2001). Linking parenting processes and self-regulation to psychological functioning and alcohol use during early adolescence. *Journal of Family Psychology, 15*, 82–93.

Cole, P. M., Michel, M. K., & Teti, L. O. (1994). The development of emotion regulation and dysregulation: A clinical perspective. *Monographs of the Society for Research in Child Development, 59* (Serial No. 240), 73–100.

Denham, S. A., & Kochanoff, A. T. (2002). Parental contributions to preschoolers' understanding of emotion. *Marriage and Family Review, 34*, 311–343.

Denham, S. A., Zoller, D., & Couchoud, E. A. (1994). Socialization of preschoolers' emotion understanding. *Developmental Psychology, 30*, 928–936.

Domitrovich, C. E., Cortes, R., & Greenberg, M. T. (2002, May). *Preschool PATHS: Promoting social and emotional competence in young children.* Paper presented at the meeting of the Society for Prevention Research, Seattle, WA.

Eisenberg, N., Cumberland, A., & Spinrad, T. L. (1998). Parental socialization of emotion. *Psychological Inquiry, 9*, 241–273.

Eisenberg, N., Cumberland, A., Spinrad, T. L., Fabes, R. A., Shepard, S. A., Reiser, M., Murphy, B. C., Losoya, S. H., & Guthrie, I. K. (2001). The relations of regulation and emotionality to children's externalizing and internalizing problem behavior. *Child Development, 72*, 1112–1134.

Eisenberg, N., Fabes, R. A., Bernzweig, J., Karbon, M., Poulin, R., & Hanish, L. (1993). The relations of emotionality and regulation to preschoolers' social skills and sociometric status. *Child Development, 64*, 1418–1438.

Eisenberg, N., Fabes, R. A., Guthrie, I. K., & Reiser, M. (2000). Dispositional emotionality and regulation: Their role in predicting quality of social functioning. *Journal of Personality and Social Psychology, 78*, 136–157.

Eisenberg, N., Fabes, R. A., Murphy, M., Maszk, P., Smith, M., & Karbon, M. (1995). The role of emotionality and regulation in children's social functioning: A longitudinal study. *Child Development, 66,* 1360–1384.

Eisenberg, N., Fabes, R. A., Nyman, M., Bernzweig, J., & Pinuelas, A. (1994). The relations of emotionality and regulation to children's anger-related reactions. *Child Development, 65,* 109–128.

Eisenberg, N., Fabes, R. A., Shepard, S. A., Murphy, B. C., Guthrie, I. K., Jones, S., Friedman, J., Poulin, R., & Maszk, P. (1997). Contemporaneous and longitudinal prediction of children's social functioning from regulation and emotionality. *Child Development, 68,* 642–664.

Eisenberg, N., Gershoff, E. T., Fabes, R. A., Shepard, S. A., Cumberland, A. J., Lososya, S. H., Guthrie, I. K., & Murphy, B. C. (2001). Mothers' emotional expressivity and children's behavior problems and social competence: Mediation through children's regulation. *Developmental Psychology, 37,* 475–490.

Eisenberg, N., Guthrie, I. K., Fabes, R. A., Shepard, S., Losoya, S., Murphy, B., Jones, S., Poulin, R., & Reiser, M. (2000). Prediction of elementary school children's externalizing problem behaviors from attentional and behavioral regulation and negative emotionality. *Child Development, 71,* 1367–1382.

Eisenberg, N., Losoya, S., Fabes, R. A., Guthrie, I. K., Reiser, M., Murphy, B. C., Shepard, S. A., Poulin, R., & Padgett, S. J. (2001). Parental socialization of children's dysregulated expression of emotion and externalizing problems. *Journal of Family Psychology, 15,* 183–205.

Eisenberg, N., & Morris, A. S. (2002). Children's emotion-related regulation. In R. Kail (Ed.), *Advances in child development and behavior,* Vol. 30 (pp. 190–229). Amsterdam: Academic Press.

Eisenberg, N., Sadovsky, A., Spinrad, T. L., Fabes, R. A., Losoya, S. H., Valiente, C., Reiser, M., Cumberland, A., & Shepard, S. A. (2005). The relations of problem behavior status to children's negative emotionality, effortful control, and impulsivity: Concurrent relations and prediction of change. *Developmental Psychology, 41,* 193–211.

Eisenberg, N., & Spinrad, T. L. (2004). Emotion-related regulation: Sharpening the definition. *Child Development, 75,* 334–339.

Eisenberg, N., Spinrad, T. L., Fabes, R. A., Reiser, M., Cumberland, A., Shepard, S. A., Valiente, C., Losoya, S. H., Guthrie, I. K., & Thompson, M. (2004). The relations of effortful control and impulsivity to children's resiliency and adjustment. *Child Development, 75,* 25–46.

Eisenberg, N., Spinrad, T. L., & Morris, A. S. (2002). Regulation, resiliency, and quality of social functioning. *Self and Identity, 1,* 121–128.

Eisenberg, N., Valiente, C., Fabes, R. A., Smith, C. L., Reiser, M., Shepard, S. A., Losoya, S. H., Guthrie, I. K., Murphy, B. C., & Cumberland, A. (2003). The relations of effortful control and ego control to children's resiliency and social functioning. *Developmental Psychology, 39,* 761–776.

Eisenberg, N., Valiente, C., Morris, A. S., Fabes, R. A., Cumberland, A., Reiser, M., Gershoff, E. T., Shepard, S. A., & Losoya, S. (2003). Longitudinal relations among parental emotional expressivity, children's regulation, and quality of socioemotional functioning. *Developmental Psychology, 39,* 2–19.

Gottman, J. M., Katz, L. F., & Hooven, C. (1997). *Meta-emotion: How families communicate emotionally.* Mahwah, NJ: Erlbaum.

Greenberg, M. T., Kusche, C. A., Cook, E. T., & Quamma, J. P. (1995). Promoting emotional competence in school-aged children: The effects of the PATHS Curriculum. *Development and Psychopathology, 7,* 117–136.

Hamre, B. K., & Pianta, R. C. (2001). Early teacher-child relationships and the trajectory of children's school outcomes through eighth grade. *Child Development, 72,* 625–638.

Hoffman, M. L. (2000). *Empathy and moral development: Implications for caring and justice.* Cambridge: Cambridge University Press.

Huffman, L. C., Mehlinger, S. L., & Kerivan, A. S. (2000). *Risk factors for academic and behavioral problems at the beginning of school.* Bethesda, MD: National Institute of Mental Health.

Kagan, J. (1998). Biology and the child. In W. Damon (Series Ed.) and N. Eisenberg (Vol. Ed.), *Handbook of child psychology,* Vol. 3, *Social, emotional and personality development.* (pp. 177–235). New York: Wiley.

Kagan, J., Snidman, N., Zentner, M., & Person, E. (1999). Infant temperament and anxious symptoms in school age children. *Development and Psychopathology, 11,* 209–224.

Kam, C.-M., Greenberg, M. T., & Kusche, C. A. (2004). Sustained effects of the PATHS curriculum on the social and psychological adjustment of children in special education. *Journal of Emotional and Behavioral Disorders, 12,* 66–78.

Kam, C.-M., Greenberg, M. T., & Walls, C. T. (2003). Examining the role of implementation quality in school-based prevention using the PATHS curriculum. *Prevention Science, 4,* 55–63.

Kochanska, G., Murray, K., & Coy, K. (1997). Inhibitory control as a contributor to conscience in childhood: From toddler to early school age. *Child Development, 68,* 263–277.

Kochanska, G., Murray, K., & Harlan, E. (2000). Effortful control in early childhood: Continuity and change, antecedents, and implications for social development. *Developmental Psychology, 36,* 220–232.

Kochanska, G., Tjebkes, T. L., & Forman, D. R. (1998). Children's emerging regulation of conduct: Restraint, compliance, and internalization from infancy to the second year. *Child Development, 69,* 1378–1389.

Landry, S. H., Smith, K. E., Miller-Loncar, C. L., & Swank, P. R. (1998). The relation of change in maternal interactive styles to the developing social competence of full-term and preterm children. *Child Development, 69,* 105–123.

Landry, S. H., Smith, K. E., Swank, P. R., Assel, M., & Vellet, S. (2001). Does early responsive parenting have a special importance for children's development or is consistency across early childhood necessary? *Developmental Psychology, 37,* 387–403.

Mischel, W., & Ayduk, O. (2004). Willpower in a cognitive-affective processing system: The dynamics of delay of gratification. In R. F. Baumeister & K. D. Vohs (Eds.), *Handbook of self-regulation: Research, theory, and applications*. New York: Guilford Press.

Murphy, B. C., Shepard, S. A., Eisenberg, N., & Fabes, R.L.A. (2004). Concurrent and across time prediction of young adolescents' social functioning: The role of emotionality and regulation. *Social Development, 13,* 56–86.

NICHD Early Child Care Research Network. (2001). Nonmaternal care and family factors in early development: An overview of the NICHD Study of Early Child Care. *Journal of Applied Developmental Psychology, 22,* 457–492.

NICHD Early Child Care Research Network. (2003). Do children's attention processes mediate the link between family predictors and school readiness? *Developmental Psychology, 39,* 581–593.

Pickering, A. D., & Gray, J. A. (1999). The neuroscience of personality. In L. Pervin & O. John (Eds.), *Handbook of personality* (pp. 277–299). San Francisco: Guilford.

Posner, M. I., & DiGirolamo, G. J. (2000). Cognitive neuroscience: Origins and promise. *Psychological Bulletin, 126,* 873–889.

Posner, M. I., & Rothbart, M. K. (1998). Attention, self-regulation, and consciousness. *Transactions of the Philosophical Society of London, B,* 1915–1927.

Rimm-Kaufman, S. E., Early, D. M., Cox, M. J., Saluja, G., Pianta, R. C., Bradley, R. H., & Payne, C. (2002). Early behavioral attributes and teachers' sensitivity as predictors of competent behavior in the kindergarten classroom. *Applied Developmental Psychology, 23,* 451–470.

Rothbart, M. K., Ahadi, S. A., Hershey, K., & Fisher, P. (2001). Investigations of temperament at three to seven years: The Children's Behavior Questionnaire. *Child Development, 72,* 1287–1604.

Rothbart, M. K., & Bates, J. E. (1998). Temperament. In W. Damon (Series Ed.) and N. Eisenberg (Vol. Ed.), *Handbook of Child Psychology,* Vol. 3, *Social, emotional, personality development* (5th ed.; pp. 105–176). New York: Wiley.

Rothbart, M. K., & Bates, J. E. (in press). Temperament. In W. Damon & R. L. Lerner (Series Eds.) and N. Eisenberg (Vol. Ed.), *Handbook of Child Psychology,* Vol. 3, *Social, emotional, personality development* (6th ed.; pp. 105–176). New York: Wiley.

Rubin, K. H., Bukowski, W., & Parker, J. G. (1998). Peer interactions, relationships, and groups. In W. Damon (Series Ed.) & N. Eisenberg (Vol. Ed.), *Handbook of Child Psychology,* Vol. 3, *Social, emotional, and personality development* (5th ed.; pp. 619–700). New York: Wiley.

Shonkoff, J. P., & Phillips, D. A. (2000). *From neurons to neighborhoods: The science of early childhood development.* Washington, DC: National Academy Press.

Tremblay, R. E., Pihl, R., Vitaro, F., & Dobkin, P. L. (1994). Predicting early onset of male antisocial behavior from preschool behavior. *Archives of General Psychiatry, 51,* 732–739.

Valiente, C., Eisenberg, N., Smith, C. L., Reiser, M., Fabes, R. A., Losoya, S., Guthrie, I. K., & Murphy, B. C. (2003). The relations of effortful control and reactive control to children's externalizing problems: A longitudinal assessment. *Journal of Personality, 71,* 1179–1205.

Chapter 7

ATTENTION DEFICITS AND HYPERACTIVITY-IMPULSIVITY IN CHILDREN: A MULTILEVEL OVERVIEW OF CAUSES AND MECHANISMS

Joel T. Nigg

Work discussed in this chapter and the chapter itself were supported in part by NIMH grant R01-MH63146 and R01-MH59105, and by NIAAA grant R01-AA12217.

BACKGROUND CONSIDERATIONS

Few child difficulties generate as much controversy and concern in our society as problems with attention and impulse control, in particular the clinical syndrome of attention-deficit/hyperactivity disorder (ADHD; American Psychiatric Association, 1994). Dramatically rising rates of medication treatments for children, particularly stimulants, have drawn the attention of social critics and clinical scientists alike. Medicalization of behavior occurs when a problem comes to fall under the purview of the medical profession—for example, American society has seen the medicalization of pregnancy and birth, drinking problems, and other processes and conditions. The medicalization of attentional problems and hyperactivity, as well as disruptive behavior more generally, has spurred controversy over the validity of ADHD as a psychiatric disorder and sparked concern. Some feel that rising medication rates may indicate an important shortage of other needed psychological or educational interventions for children. Others fear that social control is being served more than mental health in some instances. Such concerns have become heated, sometimes causing discussants to overlook the substantial evidence concerning the clinical validity of the ADHD syndrome.

Bolstering the validity case, few child mental health problems are so important or so costly. Children with ADHD are at elevated risk of academic and achievement problems, a range of health problems (including accidental injury and death), antisocial behavior, substance use and abuse, and interpersonal problems. As a result, the economic costs alone of this condition are enormous. At the same time, a substantial percentage of children with ADHD have benign outcomes, including remission of the disorder as they move through adolescence and into adulthood. Thus, a sharper understanding of the causes and determinants of ADHD's varying developmental outcomes is an important concern to society. Moreover, in view of the magnitude of the problem and the heated controversies over its management, more consideration may be warranted of "high-risk/high payoff" research strategies that can lead to new breakthroughs.

That effort does not start in a vacuum. Along with running public controversy, research on ADHD has witnessed significant advances in the past two decades. Particularly notable has been the development of more detailed neuropsychological theories that begin to integrate the various cognitive findings regarding children with ADHD (Nigg, 2001) and relate them to particular neural networks in the brain. These models emphasize the regulatory functions involved in executive control (the ability to keep behavior focused on a goal, to organize complex behavior, and to suppress unintended behavior), regulation of arousal, and related processes summarized in this chapter. At the same time, theories that integrate the role of socialization processes along with neuropsychology in the *development* of these problem behaviors have been in shorter supply. Theories that address etiology in relation to potentially preventable perinatal and prenatal insults have been limited as well.

Furthermore, ADHD is not a unitary entity but a group of disorders. Work on the clinical heterogeneity of ADHD will be essential to realizing the need for better prospective matching of children to treatment type. Most obviously, the Diagnostic and Statistical Manual of Mental Disorders (DSM-IV, the main definition criteria in the United States) now lists three subtypes that have to be considered in any account of the syndrome (See Table 7.1 sidebar for a summary).

The "Combined" Subtype (hereafter, ADHD-C) describes children who are both inattentive-disorganized, and impulsive-hyperactive. Most research on ADHD pertains to this group of children. It is related to the definition of *hyperkinetic disorder* provided by the International Classification of Diseases, 10th Edition (ICD-10, in use in Europe and elsewhere, published by the World Health Organization in 1993). However, the ICD-10 category is more restrictive (see Table 7.1). Returning to DSM-IV, the "Inattentive" subtype (hereafter, ADHD-I) describes children who are mostly inattentive-disorganized, but not extremely active or impulsive. Work on this group is less advanced, and fewer conclusions can be drawn.

Table 7.1
Number of Behavioral Symptoms Needed to Qualify for Various Types of ADHD in the Diagnostic Manuals

	Symptom Domain		
	Inattention/Disorganization (9)	Hyperactivity (6)/Impulsivity (3)	
DSM-IV Types			
ADHD-Combined	6–9	+	6–9 sx from Hyp/Imp together
ADHD-Primarily Inattentive	6–9	+	0–5
ADHD-Primarily Hyperactive-Impulsive:	0–5	+	6–9 sx from Hyp/Imp together
ICD-10			
Hyperkinetic Disorder:	6	+	3–5 Hyp + 1–3 Imp

Adults

DSM-IV specifies a diagnosis of "in partial remission" for adolescents or adults who formerly met full criteria but now have some symptoms without meeting full criteria

Co-Occurring Behavioral/Mental Disorders:

ICD-10: Specifies do not diagnose if child meets criteria for pervasive developmental disorder, manic episode, depressive episode, or anxiety disorders. Specifies conduct disorder excludes HDK diagnosis.

DSM-IV: Specifies that symptoms should not be "better accounted for" by another mental disorder.

Additional Criteria:

(a) *Onset:* Symptoms that caused impairment had to be present before 7 years of age (DSM-IV) or "onset of the disorder" is no later than age 7 (ICD-10);

(b) *Pervasiveness:* impairment must be present (DSM-IV) or criteria must be met (ICD-10) in two or more settings;

(c) *Impairment:* there must be clear evidence of clinically significant impairment in functioning (DSM-IV); impairment or distress (ICD-10).

(d) *Frequency and Duration:* Symptoms must occur "often" and must persist for at least 6 months to a degree that is maladaptive.

Source: Adapted from the DSM-IV (American Psychiatric Association, 1994) and ICD-10 (World Health Organization, 1993).

The primarily hyperactive-impulsive type (hereafter, ADHD-H) is new in DSM-IV and largely unstudied. A particular focus has concerned the relation between ADHD-C and ADHD-I, with some arguing that these are quite distinct conditions and others that ADHD-I is essentially a mild version of ADHD-C.

Our own work has approached this question of relations among subtypes by looking at the ADHD-C and ADHD-I types using family data, in which we looked at which ADHD subtype is most common in the relatives of children with a given ADHD type in both new data and in an analysis that pooled data from several existing data sets, known as a meta-analysis (Stawicki, Nigg, & Von eye, submitted). Our findings suggest that both claims about the ADHD-I to ADHD-C relation may be partially true. We found evidence of subtype specific transmission in that children with ADHD-C were more likely to have relatives with ADHD-C than with ADHD-I. However, cross-subtype transmission also emerged, but only in one direction: children with ADHD-C had an elevated likelihood of having relatives with ADHD-I versus controls, but children with ADHD-I did not have elevated rates of ADHD-C in their relatives. Thus, it is likely that the ADHD-I type includes both (a) children who have a milder version of the ADHD-C syndrome and (b) children with a partially or wholly distinct condition. Overall, clarification of relations among these clinical subtypes remains a key issue in the field.

Finally, individual differences in ADHD development relevant to gender need further elucidation. ADHD is more common in boys, for reasons that remain obscure. ADHD's neuropsychological deficits may be more severe in girls with equivalent levels of behavioral problems (Nigg, Blaskey, Huang-Pollock, & Rappley, 2002), perhaps indicating that hormones or socialization protect girls.

ADHD AND MULTIPLE LEVELS OF ANALYSIS

With these points in mind, in this chapter I approach ADHD considering multiple levels of analysis. In this subsection, I (a) overview why several levels of analysis are important in ADHD, to provide context for what follows. Then in subsequent sections, I (b) summarize work by us and others to evaluate the within-child causal mechanisms, especially neuropsychological and cognitive deficits, which may be useful eventually in designing etiologically anchored definitional criteria for the syndrome, and (c) discuss what we know about etiology outside of the child—including comments on genetics, psychosocial context, and environmental triggers.

Like few other disorders, it is important to understand ADHD at more than one level of analysis; indeed, at least four levels of analysis are essential to consider. First, if we are to consider whether it is a valid "disease entity" for mental health services, we must be concerned about the nature of the within-child problem or "dysfunction" that is contributing to the child's poor adjustment and poor self-control. We approach these within-child mechanisms in two ways. In one approach, we assess neuropsychological or cognitive mechanisms, such as attention, impulsive control, arousal, and motivation, each of which can be linked to particular neural circuits in the brain that influence the disorder. In the other approach, we assess behavioral response tendencies as measured via temperament and personality. Temperament and personality traits may be related to some of the same neural systems that underlie the neuropsychological measures (Nigg, 2000), so integrating these approaches would represent a valuable advance. Understanding ADHD in relation to temperament and personality can help clarify the boundaries between normal variation and the disorder, shed light on potential precursors to ADHD in the form of early temperament traits, and provide convergent evidence regarding the within-child regulatory mechanisms that may be at issue in ADHD. I will note work on both of these angles.

Second, the early twenty-first century is an era when genetic research is expanding exponentially; we now know that ADHD as a trait or as a disorder is marked by substantial *heritability*. Heritability, a widely misunderstood term, indicates the proportion of between-individual variation in a trait (or in risk for a disorder) that is due to variation in genetic makeup. It thus can range from zero to one. Some caveats are in order with regard to the high heritability estimates in the case of ADHD. Most notably, the highest heritability estimates (ranging above 0.80) are dependent on parent ratings of ADHD symptoms. In turn, these parent ratings are to some extent inflated by rater bias effects (called contrast effects). Studies looking at teacher ratings yield somewhat smaller estimates of heritability, although still substantial and in the range of from 0.6 to 0.7. That said, it is clear that genetic variation is an important clue to ADHD expression. Molecular genetic studies have therefore become an important line of research to note in these remarks.

Third, we must understand the disorder within the developmental context of family and peers, because they play a crucial role in the evolution and development of self-regulation. Yet this line of work is relatively underdeveloped in the case of ADHD. The relative neglect of family and peer process in studies of ADHD can be attributed to at least two issues. One is the aforementioned high heritability of ADHD as a trait or a disorder, leading many to emphasize presumed biological pathways to the disorder that may emanate from genetic effects, including a search for individual genes. However, it is important to recognize that genetic effects can be mediated by social interactions. This phenomenon is captured in genetic models by the concept of genotype-environment correlations. For example, a parent and a child may both have a genotype that makes them vulnerable to impulsive, disorganized behavior. The parent's own disorganized behavior may influence the child's development of self-regulation via poorly attuned parent–child interactions or other family or socialization processes. Alternatively, the child's difficult "ADHD-prone" genotype may elicit ineffective parenting practices that in turn further shape development of the disorder. These effects, clearly mediated by socialization, nonetheless contribute to the heritability term in twin studies.

The other reason family context is relatively neglected in studies of ADHD may be that whereas studies of attachment, parenting style, and peer relations have shown their clear association with emergence of conduct problems/aggression (which often co-occur with ADHD), parallel findings on ADHD have generally been weak when antisocial behaviors are statistically or methodologically controlled. Yet, leads with regard to family process and ADHD per se can be noted.

The co-occurrence of antisociality and ADHD bears further comment. Conduct disorder/aggression is almost invariably accompanied by, or in many cases preceded by, hyperactive-impulsive behaviors. In contrast, many children can be identified who are hyperactive-impulsive but not aggressive (Jester et al., 2005). This suggests that ADHD may be a precursor or risk factor for antisocial development. Socialization context may then moderate whether hyperactive impulsive children take a more benign or problematic course developmentally. Nigg and Hinshaw (1998) looked at family correlates of aggression in children with ADHD. They found that parent personality (rated by parents and their spouse) predicted aggression observed on the playground in a summer program if children had ADHD, but not otherwise. Perhaps children with ADHD are prone to develop antisocial behavior in a broader range of socialization contexts than other children. Additional cross-section data coincided with this finding: parenting style contributed independently to antisocial behavior patterns in children with ADHD (Hinshaw, Zupan, Simmel, Nigg, & Melnick, 1997) even when it did not do so for comparison children, even with prior child behaviors controlled. It may be that children with ADHD require parenting practices outside of the norm in many cases to prevent problematic antisocial outcomes.

Fourth, the wider societal context, including a shortage of support services for children with behavior problems, must be borne in mind. It is crucial to recognize that heritability estimates do not speak to population levels of a trait. For example, increases in height in the past century are almost certainly due to improvements in diet and other health contexts, despite the continued high heritability of height. Likewise, it is possible that societal-wide influences could affect children's overall problem levels. It is unclear whether ADHD, along with several other child mental health problems, is increasing in the population, but it may be (Achenbach, Dumenci, & Rescorla, 2002). More and better data regarding such a secular trend are urgently needed. That said, it is essential that we consider influences that may affect an entire population, which would have obvious implications for prevention. That domain might include such nonspecific factors as increased pressure on families and children (e.g., economic or academic pressures), lifestyle factors such as diet or electronic media exposure during early development, or ecological factors such as environmental toxins, pollutants, and contaminants, and even cultural differences in the meaning of the behaviors. I will reflect briefly on these possibilities as well.

Within-Child Neuro-Cognitive Mechanisms in ADHD

Hyperactive—fidgety, inattentive behaviors—entered the medical lexicon around the turn of the twentieth century, but a defining point in thought about the disorder came with the influenza epidemic of 1917–1918, in which many children suffered encephalitic infections, followed after their recovery by a syndrome of hyperactivity, impulsivity, and inattention. This led to the conjecture that diffuse neural injury was the cause of hyperkinesis, leading to the longstanding term "minimal brain dsysfunction." That term fell by the wayside in an era when neuroimaging technology was too immature to meaningfully assess such putative dysfunction, and syndromal descriptions had become overly inclusive, rendering the term of little use for research or clinical practice. It was replaced, in the 1970s, by a focus on cognitive mechanisms, beginning with interest in (a) attention and (b) arousal. Subsequent work in the 1990s emphasized (c) motivation and (d) executive functioning or cognitive control. At the same time, imaging technology underwent revolutionary advances in the 1980s and 1990s, so that current theories can appeal to a growing neuro-imaging literature on ADHD.

That literature, using magnetic resonance imaging (MRI) and related methods, indicates that ADHD is associated at the level of group averages with a reduction of about 10 percent in the total volume of right frontal cortex, a structure in the basal ganglia known as the caudate, and in the cerebellum (Swanson & Castellanos, 2002; see Fig 7.1). Additional regions may also be involved. Most important to note is that these regions are consistent with the four domains of function listed in the prior paragraph. At the same time, the small magnitude of these dysplasias, and the

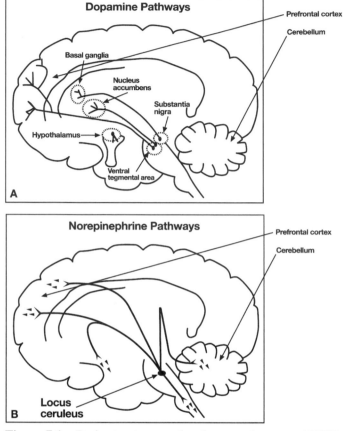

Figure 7.1   Brain structures and pathways relevant to ADHD. Dopamine pathways (related to executive functions and reward response) at top; and noradrenergic or norepinephrine pathways in the brain relevant to attention, arousal, and ADHD (bottom). Adapted with permission from Dr. Timothy Wilens.

lack of standard norms for brain development, renders them of little use for diagnostic purposes at present. I now turn to the cognitive mechanisms that have been heavily investigated in ADHD.

ATTENTION: SELECTION, ORIENTING, ALERTNESS, AND AROUSAL

Overview

Work on attention is the most advanced area of cognitive research in ADHD. As a result, we are in a position to draw conclusions with more confidence in this realm than the others. As it happens, behavior that is labeled as "inattentive" is not necessarily due to a breakdown in formally-assessed attention mechanisms in the child. Three attention functions can be identified for our purposes here: (a) orienting (where in space is attention directed), (b) selection (in a limited capacity system, we must select what we will attend even after we orient to a location), and (c) alerting or arousal.

Orienting and selection can occur either relatively reflexively and automatically, or relatively deliberately and strategically. Reflexive orienting and automatic selection processes are reliant on a posterior neural attention network that includes regions in parietal cortex and thalamus (near the hypothalamus; see Figure 7.1). The strategic or deliberate allocation of attention is reliant on an anterior attention network that includes the anterior cingulate cortex (near the brain's prefrontal cortex; see Figure 7.1). Experimental paradigms can separate reflexive orienting from strategic orienting, and early (perceptual) selection from later, strategic selection.

Posterior Attention Network

With regard to spatial orienting, more than 14 studies have examined ADHD with computerized tasks using a rapid (100 ms) cue-target event, with a cue in the form of a light onset in the peripheral visual field. The child must then respond as quickly as possible to a target (say, an "X") appearing in the peripheral visual field. Various combinations of "valid" cues (on the same side where the target will appear) and "invalid" cues (on the opposite side) test the efficiency of the reflexive attentional orienting response. We (Huang-Pollock & Nigg, 2003) reviewed all available studies and pooled the results to arrive at the best estimate of true population effects available. Despite interesting findings in individual studies, in aggregate there was no evidence of an abnormality in the posterior orienting system in ADHD.

Research on perceptual selection has been somewhat more mixed, but it is fair to say that the literature has failed to demonstrate a reliable deficit in automatic attentional selection in ADHD. We (Huang-Pollock, Nigg, & Carr, 2004) revisited this issue using a variable load paradigm, which is the newest probe from cognitive psychology. This approach varies the processing load for the child (for example, they may have to pick the target out from a set of two or a set of six alternatives) in order to manipulate automatic versus deliberate attentional selection. Our data showed perfectly normal early selection in ADHD-C, and no evidence of abnormality in ADHD-I. However, a subgroup of ADHD-I children with "sluggish tempo" (true, underactive, inattentive children) showed some atypical selection.

Overall, the posterior attention network is a poor candidate for core dysfunction in ADHD-C. Further study of ADHD-I taking into account the fact that it includes both overactive (mild ADHD-C) and underactive, sluggish, or inattentive children likely will be of value.

Anterior Attention Network

Data are mixed with regard to an ADHD deficit in *strategic* attention orienting or selection. With regard to orienting, our quantitative review and summary (Huang-Pollock & Nigg, 2003) found scant support, but studies that appropriately tested this function were few. As for selection, the picture is quite mixed. One source of data is the widely studied Stroop effect, which refers to the fact that people are much faster at naming the ink color in which words are printed if the "words" are meaningless (e.g., a row of xx's) than if they are conflicting color names (e.g., looking at the word "blue" in red ink and attempting to say the color "red"). A large number of studies have looked at this effect in ADHD, but quantitative reviews summarizing all available studies have tended to conclude that any ADHD deficit on this task is small (van Mourik, Oosterlaan, & Sergeant, 2005). Alternative designs to test selective attention have sometimes shown an ADHD deficit, but the number of appropriately designed studies again remains too few to enable firm conclusions. Thus, the jury is still out with regard to a true selection deficit in the anterior attention network in ADHD.

Alerting/Arousal

The ability to maintain an alert state and to rapidly bring attention to bear on unexpected information is mediated by a right-lateralized, noradrenergic vigilance network in the brain than runs from the brain stem to the cortex (see Figure 7.1, bottom portion). This system is important for everything from sleep regulation, to effective attention during task performance (such as when a child must stay alert in class), to regulation of mood and thought more generally (for example, someone who is tired may be more irritable and less able to handle a complex problem than someone who is well rested). The development of arousal regulation begins early in life and has dramatic implications for self-regulation and attention, because arousal modulates other attention functions (in other words, orienting or selecting information are most efficient at optimal arousal levels, and are impeded if one is under- or over-aroused). Multiple data types suggest that ADHD is associated with problems in arousal regulation, in most instances apparently due to under-arousal of cortical systems.

First, children with ADHD have difficulty responding very rapidly on fast reaction time tasks (Huang-Pollock & Nigg, 2003). A second piece of evidence comes from a very small number of studies looking at alerting to unwarned targets in laboratory orienting tasks, especially targets in the left visual field (because the alerting system is thought to be a right-lateralized neural system, problems may be easiest to detect by probing it directly with targets on the contralateral or left side, because the right hemisphere is the first to process left-sided information). Nigg, Swanson, and Hinshaw (1997) found that children with ADHD and their biological, but not adoptive, parents were very slow to alert to unwarned targets on the left side of a computer screen. This finding suggested that poor alerting may be a marker of risk for ADHD in families. However, two other studies of children's alerting to these types of cues yielded smaller effects (Huang-Pollock & Nigg, 2003), so the conclusiveness of this type of evidence remains in doubt.

A third kind of evidence comes from Continuous Performance Tasks, which ask a child to monitor an uneventful sequence of letters and detect the rare target letter (e.g., detect the "X" when most letters, appearing one at a time on the screen, are not X). This classic vigilance task yields a signal-sensitivity parameter called *d-prime*. Meta-analyses of nearly a dozen studies showed some time ago that d-prime was deficient in ADHD (Losier, McGrath, & Klein, 1996).

Finally, evidence comes from studies of scalp electrical recordings, obtained with electroencephalograph (EEG) technology. These scale electrical recordings detect brain electrical activity. Slow wave forms are interpreted as low arousal and fast wave forms signify higher arousal. A fairly large literature now documents that samples of children with ADHD are more often characterized by excess slow wave brain activity compared to other children in similar tasks, although a subgroup may have excess fast activity, indicating they are over-aroused (Clarke, Barry, McCarthy, & Selikowitz, 2001). Low cortical arousal can enable us to understand why stimulant medications tend to be helpful for children with ADHD. The stimulants likely increase cortical arousal, thus improving overall regulation of mood and behavior (many people experience an analogous effect from their daily dose of coffee).

MOTIVATION AND REWARD RESPONSE

Scientists have suspected for decades that children with ADHD may have abnormal response to incentives, failing to be motivated by the rewards that energize most children. The brain's reward response is related to dopamine circuits in the brain, running from brain stem regions to the limbic system (nucleus accumbens) and on to frontal cortex (pictured in Figure 7.1, top portion). Therefore, blunted dopamine activity in the brain would provide a mechanism for abnormal incentive response in ADHD. Stimulant medication also may work by increasing dopamine circulation in the brain synapses, thus making rewards more noticeable.

The current thinking is that children with ADHD have a steepened delay-reward gradient. This means that they put undue emphasis on short-term, small rewards, and abnormally little emphasis on delayed, larger rewards, compared to other children. This effect in turn could be due to an altered internal "clock" that causes time to seem longer than it is. Thus, if children with ADHD are allowed to complete a computer task at their own pace, they complete it quickly and make excessive errors in the process. However, if they are unable to speed the completion of the task (e.g., the pace of every trial is set by the experimenter), then they tend to perform more closely to normal (Sonuga-Barke, 2002). The internal clock is thought to be related to functioning of the cerebellum; in turn, neural circuits linking cerebellum to frontal cortex are crucial in self-regulation. Thus, recent work has begun to look both at reward response and reinforcement learning in children with ADHD, as well as at the possibility that temporal information processing (whether they can accurately estimate time by an internal "clock") is abnormal in this disorder. Reinforcement learning data are potentially of particular importance because they could shed light on micro-level socialization processes that shape the development of impulsive behavior via early learning by very young children.

EXECUTIVE FUNCTIONS AND COGNITIVE CONTROL

Executive functioning is a term from the neuropsychology literature that refers to the ability to maintain behavior on a goal set over time (Pennington & Ozonoff, 1996). It is being replaced in some literatures by the less controversial term "cognitive control." Under either rubric, multiple component operations contribute to executive functioning or cognitive control. Key operations are several. First is the ability to deliberately suppress an unintended response when it is cued (e.g., in a "check swing" in baseball, the batter is about to swing until he sees the ball break outside; he then must abruptly cancel the swing). Second is the ability to keep interfering information out of working memory (as when a child must ignore talking neighbors while working on his homework in class). Third is the ability to manipulate information in working memory (as in adding up the price of two items at the store in one's head, or as in visualizing the next two moves in a chess game). Fourth is the ability to rapidly shift mental "set" in order to integrate multiple elements of a complex task (for example, when a cook must track the beans and the turkey simultaneously in order to get the entire dinner to come out at the same time). All of these abilities rely on a series of parallel neural circuits that run from prefrontal cortex, to the basal ganglia, and on to the thalamus (see Figure 7.1). It has been theorized that all of the executive functions may depend on the basic ability to suppress an unintended or reflexive response (e.g., the urge to laugh at an inopportune time), thus making room for strategic, deliberate, or planful behavior (Barkley, 1997). Regardless, the literature on ADHD admits of three conclusions.

First, children with ADHD have difficulty with strategic response suppression. This is most readily demonstrated by a task called the stop task, in which the child must interrupt a prepared response on an occasional warning cue. The timing of the warning tone varies from early to late, making it relatively easy or difficult to interrupt the prepared response. Children with ADHD require more warning than normal in order to succeed at such interruption (Nigg, 2001; Willcutt, Doyle, Nigg, Faraone, & Pennington, 2005). EEG studies that look at evoked potentials, that is, brain electrical responses within milliseconds of a stimulus, indicate abnormal cortical responding to this task in individuals with ADHD (Plizska et al., 2000). Thus, the problem in ADHD is not merely a peripheral motor problem, but a neural processing problem in response suppression.

It is important to distinguish the effortful suppression of a motor response from the relatively automatic filtering of unimportant information. One of our primary goals has been to isolate which type of control (that is, cognitive or motoric, strategic versus automatic) is most involved in ADHD. We have adapted tasks that involve the automatic filtering of information. For example, if told to name the ink color when the word "red" is printed in blue ink, people suppress the word "red;" if they are then asked to name the color red, they take slightly longer to retrieve "red" if they have just finished ignoring "red." We showed that ability to be normal in ADHD. In contrast, the ability to deliberately suppress an eye movement was impaired in the same individuals (Nigg, Butler, Huang-Pollock, & Henderson, 2002).

It is also essential to distinguish this function from reactive response suppression, or the spontaneous, relatively automatic interruption of behavior due to anxiety. Impulsivity can also be driven by extreme low anxiety and lack of normal physiological reactions to warnings of possible punishment. This type of deficit is distinct from executive control. It is associated with unsocialized conduct disorder, which occurs in a subset of children with ADHD, but it is not clearly associated with ADHD apart from conduct disorder (Nigg, 2001).

Second, children with ADHD have difficulty protecting working memory, especially visual working memory. Work is underway to evaluate whether this includes a problem with storage in working memory, with the manipulation of information in working memory, or both. This difficulty implicates problems in the prefrontal cortex.

Third, it has been suggested that the ability to maintain response readiness (as opposed to attentional alertness) is crucial in ADHD. This ability, called "activation," may be a left-lateralized ability again involving dopamine pathways. It is measured by performance on a task over time, by response to varying event rates at which tasks occur, and by response tendencies on reaction time tasks including the Continuous Performance task. A range of evidence has suggested that this ability may be impaired in ADHD. Most notably, when events occur at a very slow or very fast event rate, children with ADHD have more difficulty than normal children at maintaining alertness or at inhibiting responses. However, when the event rate is optimized (in essence, providing external support for the weak activation ability), their performance approaches normal levels. Though this work requires further cross-validation, it may lead to ecological interventions that may assist children with ADHD to function more effectively in classroom or other settings.

PERSONALITY AND TEMPERAMENT

Key personality traits are related to regulation of behavior. Effortful control, also called constraint or conscientiousness, refers to the tendency to planfully and deliberately control attention and behavior. It is related to the idea of executive function and is a trait thought to be influenced by baseline functioning in the same frontal-subcortical neural circuits that support executive control (Nigg, 2000). Extraversion, surgency, or approach refers to the tendency to spontaneously and strongly approach potential rewards, as well as to have positive affect and be socially successful. At least two kinds of negative affect may be important as well. People tend to experience more or less anxiety and depression, especially under stress (often referred to as neuroticism)—this trait is a nonspecific correlate of most psychopathology including ADHD. People also tend to be more or less agreeable/cooperative versus hostile with others (referred to as agreeableness here). Our work (Nigg, John et al., 2002) pooled data from over 1,600 individuals from six independent samples, including parents of children with ADHD, adults with ADHD, and general population samples, collected in Michigan, Colorado, and California. We were able to show that symptoms of inattention-disorganization are strongly related to low conscientiousness, consistent with the executive or cognitive control model of ADHD.

Symptoms of hyperactivity-impulsivity were related to low agreeableness, although as might be expected, this effect was largely carried by co-occurring antisocial behaviors. Extraversion was only weakly related to ADHD symptoms, raising some question about the centrality of reward response tendencies to the disorder. However, further work is needed that isolates components of extraversion, that is, approach from positive affect and social dominance.

SUMMARY AND KEY ISSUES

This short overview makes clear that ADHD is associated with multiple, related cognitive or neuropsychological abnormalities, probably related to atypical development of key neural networks in the prefrontal cortex, regions of the basal ganglia, the cerebellum, and possibly other brain structures. Notably, attention is not the core problem in ADHD, unless by that one means vigilance or alertness. Rather, ADHD is related to low cortical arousal, poor executive or cognitive control, and possibly to abnormal time perception and consequent reinforcement response difficulties. ADHD is also related to key personality traits that, in particular, provide convergence on the role of effortful control (and associated frontal-striatal circuitry) in ADHD.

The first issue here concerns this multiplicity of findings: which ones are most important? Does one area of deficit "drive" the others? Or, alternatively, is it the case that some children with ADHD have a problem in one area or trait, and others in another area? Despite a few initial studies attempting to address these types of questions, the safest conclusion at this point is that little is known about the relative importance of these different cognitive deficits in a given child or a given sample of children. The vast majority of published studies have looked at only one or two of these major domains that contribute to self-regulation. A major need in the field is for neuropsychological studies that examine measures across these different domains.

The second key issue concerns whether these different problem areas may lead to different components of the symptom profile. Sonuga-Barke (2002) theorized that executive function problems should be related to behavior problems with inattention-disorganization, whereas poor motivation or reinforcement learning/temporal information processing should be related to symptoms of impulsivity-overactivity. Our personality data, described on the prior page, tend to agree with that suggestion. We (Nigg, Stavro et al., 2005) further tested that theory by looking at adults with ADHD on a battery of executive function tasks. We measured symptoms of inattention and hyperactivity-impulsivity, respectively, by clinician interview of the participant and two other adults who knew them well. These three sources of information were pooled. Then, the composite symptom scores were used to statistically predict overall executive functioning (recall that this refers to the ability to deliberately regulate behavior in response to goals, including the ability to suppress unintended reflexes and to control what one holds in mind, in working memory). Only symptoms of inattention were uniquely related to executive functioning; symptoms of hyperactivity-impulsivity were not. Further work along these lines is needed, looking at measures of temporal information processing, executive functioning, arousal, and motivation.

The third issue concerns whether these different components of self-regulation may in fact represent distinct developmental pathways leading to ADHD via different routes. Substantial distributional overlap exists between ADHD and normal children on any given cognitive or physiological measure. Thus, it is quite possible that many children with ADHD have "normal" development of executive functions, yet develop ADHD by a different route, such as poor reinforcement learning. It may therefore be possible to subtype children not just on the basis of clinical profile, but on the basis of neuropsychological function.

To illustrate this possibility, we (Nigg, Blaskey, Stawicki, & Sachek, 2004) divided children with ADHD into those with "normal" and "abnormal" (worse than 90th percentile) performance on a series of executive function measures. We then examined executive function performance in the first-degree biological relatives of these children and a group of normal control children with average neuropsychological functioning. The relatives of the children with ADHD plus executive function problems had significantly weaker executive function performance than the relatives of children with ADHD-alone or controls. These data suggest that there may be some etiological validity to separating children with ADHD into those with normal and abnormal neuropsychological profiles. Although much work remains to be done to solve a range of practical problems in implementing that idea, it is a crucial future direction for the field.

In summary, multiple mechanisms that shape self-regulation are affected in ADHD, but the relations among these mechanisms in ADHD remains little-studied. Most crucial is further work to illuminate heterogeneity of mechanism, to clarify whether we can identify meaningful subtypes of ADHD based on etiological mechanisms, rather than only on clinical symptoms.

Extrinsic Causal Factors in ADHD

The preceding sections addressed neuropsychological mechanisms that are intrinsic, or within the child. They may be thought of as proximal causes of the behavioral problems, although in some instances they may also be effects of the behavioral problems (e.g., a child with low arousal fails to develop strong executive functioning due to interference in socialization by his behavior problems). But where do these neuropsychological problems come from? Why do these children have atypical neural development? This brings us to more distal causes, some of which may occur very early in development. I consider in turn genetics, then family and socialization, and finally ecological risks.

MOLECULAR GENETIC FINDINGS

For ADHD, I noted that heritability is in the range of from 0.6 to 0.7 (Eaves et al., 2000), indicating that a substantial percentage of individual variation in risk for ADHD is due to genetic variation between people. In light of this replicated finding, scientists are asking which individual genes may relate to ADHD. One strategy, known as the whole genome scan, is costly and has just begun in ADHD, with too few data in hand to admit of firm conclusions as yet. The second approach therefore has been to look at theoretically identified candidate genes. For example, many scientists suspect that the several genes modulating the action of key neurotransmitters, such as dopamine and norepinephrine (Figure 7.1) may be involved in ADHD. ADHD stands apart from most psychiatric disorders in that it has yielded replicated associations with several individual genes. These are the dopamine D4 receptor gene, the dopamine transporter gene, and possibly the dopamine D5 receptor gene. However each gene accounts for only a very small portion of the genetic effect. Clearly many genes are involved. Several other genes have yielded positive findings but do not yet have the number of replications needed to have confidence in their effects. An important complexity here is that the genetic markers used are generally nonfunctional. Thus, if the markers are unluckily chosen, they can "miss" a functionally important gene variance. Therefore, recent work has looked in a more refined way at combinations of alleles and multiple markers on these alleles. Using this more refined molecular approach, we (Park et al., 2005) were able to confirm that a key noradrenergic gene (the alpha-2 receptor, important to prefrontal cortex and executive functioning) was related to ADHD. These new mapping approaches are being aggressively pursued in several centers around the world and should yield a wealth of new information about the genetic architecture of ADHD.

FAMILY AND SOCIALIZATION PROCESS

I noted that it has been difficult to identify family or parenting correlates of ADHD, in part because these effects when identified are usually carried by co-occurring antisocial or aggressive child behaviors. These results have led most observers to conclude that dysfunctional parenting is more likely to be a result, rather than a cause, of ADHD, although longitudinal research indicates that parenting style and parenting practices predict the maintenance of ADHD-related symptomatology in early childhood (Campbell, 2002). Studies that did link early family characteristics (attachment, hostility) with later ADHD generally failed to control for initial levels of child ADHD or parental ADHD or both, leaving their conclusions in doubt.

More recently, we (Jester et al., 2005) did control parent ADHD and early child behavior levels in a longitudinal family design. We followed a large sample of at-risk and control children from preschool to adolescence, examining the family and parenting predictors of four trajectories of development of attention problems (by the Child Behavior Checklist and Teacher Report Form scale, which includes hyperactivity items) and aggression. Lower emotional support and lower intellectual stimulation by the parents in early childhood predicted membership in the most problematic inattention trajectory, even when the trajectory for aggression was held constant. Conversely, conflict and lack of cohesiveness in the early family environment predicted membership in a worse developmental trajectory of aggressive behavior with ADHD symptoms held constant. Those findings provide some of the first evidence for the potential specific contribution of distinct parenting or home experiences to ADHD-spectrum and aggressive behaviors.

Thus, whereas family effects may be more prominent for aggression than for ADHD per se, continued examination of family correlates of ADHD symptom expression, course, and subtypes remains extremely important and can shed light on maintenance of the syndrome over time, as well as on moderators of benign versus very problematic outcomes.

ECOLOGICAL RISKS AND ADHD

Several ecological contexts to modern society have been theorized to contribute to an alleged rising incidence of ADHD. For some of these ideas, such as a fast pace of life or economic pressures on families, data are insufficient to warrant comment here. For others, such as dietary factors and early excessive exposure to electronic media, the possibilities suggested by initial studies are fascinating but data are still too limited to enable conclusions to be drawn about ADHD. In still other domains, causal effects on symptoms like ADHD, such as severe impulsive behavior, are established; these include certain prenatal teratogens, notably alcohol. Prenatal nicotine exposure may also play a role, although most of that evidence admits of the possibility that the association may be carried by antisocial behavior in both parent and child (Burke, Loeber, & Lahey, 2001).

Yet other ecological causes of ADHD are known. The rising survival rate of low, very low, and extremely low birth weight children has contributed to a rising incidence of secondary effects such as cerebral palsy, as well in small part the incidence of ADHD, which occurs at elevated rates in children born at low birth weight (Breslau & Chilcoate, 2000). Given that in earlier eras these children did not survive at all, this particular cause of ADHD seems well worth bearing, although systematic provision for these children's inevitable developmental needs has not been evident in the nation's health care planning.

On the other hand, industrial toxins are a potentially preventable cause of child learning and behavior problems including ADHD. Lead exposure, though dramatically reduced in the past generation thanks to earlier research and federal action eliminating lead from gasoline, remains too high, especially in urban and minority youth. Further, concern is growing about the effects of "safe" levels of lead exposure (below 10 ppb). If levels as low as 5ppb contribute to attention and learning problems, as emerging evidence suggests (Canfield et al., 2003), a substantial percentage of the child population in the United States remains at risk.

A range of other potentially damaging environmental and industrial toxins has been introduced into children's environment's with virtually no study of their effects on neurological development or on potential mental, learning, and behavioral problems in children. This leaves a serious gap in knowledge for which children may pay for decades to come, just as hundreds of thousands have already suffered from the ill-advised wholesale introduction of lead into their early environment.

A salient example of potential environmental toxicant involvement in ADHD is the family of chemicals known as polychlorinated biphenyls and their many cousins (all referred to here as PCBs, although this group includes PBBs, dioxins, and other related compounds). These compounds are of particular interest because, via their hypothesized effect on very sensitive hormone receptors in the developing fetus, they might directly influence the development of brain dopamine systems. Moreover, these compounds are ubiquitous (essentially, it is now believed that most children in the world undergo some "background level" exposure to these chemicals in utero) and remain permanently in the body. Longitudinal studies in human cohorts have now demonstrated a correlation between even these low (i.e., very widespread) exposure levels and delays in children's development of motor skills, attention, and working memory but not other functions (and not hyperactivity; Jacobson & Jacobson, 2003). Adding more concern are experimental studies showing that infant monkeys exposed to low "background" levels of PCBs (i.e., comparable to typical exposures in humans) show working memory deficits as adolescents, compared to monkeys with no PCB exposure (Rice, 1999). Thus, these correlations in human data are probably causal. Further study of the degree to which these and other chemicals may be related to ADHD and associated neuropsychological problems appears needed.

Particularly important to consider are individual differences in sensitivity to these chemicals. Contaminants may exert their effects mainly on susceptible individuals. Thus, combining of molecular genetic, neuropsychological, and contaminant approaches in the same samples represents a particularly salient high risk/high-payoff strategy for future work to identify preventable causes of ADHD.

CULTURAL EFFECTS ON ADHD

Studies in North America, Western Europe, Australia, China, Japan, India, and South America indicate that the prevalence of ADHD by DSM-IV criteria is within one order of magnitude (2–10%) cross-nationally. However, racial, ethnic, and cultural effects on ADHD symptom expression, course, comorbidity, and even structure of the symptom domains remain poorly studied and may vary for different ethnic groups (Reid et al., 1998). It also appears that culture and ethnicity can moderate how these behaviors are viewed and consequently assessed (Mueller et al., 1995). In short, lack of understanding of how ethnicity and culture may moderate the expression of ADHD remains a stark gap in knowledge today.

SUMMARY AND KEY ISSUES

When it comes to etiology of ADHD, we know that genes play a role, but we understand little about how they interact with other causal factors such as low birth weight, lead exposure, prenatal alcohol exposure, or more speculatively diet or environmental contaminants such as PCBs. Likewise, the interplay of these neural insults with family context, parenting, and other social supports to the development of self-regulation is little studied in relation to ADHD or its subtypes and outcomes. From the point of view of preventing or reducing the incidence of ADHD, a major gap in the present efforts of the nation's research portfolio concerns a concentrated examination of genotype-environment interplay that includes study of specific pre- and perinatal toxicants and contaminants, with PCBs representing one exemplar of a potential influence on the condition that is insufficiently investigated. Despite its somewhat speculative status, the high-payoff prevention potential of such work mandates its serious consideration.

Conclusions

What We Know

We know that ADHD is heterogeneous, that it is a marker for potentially very severe outcomes in a subset of youngsters, and that it is highly heritable. We know, further, that it is associated with a range of neuropsychological deficits, related to mild developmental dysplasia of key neural regions involved in the development of self-control, although such features do not characterize all children assigned this diagnosis by current criteria and so are not yet diagnostically useful. A major locus of scientific progress has been the more specific mapping and description of these cognitive problems, including definition of motor response suppression, temporal information processing, and activation and arousal functions. These effects likely contribute to the syndrome in varying subsets of children with the disorder, with perhaps some children with ADHD accounted for by problems in executive function, others by problems in motivation or arousal, and perhaps others by frank trauma. A small subset may have no dysfunction and may eventually be understood in terms of problems in adaptation or fit to context. We also know that ADHD-related syndromes can be caused by prenatal insult including teratogens such as alcohol, by low birth weight, and by post-natal lead exposure.

What We Need to Find Out

Two key gaps in knowledge about the causes of ADHD are salient. First, we need to know how the diverse cognitive problems identified with the disorder relate to one another so as to begin to identify meaningful and reliable etiological subtypes. Essential are studies that examine these many domains in the same children—a difficult proposition due to the burden on the child and the difficulty of obtaining quality data over extended testing periods. Second, we need to connect proximal (intrinsic) with distal (extrinsic) causal factors to completely explain the pathways to development of extremes of inattention, activity, and impulsivity in children. Doing so would require integrated study of (a) molecular genetics, (b) temperament, (c) neuropsychological functioning, (d) family functioning, and (e) a range of common and potentially causal insults. One under-appreciated candidate in this regard is the family of toxicants labeled here as PCBs. Such studies in their entirely have scarcely been imagined to date, due to their daunting epidemiological implications and the need for prospective studies. However, initial data could easily be obtained, simply by routine gathering of identified causal data on existing ADHD samples.

Summary

The widespread concern about ADHD reflects the fact that behavior problems characterized by inattention, overactivity, and impulsivity are a major mental health problem for today's youth, with high ancillary costs to society. Progress in understanding the mechanisms and causes of these behavior problems has been substantial, although it remains incomplete with regard to integrating proximal and distal contributors. Prevention could be markedly enhanced based on present knowledge by more concerted effort to prevent lead exposure, prenatal alcohol—and possibly nicotine—exposure, and more widespread high-quality prenatal care generally. At the same time, the bulk of future prevention potential remains to be realized in more concerned and integrative studies that link neuropsychological and etiological mechanisms in the same studies.

REFERENCES

Achenbach, T. M., Dumenci, L., & Rescorla, L. A. (2002). Is American student behavior getting worse? Teacher ratings over an 18-year period. *School Psychology Review, 31,* 428–442.

American Psychiatric Association. (1994). *Diagnostic and statistical manual of mental disorders* (4th ed.). Washington, DC: Author.

Barkley, R. A. (1997). Behavioral inhibition, sustained attention, and executive function: Constructing a unified theory of ADHD. *Psychological Bulletin, 121,* 65–94.

Breslau, N., & Chilcoate, H. D. (2000). Psychiatric sequalae of low birthweight at 11 years of age. *Biological Psychiatry, 47,* 1005–1011.

Burke, J. D., Loeber, R., & Lahey, B. B. (2001). Which aspects of ADHD are associated with tobacco use in early adolescence? *Journal of Child Psychology & Psychiatry, 42,* 493–502.

Campbell, S. B. (2002). *Behavior problems in preschool children* (2nd ed.). New York: Guilford.

Canfield, R. L., Henderson, D. R., Cory-Slechta, D. A., Cox, C., Jusko, T. A., & Lanphear, B. P. (2003). Intellectual impairment in children with blood lead concentrations below 10 microg per deciliter. *New England Journal of Medicine, 348*(16), 1517–1526.

Clarke, A. Barry, R., McCarthy, R., & Selikowitz, M. (2001). EEG-defined subtypes of children with attention-deficit/hyperactivity disorder. *Clinical Neurophysiology, 112,* 2098–2105.

Eaves, L., Rutter, M., Silberg, J. L., Shillady, L., Maes, H., & Pickles, A. (2000). Genetic and environmental causes of covariation in interview assessments of disruptive behavior in child and adolescent twins. *Behavior Genetics, 30,* 321–334.

Hinshaw, S. P., Zupan, B. A., Simmel, C., Nigg, J. T., & Melnick, S. M. (1997). Peer status in boys with and without attention-deficit hyperactivity disorder: Predictions from overt and covert antisocial behavior, social isolation, and authoritative parenting beliefs. *Child Development, 64,* 880–896.

Huang-Pollock, C. L., & Nigg, J. T. (2003). Searching for the attention deficit in attention deficit hyperactivity disorder: The case of visuospatial orienting. *Clinical Psychology Review, 23,* 801–830.

Huang-Pollock, C. L., Nigg, J. T., & Carr, T. M. (2004). Selective attention in ADHD using a perceptual load paradigm. *Journal of Child Psychology and Psychiatry, 46,* 1211–1218.

Jacobson, J. L., & Jacobson, S. W. (2003). Prenatal exposure to polychlorinated biphenyls and attention at school age. *Journal of Pediatrics, 143,* 780–788.

Jester, J. M., Nigg, J. T., Adams, K., Fitzgerald, H. E., Puttler, L. I., Wong, M. M., & Zucker, R. A. (2005). Inattention/hyperactivity and aggression from early childhood to adolescence: Heterogeneity of trajectories and differential influence of family environment characteristics. *Development and Psychopathology, 17,* 99–125.

Losier, B. J., McGrath, P. J., & Klein, R. M. (1996). Error patterns on the continuous performance test in non-medicated and medicated samples of children with and without ADHD: A meta-analytic review. *Journal of Child Psychology and Psychiatry, 37,* 971–988.

Mueller, C. W., Mann, E. M., Thanapum, S., Humris, E., Ikeda, Y., Takahashi, A., Tao, K. T., & Li, B. L. (1995). Teachers ratings of disruptive behavior in five countries. *Journal of Clinical Child Psychology, 24,* 434–442.

Nigg, J. T. (2000). On inhibition/disinhibition in developmental psychopathology: Views from cognitive and personality psychology and a working inhibition taxonomy. *Psychological Bulletin, 126,* 200–246.

Nigg, J. T. (2001). Is ADHD an inhibitory disorder? *Psychological Bulletin, 127,* 571–598.

Nigg, J. T., Blaskey, L., Huang-Pollock, C., & Rappley, M. D. (2002). Neuropsychological executive functions and ADHD DSM-IV subtypes. *Journal of the American Academy of Child and Adolescent Psychiatry, 41,* 59–66.

Nigg, J. T., Blaskey, L., Stawicki, J., & Sachek, J. (2004). Evaluating the endophenotype model of ADHD neuropsychological deficit: Results for parents and siblings of children with DSM-IV ADHD Combined and Inattentive Subtypes. *Journal of Abnormal Psychology, 113,* 614–625.

Nigg, J. T., Butler, K. M., Huang-Pollock, C. L., & Henderson, J. M. (2002). Inhibitory processes in adults with persistent childhood onset ADHD. *Journal of Consulting and Clinical Psychology, 70,* 153–157.

Nigg, J. T., & Hinshaw, S. P. (1998). Parent personality traits and psychopathology associated with antisocial behaviors in childhood attention-deficit hyperactivity disorder. *Journal of Child Psychology and Psychiatry, 39,* 145–159.

Nigg, J. T., John, O. J., Blaskey, L., Huang-Pollock, C., Willcutt, E., Hinshaw, S. H., & Pennington, B. (2002). Big five dimensions and ADHD symptoms: Links between personality traits and clinical symptoms. *Journal of Personality and Social Psychology, 83,* 451–469.

Nigg, J. T., Stavro, G., Ettenhofer, M., Hambrick, D., Miller, T., & Henderson, J. M. (2005). Executive functions and ADHD in adults: Evidence for selective effects on ADHD symptom domains. *Journal of Abnormal Psychology.*

Nigg, J. T., Swanson, J., & Hinshaw, S. P. (1997). Covert visual attention in boys with attention deficit hyperactivity disorder: Lateral effects, methylphenidate response, and results for parents. *Neuropsychologia, 35,* 165–176.

Park, L., Nigg, J. T., Waldman, I., Nummy, K. A., Huang-Pollock, C., Rappley, M., & Friderici, K. (2005). Association and linkage of α-2A adrenergic receptor gene polymorphisms with childhood ADHD. *Molecular Psychiatry, 10,* 572–580.

Pennington, B. F., & Ozonoff, S. (1996). Executive functions and developmental psychopathology. *Journal of Child Psychology and Psychiatry, 37,* 51–87.

Pliszka, S. R., Liotti, M., & Woldorff, M. G. (2000). Inhibitory control in children with attention-deficit/hyperactivity disorder: Event related potentials identify the processing component and timing of an impaired right-frontal response-inhibition mechanism. *Biological Psychiatry, 48,* 238–246.

Reid, R., DuPaul, G. J., Power, T. J., Anastopoulos, A. D., Rogers-Adkinson, D., Noll, M. B., & Riccio, C. (1998). Assessing culturally different students for attention deficit hyperactivity disorder using behavior rating scales. *Journal of Abnormal Child Psychology, 26,* 187–198.

Rice, D. C. (1999). Behavioral impairment produced by low-level postnatal PCB exposure in monkeys. *Environmental Research, 80* (2 Pt 2), S113–S121.

Sonuga-Barke, E.J.S. (2002). Psychological heterogeneity in AD/HD—A dual pathway model of behaviour and cognition. *Behavioural Brain Research, 130,* 29–36.

Stawicki, J. A., Nigg, J. T., & Von Eye, A. (in press). Familiality of ADHD combined and inattentive subtypes: New data and meta-analysis.

Swanson, J. M., & Castellanos, F. X. (2002). Biological bases of ADHD: Neuroanatomy, genetics, and pathophysiology. In P. S. Jensen & J. R. Cooper (Eds.), *Attention-deficit hyperactivity disorder: State of the science, best practices* (pp. 7-1–7-20). Kingston, NJ: Civic Research Institute.

Van Mourik, R., Oosterlaan, J., & Sergeant, J. A. (2005). The Stroop revisited: a meta-analysis of interference control in AD/HD. *Journal of Child Psychology and Psychiatry, 46,* 150–165.

Willcutt, E.G., Doyle, A.E., Nigg, J.T., Faraone, S.V., & Pennington, B.F. (2005). Validity of the executive function theory of ADHD: Meta-analytic review. *Biological Psychiatry, 57,* 1336–1346..

World Health Organization. (1993). *The ICD-10 classification of mental and behavioral disorders: Clinical descriptions and diagnostic guidelines (1992) and diagnostic criteria for research.* Geneva: World Health Organization.

Chapter 8

THE DEVELOPMENT OF
AGGRESSION IN EARLY
CHILDHOOD

Daniel S. Shaw

Much of the research reported in this paper was supported by grants
to the author from the National Institute of Mental Health, grants MH
50907, MH 01666, and MH 03876. I am grateful to the work of the staff
of the Pitt Mother & Child Project and the Pitt Early Steps Project for
their years of service, and to our study families for making the research
possible. This work was also greatly influenced by my colleagues Thomas
Dishion, Frances Gardner, and the late Richard Bell. Finally, much of the
material for this chapter originally appeared in the following volume: Shaw,
D. S., Gilliom, M., & Giovannelli, J. (2000). Aggressive behavior disorders. In C. H. Zeanah (Ed.), *Handbook of Infant Mental Health* (2nd ed.;
pp. 397–411). New York: Guilford.

INTRODUCTION

Recent consideration of developmental trends in the onset of antisocial
behavior has been focused on children who show a persistent course of
conduct problems beginning in early childhood. Termed "early starters,"
such individuals have been found to show a persistent and chronic trajectory of antisocial behavior extending from early childhood to adulthood.
Early starters represent approximately six percent of the population, yet
are responsible for almost half of adolescent crime and three-fourths of
violent crimes (Offord, Boyle, & Racine, 1991).

During the past two decades, researchers have become increasingly
interested in the possibility that early-starting children can be identified at younger and younger ages. In the 1980s, studies were initiated

during the preschool and school-age periods (Campbell, Pierce, Moore, Marakovitz, & Newby, 1996), while during the past decade predictors of early-starting pathways have been established beginning in the toddler period (NICHD Early Child Care Research Network, 2004). Longitudinal studies initiated during the toddler and early preschool periods have identified a group of early-starter children who go on to show the most chronic and severe forms of antisocial behavior. Despite the potential advantages of identifying early-starting children before they reach school-age, there are potential pitfalls to this approach. These include the following issues:

- Intentionality, an important component of aggression and other forms of disruptive behavior, is difficult to infer among infants and young toddlers.
- Most children do not have the cognitive capacity to comprehend aggression *fully* until their third or fourth year.
- For most children who show aggressive behavior prior to age three, it is likely to be transient.
- Age two represents the peak incidence rate of aggressive behavior during the life course (Tremblay, 1998), which means that the probability for predicting those children who will likely desist from showing high rates of aggression in the future is likely to be high (i.e., false positives).
- Many children who are aggressive at age two will find alternative conflict resolution strategies to replace its use by age four or five.

Alternatively, the following points support the identification and use of preventive interventions with such children.

- Children who are *not* aggressive during the toddler period are unlikely to develop clinically-elevated levels of aggressive behavior in later childhood or adulthood.
- Very few children begin showing high rates of physically aggressive behavior after age five.
- Toddlers have the capacity to inflict serious harm on siblings, parents, pets, and objects.
- Predictors of aggression and other forms of disruptive behavior are similar throughout early and later childhood.
- Interventions targeted at younger children have been shown to be more efficacious than those used with older school-age children and adolescents.

Despite caution being warranted, it is believed that work identifying factors associated with early-starting pathways of aggression and their prevention is merited, particularly given the greater malleability of children's behavior and parent–child relationships in early childhood. Thus, this chapter reviews factors associated with early-starting pathways, and preventive interventions initiated during early childhood that have been associated with the prevention of such trajectories, including basic and applied studies from the author's own laboratory. From a societal perspective, as the greatest concern is associated with the prevention of physically aggressive behavior, much of the emphasis is on the development and prevention of aggressive behavior versus other types of disruptive problem behavior, including oppositionality and hyperactivity. However, as these behaviors tend to co-occur throughout childhood, most research on the identification and treatment of antisocial behavior has aggregated together reported on multiple forms of disruptive behavior.

Defining Aggression

Intentionality lies at the heart of more recent definitions of aggression. It is perhaps the primary reason for some researchers' dismay at using the term "aggression" to describe aggressive-like behavior during infancy and the early toddler period (i.e., ages one to three). Early definitions of aggression varied. Some investigators focused solely on outcome, while others established intent to injure another person as the primary criterion. More recent interpretations assume an intent to at least threaten another and a consensus that the behavior be viewed as aggressive by the aggressor, the victim, and society. For purposes of the present discussion, aggressive behavior will be defined as an act directed toward a specific other person or object with the intent to hurt or frighten, for which there is a consensus about the aggressive intent of the act.

Aggressive acts toward others are typically subdivided into two categories: hostile and instrumental aggression. Hostile aggression refers to instances in which the major goal is inflicting injury, whereas instrumental aggression involves using force or threat of force to achieve a nonaggressive end (e.g., obtaining an object or gaining territory). Note that in both kinds of aggression, intentionality is considered to be salient in determining if a behavior is aggressive. This presents a challenge in judging whether a child has acted aggressively because of his/her limited cognitive ability and an observer's inability to interpret the meaning of the behavior.

At issue in inferring aggressive intent is the child's developmental status. According to Maccoby (1980), a child must understand the following principles to carry out an intentionally hurtful act:

1. that the intended victim can help or hinder the child's goals, knows what the child wants the victim to do, and knows that the victim can experience distress

2. that the child's actions can generate distress

3. that specific actions can cause distress in specific individuals

4. that the child can execute distress-producing actions

5. that distress can cause the victim to act in ways the child desires

6. that the victim's actions can serve the child's needs

Maccoby stresses that the child need not be conscious of these principles to act aggressively but must have some rudimentary understanding of each to act in a fully aggressive manner. At a broader cognitive level, the young child must be able to understand the nature of the other, including the other's goals and plans. Typically, a child develops the capacities to understand fully the point of view of another person at the beginning of the preschool years; however, some investigators have found that some children under the age of three are capable of demonstrating these capacities when interacting with younger siblings (Dunn & Kendrick, 1982). Given that it would be unusual for a two-year-old to understand the theoretical underpinnings of aggressive behavior, conservatism is warranted in interpreting the meaning of aggressive-like behavior, particularly from ages one to two. Just as 10 to 11-year-olds who commit murder with firearms are treated as children because of their limited ability to understand the long-term consequences of their actions, infants and toddlers who cause injury to siblings, parents, or pets need to be viewed in light of their own cognitive limitations.

Despite and because of these cognitive limitations, the age span between one and two represents a watershed period in the development of aggressive-like behavior. For infants less than a year, physical immobility limits the frequency of aggressive-like behavior. Although children less than 8 months old are clearly capable of using physical force to obtain an object, their accessibility is constrained by their inability to walk and, in most cases, crawl. With the onset of walking at 12 months and gradual increase in coordination during the second year, the accessibility issue becomes moot. The increase in physical mobility is of great concern to parents, as the emerging toddler now has the capacity to explore uncharted territory without the requisite knowledge base. In some ways, it is comparable to parents' predicament in handling the behavior of adolescents. In both instances, the child has the necessary "equipment" to engage in behavior that may cause harm to self or others without sufficient decision-making skills.

Two examples discussed by Maccoby (1980) capture the developmental transition children and parents undergo between age one and two. The first is from a study of one- to two-year-olds in groups of three to four children in a free play activity. Both one- and two-year-olds showed a comparable number of disagreements over toys; however, children's emotional intensity surrounding reactions to conflicts increased with age.

Two-year-olds were more distressed and angry when a toy was taken from them. The loss of the toy affected the quality of the child's play after the incident but also appeared to offend the child's very sense of self (Bronson, 1975). This study points out how the child comes to understand the term "mine." As Maccoby writes, "... between the ages of one and two years, is an increase in the intensity of involvement with objects, a staking out of claims, and an increasingly intense emotional reaction to encounters over possession" (1980, p. 119). As Goodenough (1931) documented over 70 years ago, angry outbursts peak in the middle of the second year for both boys and girls. Tremblay (1998) corroborated these findings with respect to aggressive behavior, reporting that by 17 months of age, 70 percent of children take toys away from other children, 46 percent push others to obtain what they want, and 21–27 percent engage in one or more of the following behaviors with peers: biting, kicking, fighting, or physically attacking. Tremblay also reports that aggression occurs more frequently for infants with siblings, especially for girls (e.g., hitting, kicking, biting), providing daily opportunities for conflicts over possessions.

A second example points to the challenge parents must face in responding to a more physically mobile and potentially destructive child beginning in the second year. The process by which parents set rules has been termed an ego devaluation crisis for infants (Ausubel, 1958). This type of parenting differs markedly from the first year, when most parents serve the infant's wishes unconditionally. In the second year, parents are also more likely to interpret the infant's misbehavior as more intentional, and as such, meriting discipline. Ego devaluation is the shock an infant must contend with in responding to a formerly servant-like parent. Children begin to realize that parents are satisfying their needs because the parents want to, not because they have to. The implication is that children come to accept their role in the family as relatively powerless beings who ultimately must yield to parental authority. Thus, it is not surprising that the second and third years are marked by increasing negativity on the part of the infant as he or she tests the limits of adult authority in response to parents' attempts to expedite socialization. Of course, the infant's day of reckoning is not a foregone conclusion. It is quite possible that in cases in which children develop early conduct problems, a very different lesson is learned; namely, if I persist long and hard enough, I can continue to get my way. Empirical support for such a coercive process is discussed later in the chapter.

The Stability of Early Aggression

Children's limited ability to understand the impact of their aggressive behavior, coupled with the developmental transitions taking place during the second and third years, make it important to examine its stability. As children are trained to desist from using aggressive conflict resolution strategies, rates of aggressive behavior gradually decrease from age two to five. The decrease in aggression is supported by data from our longitudinal study of 300 low-income boys. Using the same five items of aggressive behavior, maternal reports of boys' aggressive behavior decrease rather dramatically from age two to six. The reasons for this lessening involve children's increasing development of language skills and increasing encouragement from parents to use alternative coping strategies for resolving conflict.

Unfortunately, there are relatively few studies of the stability of aggressive behavior beginning in infancy. Studies of slightly older children suggest that continuity is moderate from the preschool to school-age period. In one of the first studies of the latter type, peer aggression was found to show a stability of .7 over a nine-month period among two- to four-year-olds (Jersild & Markey, 1935). More recently, Richman, Stevenson, and Graham, (1982) identified the top 14 percent of three-year-olds from a parental questionnaire of behavior problems, and followed them in comparison to a control group of children from similar backgrounds. Problems persisted in 63 percent of these children at age four compared to 11 percent of the control group, and 62 percent at age eight compared to 22 percent of the controls. Similarly, Campbell and colleagues have followed two cohorts of hard-to-manage children from preschool through school-age (Campbell et al., 1996). In the first cohort, children identified at age 3 showed moderate continuity of behavior problems at ages 6, 9, and 13. Fifty and 48 percent of those with problems at age 3 showed clinically significant problems at ages 6 and 9, respectively. Campbell (1994) followed a second cohort of overactive and inattentive boys and found comparable rates of continuity from preschool to school age.

The few longitudinal studies initiated prior to age three largely corroborate these results. Rose, Rose, and Feldman (1989) found a correlation of .73 on a broad factor of disruptive behavior problems between the ages two and five. In a study specifically focused on aggressive behavior conducted by Cummings, Iannotti, and Zahn-Waxler (1989), the stability from age two to five was as high as $r = .76$ for males. This study is notable because it is one of the few in which observational data were obtained at both assessment points to evaluate aggression, and because the stability was obtained while having children interact with same-age peers.

Finally, in analyzing data from our cohort of low-income boys, among boys identified at or above the 90th percentile on a broad factors externalizing symptoms at age two, 63 percent remained above the

90th percentile at age five, and 97 percent remained above the median. At age six, 62 percent remained at or above the 90th percentile and 100 percent (all 18) remained above the median. False negative rates (i.e., those not identified at age two but who went on to show high rates at school entry) were relatively low for the same factors. Only 13 and 16 percent of boys below the 50th percentile on externalizing at age two moved into the clinical range at ages five and six, respectively. When clinically elevated groups were formed at age two based solely on items involving aggressive behavior, and the outcome variable was more narrowly focused on aggressive and destructive behavior at age five, stability was even higher. Approximately 88 percent of boys identified as aggressive at age two continued to show clinically elevated symptomatology at age five (false negative rate 22 percent). These data are comparable to those reported by Patterson (1982) concerning the stability of antisocial behavior from school age to late adolescence. Of those identified in the top 5 percent, Patterson found 38.5% stayed at or above the 95th percentile and 100 percent stayed above the sample mean ten years later. Similar to Patterson's data with older children, the stability findings of early childhood also suggest that there are relatively few "late starters" who begin to show clinically elevated rates of disruptive behavior after age two.

Taken together, the results suggest that aggression shows moderate to strong continuity beginning in early childhood. The data from our own sample indicate comparable stability of clinically elevated scores as reported for older children. That 88 percent of those identified with clinically elevated scores at age two continued to maintain clinical status three to four years later is a strong endorsement of the need for early intervention programs. It should be noted that these stability levels may be limited to other high-risk samples. Still, the results suggest that aggressive behavior is relatively stable for the most aggressive children during a period of great developmental transition.

Correlates of Aggression during Early Childhood

Several factors have been theorized to influence the course of aggression and other forms of disruptive behavior in young children. Unfortunately, relatively few studies have been undertaken to validate these hypotheses with infants and toddlers. Here we review areas that have been postulated to affect early disruptive behavior and research studies that have addressed these issues. The domains include gender and child temperament, parental attributes and support, parenting, and chronic family adversity.

Sex Differences

Recently, the issue of sex differences in disruptive behavior has been of greater interest as more is known about the prevalence rates and stability of antisocial behavior during the school-age period. The emergence of boys' higher rates of externalizing behavior seems to occur during the latter part of the preschool period. While several investigators have documented the absence of sex differences in externalizing behaviors from ages one to three (Richman et al., 1982), there appears to be a shift in this pattern beginning at ages four and five (Rose et al., 1989). These differences become more dramatic during the school-age period and persist into adulthood.

In a review of studies examining sex differences in the prevalence and correlates of behavior problems among young children, Keenan and Shaw (1997) propose two explanations for the emergence of sex differences beginning at ages four to five. The first involves differential socialization practices of parents. As a result of being reinforced for sex-stereotyped behavior, girls' problems may be channeled more in the direction of internalizing difficulties. The socialization hypothesis is supported by data that during the preschool period, parents are more likely to use physical punishment with sons and more inductive techniques and reasoning with daughters (Block, 1978). Similarly, research indicates that relative to boys, mothers encourage girls to have more concern for others, to share or even relinquish toys to peers, and to behave prosocially (Ross, Tesla, Kenyon, & Lollis, 1990). Dodge and Frame (1982) have found that deficits in these affective perspective-taking skills are highly related to antisocial behavior among school-age children. It is unclear whether these differences in parental behavior initially emerge in the preschool period, or become evident at younger ages.

The second explanation attributes the greater decline in girls' externalizing problems during early childhood to their more advanced adaptive skills, which, in turn, facilitate prosocial behavior. From infancy to the preschool period, girls are found to have more rapid biological, cognitive, and social and emotional development compared to boys. Boys appear more vulnerable than girls to several neurodevelopmental disorders such as mental retardation, autism, learning disabilities, and Attention Deficit Hyperactivity Disorder. Cognitively, girls appear to have greater skills in language development (Huttenlocher, Haight, Bryk, Seltzer, & Lyons, 1991), and greater ability to maintain motivation in the face of disruption (Gold, Crombie, & Noble, 1987). In the area of social and emotional development, preschool-age girls are more likely to recommend prosocial rather than aggressive strategies in resolving conflict compared to boys

(Hay, Zahn-Waxler, Cummings, & Iannotti, 1992). Taken together, these findings provide tentative support for the validity of both the socialization and advanced maturity hypotheses in explaining the greater prevalence of boys' externalizing behavior problems. However, more work is needed in this area before firm conclusions can be drawn. For instance, it will be important to identify specific ages and specific practices at which parents begin treating girls and boys differently.

Child Temperament

Several investigators have examined the relation between early temperamental attributes and conduct problems. Most studies have focused on infant negative emotionality (Sanson, Oberklaid, Pedlow, & Prior, 1991), although more recent research has begun to focus on attention-seeking behavior, the expression of anger, and behavioral inhibition (Shaw, Gilliom, Ingoldsby, & Nagin, 2003). Negative emotionality is thought to be directly related to later oppositional and aggressive behavior, and indirectly through its effects on parenting. Studies examining direct links between infant temperament and later aggression have shown modest to moderate predictive validity (Sanson et al., 1991). However, interpretation of these findings must be tempered by the use of maternal report to assess infant difficulty *and* later behavior problems. In the few studies using multiple informants, relations between maternal report of infant difficulty and later externalizing problems have been modest or non-significant (Belsky, Hsieh, Crnic, 1998). This indicates that the direct association between infant temperament and later externalizing problems may be at least partially due to the parent's stable perception of the child rather than the child's behavior. However, such a bias may still have a significant, albeit indirect, effect on child antisocial outcome. Mothers who perceive their infants as high on negative emotionality may be less responsive to their requests for attention and use more harsh discipline strategies in response to their behavior.

In our own work, we have sought to understand the relation between infant attention seeking, maternal unresponsiveness, and early conduct problems using an interactive measure of attention seeking. Employing an observational measure developed by Martin (1981), infants are placed in a high chair with nothing to do, while mothers are instructed to complete a questionnaire *and* attend to the infant's needs. Persistent attention seeking is assessed by coding infant bids for behavior following initial bids that are unresponded to by the caregiver. Viewed from an interactional context, persistent attention seeking is likely to be aversive to the caregiver who is initially unresponsive to the infant. Thus, attention seeking may be a direct precursor of disruptive problems, but also indirectly lead to disruptive behavior by influencing caregivers' perceptions and parenting of the child. Attention seeking assessed observationally between 10 and 12 months has been directly related to conduct problems between the ages of 2 and 3.5 in three studies, including observed and maternal report of aggression at age two (Martin, 1981; Shaw et al., 1998a).

A related interest has grown in exploring individual differences in infants' expression of anger, stemming from work on the affective bases of aggression. It has been hypothesized that infants who respond to goal frustration with intense and prolonged anger may be at elevated risk for aggressive behavior problems (Calkins, 1994). Longitudinal studies from infancy to early childhood provide preliminary support for this premise. Zahn-Waxler and colleagues (1990) examined relations between aggression at age two and subsequent behavior problems in the offspring of well and depressed mothers. Both normative (object struggles, rough play) and dysregulated (hostility toward adults, out-of-control behavior) forms of infant aggression were identified. Only dysregulated aggression predicted externalizing problems reported by mothers at age five and children's reports of problem behavior at age six. Similarly, several noncompliance strategies used by two-year-olds, including passive noncompliance, simple refusal, direct defiance, and negotiation, have been identified (Kuczynski & Kochanska, 1990) Of these subtypes, only direct defiance, that is, noncompliance accompanied by poorly controlled anger, predicted externalizing problems at age five. These studies indicate that the long-term consequences of aggressive, noncompliant behavior may depend on concomitant patterns of emotion regulation.

Finally, we recently identified a group of toddlers who showed a persistent pattern of aggressive and oppositional behavior based on low levels of behavioral inhibition at age two (Shaw et al., 2003). Mothers and sons participated in an hour-long assessment during which time they were placed in a number of stressful (e.g., clean-up) and nonstressful (e.g., free play) tasks. In one such task, children were exposed to a tape recording of gorilla sounds emanating from inside a cabinet on the other side of the room from where parents and children were stationed. Only a small percentage of children approached the cabinet, but a majority of these uninhibited children showed a persistent course of conduct problems from ages two to eight.

The Family Environment: Parental Attributes, Conflict, and Support

Parental characteristics, interparental conflict, and parental support have been hypothesized and found to influence the development of child aggression in multiple ways (Shaw, Winslow, Owens, & Hood, 1998b). At an environmental level, parental maladjustment, interparental acrimony, and low social support within and outside the family may compromise parenting. In addition, these factors tend to co-occur and exacerbate one another, as parents who are impaired by psychopathology are more likely to model maladaptive problem-resolution strategies with their children and one another, engage in more verbal and physical aggression in resolving family disputes, and less actively use and seek social support from sources outside of the nuclear family. These vicious cycles further impairing their own well-being, compromise parents' ability to care for their children, and in the case of family violence, model and condone the use of aggression as a coping strategy. From a genetic perspective, maladaptive characteristics may be passed on to children, including such traits as impulsivity and low frustration tolerance. Among older children, conduct disorder and delinquency are associated with antisocial personality characteristics in both mothers and fathers (Robins, West, & Herjanic, 1975). This relationship has since been corroborated in three samples of young children. Keenan and Shaw (1994) found that familial criminality was related to boys' aggression at age two, after controlling for aggression at 18 months and maternal age—a result we have replicated in an independent and larger cohort of low-income boys (Shaw et al., 1998b). In a large sample of 17-month olds, Tremblay (1998) also found fathers' reports of antisocial behavior *before the birth of the child* to be related to infant aggression.

Parental mood disorders have also been examined as risk factors for early conduct problems. However, the majority of these studies have ascertained child disruptive behavior during preschool age or thereafter. When young children with disruptive behavior problems are compared to normal controls, mothers of children with externalizing problems report more depressive symptomatology, and these differences persist at follow-up (Campbell, 1994). Depressed parents have been found to be more passive and more critical, and less positive in responding to their children's needs, a tendency that would be expected to be exacerbated during the toddler period in the face of a more mobile, aggressive, and noncompliant child. In fact, in our own work, maternal depressive symptoms, assessed when children were 18 and 24 months old, were stronger discriminators of teachers' reports of clinically elevated conduct problems at age 8 than maternal perceptions of aggressive behavior at ages 2 to 5 or maternal depression at ages 5 or 5.5. These findings suggest that the quality of the *early* caregiving environment may play a special role in influencing the course of school-age children's disruptive behavior.

In addition to examining parental personality and adjustment, investigators have identified sources of stress and support within and outside the family system that are related to the occurrence of child behavior problems. Again, the majority of these studies begin at preschool age. Among preschoolers and school-age children, marital conflict has been found to be associated consistently with externalizing problems, particularly when conflicts involve disagreements over childrearing practices (Dadds & Powell, 1991). This finding has been corroborated repeatedly with very young children (Shaw et al., 1998b) beginning with assessments of marital satisfaction/conflict at ages one to two. In addition, quality of maternal social support outside the family has been positively related to responsive parenting, and negatively related to maternal depressive symptoms and child disruptive behavior in the first two years (Shaw et al., 1998b).

Parenting and the Family Socialization Process in Developmental Context

Parenting practices associated with child behavior problems vary with development; however, common themes persist across development that focus on parental involvement and engagement. For example, involvement is a construct that is equally valid in early childhood, middle childhood, and adolescence, taking different forms across these three developmental time periods (e.g., knowing where your children are out of the home in adolescence and monitoring children's whereabouts and his/her activities in the home during the terrible twos). In early childhood, initially the focus is on affective processes (i.e., attachment), with the advent of the terrible twos increasing the significance of behavior management practices.

Central to the emergence of early conduct problems are weak or disorganized family management practices, which can result in coercive parent–child interactions. As the child's aversive behaviors increase in intensity and frequency, the parent acquiesces, unwittingly reinforcing those behaviors (Shaw & Bell, 1993). As the child becomes increasingly irritating, the parent further escalates power assertion techniques. These cycles eventually lead to the child's open defiance or behavior problems that, in later development, include being away from home excessively, lying, stealing, and engaging in more serious behaviors such as fire-setting. Patterson, Capaldi, and Bank (1991) formalized the "early-starter model," one of two pathways by which children may emerge as chronically offending delinquent adolescents and antisocial adults. According to this model, families provide direct training in antisocial behavior for young children through their family management practices.

While the study of coercive interactions has yielded significant data about the onset of early conduct problems (Shaw et al., 1998a), there is a growing body of research showing the importance of early positive interactions between caregiver and child. For example, among three- to four-year-olds with conduct problems, Gardner (1987) showed that only 20 percent of the child's time was spent in conflict with parents. We would expect that the quality of positive interactions during the 80 percent of quieter time would have a preventive effect on early conduct problems. Consistent with this notion, Pettit and Bates (1989) found the amount of play and social contact in the first and second years to be associated with fewer conduct problems at age four.

While a predominately positive and responsive caregiver would be expected to influence the course of conduct problems during the first year, retaining a positive stance becomes a greater challenge in the second year. At this stage, parents need to minimize the toddler's exposure to forbidden and dangerous situations, which in turn prevents oppositional behavior and conflict. In the first year, contingent responsivity to the infant's bids for attention may suffice; however, greater anticipatory awareness is needed to minimize conflict with the mobile and emotionally labile toddler. Although normative increases in parent–child conflict would be expected during the "terrible twos," evidence suggests that proactive strategies to prevent aversive exchanges in the short term would improve child outcome in the long term. In particular, a mother's skills in scaffolding the child's activities predict improvements in conduct problems over time (Gardner, 1989).

By age three, mothers involved in coercive dyadic sequences, which are also marked by low levels of positive behavior and structuring of the child's environment, would be expected to be inconsistent and inflexible administrators of discipline. Mothers who initially persist in their requests for compliance may not be consistent in enforcing these demands as their children demonstrate that such efforts have little effect. They may resort to open hostility to gain submission from their children, sacrificing any semblance of a positive emotional bond. It is also reasoned that these children would be noncompliant, negative, and unenthusiastic toward their parents. The children might not trust their parents to adequately care for them or their needs. Even if some mothers are able to maintain a consistent firmness in dealing with their children, they are likely to meet greater resistance than with the average child, who would have more to lose by maintaining noncompliant behavior (i.e., loss of love). Furthermore, it is likely that these parents view their children as hostile, based on their original perceptions of the child and on the child's increasingly noncompliant behavior. The children, in turn, may come to interpret neutral or even friendly behavior as hostile. The mother's use of ineffectual disciplinary techniques fails to produce the desired outcome, reinforcing a fatalistic attitude, setting up a self-fulfilling prophecy: "He always was, and always will be, a bad child."

During the age period from 3.5 to 6 years, dyadic processes (including responsiveness and coercion) between parent and child become consolidated and extend to other family members. Coercive patterns of interaction (Patterson, 1982) become entrenched, where parents attempt to insist on certain behaviors, the child resists, conflict escalates, and the parent acquiesces, thereby reinforcing the child's problem behavior. Gardner's (1989) detailed home observational study found that this coercive pattern of reinforcement involving parental acquiescence was much more common in conduct-problem compared to nonproblem children, providing strong support for coercion theory during this developmental stage.

Other relevant normative changes during this period involve the child's increasing ability to function, both outside and inside the home, and to handle interpersonal and cognitive problems. Parents maintain the coercive intervention strategies used earlier, but now the conflict is more intense, with vacillation between ignoring rule violations and employing harsh or threatening punishments. At this stage, there is also continuity in the mother's image of her child as hostile, noncompliant, aggressive, and much more difficult to handle. At the same time, the child is applying the established pattern of aggression at home to the preschool setting, which results in complaints from teachers about the level of disruptive behavior. Equally important to the development of later antisocial behavior and deviant peer influence on substance use is that there is little internalization of parental and societal standards, even when compliance is secured. Rewards are infrequent and are used as a means of controlling behavior. All the at-risk child assimilates from infrequent conformity to authority is an extrinsic motivational system. The child performs when there is an authority figure nearby.

From follow-ups in the author's laboratory of children at risk for poor socioemotional outcomes, it is clear that coercive parent–child relationships measured in the toddler period are associated with child conflicts with peers and teachers at age six and trajectories of persistent conduct problems from ages two to eight, fueled by a child who tends to be fearless and a parent who tends to be rejecting and hostile. These results suggest that an intervention tailored to improve parenting in high-risk families at ages two to three may prove effective in preventing the problem behavior at school that is so predictive of adolescent delinquency.

Chronic Family Adversity

A number of investigators have noted that the accumulation of risk factors is related to several types of child problem behavior, including disruptive behavior problems (Sameroff, Seifer, Barocas, Zax, & Greenspan, 1987). Rutter, Cox, Tupling, Berger, & Yule (1975) were perhaps the first to suggest that the presence of multiple familial stressors may be a better predictor of child behavior problems than any specific factor alone. Consistent with this hypothesis, several investigators have found that the likelihood of behavior problems increases with the number of stressors present (Sameroff et al., 1987). In the past decade this hypothesis has been corroborated with young children (Sanson et al., 1991). In two studies of chronic family adversity assessed when children were between 1 and 2 years of age, consistent relations were found with later disruptive behavior problems between ages 2 to 3.5. Relations were more robust for externalizing versus internalizing problems. In addition, when groups were dichotomized based on clinical symptomatology, families with stressors present from four different domains had a 15 times greater probability of having clinically elevated scores than those with no stressors present. Stressor domains included maternal adjustment, family climate, parental aggressivity, and sociodemographic risk. The findings on chronic family adversity raise issues about the need to intervene with families at levels beyond the door of the therapist's office. It is also a reason the stability data are likely to be "inflated" in samples from impoverished backgrounds, because of the number and type of stressors facing such families. Preventionists and interventionists need to consider these nonpsychological factors that affect parenting ability, including social support within and outside the family, overcrowding in the home, neighborhood dangerousness, and family income.

Alternative Child Care

As more and more young children spend increasing amounts of time in day-care settings, it has become increasingly important to determine if the quality of such environments has short- or long-term impact on the development of aggressive behavior. Early studies were mixed in both the quality of the methods used and the results found. The most recent and by far the most comprehensive study of day-care effects (e.g., sample size of greater than 1,000 children) on early conduct problems found that more hours spent in any kind of nonmaternal child care from infancy to age 54 months was associated with higher ratings of externalizing problems, more so for ratings made by alternative caregivers and teachers than parents (NICHD Early Child Care Research Network, 2003). It should be noted that these effects, albeit statistically significant, tended to be of modest magnitude and did not predict trajectories of clinically meaningful problem behavior. Quality of early child care has also been found to discriminate conduct problems in a large sample of low-income children whose parents were in welfare-to-work programs (Votruba-Drzal, Coley, & Chase-Landsdale, 2004). Results indicated that many hours of day care in low-quality care were associated with higher conduct problems at school entry, whereas high-quality care served a protective function. Overall, hours spent in care and its quality have both been found to influence the course of conduct problems, and these effects are likely to be more pronounced in contexts of high risk.

Prevention and Intervention

While knowledge of the course and correlates of aggression in early childhood has increased dramatically over the past decade, relatively few psychosocial interventions that target this problem have yet to be evaluated empirically. After reviewing potential targets for preventive interventions, we review a few approaches that appear to show promise for preventing early-starting pathways.

First, early aggressive behavior must be considered within the interpersonal context in which it occurs. The research discussed above suggests that aggression in early childhood originates in and is maintained by multiple, interacting factors in the caregiving milieu, including characteristics of the child and his or her parents, as well as environmental pressures that impinge on the parent–child relationship. We assume that the reduction of child aggression requires identifying and addressing major etiological influences that are cooperating in a particular case. Hence, the focus of intervention must be broadened beyond the child to include factors such as the emotional quality of parent–child interactions, the ways in which parents respond to their child's misbehavior, and stressors that impair parents' ability to provide adequate care.

Second, aggression should be viewed from a developmental perspective. A developmental framework dictates that clinicians approach aggressive behavior in light of the salient issues of a given age period. For example, the establishment of an effective attachment relationship is a central goal of the first year of life. Aggressive behavior may be a result of an attachment relationship that is characterized by anger and frustration. Similarly, the development of autonomy is a primary task in year two, while the establishment of flexible self-regulation is a critical issue in the third year and beyond. Aggression may occur when factors within the child or family prevent the realization of these age-specific goals. It is critical that the timing and content of treatment be attuned to the developmental status of the child.

The centrality of family in general and parenting in particular suggests that interventions that focus on the family would be effective in preventing the

early-starting pathway, particularly those that account for individual differences in child attributes and other risk factors that compromise caregiving quality. The last three decades have seen an increase in the number of
family-based interventions developed for working with children and adolescents with conduct-related problems (e.g., Dishion & Kavanagh, 2003).

Prime examples of these efforts with young children are the work of
Olds (2002) and Webster-Stratton and Hammond (1997). The Olds model
engages mothers during pregnancy and immediately following the delivery
of their infants, to promote maternal health and quality of the infant–parent
relationship. Working with three samples in different regions of the United
States, Olds and colleagues have documented consistent improvements in
children's antisocial behavior extending from preschool through adolescence as a result of the home-visitation program.

Work by Webster-Stratton and colleagues focuses on parent management strategies with preschoolers and young school-age children and
has also been associated with substantial improvements in antisocial outcomes. A central focus in parent management training is helping caregivers to avoid the development of coercive interactions, wherein parent and
child each employ increasingly aversive behaviors in an attempt to control
the outcome of discipline encounters. In service of this goal, parents learn
to observe their child's behavior in an objective, unemotional manner and
to implement appropriate consequences in response to aggression.

Despite the empirical validation of these programs for infants and
preschoolers, respectively, the development of family-centered intervention programs specifically designed to meet the needs of parents with
toddlers has been lacking. Recently, we sought to fill this void by adapting Dishion's Family Check Up for toddlers (Shaw, Dishion, Supplee,
Gardner, & Arnds, in press). The Family Check Up (see Dishion &
Kavanagh, 2003) is a brief intervention designed to motivate parents
to promote more consistent parent management practices and increase
their engagement and involvement in caregiving. In addition to emphasizing behaviorally oriented behavioral management issues for parents
with toddler-age children, the Family Check Up addresses a recurring
problem of many family-centered interventions: parents' motivation
to change. Initially developed by Miller and colleagues to meet the
demands of problem drinkers (Miller & Rollnick, 2002), motivational
interviewing is used to provide families with actuarial-based data on the
likely course of problem behavior should change not occur. If change is
desired, families are then offered a flexible menu of change strategies to
achieve the desired reductions in problem behavior. Dishion successfully
adapted principles of the check up for families with adolescents before
applying it to families meeting the challenges of the terrible twos. Our

initial findings using the Family Check Up with toddlers show promise. Using 120 male toddlers at extreme risk for early-starting pathways based on the presence of sociodemographic, family, and child risk factors, those families randomly assigned to the Family Check Up showed reductions in destructive and aggressive behavior at ages three and four, and increased parental involvement with their child from ages two to four. We are currently attempting to validate these findings with a sample of 720 boys *and* girls from urban, rural, and suburban areas of the United States, the results of which should be forthcoming in the next few years.

SUMMARY

This chapter has described the current state of knowledge on the development of aggression and its prevention in early childhood. Despite cognitive limitations in fully understanding aggression and the high frequency of the behavior, aggressive behavior in early childhood shows comparable stability and similar correlates to aggressive behavior at older age periods during childhood. These findings suggest that prevention and intervention efforts should be directed at similar targets as they are for older children, with special attention to parent–child relationships and factors that compromise the quality of the caregiving environment. Preventive interventions that are targeted to address developmental transition points are recommended to capitalize on parental anxieties in handling the demands of a rapidly changing child. Examples include Olds's work during infancy and our ongoing work addressing the challenges of the terrible twos.

REFERENCES

Ausubel, D. P. *Theory and problems of child development.* New York: Grune and Stratton.

Belsky, J., Hsieh, K., & Crnic, K. (1998). Mothering, fathering, and infant negativity as antecedents of boys' externalizing problems and inhibition at age 3 years: Differential susceptibility to rearing experience? *Development and Psychopathology, 10,* 301–320.

Block, J. H. (1978). Another look at sex differentiation in the socialization behavior of mothers and fathers. In J. Sherman & F. L. Denmark (Eds.), *The psychology of women: Future directions of research* (pp. 29–87). New York: Psychological Dimensions.

Bronson, W.C. (1975). Developments in behavior with age mades during the second year of life. In M. Lewis & L. A. Rusenblum (Eds.), *The origins of behavior: Friendship and peer relations.* New York: Wiley.

Calkins, S. (1994). Origins and outcomes of individual differences in emotion regulation. In N. A. Fox (Ed.), *The development of emotion regulation: Biological and behavioral considerations. Monographs of the Society for Research in Child Development* (pp. 53–72). Chicago: University of Chicago Press.

Campbell, S. B. (1994). Hard-to-manage preschool boys: Externalizing behavior, social competence, and family context at two-year-follow-up. *Journal of Abnormal Child Psychology, 22,* 147–166.

Campbell, S. B., Pierce, E. W., Moore, G., Marakovitz, S., & Newby, K. (1996). Boys' externalizing problems at elementary school: Pathways from early behavior problems, maternal control, and family stress. *Development and Psychopathology, 8,* 701–720.

Cummings, E. M., Iannotti, R. J., & Zahn-Waxler, C. (1989). Aggression between peers in early childhood: Individual continuity and developmental change. *Child Development, 72,* 887–895.

Dadds, M. R., & Powell, M. B. (1991). The relationship of interparental conflict and global marital adjustment to aggression and immaturity in aggressive and nonclinic children. *Journal of Abnormal Child Psychology, 19,* 553–567.

Dishion, T. J., & Kavanagh, K. (2003). *Intervening in adolescent problem behavior: A family-centered approach.* New York: Guilford Press.

Dodge, K. A., & Frame, C. M. (1982). Social cognitive biases and deficits in aggressive boys. *Child Development, 53,* 620–635.

Dunn, J., & Kendrick, C. (1982). *Siblings: Love, envy, and understanding.* Cambridge, MA: Harvard University Press.

Gardner, F. E. M. (1987). Positive interaction between mothers and conduct-problem children: Is there training for harmony as well as fighting? *Journal of Abnormal Child Psychology, 15,* 283–293.

Gardner, F. E. M. (1989). Inconsistent parenting: Is there evidence for a link with children's conduct problems? *Journal of Abnormal Child Psychology, 17,* 223–233.

Gold, D., Crombie, G., & Noble, S. (1987). Relations between teachers' judgments of girls' and boys' compliance and intellectual competence. *Sex Roles, 16,* 351–358.

Goodenough, F. L. (1931). *Anger in young children.* Minneapolis: University of Minnesota Press.

Hay, D. F., Zahn-Waxler, C., Cummings, E. M., & Iannotti, R. J. (1992). Young children's views about conflict with peers: A comparison of the daughters and sons of depressed and well women. *Journal of Child Psychology and Psychiatry, 33,* 669–683.

Huttenlocher, J., Haight, W., Bryk, A., Seltzer, M., & Lyons, T. (1991). Early vocabulary growth: Relation to language input and gender. *Developmental Psychology, 27,* 236–248.

Jersild, A. T., & Markey, F. V. (1935). Conflicts between preschool children. *Child Development, 21,* 170–181.

Keenan, K., & Shaw, D. S. (1994). The development of aggression in toddlers: A study of low-income families. *Journal of Abnormal Child Psychology, 22,* 53–77.

Keenan, K., & Shaw, D. S. (1997). Developmental influences on young girls' behavioral and emotional problems. *Psychological Bulletin, 121,* 95–113.

Kuczynski, L., & Kochanska, G. (1990). Development of children's noncompliance strategies from toddlerhood to age 5. *Developmental Psychology, 26,* 398–408.

Maccoby, E. E. (1980). *Social development.* New York: Harcourt Brace.

Martin, J. (1981). A longitudinal study of the consequences of early mother-infant interaction: A microanalytic approach. *Monographs of the Society for Research in Child Development, 46,* Serial Number 190.

Miller, W. R., & Rollnick, S. (2002). *Motivational interviewing: Preparing people for change* (2nd ed.). New York: Guilford.

NICHD Early Child Care Research Network (2003). Does the amount of time spent in child care predict socioemotional adjustment during the transition to kindergarten? *Child Development, 74,* 976–1005.

NICHD Early Child Care Research Network (2004). Trajectories of physical aggression from toddlerhood to middle childhood: Predictors, correlates, and outcomes. *Monographs of the Society for Research in Child Development, 69,* Serial Number 278.

Offord, D. R., Boyle, M. H., & Racine, Y. A. (1991). The epidemiology of antisocial behavior in childhood and adolescence. In D. J. Pepler & K. H. Rubin (Eds.), *The development and treatment of childhood aggression* (pp. 31–54). Hillsdale, NJ: Lawrence Erlbaum Associates.

Olds, D. (2002). Prenatal and infancy home visiting by nurses: From randomized trials to community replication. *Prevention Science, 3,* 153–172.

Patterson, G. (1982). *Coercive family processes* (Vol. 3). Eugene, OR: Castalia.

Patterson, G. R., Capaldi, D. M., & Bank, L. (1991). An early starter model for predicting delinquency. In D. Pepler & R. K. Rubin (Eds.), *The development and treatment of childhood aggression.* Hillsdale, NJ: Erlbaum.

Pettit, G., & Bates, J. (1989). Family interaction patterns and children's behavior problems from infancy to 4 years. *Developmental Psychology, 25,* 413–420.

Richman, M., Stevenson, J., & Graham, P. J. (1982). *Preschool to school: A behavioral study* . London: Academic Press.

Robins, L., West, P., & Herjanic, B. (1975). Arrests and delinquency in two generations: A study of black urban families and their children. *Journal of Child Psychology and Psychiatry, 16,* 125–140.

Rose, S. L., Rose, S. A., & Feldman, J. F. (1989). Stability of behavior problems in very young children. *Development and Psychopathology, 1,* 5–19.

Ross, H., Tesla, C., Kenyon, B., & Lollis, S. (1990). Maternal intervention in toddler peer conflict: The socialization of principles of justice. *Developmental Psychology, 26,* 994–1003.

Rutter, M., Cox, A., Tupling, C., Berger, M., & Yule, W. (1975). Attainment and adjustment in two geographical areas: 1. The prevalence of psychiatric disorder. *British Journal of Psychiatry, 126,* 493–509.

Sameroff, A.J., Seifer, R., Barocas, R., Zax, M., & Greenspan, S. (1987). IQ scores of 4-year-old children: Social-environmental risk factors. *Pediatrics, 79,* 343–350.

Sanson, A., Oberklaid, F., Pedlow, R., & Prior, M. (1991). Risk indicators: Assessment of infancy predictors of pre-school behavioural maladjustment. *Journal of Child Psychology and Psychiatry, 32,* 609–626.

Shaw, D.S., & Bell, R.Q. (1993). Developmental theories of parental contributors to antisocial behavior. *Journal of Abnormal Child Psychology, 21,* 493–518.

Shaw, D.S., Dishion, T.J., Supplee, L., Gardner, F., & Arnds, K. (in press). A family-centered approach to the prevention of early-onset antisocial behavior: Two-year effects of the family check-up in early childhood. *Journal of Consulting and Clinical Psychology.*

Shaw, D.S., Gilliom, M., Ingoldsby, E.M., & Nagin, D (2003). Trajectories leading to school-age conduct problems. *Developmental Psychology, 39,* 189–200.

Shaw, D.S., Winslow, E.B., Owens, E.B., & Hood, N. (1998b). Young children's adjustment to chronic family adversity: A longitudinal study of low-income families. *Journal of the American Academy of Child and Adolescent Psychiatry, 37,* 545–553.

Shaw, D.S., Winslow, E.B., Owens, E.B., Vondra, J.I., Cohn, J.F., & Bell, R.Q. (1998a). The development of early externalizing problems among children from low-income families: A transformational perspective. *Journal of Abnormal Child Psychology, 26,* 95–107.

Tremblay, R. (1998). On the origins of physical aggression. Presented at the meeting of the Life History Society, Seattle, WA.

Votruba-Drzal, E., Coley, R.L., & Chase-Landsdale, P.L. (2004). Child care and low-income children's development: Direct and moderated effects. *Child Development, 75,* 296–312.

Webster-Stratton, C., & Hammond, M. (1997). Treating children with early-onset conduct problems: A comparison of child and parent training interventions. *Journal of Consulting and Clinical Psychology, 65,* 93–109.

Zahn-Waxler, C., Iannotti, R.J., Cummings, E.M., & Denham, S. (1990). antecedents of problem behaviors in children of depressed mothers. *Development and Psychopathology, 2,* 271–292.

Chapter 9

CHILD ABUSE AND NEGLECT: CONSEQUENCES OF PHYSICAL, SEXUAL, AND EMOTIONAL ABUSE OF CHILDREN

Ellen E. Whipple

Parenting is one of the most profound responsibilities a person will ever assume, yet becoming a parent requires no education, training, or other requirements that might help prepare one for the challenging road ahead. In an increasingly mobile and diverse American society, children are frequently raised geographically distant from extended families, and new parents are often left alone to grapple with how to handle innumerable daily interactions with their children; an integral part of the socialization process (Baumrind, 1973). From 1970 to 1996, the percentage of children under age 18 living with two parents decreased steadily from 85 percent to 68 percent, stabilizing at 68 percent during the 1990s through 2003. In 2003, 36 percent of black children were living with two parents, compared to 77 percent of non-Hispanic white children and 65 percent of Hispanic children. In 2002, 82 percent of Asian and Pacific Islander children lived in two-parent families. Since 1995, the percentage of births to unmarried women in the United States has declined slightly among black women while continuing to climb among Hispanics and non-Hispanic whites. Women who give birth outside of marriage, and their children, tend to be more disadvantaged than their married counterparts. Unmarried mothers generally have lower incomes, lower education levels, and greater dependence on welfare assistance than married mothers. Children born to unmarried mothers are more likely to grow up in a single-parent household, experience instability in living arrangements, live in poverty, and display socioemotional problems.

The relationship between parental stress and child maltreatment is well documented. Stressors that often place families at higher risk for physical child abuse include early motherhood, high geographic mobility, large family size, poverty, and ethnic minority group status, although the role of ethnicity is complex (Earls, McGuire, & Shay, 1994). Poverty, and its associated correlates of single parenthood, low education levels, and unemployment, has repeatedly been found to negatively impact childrearing. According to the third National Incidence Study of child abuse and neglect (NIS-3), rates of child maltreatment have climbed steadily, from 9.8 per 1,000 children in 1980, to 14.8 in 1986 and 23.1 in 1993 (Sedlak & Broadhurst, 1996). There were 1.8 million substantiated Child Protective Service (CPS) reports across the United States during 2002. More than 60 percent of child victims experienced neglect; almost 20 percent were physically abused; 10 percent were sexually abused; and 7 percent were emotionally maltreated. Children aged birth to three years had the highest rates of victimization at 16 percent per 1,000 children. Three-quarters (76 percent) of children who died due to abuse or neglect were younger than four years old. More than 80 percent of perpetrators were parents; other relatives accounted for 7 percent; and unmarried partners of parents accounted for 3 percent of the perpetrators. This chapter focuses on infants to five year old children and their families who are at heightened risk for physical child abuse and provides a framework for assessment and treatment approaches that aim to prevent discipline interactions from "crossing the line."

THE PHYSICAL DISCIPLINE–PHYSICAL CHILD ABUSE CONTINUUM

Despite decades of research, in tandem with heightened public awareness about physical child abuse (and other types of aggression), there are no national or scientific standards for what constitutes acceptable levels of physical discipline in the United States. One of the most frequently used strategies to discipline a child, especially a younger child, is spanking. Research suggests that about 90 percent of parents in the United States report having spanked their children. In 2000, 79 percent of men and 71 percent of women agreed that spanking a child is sometimes necessary. Adults who are college graduates are less likely than adults without a high school diploma to say that spanking is sometimes necessary. For both men and women, black adults are more likely than both white and Hispanic adults to sanction spanking. This summary builds on previous work in which an empirical link between corporal punishment and physical child abuse was established. Physically abusive mothers were found to spank their children significantly more than nonabusive mothers, which accounted for a significant portion of the variance in a predictive model (Whipple & Webster-Stratton, 1991). A current critical question for practitioners working with parents of very young children is: "What constitutes *crossing the line* from physical discipline to abuse in parent–child discipline interactions?" Clarifying this line is important because physical abuse so often occurs within the context of a discipline episode. It is most likely that when physical discipline or corporal punishment fails to reduce a child's misdeed, punishment is increased over long periods of time, ultimately resulting in child abuse (Carey, 1994). That is, less competent parents who use spanking ineffectively may become more frequent spankers. Thus, clarifying frequencies of mild, moderate, and high corporal punishment must be a central focus for guiding policy and practice (Larzelere, 1986).

Physical abuse has been defined as "cruelty to children," with allegations of a specific individual "knowingly and willfully inflicting unnecessarily severe corporal punishment or physical suffering upon the child" (Widom, 1989). Physical child abuse includes forms of parental behaviors that Straus and Gelles (1990) term "very severe violence" (e.g., kicking, biting, hitting, beating up; burning or scalding; threatening to or actually using a knife or gun). They further state that child abuse is the point at which all societies and groups draw a line (often legally), and includes such visible injuries as bruises, cuts, burns, or broken bones. *Corporal punishment* has been defined by Straus and Gelles (1990) as "a legally permissible violent act carried out as part of the parenting role," and includes parental "severe violence" such as hitting with an object (paddling). They employ the category "minor violence" to describe such parental behaviors as throwing something, grabbing or shoving, and slapping or spanking. While *physical discipline* may be viewed as a positive aspect of parenting that provides children with the necessary structure for growth, corporal punishment involves inflicting pain partly for retribution and teaches a child that those in power can force others to obey (Greven, 1990). In the long run the degrading aspects of corporal punishment may be more likely to cause resentment and a desire to defy the parent and others.

KEY COMPONENTS FOR EARLY IDENTIFICATION OF PHYSICAL CHILD ABUSE

Comprehensive assessment of physical child abuse involves distinguishing it from corporal punishment and physical discipline. Parents who physically abuse routinely employ harsh, unreasonable discipline inappropriate to the child's age or transgression (Wolfe, 1991). Taking a behavioral discipline history should be a part of assessment of all families with young children. Other factors associated with abuse include high levels of parental stress, especially when combined with difficult child behavior or temperament (Mash, Johnston, & Kovitz, 1983). Higher rates of severely violent behavior often characterize families where alcoholism is combined with antisocial personality disorder and/or recurrent parental depression (Bland & Orn, 1986; Whipple, Fitzgerald, & Zucker, 1995). One community-based sample of 595 mothers of newborns identified as at risk for child maltreatment found that severe child physical assault was significantly associated with maternal depression and partner violence in particular (Windam, Rosenberg, Fuddy, McFarlane, Sia, & Duggan, 2004). Since stress and depression can further reduce a parent's tolerance for child misbehavior, abusive families often get caught in a viscous circle of child maladaptive responses and negative parental reactions (Patterson, 1986).

In an effort to elucidate factors associated with corporal punishment and physical discipline, studies examining punitive child-rearing practices were reviewed. Since few studies distinguish between these two constructs they are combined here and referred to as physical punishment. Four primary factors are associated with parental use of physical punishment: intergenerational history of aggressive parenting styles, personality factors, religiosity, and cultural acceptance, and should be part of a comprehensive assessment. Of these, the intergenerational transmission of aggression has received the most attention. The Environmental Risk Longitudinal Twin Study with a nationally representative 1994–1995 birth cohort of 565 twin pairs suggest that children's difficult and coercive behavior provokes harsh discipline from adults (Jaffee et al., 2004). Using a genetically sensitive design, the authors found that environmental factors accounted for most of the variation in corporal punishment and physical child abuse. Corporal punishment, however, was genetically mediated in part, and these factors were largely the same as those that influenced children's antisocial behavior, suggesting a child effect. Additionally, Jaffee, Caspi, Moffitt and Taylor (2004) found that physical abuse played a major causal role in the development of children's antisocial behavior and that preventing maltreatment can prevent its violent sequelae.

Personality characteristics associated with punitive child-rearing practices include a strong belief by parents in authoritarian means of control and in physical punishment as a means to correct perceived child misconduct. These parents also tend to view their children's transgressions as more wrong and use more power assertion and fewer reasoning techniques. One cross-sectional survey of 204 mothers recruited from pediatric practices found that belief rather than impulse largely explained spanking of young children. The parenting styles of mothers with higher abuse potential have been characterized by rejection, negativity, and punitiveness in situations of higher stress. Parental reliance on physical punishment also appears to have deep roots in religiosity (Carey, 1994; Greven, 1990). Parents with religious denominations subscribing to a literal belief in the Bible (e.g., the Bible, being from God, cannot be wrong) have been found to value the use of corporal punishment more than those with nonliteral views (Wiehe, 1990).

Understanding the connection between cultural sanctioning of physical punishment and incidence of child abuse poses one of the greatest challenges. Straus and Gelles (1990) contend that the difference between violence and abuse is a matter of societal norms. Still, within most societies, parameters exist that distinguish between acceptable and unacceptable forms of adult physical aggression toward children. Cultural analyses of this question have identified two parameters. The first examines *legal sanctions* that spell out what is or is not socially acceptable. For example, the prohibition of physical punishment in Sweden has decreased the tolerance for and incidence of physical abuse, as well as helped guide the movement against spanking in other Scandinavian countries and Austria (Straus, 1994). The second parameter considers parents' rationalizations of abusive behavior based on *culturally sanctioned* childrearing practices: an area in great need of further research. Ortega (2001) found that mothers with high cultural connection were less aggressive parents and felt more responsible for their child's behavior. Similarly, Ferrari (2002) found that fathers who held familism in low regard were more likely to use physical punishment to discipline their children, controlling for ethnicity in a study of 150 ethnically diverse American families.

Table 9.1 provides a summary of factors to consider in assessment of at-risk families. Physical child abuse may be at the extreme and unfortunate end of a complex continuum of behaviors including spanking, which are forms of physical discipline and corporal punishment. Consequently, there appears to be a pressing need for those who work with young children to uniformly gather behavioral frequencies of parental spanking and other discipline-related acts, and to better understand how and when escalation into abuse occurs (Graziano, 1994). Barber (1992) proposes limiting the time frame for assessing parental responses to the previous 24-hours, in order to increase the reliability of self-reporting frequently occurring and/or socially embarrassing behaviors. Greater attention also needs to focus on contextual factors surrounding physical punishment (e.g., with or without positive communication), which may be just as important as how often it is employed. For example, Larzelere (1986) found that the context in which punishment occurs can negate the influence of "teaching" a child to use violence as a means of problem solving. Darling and Steinberg (1993) propose that physical discipline administered in a supportive, reasonable context is likely to have different developmental outcomes than interactions that stem from unpredictable outbursts. Similarly, Grusec and Goodnow (1994) maintain that the effects of discipline will

Table 9.1
Factors to Consider in Assessment of Families at Risk of Physical Child Abuse

---

Risk factors to assess:
  Parental stress, depression, anxiety, and other mental disorders
  Child temperament, difficult child behavior, and child mental disorders
Psychosocial stressors:
  Young parenthood, high geographic mobility, large family size, ethnic
  minority group status
Poverty:
  Low income, low educational level, unemployment or under-employment
  Intergenerational history of child abuse or neglect
  Parental belief in authoritarian means of control
  Parental perceptions of children's transgressions as seriously wrong
  Parental sanctioning of the use of physical punishment
  High religiosity, especially a literal interpretation of the Bible
Other factors to assess:
  Gather behavioral frequencies of parental spanking and other discipline-related acts
  Differentiate physical discipline, corporal punishment, and physical child abuse
  Nature of the child's misbehavior
  Parent's knowledge of normal child developmental stages
  Contextual factors surrounding the discipline episode (e.g., positive communication)
  Child's interpretation of the events surrounding the discipline episode
  Child's chronological and developmental age
  Sequence of parent–child physical discipline interactions
  Whether parents tried alternative discipline strategies first

---

vary depending on the child's interpretation and evaluation of particular methods, the quality of the parent–child relationship, and parental goals.

Areas for Further Attention

Consequences of physical punishment must be considered developmentally, as the impact may differ based on tasks the child was negotiating, and on the child's level of internalization (Grusec & Goodnow, 1994). As children get older, they may be better able to understand the parent's intention, recognize departures from the parent's usual style, and interpret parental affective cues that indicate the significance of a child's misbehavior. *Very young children, especially preverbal, have few mechanisms available to them to understand parental aggression.* Thus, additional attention is needed to more specifically assess relationships between child age and parental competence, especially differential rates of physical punishment, subsequent developmental trajectories, and child outcomes. Another area in need of greater understanding surrounds the sequential aspects of parent–child discipline interactions. For example, future inquiries could address the nature of the misbehavior and whether the parent tried alternative discipline strategies first. Grusec and Goodnow (1994) encourage parents to be flexible in their disciplinary actions, matching their action to the child's perceptions of and cognitive and emotional reactions to the conflict situation. Practitioners working with at-risk families need more specific guidelines, which go beyond the overly legalized definitions of visible injuries to children, as to what constitutes *crossing the line* from discipline to abuse. Earlier detection and monitoring of excessively high rates of parental spanking could help reach unsubstantiated abuse cases among families who are reluctant to seek services. Gracia (1995) suggests that it is in cases where abuse is "not serious enough" to be reported that early interventions (which are less punitive, intrusive, and stigmatizing) are more likely to succeed.

THE RECIPROCAL INTERPLAY OF CHILD ABUSE AND MENTAL HEALTH

The long-term socioemotional consequences of a physically abusive childhood are profound, including lower peer status among child victims; later development of aggressive and violent behavior; interpersonal, academic, and vocational difficulties over the life span; psychopathology, such as posttraumatic stress disorder, depression, and alcoholism; and the intergenerational transmission of impaired parenting. One especially well-controlled study found that physical abuse during childhood was a risk factor for later aggressive behavior even when controlling for ecological and biological factors (Dodge, Bates, & Pettit, 1990). More recently, Zeanah, Scheeringa, Boris, Heller, Smyke, and Trapani (2004) found that both types of Reactive Attachment Disorder (RAD) could be reliably identified in maltreated toddlers. According to the *Diagnostic and Statistical Manual of Mental Disorders, Fourth Edition* (DSM-IV), in inhibited RAD, the child does not initiate and respond to social interactions in a developmentally appropriate manner. It is a disorder of nonattachment and is related to the loss of the primary attachment figure and the lack of opportunity for the infant to establish a new attachment with a primary caregiver. In disinhibited RAD, the child participates in diffuse attachments, indiscriminate sociability, and excessive familiarity with strangers. The child has repeatedly lost attachment figures or has had multiple caregivers and has never had the chance to develop a continuous and consistent attachment to at least one caregiver. Zeanah, et al. (2004) found both types of RAD were identified in children with and without an attachment figure. Within this maltreated group, toddlers whose mothers had a history of psychiatric disturbance were more likely to be diagnosed with attachment disorders.

The authors suggest that the prevalence of RAD among children who have a history of maltreatment appears to be increased substantially. Indeed, the continuity of attachment relationships into adulthood is well established (Siegel, 1999).

It is important to recognize the psychiatric co-morbidity in parents and children involved in maltreatment. DeBellis et al, (2001) examined lifetime incidence of mental disorders in caregivers involved in child maltreatment. Mothers of maltreated children exhibited a significantly greater lifetime incidence of anxiety disorders (especially post-traumatic stress disorder), mood disorders, alcohol and/or substance use or dependence disorder, suicide attempts, and co-morbidity of two or more psychiatric disorders when compared to similar nonmaltreating families. The majority of maltreated children and adolescents reported anxiety disorders, especially PTSD (from witnessing domestic violence and/or sexual abuse), mood disorders, suicidal ideation and attempts, and disruptive disorders. Childhood maltreatment and parental drug problems are two distinct conditions that co-occur about 30 percent of the time. Further, when they co-exist, greater problems characterized by global parental dysfunction are likely, and are more strongly related for men (Locke & Newcomb, 2003). Substance abuse has been identified as one of the strongest predictors of physical neglect (Cash & Wilke, 2003; Ondersma, 2002). Cocaine-using mothers have been found to have symptoms of PTSD, experience or witness community violence, and use negative discipline with their children (Eiden, Peterson, & Coleman, 1999). While domestic violence and child abuse are known to be highly correlated, their relationship is complex. One study found high levels of abuse and associated trauma disorders in both children and their mothers, and affected mothers were less likely to seek mental health services for their children (Chemtob & Carlson, 2004). Mental health problems, especially the possible presence of a personality disorder in the maltreating caregiver, are largely ignored, resulting in the provision of inappropriate and/or inadequate intervention programs for the family as a whole. It is essential that clinicians working with maltreating families consider the likelihood of a mental disorder and be certain that both parents and children receive appropriate treatment, such as therapy or medication. The current under-funding of mental health centers and psychiatric facilities is a critical issue in today's era of managed care and cost containment.

DiLauro (2004) found that physical neglect and physical abuse were associated with very different stressors that affect family functioning and that risk factors must be more accurately detected, such that successful treatment plans can be designed. External stressors related to socioeconomic and environmental factors were more associated with neglect. Stressors due to interpersonal issues, such as deficits in a parent's ability to interact with others and form viable relationships, were more associated with physical child abuse. DiLauro suggests that interventions for physical abusers should be designed to challenge faulty thinking and develop more appropriate coping mechanisms when conflicts arise. Mastering techniques to minimize the behavioral fight or flight response was also deemed as critical. Parents who both physically abuse and neglect seem to have the most trouble coping with their children's behavior, implicating the need for interventions to focus on the parent–child relationship in order to better understand the triggers that cause the parent to react. Also important for the practitioner to consider is the importance of working intensively with the child to address behavior problems. An emphasis on creating a new dialogue between parent and child should be a focus in family sessions so that productive communication can emerge.

Early Intervention in an Ecological Context

The ecological model was chosen to provide an intervention framework as it provides a way to view families from multiple dimensions, and not solely on one aspect of an individual, to explain or predict outcomes (Cash & Wilke, 2003). The ecological model was developed by Uri Brofennbrenner and elaborated on by James Garbarino to conceptualize child maltreatment as a social-psychological phenomena that is multiply determined by forces across numerous dimensions. The first level, the individual (ontogenic development), includes the individual mother, father, and child. Second is the family (microsystem), which includes the parenting dyad and the nuclear and extended family. The community (exosystem) considers social supports, neighborhoods, and other factors related to the context in which the family lives. Finally, the culture (macrosystem) addresses not only ethnicity, but social structure, such as policies, and societal standards. A major assumption underlying the ecological model of child maltreatment is that the causes and consequences are multilayered, much like a set of Russian nesting dolls. In search of the "truth" of a child's lived experience, clinicians must consider the layers of personal history, family, community, and culture (Steele, 2004). Recognizing the wide array of treatment approaches to address physical child abuse of very young children, those presented here have strong empirical support, although this is not intended as an inclusive summary of all interventions. Additional model programs are presented later in the text.

INDIVIDUAL PARENTS AND CHILDREN (ONTOGENIC DEVELOPMENT): PARENTAL ATTRIBUTIONS AND REGULATIVE COMMUNICATION

Parenting involves frequent attempts to regulate children's behavior. According to one model of physical child abuse, Milner (1993) analyzes relationships among three sets of variables: parent/family factors (e.g., parental education, child age, family structure); information-processing factors (e.g., parental attributions for child misbehavior, dysfunctional childrearing beliefs); and parental regulative communication. Others focus more specifically on the critical role of regulative communication in physical child abuse (Wilson, Whipple, & Grau, 1996; Wilson, Cameron, & Whipple, 1997), recognizing the interactional components. Parents do not strike their children at random moments, but rather at recognizable moments that unfold as part of larger conversations. Most research on regulative communication by physically abusive parents is grounded in Hoffman's (1980) distinction between power-assertive and inductive discipline. Power-assertion provides the child no rationale for altering his or her behavior other than to avoid punishment. Broadly defined, induction includes any message that provides explanations for requiring behavior change. Reasons can appeal to the child's pride, mastery strivings, or concern for others. Especially important for promoting internalization is "other-oriented induction," which highlights implications of the child's behavior for other people.

Physically abusive and nonabusive parents differ in their attempts to regulate perceived child misbehavior (Wilson & Whipple, 2001). Physically abusive parents issue more requests and commands during conversations with their children. Physically abusive parents also use: a larger percentage of requests and commands without any explanation when responding to perceived child misbehavior; more power-assertive strategies and fewer inductive strategies, both before and after encountering child resistance; and more intense or severe forms of physical discipline, such as slapping or hitting a child (Trickett & Kuczynski, 1986). Physically abusive parents display more noncontingent responses than nonabusive parents when attempting to regulate children's behavior. Abusive parents are more likely to continue seeking a child's compliance even after the child has complied, and to scold as opposed to praise a child immediately after the child complies. Finally, physically abusive parents are less successful than nonabusive parents at gaining their child's compliance.

In light of such findings, programs designed to prevent or treat physical child abuse should include curriculum on parental regulative communication. In an effort to organize parental cognitions associated with physical child abuse, a four-stage social information-processing model delineates how abusive parents may display greater biases and errors than nonabusive parents (Milner, 1993; 2003). The model assumes that abusive parents possess pre-existing schema that bias their perceptions, interpretations, and responses to children's behavior. At Stage 1 (Perception), physically abusive parents are believed to be less attentive to and aware of child-related behavior. At Stage 2 (Interpretation and Evaluation), physically abusive, relative to nonabusive, parents are assumed to make less charitable interpretations and judgments about their child's behavior. Abusive parents also view themselves as less responsible for unpleasant interactions with their children and give their children less credit for pleasant interactions. At Stage 3 (Information Integration and Response Selection), abusive parents may fail to adequately integrate information and are thought to possess less complex plans for regulating child misbehavior. At Stage 4 (Response, Implementation, and Monitoring), abusive parents are thought to be less skilled at implementing, monitoring, and modifying responses.

Although Milner's (1993) social information-processing model focuses on parental cognitions associated with physical child abuse, the model assumes that child, family, community, and cultural-level factors influence abusive parents' cognitions, and hence their behavior during regulative episodes with children. Factors such as young parental age, limited education, single parenthood, or unemployment may be associated with pre-existing schema (i.e., dysfunctional childrearing beliefs) that bias attributions and responses to perceived child misbehavior. These parents may be less able to "connect the dots," as they are often concrete thinkers who may not think systemically. Community-level factors, such as inadequate housing and neighborhoods, also may increase levels of parenting stress and depression, which predisposes parents to shift toward automatic thoughts as opposed to more careful processing at each stage of the model. Greater automatic processing, in turn, increases the influence of pre-existing schema as parents engage in harsher judgments about their child's behavior.

Practice Implications

One successful implementation of this cognitive model was via a parent education and support program, the Family Growth Center (described in greater detail in the following section). Wilson and Whipple (2001) evaluated parental attributions and regulative communication of 30 parents of preschoolers in a community-based program. Participants described aloud what they would say or do in response to three hypothetical scenarios in which one of their children had misbehaved, and later made attributions for each misbehavior. Three classes of variables were assessed (information-processing; sociodemographic; indices of parental regulative communication) and Milner's social information-processing model was used to organize and justify predictions about relations among the variables. Findings revealed that parents with less education and from lower-income backgrounds were more likely to endorse dysfunctional beliefs, such as inappropriate developmental expectations for children, and had a strong belief in the necessity of physical punishment. Parents who endorsed such beliefs blamed the child more for misbehaving. On encountering child resistance, these parents were less likely to use inductive strategies in their responses to the scenarios or to vary their regulative strategies depending on how the child had misbehaved. Parents with higher levels of depression were more likely to perceive that specific misbehaviors reflected how their child behaved in general; these parents were also more likely to attribute the same level of knowledge to their child regardless of how the child had misbehaved. Further, as depression increased, parents were less likely to include inductive strategies in their regulative messages or to vary their regulative strategies across different types of child misbehavior, both before and after encountering child resistance (Wilson & Whipple, 2001).

Parents, Children, and the Family System (the Microsystem): Education and Support

Parent education and support programs are one of the most effective methods of reaching at-risk families. Three primary goals of most programs are to help parents achieve more harmonious relations with their children, to teach parents how to cope more effectively with their children's misdeeds, and to assist parents in modifying a child's behaviors as they deem appropriate. Current questions center around better understanding "what works for whom" across types of abuse and neglect, "dosage" (how much service is needed), how to effectively target programs based on age of the children and characteristics of the parents, the merits of home visiting versus center-based programs, level and type of training needed to effectively deliver program content (i.e., paraprofessionals versus professionals), and the role of the parent-worker relationship in program effectiveness. The National Research Council (1993) found that parent education programs represented the majority of existing prevention efforts, especially those targeting parental practices in families with young children. Specific dimensions varied by delivery system (home, school, community center, clinic), primary target (family, parent, child), timing of onset (prenatal through adolescent), intensity (amount of programming per week), duration (length of program), uniformity of services to client, number of services offered, training of service provider, and curriculum content. A time commitment of 6 to 12 months was needed to change attitudes and strengthen parenting. Short-term, low-intensity programs were not found to be sufficient, by themselves, to alter long-term parent–child relationships.

The Family Growth Center (FGC) as a Model Program

The FGC offers behaviorally grounded parent education and support programs at three sites in a moderate-sized Midwestern city. Administered by Child Abuse Prevention Services (CAPS), the FGC allows families to determine their level of program involvement based on need and offers a multitude of programs to a wide variety of families. CAPS maintains a membership in the Prevention Providers, a wide base of community-based professionals who keep each other informed of program trends and explore solutions to service delivery gaps. The relatively small agency size allows for quick adaptability to current practice needs. For example, when the state implemented their welfare reform program, a large demand for child care was created. The FGC was able to quickly increase the availability of on-site child-care providers, a luxury not afforded to larger, more heavily bureaucratic organizations. CAPS cooperates with many agencies to increase its effectiveness in the community at the most efficient cost.

The FGC offers a continuum of parent education and support programs, increasing in both duration and intensity. It is the only such facility in the metropolitan area that offers free/low cost respite services for parents of young children. An ongoing support group, Helping Ourselves Parent Effectively (HOPE), meets weekly for two hours and facilitates the development of positive parenting techniques, knowledge of child development, and anger management skills. The group has an open door policy with no preregistration necessary in an effort to reach especially risky or reluctant parents. The ongoing nature of this program is also utilized by parents in need of a reminder about how to use appropriate discipline in times they feel they could *cross the line*. Stress Management classes are administered through community mental health and teach positive life coping strategies to low-income mothers and women who are at risk for chronic depression, especially those from violent households (e.g., battered women). Early Childhood Development (ECD) targets families with four-year-old children at risk for school failure, with a 30-week commitment and a mandatory child component (with transportation provided). ECD utilizes a wraparound approach through the use of a team of family members, natural supports, and community services working together in partnership to create a culturally competent and strengths-based approach to meeting goals.

In the original evaluation, data were collected at three points in time using a combination of questionnaires, interviews, and telephone contacts with 34 families over nine months. Parental depression and stress as risk factors were significantly reduced, while social support and child misbehaviors were not (Whipple & Wilson, 1996). Further, parents who participated in three to five programs over a two-year time period showed the most significant improvement, supporting duration of program involvement. The second evaluation involved observational and self-report data on 116 families over a 15-month time frame and found that parents who completed the most intensive 30-week program were better able to provide a home environment to foster their four-year-olds' development, demonstrated clear decreases in parental stress, and learned how to negotiate conflict with their children in a less violent manner (Whipple, 1999).

Social Support and Community Factors (the Exosystem): Neighborhoods and Outreach

The concept of community can be defined in multiple ways: as a network of social connections, a target for resource allocation, and simply a physical space (Shonkoff & Phillips, 2000). A community is a social system that performs production/distribution/consumption, socialization, social control, social participation, and mutual support. As practitioners come to view communities as social systems, various elements must be considered, including beliefs, values, norms, roles, status and rank (social stratification), power, and sanctions. Several decades of research have documented a link between community characteristics and child maltreatment. One well-controlled study of 400 families systematically selected from neighborhoods found four factors explained almost two-thirds of the variance in parents' etiological views on the definition of child maltreatment: poverty and family disruption, substance abuse and stress, lack of moral and family values, and individual psychopathology (Korbin, Coulton, Linstrom-Ufuti, & Spilsbury, 2000). These factors were related to neighborhood conditions, perceptions of neighborhoods, and individual characteristics.

Molnar, Buka, Brennan, Holton, and Earls (2003) implemented a multilevel approach to examine whether neighborhoods affect the amount of corporal punishment and/or physical child abuse used by individual families. Neighborhoods with greater concentrations of immigrants had lower rates of physical aggression. Among Hispanic families, a high density of social networks in the neighborhood was especially important, above and beyond social support received from their families. At both neighborhood and family levels, socioeconomic disadvantage, unemployment, and female single parent households were associated with higher rates of parent-to-child aggression. This research suggests that individually targeted programs are not the sole means of decreasing physical child abuse. Rather, programs that reduce neighborhood disadvantage, reduce community violence, and increase social networks may prove most effective. They call specifically for effective public health strategies that do not endorse corporal punishment as a method of discipline.

In most industrialized countries, home visiting programs are part of a universal comprehensive health care system for women and children that have been well established for over 60 years. Early home visiting programs that seek to promote family wellness and prevent child abuse and neglect have flourished over the past decade in the United States, serving a very heterogeneous population across a wide range of settings. Whether or not such programs should be universal or target high-risk populations is an area for debate. Home visiting is not a single, uniform intervention but rather a *strategy* for service delivery, which typically seeks to create change by providing parents with social support, practical assistance via case management, and education about parenting and child development. Desired outcomes typically include improving health-related outcomes for children, enhancing child development, decreasing rates of child abuse and neglect, and improving parents' life courses. Based on results from a meta-analytic review of 19 studies of 4,200 families enrolled in early home visitation programs to prevent physical child abuse and neglect, Gutterman (1999) advocates careful examination of subgroup findings, such as sociodemographic and regional characteristics, to determine how well program elements such as service intensity, duration, content, and level of engagement will predict positive outcomes in various demographic groups.

Healthy Families America (HFA) as a Model Program

An initiative of Prevent Child Abuse America (PCA), Healthy Families America (HFA) is a voluntary home visiting program with four overarching goals: to systematically assess family strengths and needs and refer as needed; to enhance family functioning by building trusting relationships, teaching problem-solving skills, and improving the family's support system; to promote positive parent–child interactions; and to promote healthy childhood growth and development. HFA is a model of change that outlines a specific population (all newborns and their parents) and identifies key program elements, including mechanisms targeted for change among program participants (parent–child interactions, health care utilization, formal and informal social support, and child cognitive and social development) as well as change within communities (normative standards for parenting, community responsibility for child well-being, and coordination of program intake and referral procedures). In a review of selected evaluations of HFA programs across 20 different HFA sites in multiple states, Daro and Harding (1999) found that many programs are not well integrated into existing child welfare response systems, nor have they become an integral part of public health-care systems. The target population for HFA is identified by assessing women in local hospitals around the time of birth for risk factors related to child abuse and neglect. Women with positive screens are then contacted by a family worker and offered a home visit and further in-depth assessment using the Kempe Family Stress Checklist (FSC). HFA programs draw from a multitude of empirically supported parenting curricula available nationwide.

The evaluation presented here included a two-county rural PCA site-licensed HFA program in a Midwestern state (Whipple & Nathans, 2005). The program grew from a recognized need for child abuse prevention based on a heightened incidence of shaken baby syndrome cases seen by a probate judge in his courtroom in the early 1990s. A small task force was created that evolved into a community coalition that selected the HFA model as the approach most needed to address child abuse prevention. The sample included 115 families, with six months or greater of program involvement over a five-year time frame. Findings reflected a rural sample composed of predominantly young white mothers with low education levels, variable employment histories, and relatively little support from the babies' fathers. Indeed, it was these sociodemographic characteristics that reflected the biggest impact on program effectiveness. As might be expected, mothers who were older, married, or maintained a relationship with the babies' fathers, with higher education levels and fewer children, demonstrated the most positive outcomes. Concrete goals, such as linking families to additional services, securing a medical home, decreasing childhood illnesses, accidents, childhood immunizations, and the number of emergency room visits were successfully achieved, even among families with less program involvement. Mothers with more stable sociodemographic traits stayed involved longer in the program and were more likely to achieve abstract program goals, such as improving the home environment, decreasing parental stress, and improving parent–child interactions. It seems that parents operating from a relatively secure base were the most able to reap program benefits (Whipple & Nathans, 2005).

These maternal sociodemographic characteristics were also associated with higher program engagement, both progressing through the program and overall heightened duration and intensity of involvement. These findings illuminate an important ethical question of how early intervention programs can best engage those who present with the greatest challenges. All of the families in this study showed the potential and willingness to engage with workers for at least six months. This was accomplished with even the riskiest families through the flexibility in the HFA model to start treatment by addressing the primary stressor for the parent, such as housing or financial assistance. Through the use of multiple curricula, workers tailored each home visit based on the babies' age and the mothers' comfort level. Despite these efforts, some families faced too many barriers and were allowed to utilize Creative Outreach in order to stay connected to the program (yet be less involved) for up to three months. This HFA program was implemented via the public health department with paraprofessional service providers. While Olds (2002) has argued that such outcomes are more effectively achieved when nurses are service providers, this study and others (Gutterman, 1997; Macleod & Nelson, 2000) propose that it is a proactive ecological framework that produces the most robust findings. Macleod and Nelson (2000) found that multicomponent programs had the most effective outcomes. In a review of 18 controlled evaluations, Gutterman (1997) found the strongest treatment group effects were those that used paraprofessional helpers.

The HFA model implemented in rural settings may function most effectively as a first line triage case management model with a strong outreach component, a largely unrecognized role of a national program model that is typically considered a "micro service delivery" venue. In this evaluation, the majority of families utilized five additional services to aid in the life of their young child, including WIC, financial assistance, Medicaid, food stamps, and Infant Mental Health Services. Linking otherwise isolated families with necessary formal and/or informal support is essential in reducing maltreatment risk (Koeske & Koeske, 1990). Study findings point to the need to better integrate early intervention with other service delivery systems, especially child welfare, mental health, and health care. The vast array of stressors faced by families served, including such macro-practice issues as education, employment, and income level, must be addressed through a comprehensive ecological model.

Social Structure (The Macrosystem): Policy and Culture

Social change is a very complex and dynamic process. Many practitioners say they are not political and have no desire to become involved in the "messy" process of social action. The United States is currently at a crossroads between identifying itself as an elitist or pluralistic societal structure, and the impact on low-income families is palpable. Based on an extensive review of state-of-the-art knowledge about early childhood development, Shonkoff and Phillips (2000) offer four over-arching themes for the implementation of policies in this area: all children are born ready to learn; early environments matter and nurturing rela-tionships are essential; society is changing and the needs of young chil-dren are not being addressed; and interactions among early childhood science, policy, and practice are problematic and demand dramatic rethinking. Early childhood policies are highly fragmented, with com-plex and confusing points of entry that are particularly problematic for underserved segments of the population. Americans as a whole need to make the link between societal economic prosperity and the well-being of its citizens. The youngest and most vulnerable children suffer the highest poverty rates of any age group in the United States. Nearly one in five children under age six lives in poverty, and the number is rising (Lynch, 2004). The problems for children and society that result from childhood poverty are *desperate* for effective policy solutions.

Poor children often have inadequate food, safety, shelter, and physical and mental care. In school, poor children too often fall far short of achiev-ing their academic potential, making them more likely to enter adulthood lacking the skills to compete in the global labor market. As adults, they are more likely to suffer from impaired physical and mental health and participate in crime and other antisocial behavior; these children are also less likely to grow up to be gainfully employed and contribute to economic growth and community well-being. There is a strong consensus among experts who have studied high-quality early intervention programs that these programs have substantial payoffs. A recent study by the Economic Policy Institute clearly demonstrates that investments in high-quality early intervention programs consistently generate benefit-cost ratios exceeding three to one—or more than a $3 return for every $1 invested—well above the one-to-one ratio needed to justify such investments. Follow-up studies of poor children who participated in these programs found solid evidence of markedly better academic performance, decreased rates of criminal conduct, and higher adult earnings than among their nonpartici-pating peers (Lynch, 2004). The five programs included in this analysis were selected because they were considered representative examples of well-conceived programs, and all had long-term follow-up studies that analyzed program outcomes until the children were 15 to 41 years old. Early childhood development programs included in this analysis included the Perry Preschool Project (Ypsilanti, Michigan); the Prenatal/Early

Infancy Project (Elmira, New York); the Abecedarian Early Childhood Intervention (North Carolina); the Chicago Child–Parent Center; and Head Start and Early Head Start (nationwide). While these large well-funded programs are best-practice models, they may not be suited to the unique needs of all diverse communities across the United States.

Coercion as a reason for change can be understood within the context of governmental policy. There are currently a number of controversial efforts across the United States to legislate marriage and family life. For example, in the state of Michigan, Marriage and Family Preservation Bills have been approved by the House of Representatives and are being considered by the Senate. Included in the package are bills to encourage premarital education and require divorcing parents to complete a "divorce effects" program. The premarital education program would emphasize skill-building strategies and would include conflict management, communication skills, financial matters, and if the couple has or intends to have children, child and parenting responsibilities (House Bill 5467). It is expected that couples would pay for a minimum of four hours of premarital education, and while providers are encouraged to offer a sliding scale, access for low-income families will likely present yet another barrier. Couples seeking a divorce would be required to complete a divorce effects educational program that addresses the child's developmental stages; responses to divorce; the adults' communication skills; conflict resolution skills; emotional, family, and work adjustments; stress reduction; parallel and cooperative parenting techniques; reconciliation and counseling options; and substance abuse information and referral (House Bill 5470). Until such policies work in tandem with socioeconomic restraints, they are likely to produce a new set of problems rather than solve old ones (e.g., welfare reform requiring parents to seek employment without access to high quality child care).

Another trend in state government is to require some early intervention programs to implement curricula that promotes marriage (in order to stay funded). In Michigan for example, the Family Independence Agency (FIA) contracted with a university extension program to develop a "Caring for My Family" curriculum to target new mothers with infants aged 7 to 12 weeks (who are receiving cash assistance) and mandate participation in order to maintain benefits. The curriculum is designed to help new mothers and fathers make healthy decisions about their relationships, with a primary goal of increasing father involvement in family life. Father involvement per se is not necessarily linked to positive outcomes for children. Rather, it is the variety of ways in which fathers take responsibility for their children that many now believe is the most important component of fathering. This entails not only financial responsibility, but supportive and emotional aspects as well. There is almost no research on how the roles of fathers (and other men in young children's lives) are involved within the context of culturally diverse values and family structure (Shonkoff & Phillips, 2000).

There is growing interest in how single parenting comes about and what alternative forms of support exist. The circumstances surrounding single-parent families vary greatly, as do the amount and types of resources they have available to their children. Among the many unanswered questions include: how does divorce, versus other routes to single parenthood, differ in effects on children? Are these differences caused by the family structure, or do they reflect preexisting differences between children in intact and single-parent families? Does the effect of single-parent family structure depend on age of the child? Unfortunately, research to date has not supplied clear answers to these questions (Shonkoff & Phillips, 2000). Until these factors are disentangled and well understood, legislation about marriage and family life (some of which specifically targets poor families) is a severe misuse of power and appears to be an effort to regulate the poor.

Extensive research from a variety of service system perspectives pivots on the ethical principle that effective intervention demands an individualized approach that matches well-defined goals to the specific needs and resources of the children and families who are served. There is scant support for a one-size-fits-all model of early childhood intervention (Shonkoff & Phillips, 2000). If young, single, poor mothers are indeed at highest risk for abusing or neglecting their children, then the greatest window of opportunity is *before* a woman becomes pregnant. Parents, family members, teachers, neighbors, community programs (e.g., teen health clinics), and other supports can play a critical role in facilitating pathways to education, employment, and planned parenthood.

Culture influences every aspect of human development and is reflected in childrearing beliefs and practices designed to promote healthy adaptation. Culture is both reproduced and transformed within each child. The socialization process that is embedded in the development of early relationships is influenced by the transmission of values and behaviors from one generation to the next (Shonkoff & Phillips, 2000). Another important aspect of the context of child abuse and neglect is the cultural acceptability of physical aggression and violence within a society. Of relevance here is Straus's (1994) discussion of the cultural spillover theory, whereby cultural norms that endorse violence for socially approved purposes are applied toward nonlegitimate acts. For example, a society such as the United States that sanctions corporal punishment of children, and other forms of violence (e.g., war, violent media images), is more likely to foster spillover of physical discipline into physical abuse. Clearly, innovative program implementation and rigorous evaluation needs to continue to be able to meet the ongoing changes in family structure and needs of families with very young children. Implementation of managed care, brief treatment models for complex psychosocial issues, and overall decreased funding for mental health presents enormous challenges. Some answers lie in the relevance and availability of pre- and post-service training and education in such areas as child welfare and early intervention. One powerful mechanism toward this end is through university partnerships, where communities and universities come together to begin to solve some of society's most vexing social problems, such as the persistence of child abuse and neglect, and the seemingly unending subsequent cycle of poverty and mental illness.

Conclusion

Poverty, in combination with low education levels, single parenthood, unemployment, high mobility, and large family size are especially tenacious risk factors for child abuse and neglect. Parent education and support, home visiting, and other early intervention programs would best benefit families by collaborating closely with larger service delivery systems and organizations (e.g., high schools, community colleges, neighborhood centers, job training programs, community agencies, employers) to ensure that parents with very young children have the opportunity to rise above poverty. As families migrate across America, often in pursuit of educational or employment opportunities, societal social structure simply must become more flexible and accommodating of the vast array of lifestyles in the United States. Low-income families perpetually face the greatest barriers with fewer resources to help cope with stress. It is time to level the playing field.

Philosophical and legal debate as to whether parents should ever physically strike their children will be an ongoing issue. In American society, interpersonal aggression continues to be perceived as a socially acceptable expression of strong emotions in numerous situations. Among child abuse specialists, who see the terrible and lasting consequences of child maltreatment, it is understandable that all instances of parents hitting children are viewed as physical assault and the foundation of child abuse (Garbarino, 1996). Despite the appeal of endorsing nonviolence in all interpersonal relations, the complex sociocultural composition of American society suggest that for many parents, physical punishment, when used in moderation as a form of discipline, is relatively common. Like alcohol consumption, which continues to be socially and legally permissible when used moderately and within certain boundaries, physical punishment of young children appears to be found permissible by many "normal," nonabusive American parents if utilized within the context of competent parenting. This said, few parents who do *cross the line* start out with the intention of becoming abusive. Early intervention programs have a unique and valuable opportunity to provide a safe haven for parents to discuss discipline strategies, and if armed with some clear standards of comparison, are well positioned to meet the needs of families functioning in the "gray zone" between physical punishment and abuse, and intervene to prevent negative outcomes.

REFERENCES

Barber, J.G. (1992). Evaluating parent education groups: Effects on sense of competence and social isolation. *Research on Social Work Practice, 2*(1), 28–38.

Baumrind, D. (1973). The development of instrumental competence through socialization. In A. D. Pick (Ed.), *Minnesota symposia on child psychology* (Vol. 7, pp. 3–46). Minneapolis: University of Minnesota Press.

Bland, R., & Orn, H. (1986). Family violence and psychiatric disorder. *Canadian Journal of Psychiatry, 31,* 129–137.

Carey, T.A. (1994). Spare the rod and spoil the child. Is this a sensible justification for the use of punishment in child rearing? *Child Abuse & Neglect, 18*(12), 1005–1010.

Cash, S.J., & Wilke, D.J. (2003). An ecological model of maternal substance abuse and child neglect: Issues, analyses, and recommendations. *American Journal of Orthopsychiatry, 73*(4), 392–404.

Chemtob, C.M., & Carlson, J.G. (2004). Psychological effects of domestic violence on children and their mothers. *International Journal of Stress Management, 11*(3), 209–226.

Darling, N., & Steinberg, L. (1993). Parenting style as context: An integrative model. *Psychological Bulletin, 113*(3), 487–496.

Daro, D.A., & Harding, K.A. (1999). Healthy families America: Using research to enhance practice. *The Future of Children* (The David and Lucille Packard Foundation), *9*(1), 152–176.

De Bellis, M.D., Broussard, E.R., Herring, D.J., Wexler, S., Moritz, G., & Benitez, J.G. (2001). Psychiatric co-morbidity in caregivers and children involved in maltreatment: A pilot research study with policy implications. *Child Abuse & Neglect, 25,* 923–944.

DiLauro, M.D. (2004). Psychosocial factors associated with types of child maltreatment. *Child Welfare, 83*(1), 69–99.

Dodge, K.A., Bates, J.E., & Pettit, G.S. (1990). Mechanisms in the cycle of violence. *Science, 250,* 1678–1683.

Earls, F., McGuire, J., & Shay, S. (1994). Evaluating a community intervention to reduce the risk of child abuse: Methodological strategies in conducting neighborhood surveys. *Child Abuse and Neglect, 18*(5), 473–485.

Eiden, R.D., Peterson, M., & Coleman, T. (1999). Maternal cocaine use and the caregiving environments during early childhood. *Psychology of Addictive Behaviors, 13*(4), 293-302.

Ferrari , A.M. (2002). The impact of culture upon child rearing practices and definitions of maltreatment. *Child Abuse & Neglect, 26,* 793–813.

Garbarino, J. (1996). CAN reflections on 20 years of searching? *Child Abuse & Neglect, 20*(3), 157–160.

Gracia, E. (1995). Visible but unreported: A case for the "not serious enough" cases of child maltreatment. *Child Abuse & Neglect, 19*(9), 1083–1093.

Graziano, A.M. (1994). Why we should study subabusive violence against children. *Journal of Interpersonal Violence, 9*(3), 412–419.

Greven, P. (1990). *Spare the child: The religious roots of punishment and the psychological impact of physical abuse.* New York: Knopf.

Grusec, J.E., & Goodnow, J.J. (1994). Impact of parental discipline methods on the child's internalization of values: A reconceptualization of current points of view. *Developmental Psychology, 30*(1), 4–19.

Gutterman, N.B. (1997). Early prevention of physical child abuse and neglect: Existing evidence and future directions. *Child Maltreatment, 2*(1), 12–34.

Gutterman, N.B. (1999). Enrollment strategies in early home visitation to prevent physical child abuse and neglect and the "universal versus targeted" debate: A meta-analysis of population-based and screening-based programs. *Child Abuse & Neglect, 23*(9), 863–890.

Hoffman, M.L. (1980). Moral development in adolescence. In J. Adelson (Ed.), *Handbook of adolescent psychology* (pp. 295–343). New York: Wiley.

Jaffee, S.R., Caspi, A., Moffitt, T.E., Polo-Tomas, M., Price, T., & Taylor, A. (2004). Physical maltreatment victim to antisocial child: Evidence of an environmentally mediated process. *Journal of Abnormal Psychology, 113*(1), 44–45.

Jaffee, S.R., Caspi, A., Moffitt, T.E., & Taylor, A. (2004). The limits of child effects: Evidence for genetically mediated child effects on corporal punishment but not on physical maltreatment. *Developmental Psychology, 40*(6), 1047–1058.

Koeske, G.F., & Koeske, R.D. (1990). The buffering effect of social support on parental stress. *American Journal of Orthopsychiatry, 60*(3), 440–451.

Korbin, J.E., Coulton, C.J., Lindstrom-Ufuti, H., & Spilsbury, J. (2000). Neighborhood views on the definition and etiology of child maltreatment. *Child Abuse & Neglect, 24*(12), 1509–1527.

Larzelere, R.E. (1986). Moderate spanking: Model or deterrent of children's aggression in the family? *Journal of Family Violence, 1*(1), 27–35.

Locke, T.F., & Newcomb, M.D. (2003). Childhood maltreatment, parental alcohol/drug-related problems, and global parental dysfunction. *Professional Psychology: Research & Practice, 34*(1), 73–79.

Lynch, R.G. (2004). *Exceptional returns: Economic, fiscal, and social benefits of investment in early childhood development.* Washington, DC: Economic Policy Institute.

MacLeod, J. & Nelson, G. (2000). Programs for the promotion of family wellness and the prevention of child maltreatment: A meta-analytic review. *Child Abuse & Neglect, 24*(9), 1127–1149.

Mash, E. J., Johnston, C., & Kovitz, K. (1983). A comparison of the mother-child interactions of physically abused and non-abused children during play and task situations. *Journal of Clinical Child Psychology, 12*(3), 337–346.

Milner, J. S. (1993). Social information processing and physical child abuse. *Clinical Psychology Review, 13,* 275–294.

Milner, J. S. (2003). Social information processing in high-risk and physically abusive parents, *Child Abuse & Neglect, 27,* 7–20.

Molnar, B. E., Buka, S. L., Brennan, R. T., Holton, J. K., & Earls, F. (2003). A multi-level study of neighborhoods and parent-to-child physical aggression: Results from the project on human development in Chicago neighborhoods. *Child Maltreatment, 8*(2), 84–97.

National Research Council (1993). *Understanding child abuse and neglect.* Washington, DC: National Academy Press.

Olds, D. L. (2002). Home visiting by paraprofessionals and by nurses: A randomized, controlled trial. *Pediatrics, 110*(3), 486–496.

Ondersma, S. J. (2002). Predictors of neglect within low-SES families: The importance of substance abuse. *American Journal of Orthopsychiatry, 72*(3), 383–391.

Ortega, D. M. (2001). Parenting efficacy, aggressive parenting, and cultural connections. *Child and Family Social Work, 6,* 47–57.

Patterson, G. R. (1986). Performance models for antisocial boys. *American Psychologist, 41*(4), 432–444.

Sedlak, A. J., & Broadhurst, D. D. (1996). *Third national incidence study of child abuse and neglect.* Washington, DC: U.S. Department of Health and Human Services.

Shonkoff, J. P., & Phillips, D. A., Eds. (2000). *From neurons to neighborhoods: The science of early childhood development.* Washington, DC: National Academy Press.

Siegel, D. J. (1999). *The developing mind: How relationships and the brain interact to shape who we are.* New York: Guilford.

Steele, L. C. (2004). How old are you and do you have a dog? *National Child Advocate, 6*(1and 2), 1–16.

Straus, M. A. (1994). *Beating the devil out of them: Corporal punishment in American families.* New York: Lexington Books.

Straus, M. A., & Gelles, R. J. (1990). *Physical violence in American families: Risk factors and adaptations to violence in 8,145 families.* New Brunswick, NJ: Transaction Publishers.

Trickett, P. K., & Kuczynski, L. (1986). Children's misbehaviors and parental discipline strategies in abusive and nonabusive families. *Developmental Psychology, 22,* 115–123.

Whipple, E. E. (1999). Reaching families with preschoolers at risk of physical child abuse: What works? *Families in Society, 80*(2), 148–160.

Whipple, E. E., Fitzgerald, H. E., & Zucker, R. A. (1995). Parent–child interactions in alcoholic and non-alcoholic families. *American Journal of Orthopsychiatry, 65*(1), 153–159.

Whipple, E. E., & Nathans, L. L. (2005). Evaluation of a rural Healthy Families America (HFA) program: The importance of context. *Families in Society, 86*(1), 71–82.

Whipple, E. E., & Webster-Stratton, C. (1991). The role of parental stress in physically abusive families. *Child Abuse and Neglect: The International Journal, 15*(3), 279–291.

Whipple, E. E., & Wilson, S. R. (1996). Evaluation of a parent education program for families at risk of physical child abuse. *Families in Society, 77*(4), 227–239.

Widom, C. S. (1989). Child abuse, neglect, and adult behavior: Research design and findings on criminality, violence, and child abuse. *American Journal of Orthopsychiatry, 59*(3), 355–367.

Wiehe, V. R. (1990). Religious influence on parental attitudes toward the use of corporal punishment. *Journal of Family Violence, 5*(2), 173–186.

Wilson, S. R., Cameron, K. A., & Whipple, E. E. (1997). Regulative communication strategies within mother-child interactions: Implications for the study of reflection-enhancing parental communication. *Research on Language and Social Interaction, 30*(1), 73–92.

Wilson, S. R., & Whipple, E. E. (2001). Attributions and regulative communication by parents participating in a community-based child physical abuse prevention program. In V. Manusov & J. H. Harvey (Eds.), *Attribution, communication, behavior and close relationships* (pp. 227–247). New York: Cambridge University Press.

Wilson, S. R., Whipple, E .E., & Grau, J. (1996). Reflection-enhancing regulative communication: How do parents vary across situations and child resistance? *Journal of Social and Personal Relationships, 13*(4), 553–569.

Windam, A. M., Rosenberg, L., Fuddy, L., McFarlane, E., Sia, C., & Duggan, A. K. (2004). Risk of mother-reported child abuse in the first 3 years of life. *Child Abuse & Neglect, 28,* 645–667.

Wolfe, D. A. (1991). *Preventing physical and emotional abuse of children.* New York: The Guilford Press.

Zeanah, C. H.., Scheeringa, M., Boris, N. W., Heller, S. S., Smyke, A. T., & Trapani, J. (2004). Reactive Attachment Disorder in maltreated toddlers. *Child Abuse & Neglect, 28,* 877–888.

Chapter 10

WELFARE AND ANTIPOVERTY POLICY EFFECTS ON CHILDREN'S DEVELOPMENT

Pamela A. Morris and Lisa Gennetian

INTRODUCTION

During the past 30 years, welfare and other public policies for families living in poverty have developed a primary objective of increasing parents' self-sufficiency by requiring and supporting employment. Fortunately, there now is consistent evidence from well-designed studies about whether promoting work among low-income single parents helps or hurts children, and under what conditions it does so. This chapter summarizes the results on children from a set of research conducted as part of MDRC's Next Generation project, relying on data from a set of welfare experiments aimed at increasing the self-sufficiency of low-income parents in the United States and Canada. Such research provides critical information to advance developmental research on the effects of changes in parents' employment and income on the development of low-income children, in addition to informing the decisions policymakers will make regarding their welfare policy.

POLICY CONTEXT

The Personal Responsibility and Work Opportunity Reconciliation Act (PRWORA), passed in 1996, was the culmination of several decades of efforts to promote work and reduce long-term welfare receipt among single-parent families. As a result of these efforts, Aid to Families with Dependent Children (AFDC), which had guaranteed aid for low-income families with children, was eliminated, and was replaced with Temporary Assistance for Needy Families (TANF), which provided block grants to states, introduced time limits on cash assistance, and imposed work requirements on recipients. At the same time, benefits for working-poor families were expanded to reward work outside the welfare system through the Earned Income Credit (EIC, the federal tax credit that supplements the earnings of low-income families), publicly funded health insurance, and child-care assistance. In the wake of all of these developments, there has been very little research to inform our understanding of how these changes may have affected children. Yet, because these changes encourage parental employment and weaken the safety net for families in which parents do not maintain employment, they may have important consequences for children.

In this chapter, we summarize the findings on children of a set of welfare and employment policy experiments. Notably, these analyses do not provide a bottom-line assessment of the effects of the post-1996 welfare reform changes. In part this is because the new law provided states with considerable latitude in designing their own welfare programs—the result is, in effect, a different constellation of welfare policy components across states. But what these data can tell us are the effects of specific welfare reform policy choices that are currently being used by states, and they can address whether promoting work among low-income single parents helps or hurts children, and under what conditions it does so. In so doing, it informs decisions policymakers are currently making as their welfare policies continue to evolve.

The welfare and antipoverty policies we examine here target parents' economic outcomes and are likely to affect children only indirectly, through changes in their parents' economic circumstances. Therefore, our findings build on and contribute to a wealth of developmental, economic, and policy research, relying on both nonexperimental and experimental data that suggest that changes in parents' employment and family income can affect children's development. Economic and psychological theory provide frameworks for understanding the mechanisms by which parents' employment and income can have such effects, by emphasizing both the role and distribution of material and social resources (Becker, 1981; Bergstrom, 1997; Coleman, 1988) and family psychological processes (Chase-Lansdale & Pittman, 2002; McLoyd, 1990, 1997, 1998; McLoyd, Jayartne, Ceballo, & Borquez, 1994). More specifically, economic theory would suggest that employment and income may affect children's social behavior and academic achievement by affecting the goods parents purchase for children (books, toys, and child care) and the time parents spend with children. Psychological theory emphasizes the effects of employment and income on parental emotional well-being (stress and depression), and, in turn, on parenting behavior, as one pathway by which parents' employment and income affect children's development.

For low-income families headed by single mothers, the associations between maternal employment and children's cognitive and social development tend to be positive, but much of this difference is a function of preexisting differences between mothers who are and are not employed (Harvey, 1999; Huston, 2002; Vandell & Ramanan, 1992; Zaslow & Emig, 1997). The effects of maternal employment on children's development also depend on the characteristics of employment—its quality, extent, and timing—and on the child's age (Brooks-Gunn, Han, & Waldfogel, 2002; Harvey, 1999; Parcel & Menaghan, 1994). Highly routinized jobs that pay very low wages and afford little autonomy lead to low levels of home environmental stimulation, which in turn affect children's development adversely (Moore & Driscoll, 1997; Parcel & Menaghan, 1994, 1997). Some evidence suggests that employment in the first year of a child's life may be associated with increased risks, but the findings are not consistent (Baydar & Brooks-Gunn, 1991; Brooks-Gunn et al., 2002).

The effects of parent employment also depend in part on the type and quality of child care received when parents are working (Huston, 2002; Zaslow, Moore, Morrison, & Coiro, 1995). The child-care options that parents use depend, in turn, on both income and policies that subsidize care. Higher-income families use more formal center-based care than do low-income families, and low-income parents who receive subsidies and other forms of child care support use more formal center-based care in comparison to home-based care (Fuller, Kagan, Caspary, & Gauthier, 2002). Both longitudinal and experimental studies show that high-quality care during preschool is associated with better cognitive outcomes than low-quality or no care, particularly for children from low-income families (Lamb, 1998; McLoyd, 1998; NICHD Early Child Care Research Network, 2002; NICHD Early Child Care Research Network & Duncan, 2003; Peisner-Feinberg et al., 1999; Scarr, 1998; Shonkoff & Phillips, 2000). Formal center-based care appears to confer more cognitive benefits to children than home-based care, even after controlling for differences in quality, but the effects on social behavior are more mixed (Fuller et al., 2002; Loeb, Fuller, Kagan, & Carrol, 2004; NICHD Early Child Care Research Network & Duncan, 2003). One reason may be that centers provide higher-quality care than the home-based settings used by low-income families (Coley, Chase-Lansdale, & Li Grining, 2001). There is some evidence, however, that center-based care may increase behavior problems, although the findings are less consistent (NICHD Early Childhood Research Network, 2003).

Poverty has consistently negative associations with children's development, but there is considerable controversy about the causal role of income per se, as opposed to other correlates of poverty (Bradley & Corwyn, 2002;

Duncan & Brooks-Gunn, 1997; Duncan, Brooks-Gunn, & Klebanov, 1994; Mayer, 1997; McLoyd, 1998). In one set of analyses, income was more consistently related to cognitive performance than to behavior and health, so understanding its effects across a range of child outcomes appears to be critical (Duncan & Brooks-Gunn, 1997; Klerman, 1991; Korenman & Miller, 1997). Income effects are often found to be nonlinear—increments to low levels of income appear more important than increments to higher levels, and chronic poverty has stronger associations with child outcomes than transitory poverty (Bolger, Patterson, Thompson, & Kupersmidt, 1995; Bradley & Corwyn, 2002; Dearing, McCartney, & Taylor, 2001; Duncan & Brooks-Gunn, 1997; Duncan et al., 1994; McLoyd, 1998). Finally, early childhood poverty (when the child is age 0 to 5) has been found to be more strongly associated with children's completion of schooling in adolescence than was poverty from age 6 to 15 (Duncan & Brooks-Gunn, 1997).

STUDIES

Our analysis utilizes 7 random-assignment studies that together evaluate the effects of 13 welfare and employment programs in the United States and two provinces in Canada (see Table 10.1). All were begun in the early to mid-1990s and designed to estimate the effects on low-income families and children of programs designed to increase parental employment. Many were pilot programs tested by individual states under waivers of the rules governing Aid to Families with Dependent Children (AFDC), the welfare system that was replaced in 1996 by Temporary Assistance for Needy Families (TANF). All were designed as "employment" treatments of one form or another—all were intended to reduce welfare and increase employment, without direct intervention components targeted at parents' mental health, parenting, or outcomes for children directly. Although many policies were tested, the approaches can be grouped into several categories: *generous earnings-supplement policies* that are designed to encourage work and increase income via make-work-pay strategies; and *mandatory employment services and time-limited programs,* which attempt to encourage work via sanctions and benefit termination strategies. A third important dimension of some of these programs is *expanded child-care assistance,* aimed at enhancing the use of subsidies or more formalized child-care settings.

More specifically, generous earnings supplements are designed to make work more financially rewarding, usually by increasing the earnings disregard (the amount of earnings that is not counted as income in calculating a family's welfare benefit) so that families can keep part of their welfare dollars when they go to work. Mandatory employment services are

Table 10.1
Descriptions of the Studies

Study	Sites	Key Policy Features Tested				When Study Began and Length of Follow-Up	Primary Source(s)
		Generous Earnings Supplements	Mandatory Employment Services	Time Limits	Expanded Child Care Assistance		
Connecticut Jobs First Evaluation	New Haven and Manchester, CT	✓	✓	✓		1996 36 months	Bloom et al., 2002
Family Transition Program (FTP)	Escambia County, FL		✓	✓	✓	1994 48 months	Bloom et al., 2000
Minnesota Family Investment Program (MFIP)	Seven counties in Minnesota	✓	✓		✓	1994 36 months	Gennetian and Miller, 2000
National Evaluation of Welfare-to-Work Strategies (NEWWS)	Atlanta, GA; Grand Rapids, MI; Riverside, CA; and Portland, OR		✓			1991 24 months 60 months	Hamilton et al., 2002; and McGroder et al., 2000
New Hope Project	Milwaukee, WI	✓			✓	1994 24 months 60 months	Bos et al., 1999
Los Angeles Jobs-First Greater Avenues for Independence (GAIN) Evaluation	Los Angeles County		✓			1996 24 months	Freedman et al., 2000
Self-Sufficiency Project (SSP)	New Brunswick, British Columbia	✓				1992 36 months 54 months	Morris and Michalopoulos, 2000

Notes: All sites used a random assignment design that consisted of one or more program group and a control group. The control group in each case was the traditional welfare system in place at the time of the study (typically AFDC).

requirements that recipients participate in employment-related activities as a condition of receiving their welfare benefits. The primary tool used to enforce participation mandates is sanctioning, whereby a recipient's welfare grant is reduced if she or he does not comply with program requirements. Finally, time limits intended to reduce welfare dependence were a feature of two studies, although the limits were bundled with other program features like mandatory services and earnings supplements. In several cases, programs mixed the aforementioned policies with expansions in child-care assistance through enhanced resource and referral, encouragement of formal care, higher income eligibility limits, direct payment to providers, and reduced bureaucratic barriers.

The following evaluation studies were included in this analysis: Connecticut Jobs-First (CT Jobs First; Bloom et al., 2002), Florida's Family Transition Program (FTP; Bloom et al., 2000), Los Angeles Jobs First GAIN (LA GAIN; Freedman, Knab, Gennetian, & Navarro, 2000), Minnesota Family Investment Program (MFIP; testing the effects of two programs, Full MFIP and MFIP Incentives Only; Gennetian & Miller, 2000), National Evaluation of Welfare to Work Strategies (NEWWS; testing the effects of six programs in three sites across two follow-up points; Hamilton et al., 2001; McGroder, Zaslow, Moore, & LeMenestrel, 2000), New Hope (testing the effects of one program at two follow-up points; Bos et al., 1999; Huston et al., 2003), and the Canadian Self-Sufficiency Project (SSP; testing the effects of one program at two follow-up points; Morris & Michalopoulos, 2000; Michalopoulos et al., 2002). Notably, the inclusion of the Canadian study (SSP) is appropriate given that prior work has shown very similar effects across generous supplement policies in the United States and Canada (Berlin, 2000), despite any differences in the policy context (e.g., that Canada has national health insurance).

All of these studies had a common design. In each study, sample members were randomly assigned at baseline to one or more program groups that were subject to a new set of welfare rules and benefits or to a control group that received the prevailing AFDC welfare benefits package and rules (or other benefits largely available to low-income families). In all but one of the studies, parents were applying for welfare or renewing eligibility when they were randomly assigned. (In the case of the New Hope Study, all geographically eligible low-income parents were eligible to participate). This process of random assignment ensures that there are no systematic differences between the two groups at the beginning of the study and that any differences between the two groups observed later can confidently be attributed to the intervention being examined. These experiments, akin to medical clinical trials often conducted to test the effectiveness of a particular drug or treatment, are the most rigorous way to examine the effects of welfare policies on children.

To estimate effects in any single study, differences in the average outcomes between children of parents assigned to the control group and children of parents assigned to the program group are computed. These program *impacts* are estimated for various measures of children's development, and for each we determined if the impact was *statistically significant* or unlikely to arise from chance. Our initial research conducted program impacts by study, comparing and contrasting effects across program models. Our second phase relied on meta-analytic techniques to address average impacts across sets of studies. Finally, our most recent work pools the microdata from the studies, allowing us not only to estimate program impacts but also to use these data to estimate the effects of key targets of these programs (in our case, employment, income, and child care) on outcomes for children.

Children range in age from 2 to 15 at the point of random assignment. Random assignment is a critical point of reference because it marks the point at which children begin to experience the policy-induced changes in employment and income on the part of their parents. Children's achievement was assessed at least two and sometimes as long as seven years after parents entered the programs, so that most children were in school when we assessed their achievement outcomes. Children's achievement is based on parents', teachers', and children's own reports of how children are doing in school. Children's behavioral outcomes were typically collected for the youngest of these children (with the most in-depth measures collected for children who were preschoolers and in elementary school at parents' entry into the programs). For older children, our best assessments of behavior come from the single Canadian study (SSP), with the only cross-study information being older children's behavior in school, and based only on parent report assessments (school suspensions and drop out).

FINDINGS ON THE EFFECTS OF WELFARE AND EMPLOYMENT POLICIES

We find that welfare reform policies affect children differently depending on their age, the outcome under consideration (school achievement vs. social behavior) and, for at least one group of children, the welfare policy approach under consideration. We also discuss what we know about the likely predictors of these effects, drawing from some more recent nonexperimental analyses that allow us to extend our experimental findings to address some of the likely mediators of program impacts on children.

Effects of Welfare and Antipoverty Programs on Preschool and Early School-Age Children

Our findings suggest that welfare reform policies can benefit younger children, when designed in ways to increase both the employment and the income of single parents. More specifically, for children who were preschool and elementary-school ages at the point of their parents' random assignment to program and control groups, programs that were designed to increase both employment and income (through earnings supplements) led to small, but consistently positive effects, on children's developmental outcomes (Morris, Huston, Duncan, Crosby, & Bos, 2001). By contrast, programs that encourage employment without earnings supplements (through mandatory approaches and, in one case, time limits) typically increase employment among parents (and reduce welfare use) but not their income, and have few and inconsistent effects on young children's development (Morris et al., 2001; McGroder et al., 2000; Morris et al., 2001).

The benefits of earnings supplement programs appear to be most consistent for school achievement and cognitive test scores as compared to measures of children's social behavior. More specifically, we find benefits of earnings supplement programs for children's achievement in school, as reported by parents, teachers, and in some cases, by test scores or the children themselves. Our early work examined these effects separately in four programs that all increased parents' employment and income, and found benefits in all four (Morris et al., 2001). More specifically, we find benefits of generous supplement programs of about 10 percent to 15 percent of the average variation in the control group, a small, but statistically significant secondary benefit of these program models.

This same research examined effects on children's social behavior as well. We reported findings for three generous supplement programs on children's externalizing behavior problems (e.g., acting out behavior; Morris et al., 2001). While there was a reduction in children's behavior problems in one of the three programs, two had neutral effects. Turning to children's positive behavior (positive social interactions with others), we see similar results, with increases in children's positive behavior in two of three programs. These findings suggest that, if these programs influence children's behavior at all, their effects are favorable. But it is not clear that the implementation of generous earnings supplement policies will necessarily lead to significant effects on children's emotional and behavior adjustment.

Our more recent work relies on a pooled dataset across these evaluations, allowing us to examine in more detail the precise age group of children affected by welfare reform policies, and, at the same time, allowing us to more flexibly test alternative hypotheses to any effects observed (Morris, Duncan, & Clark-Kauffman, in press). For this analysis, we focused on children's academic achievement—the outcome for which effects are most consistent and for which we could examine the effects across the widest age range. We find benefits of earnings supplement programs for children making the transition to middle childhood and elementary school (age four to five when parents entered the programs) more so than for children already in elementary school. Smaller positive effects approaching significance are also found for children ages two to three years old, but neutral effects are found for children already in middle childhood at parents' entry into the programs.

Why might this period of development be most sensitive to welfare and employment policies? First and foremost, we ascertained whether these findings were due to differences in parents' response to these programs depending on the age of their children—that is, whether parents of younger children did not increase their employment as much as those of older children to the same incentives and requirements. However, consistent with the goals of the programs, welfare and antipoverty programs have consistent effects on earnings and income across age groups of children. Second, we wanted to ensure that these differences were not caused by differences in the family ecology of families with older and younger children. For example, younger children are more likely to have younger mothers, and parents' age, rather than child's age, may be the more important factor in how employment policies affect children's development. Our findings are robust to tests of this confound, as results show that our findings cannot be attributed to family characteristics that differ for children of different ages.

Developmental theory provides some guidance for hypothesizing why this pattern of effects occurred. Because of the reorganization that occurs with developmental transitions (Cicchetti, 1991; Sroufe, 1990), children's development may be most open to change during these periods. In addition, these effects may have been driven, at least in part, by the increased plasticity of development during early childhood. Moreover, the fact that the family system has such a strong direct effect on early childhood development (Bronfenbrenner & Morris, 1998) makes this period of development most sensitive to policy changes targeting the parent and family. Finally, the transition to elementary school may have supported children's development during their parents' increased employment. Regardless of whether or not a parental transition to employment occurs, these children will make the transition to elementary school. Unlike the low-income child-care environment, school may provide a stable context for young children's development as parents in poverty make the transition into employment.

Effects of Welfare and Antipoverty Programs on Older Children

Notably, the pattern of effects for older children is much different than for their younger peers. While much of the concern over the potentially harmful effects of welfare policies on young children did not materialize, unexpected negative effects appeared in several of the experimental evaluations (e.g. see Brooks, Hair, & Zaslow, 2001). A synthesis of these findings across eight of the evaluation studies provided further systematic evidence that these welfare and work policies indeed had small adverse effects on some school outcomes among adolescents aged 12–18 years old at follow-up (Gennetian et al., 2002, Gennetian, Duncan et al., 2004). The adverse effects were observed mostly for school performance outcomes (although our ability to assess effects on other outcomes is severely limited by the data collection strategies employed) and occurred in programs that required mothers to work or participate in employment-related activities and those that encouraged mothers to work voluntarily. The most pronounced negative effects on school outcomes occurred for the group of adolescents who had a younger sibling. More specifically, among adolescents with younger siblings at study entry, the programs increased the percentages who received special educational services, were suspended, and dropped out of school. Among adolescents who did not have younger siblings, in contrast, the programs had no effect on receipt of special educational services or dropping out and actually decreased rates of suspension by nearly eight percentage points. Note that effects on suspensions or expulsions and on dropping out did not occur for the full sample of adolescents. As they increased their employment, parents may have had less time to monitor their adolescents' schooling and might have expected adolescents, especially female adolescents, to take on more responsibilities in the home or otherwise.

Limited information about adolescents' childbearing and other behavioral measures are available from some of the studies (Gennetian et al., 2002). With regard to teen parenting, these program had neutral effects. Of the six programs for which information about school behavior is available, only one led to a statistically significant effect, namely, an increase in school behavior problems. The program for which information about delinquent behavior and substance use is available increased the frequency of minor delinquent activity (such as skipping school) and drinking once a week or more[1] and had no effects on major delinquent behavior such as drug use and being involved with gangs. These effects did not appear to translate into negative outcomes at a later follow-up point. Finally, of the three programs that had information about police involvement, one showed increased involvement with the police.

What these findings highlight is the importance of considering the spectrum of children across their developmental stages in evaluating the effects of policies. Compared to what we have learned about the effects of welfare policies—and maternal employment more generally—on young children, we know relatively less about how maternal employment and experience with welfare affects children during early and late adolescence. Some recent studies using data with welfare populations suggest that movement off of welfare reduces the incidence of suspensions or expulsions (Dunifon & Kalil, 2003). Other recent studies suggest that increased employment improves the self-esteem of low-income adolescents (Chase-Lansdale et al., 2003).

As with the younger children, further analyses were conducted to ensure it was age and not family characteristics driving the differences in effects on children of these welfare and employment policies. Again, differences in effects could not be accounted for by family characteristics that differed for children across the childhood age span (Morris, Duncan, & Clark-Kauffman, in press). Moreover, this analysis again pointed to the potential sensitivity of developmental transitions—as we find the most negative effects on children's achievement for the children making the transition into adolescence. The increased sensitivity during this period may be a result of the heightened biological and socioemotional growth that occurs at this point in development (Brooks-Gunn & Petersen, 1983; Hamburg, 1974). The increase in maternal employment as a result of these welfare policies may result in the absence of the parent at the moment when children need the most support in navigating this transition. Moreover, parents' employment may restructure children's own roles in the household during this critical period of identity development.

A Summary of the Effects of Welfare and Work Policies across Childhood

To summarize the findings across the childhood age spectrum on one outcome—children's achievement—we interacted treatment status (e.g., whether in the experimental or control group) with children's age (0–1, 2–3, 4–5, 6–7, 8–9, 10–11, or 12–15 at baseline; Figures 10.1 and 10.2; Morris, Duncan, & Clark-Kauffman, in press). Each value can be interpreted as the percent of standard deviation, or average variation in the control group, that child achievement is changed as a result of parents' assignment to the program group (relative to the control group).

Thus, each bar is the effect, or impact, of the welfare and work policies. Stars indicate those effects that are statistically significant, or that can be distinguished from zero. We show effects for all programs considered together in the first figure, and separately for generous supplement and the other policy approaches in figure 10.2.

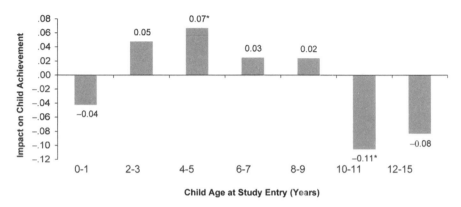

Figure 10.1   Effects on children's school achievement by age at study entry

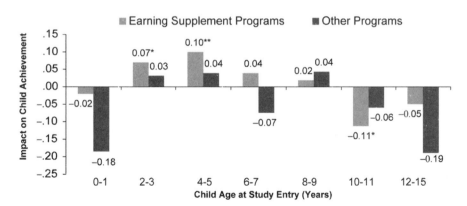

Figure 10.2   Effects on children's school achievement by age at study entry and by program type

Notes. Data include assessments of children's school achievement on parent report, test score, and teacher reports two to five years after parents entered the programs (see Morris, Duncan, & Clark-Kauffman, in press).

Each bar represents the average "impact" (the difference between randomly assigned experiment and control groups) across programs for each age group. Bars above the horizontal axis indicate a positive impact of the programs. Bars below indicate a negative impact.

Stars indicate those impacts that are statistically significant (i.e. can be differentiated from zero).

Statistical significance levels are indicated as: *p<.05, **p<.01, † p<0.10.

As indicated in the earlier discussion, and summarized here, these figures make clear how welfare reform and antipoverty programs affect children differently depending on their age and stage in development. For children making the transition into middle childhood, we find improvements in child achievement of about 7 percent of a standard deviation change as a result of the new welfare reform program, and reductions of these same policies for children making the transition to adolescents of about 10 percent of a standard deviation. When considering generous supplement policies separate from other policy approaches, we find statistically significant and positive (albeit small) experimental impacts for the two preschool age groups of children in these programs (those children age two to three and four to five at the point of parents' entry into the programs—of about 7 to 11 percent of a standard deviation change. Translated to an IQ-type scale, this amounts to one to two points increase as a result of parents' assignment to the experimental program—small but statistically significant improvements.

What Are the Effects of Income and Child Care on Children?

We now turn to nonexperimental analyses that leverage these data to address how the changes in parents' income and employment, and changes in children's use of child-care arrangements, all of which occurred as a result of these programs, affected developmental outcomes for children. Our findings show that increases in parents' income, and increases in the use of center-based child care, can benefit children's achievement in school. At the same time, we find very little evidence showing an effect of center-based care on children's externalizing or internalizing behavior.

To answer these questions, we took advantage of both sample size and policy variation available across these studies to estimate the effects of economic circumstances and child-care arrangements on outcomes for children. Key to our approach is the fact that random assignment of parents to program and control groups serves as a source of variation in our predictors of interest (income and child care) that is unrelated to characteristics of families and children before they entered the programs. Our analyses, using an instrumental variables approach, used *only* the variation in income and child care caused by random assignment to estimate the impacts of these two variables (Gennetian, Morris, Bos, & Bloom, 2005). By comparison, most research to date has been forced to rely on naturally occurring variation in income, child care, and outcomes for children, and is thus subject to biases that are extremely difficult to identify or control for. Furthermore, since we simultaneously estimate the effects of employment, income, welfare use, and child care, we are able to untangle the separate effects of these multiple mediating pathways. These findings are described in more detail in Morris, Duncan, and Rodrigues (2004), and Gennetian, Crosby, Dowsett and Huston (2004). Notably, however, because these analyses are a nonexperimental analysis of experimental data, the findings do not meet the same standards of causality as pure experimental impacts in our well-designed random-assignment studies.

First, with regard to effects on income, we rely on data from four of our welfare-to-work experiments (Connecticut Jobs First; Los Angeles Jobs First GAIN; the New Brunswick and British Columbia sites of the Canadian Self-Sufficiency Project [SSP]; and the Atlanta, GA, Grand Rapids, MI, and Riverside, CA Labor Force Attachment tests in the National Evaluation of Welfare to Work Strategies [NEWWS]). The four studies provide us with nearly 20,000 observations of children age 2 to 15 at the time of random assignment.

Our analyses show that young children's school achievement is improved by the income gains generated by these programs but is not affected by changes in parental employment and welfare receipt occurring at the same time. Figure 10.3 presents how, across our welfare and work policies, the impacts on income are related to the impacts on children's school achievement. Each point on the figure represents the impact from a single study. Our findings are based on an estimation strategy that relies on these impacts (although they allow us to simultaneously consider other important factors that are likely to affect children, such as the programs' impacts on parents' employment and income). As shown in Figure 10.3, we find a positive relation between program impacts on income and program impacts on children's school achievement—those programs that increase income the most also appear to increase children's achievement the most.

To put some numbers behind these positive effects, our instrumental variables analyses find that a $1,000 increase in annual income sustained for between two and five years boosts child achievement by six percent of a standard deviation. These effects are similar in size with and without accounting for other changes the programs produced at the same time—employment and welfare receipt. Translated into an IQ-type scale, this amounts to about one point. Translated into one of the achievement tests use in these studies—the Bracken Test of School Readiness—these effect sizes translate into one additional correct answer in a 61-question test regarding colors, letters, numbers/counting, comparisons, and shapes. The earnings supplement programs in our study boosted family income for younger children by between $800 and nearly $2,200 per year, which corresponds

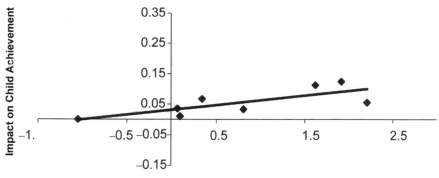

Figure 10.3   Individual study impacts on parents' income and child achievement for 2- to 5-year-olds

to achievement effect sizes ranging from 5 to 12 percent of a standard deviation. For the older age groups, generally nonsignificant effects of income are found, at least when employment and welfare receipt are considered alongside income.

Results from nonexperimental studies are quite consistent with those we find here—that family income has benefits for children, although more so for cognitive outcomes than for child behavior and health, and more so for younger than for older children (Duncan & Brooks-Gunn, 1997; Duncan, Yeung, Brooks-Gunn, & Smith, 1998; Haveman & Wolfe, 1995; Klerman, 1991; Korenman & Miller, 1997). This research also suggests that family economic conditions matter because they enhance the material and social resources available to children (e.g., the kinds of books and toys parents can purchase for their children; Becker, 1981; Bergstrom, 1997; Coleman, 1988) and may improve family psychological processes (e.g., parental emotional well-being and parenting; Chase-Lansdale & Pittman, 2002; McLoyd, 1990, 1997, 1998; McLoyd, Jayartne, Ceballo, & Borquez, 1994).

Given this prior work suggesting that income benefits children through parents' increased ability to purchase opportunities for their children, like quality care, we next addressed whether the use of center-based care partially explained the positive effects of income on children's achievement. As with the effects of income on children's achievement, we first present the relation between impacts of our programs on income and impacts on children's child care arrangements, and again we observe a positive association (see Figure 10.4). In fact, when analyses are conducted to test the effects of income on center-based care, we find that a $1,000 increase in average quarterly income increases participation in the exclusive use of center-based care by about nine percentage points.

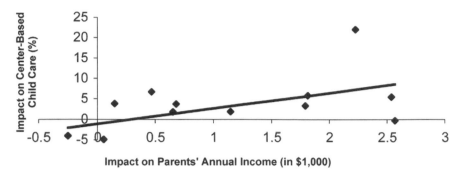

Figure 10.4   Individual study impacts on parents' income and center-based child care for 3- to 5-year-olds

In addition to investigating the relationship between increased income and center-based care, we estimated the direct effects of center-based care on children's achievement and problem behavior (Gennetian, Crosby, Dowsett, & Huston, 2004; Crosby, Dowsett, Gennetian, & Huston, 2004). While several of these programs—particularly those with an earnings supplement—increased employment and income, and center-based care, some programs, whether or not they had an earning supplement policy, offered expanded child-care assistance. Such assistance included expanded[2] financial and nonfinancial child-care resources, primarily aimed at facilitating the use of center-based or licensed care, that were otherwise not available. Our prior work shows that programs with expanded child-care assistance increased the use of center-based care more so than the use of home-based care, whereas other programs were more likely to increase the use of home-based care than center-based care, especially for preschool-aged children (Crosby, Gennetian and Huston, 2005). Controlling for employment, earnings, and income, we use this unique variation in the use of center-based care arrangements to estimate the effects of center-based care.

Data for these analyses are from seven different employment and welfare studies that together represent 13 welfare or employment programs.[3] These analyses focus on two groups of children—those who were two to five years old and not yet in kindergarten when their parents entered these studies, and those who were in kindergarten to second grade. We assess the effects of exclusive participation in center-based care, and for a subset of studies with data, the effects of total months in center-based care.

Our findings suggest that use of center-based care, as opposed to care in someone's home,[4] during a child's preschool years (while their mother

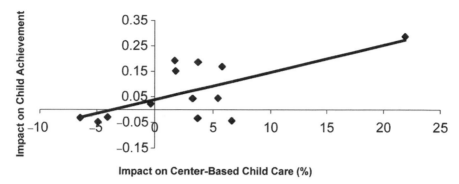

Figure 10.5 Individual study impacts on center-based child care and child achievement for 3- to 5-year-olds

is employed) has a positive effect on school achievement in the early grades of elementary school. Summarized in Figure 10.5, we find that, as with impacts on income, greater impacts on children's use of center-based care are associated with greater impacts on children's achievement. But of course, these programs also change income and employment of parents—yet, analyses controlling for program impacts on parents' economic outcomes find that these positive effects still hold even after accounting for these effects. This positive effect of center-based care partly accounts for the positive effect of income for this same age group. Effect sizes are small—an increase in .10 of probability of being exclusively in center-based care during the preschool years increases achievement by about 10 percent of a standard deviation—but, nevertheless, provide confirming evidence that organized center-based care that is generally available to low-income families can be beneficial to low-income children's cognitive functioning and preacademic preparation. These findings are consistent with prior nonexperimental work showing the benefits of participation in structured, center-based programs for children's cognitive functioning, even when controlling for the quality of care (Currie, 2001; Currie & Thomas, 1995; Garces, Currie, Thomas, 2002; Loeb et al. 2004; NICHD Early Child Care Research Network, 2002, 2003), as well as with our own hypotheses about the way in which the increased income may have benefited children.

Using a similar estimation technique with the same data, we also examine the effects of center-based care on children's externalizing (acting out) and internalizing (depressed/withdrawn) behavior, based on maternal as well as teacher reports (Crosby et al., 2004). Here we find positive associations of center-based care in the preschool years with problem behavior in the school years using ordinary least squares techniques (i.e., increases in problem behavior with more center care); these effects are negligible when estimated using instrumental variables analysis. The one estimate that does hold up in the instrumental variables analysis—higher maternal-reported internalizing problems due to center-based care—is no longer statistically significant when controls for maternal depressive symptoms are included in the model. By contrast, we find that center-based care during the preschool years *reduces* teacher reports of externalizing problem behavior while children are elementary school-aged.

DISCUSSION

This chapter summarizes research conducted to understand how macro-policies—welfare and antipoverty policies—affect the well-being of children and adolescents. Our research has shown that welfare reforms targeted at parents can have important consequences for their children. Specifically, the findings reported here demonstrate that policies that aim to improve the economic security of families can benefit elementary school-age children, particularly with regard to their school achievement. These benefits appear to be due to the increased income generated as a result of these programs, and, partially due to increased use of center-based care arrangements.

At the same time, there are some important cautions in this research. First, for adolescents, the results suggest that policies that increase parental employment may have some negative effects on schooling outcomes, suggesting a need for policymakers to develop strategies that can effectively engage low-income youth and help them move successfully into adulthood. Second, our findings with regard to child care show that the benefits to increased use of center-based care are primarily for children's cognitive development, leaving open the question about how to best simultaneously improve socioemotional development, a key predictor of future achievement in school.

Our best and most consistent evidence across this set of welfare and work policies are the effects on children's school achievement. Improvements in children's mental health outcomes may require more intensive treatment strategies than the welfare and employment policies we evaluated here. One promising model that is currently being evaluated in the context of a large-scale federally-funded experimental study addresses how a telephonic clinical care management model can reduce depression and increase employment among Medicaid recipients diagnosed with depression (currently being evaluated by MDRC as part of the Enhanced Services for the Hard-to-Employ Demonstration and Evaluation Project, funded by the Department of Health and Human Services). As one of a set of studies being conducted on families facing significant barriers to their employment, this model shows promise in meeting the mental health needs of hard-to-employ welfare-recipient parents, and, if successful in this regard, is likely to reduce some of the risks associated with living with a depressed parent for children as well (including the risk of greater mental health problems for the children themselves).

Other macro-policies that may address children's socioemotional adjustment are programs that are intended to reduce marital conflict among two-parent, low-income families (also being evaluated by MDRC in a federally-funded effort, "Supporting Healthy Marriages"), and two-generation approaches, providing services to improve economic outcomes for parents as well as the developmental needs of children. These kinds of policies may have stronger and more robust effects on children's behavioral outcomes than those we find in the context of these welfare and employment policies.

At the same time, the history of these macro-policies is replete with discussions of concerns for children, particularly young children, of requiring or even encouraging low-income single parents to go to work. The fact that no clear and consistent detriments to young children's mental health were found as a result of these efforts is noteworthy. While state policies that are more stringent than those we evaluated here may have a differing pattern of effects, the fact that these programs increased employment and had few effects on young children's behavior should allay concerns about harm to young children of the kinds of policies that we evaluated here.

We end by noting the significance of these findings for program and policy. For a fraction of the cost of high-quality preschool programs, these policies aimed at single welfare-recipient parents can indeed affect the well-being of low-income preschool children. While the effects are small, they do suggest that policymakers who wish to use welfare policy as a means to address the developmental needs of young children may want to consider these kinds of income-boosting policies. For older children, the findings imply that changes in welfare policy need to be paired with policies designed to support adolescents—the most obvious being after-school programs, although the fact that sibling care may have played a role here suggests that expansions in child-care programs serving younger siblings of these adolescents might make a difference as well.

NOTES

1. For further discussion of these effects, see Morris and Michalopoulos, 2000.

2. In all studies, parents in the control groups were eligible for child care subsidies offered through Aid to Families of Dependent Children (AFDC) (prior to 1996) and for some subsidies outside the welfare system. In some of the experiments, members of the program groups had the same "standard" child-care subsidies as their control counterparts, but other programs included a range of additional policy components that we have labeled "enhanced child-care assistance." These policies can be grouped into five sets: resource and referral, encouragement of formal care, higher income eligibility limits, direct payment to providers, and reduced bureaucratic barriers.

3. In addition to the studies listed in Table 10.1, we also relied on data from the New Chance evaluation (Quint, Bos, & Polit, 1997), an experimental study of a voluntary service program for young welfare-recipient parents, for these analyses.

4. Because most of the increased use of child care in these programs is prompted by increases in maternal employment and because we control for employment, the resulting estimates of center-based care are relative to the effects of home-based care arrangements (rather than to no child care).

REFERENCES

Baydar, N., & Brooks-Gunn, J. (1991). Effects of maternal employment and child-care arrangements in infancy on preschoolers' cognitive and behavioral outcomes, evidence from the children of the NSLY. *Developmental Psychology, 27*(6), 932–945.

Becker, G.S. (1981). *A treatise on the family.* Cambridge, MA: Harvard University Press.

Bergstrom, T. (1997). A survey of theories of the family. In M. Rosenzweig & O. Stark (Eds.), *Handbook of population and economics* (pp. 21–74), New York: North Holland.

Berlin, G. (2000). *Encouraging work, reducing poverty: The impact of work incentive programs.* New York: MDRC.

Bloom, D., Kemple, J.J., Morris, P., Scriverner, S., Verma, N., & Hendra, R. (2000). *The family transition program: Final report on Florida's initial time-limited welfare program.* New York: MDRC.

Bloom, D., Scrivener, S., Michalopoulos, C., Morris, P.A., Hendra, R., Adams-Ciardullo, D., & Walter, J. (2002). *Jobs First: Final report on Connecticut's welfare reform initiative.* New York: MDRC.

Bolger, K.E., Patterson, C.J., Thompson, W.W., & Kupersmidt, J.B. (1995). Psychosocial adjustment among children experiencing persistent and intermittent family economic hardship. *Child Development, 66,* 1107–1129.

Bos, J., Huston, A., Granger, R., Duncan, G., Brock, T., & McLoyd, V. (1999). *New hope for people with low incomes.* New York: MDRC.

Bradley, R. H., & Corwyn, R. (2002). Socioeconomic status and child development. *Annual Review of Psychology, 53,* 371–399.

Bronfenbrenner, U., & Morris, P. (1998). The ecology of developmental processes. In R. M. Lerner (Ed.), *Theoretical models of human development,* Vol. 1, *Handbook of child psychology* (5th ed., pp. 993–1028). Editor-in-chief: William Damon. New York: Wiley.

Brooks, J. L., Hair, E. C., & Zaslow, M. (2001). *Welfare reform's impacts on adolescents: Early warning signs.* Child Trends Research Brief. Washington, DC: Child Trends.

Brooks-Gunn, J., Han, W., & Waldfogel, J. (2002). Maternal employment and child cognitive outcomes in the first three years of life: The NICHD study of early child care. *Child Development, 73*(4), 1052–1072.

Brooks-Gunn, J., & Petersen, A. C. (Eds.). (1983). *Girls at puberty: Biological and psychosocial perspectives.* New York: Plenum Press.

Chase-Lansdale, P. L., Moffitt, R. A., Lohman, B. J., Cherlin, A. J., Coley, R. L., Pittman, L. D., Roff, J., & Votruba-Drzal, E. (2003). Mothers' transitions from welfare to work and the well-being of preschoolers and adolescents. *Science, 299,* 1548–1552.

Chase-Lansdale, L., & Pittman, L. (2002). Welfare reform and parenting: Reasonable expectations. *Future of Children, 12,* 167–185.

Cicchetti, D. (1991). Fractures in the crystal: Developmental psychopathology and the emergence of self. *Developmental Review, 11,* 271–287.

Coleman, J. S. (1988). Social capital in the creation of human capital. *American Journal of Sociology, 94,* S95-S120.

Coley, R. L., Chase-Lansdale, P. L., & Li Grining, C. P. (2001, April). *Low-income families and child care: Quality, options, and choices.* Paper presented at the Biennial Meeting of the Society for Research in Child Development, Minneapolis, MN.

Crosby, D., Dowsett, C., Gennetian, L., & Huston, A. (2004). The effects of center-based care on the problem behavior of low-income children with working mothers. Unpublished Manuscripts. New York: NY MDRC.

Crosby, D., Gennetian, L., & Huston, A. (2005). Child care assistance policies can affect the use of center-based care for children in low-income families. *Journal of Applied Developmental Science, 9,* (2), 86–106.

Currie, J. (2001). Early childhood intervention programs: What do we know? *Journal of Economic Perspectives, 15*(2), 218–238.

Currie, J., & Thomas, D. (1995). Does Head Start make a difference? *The American Economic Review, 85*(3), 341–364.

Dearing, E., McCartney, K., & Taylor, B. A. (2001). Change in family income-to-needs matters more for children with less. *Child Development, 72,* 1779–1793.

Duncan, G. J., & Brooks-Gunn, J. (1997). Income effects across the life span: Integration and interpretation. In G. J. Duncan & J. Brooks-Gunn (Eds.), *Consequences of growing up poor* (pp. 596–610). New York: Russell Sage Foundation.

Duncan, G.J., Brooks-Gunn, J., & Klebanov, P.K. (1994). Economic deprivation and early childhood development. *Child Development, 65*, 296–318.

Duncan, G.J., Yeung, W., Brooks-Gunn, J., & Smith, J.R. (1998). Does poverty affect the life chances of children? *American Sociological Review, 63*(3), 406–423.

Dunifon, R.E., & Kalil, A. (2003). *Maternal welfare and work combination and adolescents' school progress.* Working Paper. Ford School of Public Policy, University of Michigan.

Freedman, D., Knab, J., Gennetian, L., & Navarro, D. (2000). The Los Angeles Jobs-First GAIN evaluation: Final report on a work first program in a major urban center. New York: MDRC.

Fuller, B., Kagan, S. L., Caspary, G., & Gauthier, C. (2002). Has welfare reform advanced child-care options for poor families? *The Future of Children, 12*(1), 97–119.

Fuller, B., Kagan, S., Loeb, S., Carroll, J., McCarthy, J., Krelcher, G., Carrol, B., Cook, G., Chang, Y., & Sprachman, S. (2002). *New lives for poor families? Mothers and young children move through welfare reform.* The University of California, Berkeley; Teacher's College, Columbia University; Stanford University; Yale University: The Growing Up in Poverty Project.

Garces, E., Currie, J., & Thomas, D. (2002). Longer term effects of Head Start. *American Economic Review, 92*(4), 999–1012.

Gennetian, L.A., Morris, P., Bos, J., & Bloom, H. (2005). Constructing instrumental variables from experimental data to explore how treatments produce effects. In H. Bloom (Ed.), *Learning more from social experiments: Evolving analytic approaches.* New York: Russell Sage Foundation.

Gennetian, L., Duncan, G., Knox, V., Vargas, W., Clark-Kauffman, E., & London, A. (2004). How welfare policies affect adolescents' school outcomes: A synthesis of evidence from experimental studies. *Journal of Research on Adolescence, 14*(4), 399–423.

Gennetian, L.A., Crosby, D.A., Dowsett, C., & Huston, A.C. (2004). Center-based care and the achievement of low-income children: Evidence using data from experimental employment-based programs. Unpublished manuscript. New York: MDRC.

Gennetian, L.A., Huston, A.C., Crosby, D.A., Chang, Y.E., Lowe, E.D., & Weisner, T. (2002). *Making child care choices: How welfare and work policies influence parents' decisions.* New York: MDRC.

Gennetian, L.A., & Miller, C. (2000). *Reforming welfare and rewarding work: Final report on the Minnesota Family Investment Program,* Vol. 2, *Effects on Children.* New York: MDRC.

Hamburg, B. A. (1974). Early adolescence: A specific and stressful stage of life. In G. V. Coelho, D. A. Hamburg, & J. E. Adams (Eds.), *Coping and adaptation* (pp. 101–124). New York: Basic.

Hamilton, G., Freedman, S., Gennetian, L.A., Michalopoulos, C., Walter, J., Adams-Ciardullo, D., Gassman-Pines, A., McGroder, S., Zaslow, M., Brooks, J., & Ahluwalia, S. (2001). National evaluation of welfare-to-work strategies: How effective are different welfare-to-work approaches? Five-year adult and child impacts for eleven programs. Executive Summary. Washington, DC: U.S. Department of Health and Human Services, Administration for Children and Families and Office of the Assistant Secretary for Planning and Evaluation, and U.S. Department of Education.

Harvey, E. (1999). Short-term and long-term effects of early parental employment on children of the National Longitudinal Survey of Youth. *Developmental Psychology, 35*(2), 445–459.

Haveman, R., & Wolfe, B. (1995). Short-term effects of early parental employment on children of the National Longitudinal Survey of Youth. *Developmental Psychology, 35*(2), 445–459.

Huston, A. (2002). Reforms and child development. *Future of Children, 12*(1), 59–78.

Huston, A.C., Miller, C., Richburg-Hayes, L., Duncan, G.J., Eldred, C.A., Weisner, T.S., Lowe, E., McLoyd, V.C., Crosby, D.A., Ripke, M.N., Redcross, C. (2003). *The New Hope Project effects on families and children after five years*. New York: MDRC.

Klerman, L. (1991). The health of poor children: Problems and programs. In A. Huston (Ed.), *Children and poverty* (pp. 136–157). Cambridge and New York: Cambridge University Press.

Korenman, S., & Miller, J.E. (1997). Effects of long-term poverty on physical health of children in the National Longitudinal Survey of Youth. In G.J. Duncan & J. Brooks-Gunn (Eds.), *Consequences of growing up poor* (pp. 70–99). New York: Russell Sage Foundation.

Lamb, M. (1998). Nonparental child care: Context, quality, correlates and consequences. In I.E. Sigel and K.A. Renninger (Eds.), *Handbook of child psychology* (5th ed., vol. 4). New York: John Wiley and Sons.

Loeb, S., Fuller, B., Kagan, S.L., & Carrol, B. (2004). Child care in poor communities: Early learning effects of type, quality, and stability. *Child Development, 75*, 47–65.

Mayer, S. (1997). *What money can't buy: The effect of parental income on children's outcomes*. Cambridge, MA: Harvard University Press.

McGroder, S.M., Zaslow, M.J., Moore, K.A., & LeMenestrel, S.M. (2000). *Impacts on young children and their families two years after enrollment: Findings from the Child Outcomes Study*. National Evaluation of Welfare-to-Work Strategies. Washington, DC: U.S. Department of Health and Human Services, Office of the Assistant Secretary for Planning and Evaluation and Administration for Children and Families; and U.S. Department of Education, Office of the Under Secretary and Office of Vocational and Adult Education.

McLoyd, V.C. (1990). The impact of economic hardship on black families and children: Psychological distress, parenting and socioemotional development. *Child Development, 61*, 311–346.

McLoyd, V.C. (1997). The impact of poverty and low socioeconomic status on the socioemotional functioning of African American children and adolescents: Mediating affects. In R.D. Taylor & M.C. Wang (Eds.), *Social and emotional adjustment and family relations in ethnic minority families* (pp. 7–34). Mahwah, NJ: Lawrence Erlbaum.

McLoyd, V.C. (1998). Children in poverty, development, public policy, and practice. In I.E. Siegel & K.A. Renninger (Eds.), *Handbook of child psychology* (4th ed.), New York: Wiley.

McLoyd, V.C., Jayartne, T.E., Ceballo, R., & Borquez, J. (1994). Unemployment and work interruption among African-American single mothers, effects on parenting and adolescent socioemotional functioning. *Child Development, 65,* 562–589.

Michalopoulos, C., Tattrie, D., Miller, C., Robins, P.K., Morris, P., Gyarmati, D., Redcross, C., Foley, K., & Ford, R. (2002). *Making work pay: Final report on the Self Sufficiency Project for long-term welfare recipients.* New York: MDRC.

Moore, K., & Driscoll, A. (1997). Low-wage maternal employment and outcomes for children: A study. *Future of Children, 7*(1), 122–127.

Morris, P., Duncan, G., & Clark-Kauffman, E. (in press). Child well-being in an era of welfare-reform: The sensitivity of transitions in development to policy change. *Developmental Psychology.*

Morris, P., Duncan, G., & Rodrigues, C. (2004). *Does money really matter? Estimating impacts of family income on children's achievement with data from random assignment experiments.* Unpublished manuscript. New York: MDRC.

Morris, P., Huston, A.C., Duncan, G.J., Crosby, D.A., & Bos, J.M. (2001). *How welfare and work policies affect children: A synthesis of research.* New York: MDRC.

Morris, P., & Michalopoulos, C. (2000). *The Self Sufficiency Project at 36 months: Effects on children of a program that increased employment and income.* New York: MDRC.

NICHD Early Child Care Research Network (2002). Early child care and children's development prior to school entry: Results from the NICHD Study of Early Child Care. *American Educational Research Journal, 39,* 133–164.

NICHD Early Child Care Research Network (2003). Type of child care and children's development at 54 months. Mimeo.

NICHD Early Child Care Research Network, & Duncan, G.J. (2003). Modeling the impacts of child care quality on children's preschool cognitive development. *Child Development, 74,* 1454–1475.

Parcel, T.L., & Menaghan, E.G. (1994). *Parent's jobs and children's lives.* New York: Aldine de Gruyter.

Parcel, T.L., & Menaghan, E.G. (1997). Effects of low-wage employment on family well-being. *Future of Children, 7*(1), 116–121.

Peisner-Feinberg, E.S., Burchinal, M.R., Clifford, R.M., Culkin, M.L., Howes, C., Kagan, S. L., Yazsjian, N., Byler, P., Rustici, J., & Zelazo, J. (1999). *The children of the cost, quality, and outcomes study go to school.* (Technical Report). Chapel Hill: University of North Carolina.

Quint, J., Bos, J., & Polit, D. (1997). *New chance: Final report on a comprehensive program for young mothers in poverty and their children.* New York: MDRC.

Scarr, S. (1998) American child care today. *American Psychologist, 53*(2), 95–108.

Shonkoff, J.P., & Phillips, D.A. (Eds.). (2000). *From neurons to neighborhoods: The science of early childhood development.* Washington, DC: National Academy Press.

Sroufe, L.A. (1990). An organizational perspective on the self. In D. Cicchetti & M. Beeghly (Eds.), *The self in transition: Infancy to childhood* (pp. 281–307). Chicago: University of Chicago Press.

Vandell, D.L., & Ramanan, J. (1992). Effects of early and recent maternal employment on children from low-income families. *Child Development, 63*(4), 938–949.

Zaslow, M.J., & Emig, C.A. (1997). When low-income mothers go to work: Implications for children. *Future of Children, 7*(1), 110–115.

Zaslow, M.J., Moore, K.A., Morrison, D.R., & Coiro, M.J. (1995). The Family Support Act and children: Potential pathways of influence. *Children and Youth Services Review, 17*(1–3), 231–249.

Chapter 11

RESPONDING TO THE CRISIS IN AMERICAN INDIAN AND ALASKA NATIVE CHILDREN'S MENTAL HEALTH

Paul Spicer and Michelle Christensen Sarche

Funds for writing this chapter were provided by grants from the National Institute of Child Health and Human Development (HD 42760; P Spicer, PI), the National Institute of Mental Health (MH 63260; M Sarche, PI), and the Robert Wood Johnson Foundation (SAPRP 47400; P Spicer, PI).

INTRODUCTION

Our goal in this chapter is to summarize what the available evidence suggests regarding the mental health service needs of American Indian and Alaska Native infants, children, and adolescents and to document, in the most forceful terms possible, the lack of resources to fund appropriate services for them and their families. American Indian and Alaska Native families face numerous adversities with minimal support from formal mental health systems. In this chapter, we highlight the results of an ongoing program of research on the relationships between children's mental heath and parental problems and the opportunities to address the issues that arise in the context of a broader focus on Indian child welfare and other systems of care. We begin, however, with an overview of what little is known about the mental health needs of Indian and Native children and families.

THE BROADER CONTEXT OF INDIAN AND NATIVE CHILDREN'S MENTAL HEALTH NEEDS

In the broader literature dedicated to understanding children's social and emotional development and experiences, strikingly little research exists to document the experience of American Indian and Alaska Native children of any age. In total, American Indian and Alaska Native people today represent roughly 1.5 percent of the total U.S. population (U.S. Census Bureau, 2000). With 33.9 percent of this population under the age of 18 (U.S. Census Bureau, 2001) and fertility rates higher than the general U.S. population and other minority populations (U.S. Census Bureau, 1990), the Indian and Native population is among the youngest and fastest-growing in the country. High quality data are difficult to obtain on many aspects of Indian and Native life, owing in large part to difficulties in sampling these small, isolated, diverse, and culturally distinct populations (Beals, Manson, Mitchell, Spicer, & AI-SUPERPFP Team, 2003; Grossman, 2003; Norton & Manson, 1996). Yet, based on existing data, there can be little doubt that the Indian and Native population as a whole is confronted with vast disparities in health and health care (Beals, Novins et al., 2005; Gone, 2004; Katz, 2004; Spicer et al., 2003; Zuckerman, Haley, Roubideaux, & Lillie-Blanton, 2004). American Indian and Alaska Native populations also wrestle with the legacy of centuries of dispossession at the hands of the U.S. government as the result of policies and practices intentionally designed to break apart American Indian culture, communities, family, and identity (Bird, 2002; Brave Heart & Spicer, 2000; Duran, 1990; Harris, 2002; Roubideaux, 2002).

According to the U.S. Census Bureau (2003), 23.2 percent of American Indian and Alaska Native people are living at or below the poverty level based on a recent three-year average (2000–2002). This rate is nearly twice that of the U.S. all races rate (11.7%) and is the highest of all races, except African Americans for whom it is the same. Census Bureau statistics (2000) reveal that 32 percent of American Indian/Alaska Native children under the age of 18 are living in poverty, a rate that is again twice that of the U.S. all races rate of 16.1 percent. The same Census Bureau statistics reveal that 22 percent of all American Indian/Alaska Native families live at or below the poverty level, compared with 9.2 percent of families in the general population. American Indian/Alaska Native families with children under the age of five are especially likely to be living in poverty compared to both American Indian/Alaska Native families in general and families in the general population with children under five years of age (35% versus 22% and 17%, respectively). Census data also reveal discrepancies in education and employment for American Indian and Alaska Native people relative to the general population. Although American Indian and Alaska Native people are as likely to have a high school diploma or general education diploma, some college, or an associate's degree, they are less likely to attain a bachelor's (7.6% versus 15.5%) or professional (3.9% versus 8.9%) degree, and less likely to have completed high school

(70% versus 90.4%). According to the School and Staffing Surveys (National Center for Educational Statistics, 1997), educational discrepancies are apparent early for Indian and Native students, with Bureau of Indian Affairs and tribal school students being approximately three times more likely to drop out or withdraw from school (9.5% versus 2.7%) and almost twice as likely to be retained a grade (11.7% versus 6.5%) compared to national data from the same survey. In terms of employment, Indian and Native people are unemployed at twice the rate of the general population (7.5% versus 3.7%), and for reservation communities, the unemployment rate is estimated to be far greater (Indian Health Service, 1999).

Given the economic and social inequalities experienced by their communities, it is not surprising that marked disparities in health have been documented for Indian and Native people of all ages. According to the Indian Health Service, the federal health care agency that provides medical care to roughly 1.6 million American Indian and Alaska Native people, the age-adjusted death rate for Indian and Native adults exceeds that of the general population by almost 40 percent (699.3/100,000 versus 503.9/100,000). The physical health disparities most affecting Indian and Native adults include deaths due to diabetes, chronic liver disease and cirrhosis, and accidents, all of which occur at three times the national rate. Deaths due to tuberculosis, pneumonia, influenza, suicide, homicide, and heart disease also exceed those of the general population.

Few data exist to document the health status of the many Indian and Native people not served by the Indian Health Service (Forquera, 2001), yet those that do exist suggest similarly higher rates of accidents, alcohol-related deaths, tuberculosis, and sexually transmitted diseases relative to white populations from the same geographic area (Grossman, Krieger, Sugarman, & Forquera, 1994). According to the most recently available data, death due to suicide among Indian and Native people of all ages is 72 percent higher than in the general population, while death due to chronic liver disease and cirrhosis is nearly five times the national rate (Indian Health Service, 1999). Furthermore, the impact of one individual's mental health problems often reaches well beyond that individual's own experience, creating not only hardship and suffering for his or her family, but extended family and entire community as well, due to the close and interwoven nature of relationships in Indian and Native communities (Robin, Chester, & Goldman, 1996).

While mortality data provide some traces of evidence on the mental health needs of Indian and Native communities, especially for deaths from suicide and alcoholism, systematic epidemiological evidence on the level of mental health problems has only recently become available as our team has published the results of the largest study of psychiatric epidemiology ever attempted in American Indian communities (Beals et al., 2003; Beals,

Novins et al., 2005; Beals et al., 2004; O'Connell, Novins, Beals, Spicer, & The AI-SUPERPFP Team, 2005; Spicer et al., 2003). In this study our team assessed the prevalence of nine DSM-III-R or DSM-IV disorders among 3,086 American Indian men and women between the ages of 15 and 54 from two different tribal backgrounds (one reservation in the Southwest and two tribally-related reservations on the Northern Plains). Instrumentation on this effort was a culturally modified version of that used in the original National Comorbidity Survey (Kessler et al., 1994) and was designed to permit explicit comparisons to those rates. Because of the time between our study and the original National Comorbidity Survey, we also modified the measure to permit us to address DSM-IV diagnoses. We focus here on the explicit comparison to published rates from the original National Comorbidity Survey, using DSM-III-R criteria. The highest lifetime rates of disorder for Indian women were post-traumatic stress disorder (Southwest 22.5; Northern Plains 20.2), alcohol dependence (Southwest 8.7; Northern Plains 20.2), and major depression (Southwest 14.3; Northern Plains 10.3). For Northern Plains women, alcohol abuse was also among the most likely diagnoses (10.3 lifetime prevalence). The highest lifetime rates of disorder for men were alcohol dependence (Southwest 31.1; Northern Plains 30.5), post-traumatic stress disorder (Southwest 12.8; Northern Plains 11.5), and alcohol abuse (Southwest 11.2; Northern Plains 12.8). In an explicit and planned comparison to the National Comorbidity Survey (Kessler et al., 1994), rates of post-traumatic stress disorder were significantly higher for American Indian men and women from both tribal backgrounds, ranging from two to three times the national rate. Alcohol dependence was also significantly higher among both Southwest and Northern Plains men (50% higher) and among Northern Plains women (100% higher) compared to the national sample. Surprisingly, major depression was significantly lower among both Southwest and Northern Plains women compared to the national sample (one-third lower for Southwest women, and 50% lower for Northern Plains women), although a variety of cultural and methodological problems in the assessment of depression suggest caution in interpreting these results (Beals, Manson et al., 2005).

DIRECT EVIDENCE ON THE MENTAL HEALTH NEEDS OF AMERICAN INDIAN AND ALASKA NATIVE CHILDREN

Mortality data provides some indirect evidence for the level of mental health service needs among Indian and Native children, with suicide among young people in 1997–1998 (the latest published data) occurring at a rate of 9.1 per 100,000 children, which was three times the white rate, four times the black rate, and in certain regions, was as much as six times the national rate (Centers for Disease Control and Prevention, 2003). Though small in quantity, available research studies directly assessing mental health status suggest that American Indian and Alaska Native children face significant challenge both in terms of mental health risk and mental health problems. In one of the largest studies of American Indian and Alaska Native youth mental health, Blum and colleagues surveyed 13,454 Indian and Native youth in grades 7–12 and found high rates of both physical and mental health risk behavior and experiences (Blum, Harmon, Harris, Bergeisen, & Resnick, 1992). In this sample, physical and sexual abuse was reported by 10 percent and 13 percent of youth, respectively. For girls, these rates were higher with 23.9 percent reporting physical abuse and 21.6 percent reporting sexual abuse by twelfth grade. An alarming 17 percent of children had attempted suicide, while 11 percent knew someone who had committed suicide. Weekly or more alcohol use was reported by 8.2 percent of seventh graders, whereas by twelfth grade, 14.1 percent of children reported weekly or more alcohol use. Overall, 6 percent of children reported signs of severe emotional distress. Children in this study also placed themselves at high risk for physical injury and trauma, reporting never wearing a seatbelt (44%), drinking and driving (37.9% of drivers), and riding with a driver who had been drinking (21.8%).

Explicitly comparative work presents a more mixed picture of the mental health status of Indian and Native children. In a study of 1,251 American Indian students in grades 2 and 4, Dion, Gotowiec, and Beiser (1998) found that white children experienced more depressive symptoms according to self and parent report on a standardized behavioral checklist than did Indian children of the same age. In a study of 404 seventh, ninth, and eleventh grade students (112 of whom were Indian), by contrast, Fisher, Bacon, & Storck (1998) compared rates of psychiatric symptomatology for American Indian children on the same standardized behavioral checklist based on self, teacher, and parent report. Specifically, they found higher ratings of somatic complaints (self, teacher), delinquency (self, teacher, parent), withdrawal (teacher), anxiety/depression (teacher), attention problems (teacher), and aggression (teacher) for American Indian boys. For American Indian girls they found higher ratings of anxiety/depression (self), social problems (self), delinquency (self), and overall problems (parent). They also found that overall, American Indian children had more mental health risk factors than did other children, including single-parent households, a family member who attempted or completed suicide, a friend who committed suicide, and lower grades.

Research using explicit diagnostic criteria has also shown mixed results. In a study of 323 American Indian children, Costello, Farmer, Angold, Burns, & Erkanli (1997) assessed the three-month prevalence rate of

ICD-10 and DSM-III-R and IV disorders for children 9–13 years old. Overall, the authors found that conduct and oppositional defiant disorder, anxiety disorders, and separation anxiety were the most common diagnoses and occurred at similar rates for Indian and white children from the same area. Though substance abuse and dependence were rare for both groups, American Indian children were significantly more likely to be diagnosed with an abuse or dependence disorder than were white children (Costello et al., 1997). In contrast, Beals et al. (1997) found higher rates of disorder among older American Indian children for a greater number of DSM-III-R disorders in a school-based sample of 109 14–16-year-old children from a Northern Plains reservation community compared to published rates of disorder for similarly aged and similarly assessed non-American Indian children. In this sample, substance use disorders were the most common, with 18.3 percent of American Indian children meeting criteria for either abuse or dependence within the last six months. Disruptive behavior disorders, anxiety disorders, mood disorders, and other substance use disorders were diagnosed in 13.8 percent, 5.5 percent, 4.6 percent, and 3.9 percent of American Indian children, respectively. In comparison, rates of attention deficit hyperactivity disorder, substance abuse/dependence, and conduct and oppositional defiant disorder were elevated relative to previously published rates for other children.

CHILD ABUSE AND NEGLECT

The high rates of teen pregnancy, poverty, and single-parent, female-headed households noted above, as well as the persistent indications of high rates of alcohol abuse in some American Indian/Alaska Native communities (May, 1996; Spicer et al., 2003), all contribute to the documented high rates of child abuse and neglect that have been found (DeBruyn, Lujan, & May, 1992; Fischler, 1985; Lujan, DeBruyn, May, & Bird, 1989; Piasecki et al., 1989). Research on child abuse and neglect in Indian and Native communities lags behind that in the general population, but a growing body of literature has explored these phenomena. Isolated reports on child maltreatment in American Indian tribes have existed since the late 1970s (Fischler, 1985; Hauswald, 1987; White, 1981; Wichlacz, Lane, & Kempe, 1978). But systematic national data, permitting comparisons to other racial and ethnic groups, has only recently been available. The most recent report on child maltreatment from the National Child Abuse and Neglect Data System reported that rates of maltreatment for Indian children in 2002 were 21.7 per 1000, which is more than twice the rate for white children (10.7 per 1000) (National Child Abuse and Neglect Data System, 2004). Moreover, given persistent problems in data reporting in many American Indian/Alaska

Native jurisdictions (Earle, 2000), these rates are likely to underrepresent the extent of the problem.

What we know about the patterns of abuse and neglect in Indian communities suggests that alcohol plays a crucial role, especially in cases of neglect (Fischler, 1985; White, 1981). In a survey of federal survey providers in the Southwest, Piasecki et al. (1989) found that those American Indian children who were abused or neglected were significantly more likely to come from homes where there was parental alcohol abuse, divorce, a single parent, and a chaotic family. With only a few exceptions, these children were also significantly more likely to have been placed in boarding schools, foster care, or other institutions. Research by Lujan and colleagues (1989), also in the Southwest, provides even more insight into these dynamics, with evidence of alcohol abuse found in 85 percent of neglect cases and 63 percent of abuse cases. While subsequent research by the same team indicated that alcohol abuse was not the only cause of child maltreatment, occurring as it did in the context of multiple other risk factors (DeBruyn et al., 1992), it clearly appeared to be a major contributing factor to involvement with the child welfare system for American Indian and Alaska Native parents. Most recently, Kunitz and Levy (2000) found that the only women to lose custody of children in their sample from the Navajo Nation were those who met criteria for alcohol dependence. Thus, it would appear that substance abusing American Indian/Alaska Native parents come to the attention of the child welfare system at very high rates. Unfortunately all too often they encounter a system ill-equipped to address their needs.

Work by our own team (Libby et al., in press), underscores the extent to which systems designed to serve American Indian/Alaska Native families whose children are at risk for out-of-home placement do not adequately meet the needs of parents. Utilizing data from the National Study of Child and Adolescent Wellbeing, which is based on a random sample of children and families involved with child welfare systems across the United States, we examined the level of need for alcohol, drug, and mental health services for American Indian/Alaska Native parents involved in child welfare and the extent to which these needs were met with services. We focused only on those cases where the child remained in the home, thereby ensuring consistent data on the caregiver. At the time of the Child Protective Services investigation, 27 percent of these American Indian/Alaska Native caregivers had alcohol, drug, or mental health problems indicated by their caseworkers, but only 14 percent of them received a formal assessment. About one-quarter were referred for services, but only 12 percent of the caregivers with these problems received any type of specialty service in the 18 months following the opening of their case. Interestingly, American Indian Alaska Native caregivers were significantly less likely to receive services than Hispanic caregivers, but their service receipt was not significantly different from that of white or black caregivers, underscoring the extent to which the problems impacting upon American Indian and Alaska Native parents involved with child welfare are more systemic and not necessarily unique to them.

Nevertheless, we did detect disparities in a surprising area. In currently unpublished analyses of these data we examined levels of unmet need by service sector (substance abuse and mental health). In these analyses we found that the level of need was actually highest for American Indian and Alaska Native parents in mental health, not substance abuse, and that American Indian and Alaska Native caregivers were least likely to receive specialty mental health services compared to parents from other racial/ethnic groups. In contrast, they were most likely to receive services for substance abuse. Thus it would appear that a valuable opportunity to intervene in the lives of American Indian and Alaska Native families on mental health problems is lost when they come into contact with child welfare systems, as they continue to do with great frequency.

CHILD WELFARE AND AMERICAN INDIAN AND ALASKA NATIVE CHILDREN

Surveys by the association of American Indian Affairs in the late 1960s and repeated in the early 1970s indicated that 25–35 percent of all Indian children had been separated from their families and placed in foster homes, adoptive homes, or institutions, rates that were often dramatically higher than those for non-Indian children. For example, the rate of out-of-home placement for Indian children in South Dakota was 16 times higher and in Washington 19 times higher than the rates for non-Indians in the same states (Byler, 1977). In part as a response to these very high rates of out-of-home placement, Congress passed the Indian Child Welfare Act of 1978 (Ishisaka, 1978; Mannes, 1995). The Indian Child Welfare Act requires states to determine possible tribal affiliations of Indian and Native children involved in proceedings regarding foster care placements, termination of parental rights, and preadoptive and adoptive placements within their jurisdictions. The act further requires that these agencies give notice to the child's parents or custodians and tribe regarding the commencement of any of these proceedings and their right of intervention, and it establishes preferences for the placement of Indian and Native children in their families or in tribally approved placements (Jones, Gilette, Painte, & Paulson, 2000). In addition, the act mandates that the party seeking placement or termination of parental rights demonstrate unsuccessful but active efforts to provide remedial services and rehabilitative programs to prevent the breakup of the family.

Thus Indian Child Welfare Act provisions must be invoked for children identified as American Indian or Alaska Native. This makes it important for states and counties to have procedures in place to identify all American Indian and Alaska Native children at the beginning of an investigation by Child Protective Services. State social service agencies were not required to report their clients' race until 1997, when the Adoption and Safe Families Act (Public Law Number 105-89) changed the practice. States are now required to report by race and are sanctioned if they fail to do so. The act requires compliance in identifying a client by race, but how this law is implemented varies from state to state, and from tribal nation to tribal nation (Goodluck & Willeto, 2000). If a child's race is not ascertained, the agency might well overlook the need to implement Indian Child Welfare provisions for that child.

There have long been concerns about the extent to which non-tribal child welfare agencies implement the required provisions of the law and the extent to which tribes have the resources to assume jurisdiction of those cases of which they are notified. Earlier studies suggest that the largest reported barriers to compliance with Indian Child Welfare Act were at the federal and state policy levels. According to Cross, Earle, and Simmons (2000), these include the following: lack of funding, jurisdictional barriers (i.e., the relationship between states and tribes), lack of trained personnel, lack of information about the extent of the problem, and lack of appropriate service models.

In addition, many tribes do not have their own courts or child welfare programs or specialists and consequently do not have trained personnel to advocate for Indian or Native children or navigate the judicial and child welfare systems (Earle, 2000). When these structures are not in place, it may be difficult for child welfare agencies to establish a child's tribal memberships or eligibility. Furthermore, tribal nations have historically related directly to the federal government rather than to the states in which they are located. This relation complicates the investigation and reporting of child abuse and neglect, as states bear the primary responsibility for these tasks in the United States (Earle, 2000).

The Adoption and Safe Families Act has further complicated issues related to the treatment of American Indian children who have been abused and/or neglected. While this act does not contradict any Indian Child Welfare Act provisions, there are concerns that it will result in increased pressure to find permanent placements for Indian and Native children, especially in non-tribal jurisdictions (Simmons & Trope, 1999). To ensure that these potentially competing laws are interpreted and followed correctly, there are calls for more training for anyone dealing with child abuse and neglect of Indian children, including state and county personnel, law enforcement, courts, and even tribal council members (Earle, 2000). But for tribes that are trying to do their own work in this area, lack of resources is a major issue. In Earle's descriptive study, tribal workers reported that the workload is too much for the personnel they are currently able to hire, and they also expressed the need to have their own specialized staff such as a criminal investigator. Thus, issues of funding are crucial, as there has not even been enough money made available to support legislation already passed requiring tribes to handle abuse and neglect cases, let alone new requirements (Earle, 2000). Cross and colleagues estimate that initial funding under the Indian Child Welfare Act could meet only 25 percent of the need and, even now, leaves many tribes with only one case worker (Cross, Earle, & Simmons, 2000). Tribal access to other federal monies provided under the Social Security Act is complicated by the fact that these laws were written with little consideration of the unique status of American Indian/Alaska Native tribes, meaning that tribes often must negotiate with states to access these federal dollars (Brown, Whitaker, Clifford, Limb, & Munoz, 2000; Cross et al., 2000). And even where tribes may compete for funds directly, current levels of funding received by them are generally quite inadequate (Cross et al., 2000). Compounding the difficulties tribes face are even more serious shortfalls in the funding of health care for tribes.

HEALTH AND MENTAL HEALTH OF AMERICAN INDIAN AND ALASKA NATIVE CHILDREN

Health services to the American Indian/Alaska Native population are provided through three interrelated approaches: Indian Health Service operated clinics and hospitals; tribally operated health programs (largely funded through Congressional appropriations administered through the Indian Health Service), and urban programs governed by Indian Health Boards in metropolitan areas, partially funded by Indian Health Service (Noren, Kindig, & Sprenger, 1998). The Indian Health Service is the primary source of health services for 55 percent of the estimated 2.4 million Indian people. The majority of Indian people served by the Indian Health Service live on or near reservations, often in some of the most remote and poverty stricken areas of the country where other sources of health care are much less available. The Indian Health Service was founded on the idea that a direct service organization and government health program would be required to meet the federal trust responsibility for the health of Indian and Native people. Because of the geographic access problems in many of the rural areas where reservations are located, the Indian Health Service is often the only source of care available for these populations.

The 1990s saw interesting developments in the organization of health care for American Indian and Alaska Native tribes. After statutory changes in the late 1980s, tribal governments became more involved in operating their own health care delivery systems. Individual tribes and tribal (or village) consortiums took over the administration of health programs for their members. Provisions within the Indian Self-Determination and Education Act of 1975, with amendments, permitted tribes the opportunity to shape their delivery systems to meet their self-identified needs. In the process of this transformation, administrative funds were made available to tribes to fulfill needs that did not require the involvement of a federal employee. In accepting these responsibilities, tribes were funded with money previously used to pay Indian Health Service administrative personnel and headquarters functions such as technical assistance, quality control, patient information management, and long-term planning. Of necessity, the Indian Health Service was redesigned and transformed into a partnership between the federal program, tribes, and urban programs (Manson, 2000; Pfefferbaum, Pfefferbaum, Rhoades, & Strickland, 1997).

In addition, there are 34 urban projects, ranging from community health to comprehensive primary health care services. Urban health programs, established in recognition of the growing trend of Indian people moving away from reservations, also face unique funding problems. Despite that fact that more than half of American Indians and Alaska Natives live in metropolitan areas, only one percent of the total Indian Health Service budget went toward Urban Indian Health Programs in 1994. This budget allocation met an estimated 22 percent of the identified need for services at existing urban sites (Noren et al., 1998). Urban projects may receive funding from non-IHS sources as well as from IHS. They treat non-Indians as well as Indians and are likely to request payment from both, based on an income-based sliding scale. Despite this shift to metropolitan areas, demand for care at local Indian Health Service facilities continues to increase (Dixon, 2001; Pfefferbaum et al., 1997).

The Indian Health Service is not an entitlement program, and funds are therefore somewhat unpredictable since they are obtained through annual appropriations by the U.S. Congress. So, even when Indian Health Service facilities are located in needy locations, sufficient resources may not be available to provide the needed health services (Dixon, 2001; Noren et al., 1998). This is particularly true for Contract Health Services, including more expensive diagnostic and treatment services, which are often denied or delayed. Due to these limitations, American Indian and Alaska Native people have increasingly depended on other sources of health care (Noren et al., 1998).

While the federal government's overall responsibility for health care to American Indian and Alaska Native people has been unambiguous, continued unresolved disputes have resulted from the failure of legislation to explicitly define the rights and responsibilities of the federal government, states, and county agencies. Because Indian and Native people are citizens of tribes, as well as citizens in the counties and states in which they reside, they are also entitled to the benefits to which all citizens are entitled. Indeed, appropriations for the Indian Health Service are based on the assumption that Indian and Native people are entitled to care provided in conjunction with these other programs they qualify for as U.S. and state citizens (Pfefferbaum et al., 1997). Thus an Indian or Native person who meets eligibility criteria for a state Medicaid program or state Children's Health Insurance Program may enroll and have payments made for their services at state or federal expense. But accessing these services is not always straightforward. According to Pfefferbaum (1997), while this dual entitlement is established in law, receipt of services through public programs usually only follows after extensive negotiation or litigation to overcome denials and delays.

Moreover, persistent shortfalls in funding have left the Indian Health Service severely underresourced. Funds for health care in American Indian and Alaska Native tribes, adjusted for medical inflation and population growth, saw steady declines throughout the 1990s (Henry J. Kaiser Family Foundation, 1999), and even a record increase for the Indian Health Service in 2001 was barely sufficient to keep up with medical inflation in that year (Dixon, 2001). Thus, tribes find themselves with funds that are increasingly insufficient for even the most basic health care needs of their people. A United States Commission on Civil Rights report (U.S. Commission on Civil Rights, 2003) recently documented that the Indian Health Service is so severely underfunded that it spends just $1,914 per patient per year, half the amount ($3,803) spent on a federal prisoner in a year.

Not surprisingly, with regard to mental health services in particular, most tribal communities lack the infrastructure to support an effective mental health system (Manson, 2001). According to providers in 10 out of the total 12 Indian Health Service areas, mental health was identified as the number one health problem confronting American Indian and Alaska Native people and communities today, and along with social problems, was estimated to contribute to more than one-third of the demands for services (Johnson & Cameron, 2001). Despite such a demand, the Indian Health Service allocates only seven percent of its already limited to budget to mental health and substance abuse services (Gone, 2004). The impact of this on the availability of mental health services is dramatic. For example, by recent accounts there were only two psychiatrists and four psychologists per 100,000 people served by the Indian Health Service, one-seventh the number of psychiatrists and one-sixth the number of psychologists available to the general population (Gone, 2004). A report from the Office of Technology Assessment in 1990 reported that there were only 17 child-prepared mental health professionals within the entire IHS system (Office of Technology Assessment, 1990), or an average of 0.43 providers per 10,000 children, which was only 10 percent of the recommended number of providers. Manson (2001) also reports that 4 of the 12 Indian Health Service areas have no mental health care providers trained in pediatric or adolescent medicine. This lack of capacity makes it quite likely that American Indian and Alaska Native children are not receiving the mental health services they need.

CIRCLES OF CARE: INITIATING AND SUPPORTING INNOVATIVE SERVICES FOR CHILDREN AND FAMILIES IN AMERICAN INDIAN AND ALASKA NATIVE COMMUNITIES

As a partial remedy to this dire situation in American Indian and Alaska Native children's mental health services, the Circles of Care Initiative, funded by the Federal Center for Mental Health Services, with additional support from the Indian Health Service and the National Institute of Mental Health, has attempted to help Indian and Native communities respond to long-standing concerns regarding the availability, accessibility, and acceptability of mental health services for American Indian and Alaska Native children and adolescents and their families in the context of the unique set of cultural, epidemiological, fiscal, jurisdictional, and operational challenges to developing such systems. While service demonstration grants issued under the Comprehensive Community Mental Health Services for Children and their Families Program had funded three American Indian tribal organizations, many more American Indian and Alaska Native organizations had submitted unsuccessful applications under this initiative. It was the assessment of the Center for Mental Health Services, as well as a number of outside experts that served on an advisory board to this agency, that American Indian and Alaska Native communities would be more competitive for grants under this and other initiatives if they were able to pursue a community-based strategic planning effort that could form the foundation for their applications, a planning effort that has been explicitly supported by the Circles of Care initiative.

Reflecting on their experiences in this effort, the first round of grantees (a second round of grantees has also completed their planning efforts and a third round will be funded in 2005) pointed to a number of positive outcomes from their efforts to better understand the systems of care that serve children with severe emotional disturbances and their parents

(Duclos, Phillips, & LeMaster, 2004). These included the development of written products documenting need, existing services, and future plans; better attention to data collection in local agencies; and the development of new programs. Grantees also pointed to gains in integrating cultural approaches into their services plans, training staff, mobilizing the community on children's mental health, and developing new collaborations. Grantees also encountered, but in general were able to address, significant obstacles in recruiting and retaining staff, establishing working relationships with leadership at the tribal and agency levels, mistrust of research and evaluation, and responding to community concerns. While publications to date have emphasized the experience of grantees with the evaluation process, important programmatic lessons have also emerged, including the potential value of integrating traditional healing and community-based activities focusing on intergenerational dynamics in children's mental health and healing (Simmons, Novins, & Allen, 2004), insights that have also emerged in our earlier work (Brave Heart & Spicer, 2000; Spicer & Fleming, 2000).

CONCLUSIONS AND NEXT STEPS

The experiences of the communities funded under Circles of Care underscore the creativity that exists in many Indian and Native communities, which can be tapped to address the profound needs of Indian and Native children and families if properly supported. Indeed, in the context of considering issues in American Indian infant mental health and children of alcoholics, we have already documented the potential power of intergenerational approaches to address the needs of parents and their children simultaneously, approaches that draw, in powerful ways, on dominant cultural themes of family and community histories in American Indian and Alaska Native communities (Brave Heart & Spicer, 2000; Spicer & Fleming, 2000). And our work in the context of the child welfare system, reported previously, emphasizes the possibilities for such interventions that appear to be tailor-made for that context. Unfortunately there is a stunning lack of financial commitment at state and federal levels to support any innovation, a neglect that is even more striking given the unequivocal indications of need that we have reviewed here. Three very powerful messages thus emerge from this review: (1) American Indian and Alaska Native children suffer disproportionately from levels of stress and serious mental health problems; (2) they do so with little formal support from mental health systems; but (3) with proper support their communities display tremendous resourcefulness and creativity in addressing their needs. We can only hope that this contribution provides much needed impetus for governments at all levels to honor their obligations to the health and well-being of the original inhabitants of this land.

REFERENCES

Beals, J., Manson, S. M., Mitchell, C. M., Spicer, P., & AI-SUPERPFP Team. (2003). Cultural specificity and comparison in psychiatric epidemiology: Walking the tightrope in American Indian research. *Culture, Medicine, and Psychiatry, 27*, 259–289.

Beals, J., Manson, S. M., Whitesell, N. R., Mitchell, C. M., Novins, D. K., Simpson, S., Spicer, P., & the AI-SUPERPFP Team. (2005). Prevalence of major depression in two American Indian reservation populations: Unexpected findings with a structured interview. *American Journal of Psychiatry, 162*, 1713–1722.

Beals, J., Novins, D. K., Spicer, P., Orton, H. D., Mitchell, C. M., Manson, S. M., & the AI-SUPERPFP Team. (2004). Challenges in operationalizing the DSM-IV clinical significance criterion. *Archives of General Psychiatry, 61*, 1197–1207.

Beals, J., Novins, D. K., Whitesell, N. R., Spicer, P., Mitchell, C. M., Manson, S. M., & the AI-SUPERPFP Team. (2005). Mental health disparities: Prevalence of mental disorders and attendant service utilization of two American Indian reservation populations in a national context. *American Journal of Psychiatry, 162*, 1723–1732.

Beals, J., Piasecki, J., Nelson, S., Jones, M., Keane, E., Dauphinais, P., Red Shirt, R., Sack, W. H., & Manson, S. M. (1997). Psychiatric disorder among American Indian adolescents: Prevalence in Northern Plains youth. *Journal of the American Academy of Child and Adolescent Psychiatry, 36*(9), 1252–1259.

Bird, M. E. (2002). Health and indigenous people: Recommendations for the next generation. *American Journal of Public Health, 92*, 1391–1392.

Blum, R. W., Harmon, B., Harris, L., Bergeisen, L., & Resnick, M. D. (1992). American Indian—Alaska Native youth health. *Journal of the American Medical Association, 267*, 1637–1644.

Brave Heart, M.Y.H., & Spicer, P. (2000). The sociocultural context of American Indian infant mental health. In J. D. Osofsky & H. E. Fitzgerald (Eds.), *WAIMH handbook of infant mental health* (Vol. 1, pp. 151–179). New York: John Wiley & Sons.

Brown, E. F., Whitaker, L. S., Clifford, C. A., Limb, G. E., & Munoz, R. (2000). *Tribal/state Title IV-E intergovernmental agreements: Facilitating tribal access to federal resources.* Portland, OR: National Indian Child Welfare Association.

Byler, W. (1977). The destruction of American Indian families. In S. Unger (Ed.), *The destruction of American Indian families* (pp. 1–11). New York: Association on American Indian Affairs.

Centers for Disease Control and Prevention. (2003). Injury mortality among American Indian and Alaska Native children and youth—United States, 1989–1998. *Morbidity & Mortality Weekly Report, 52*, 697–701.

Costello, E. J., Farmer, E. M., Angold, A., Burns, B. J., & Erkanli, A. (1997). Psychiatric disorders among American Indian and white youth in Appalachia: The Great Smoky Mountains Study. *American Journal of Public Health, 87*, 827–832.

Cross, T.A., Earle, K.A., & Simmons, D. (2000). Child abuse and neglect in Indian country: Policy issues. *Families in Society, 81*, 49–58.

DeBruyn, L.M., Lujan, C.C., & May, P.A. (1992). A comparative study of abused and neglected American Indian children in the Southwest. *Social Science and Medicine, 35*, 305–315.

Dion, R., Gotowiec, A., & Beiser, M. (1998). Depression and conduct disorder in Native and non-Native children. *Journal of the Academy of Child and Adolescent Psychiatry, 37*, 736–742.

Dixon, M. (2001). Access to care for American Indians and Alaska Natives. In M. Dixon & Y. Roubideaux (Eds.), *Promises to keep: Public health policy for American Indians and Alaska Natives in the 21st century* (pp. 61–87). Washington, DC: American Public Health Association.

Duclos, C.W., Phillips, M., & LeMaster, P.L. (2004). Outcomes and accomplishments of the Circles of Care planning efforts. *American Indian & Alaska Native Mental Health Research, 11*(2), 121–138.

Duran, E. (1990). *Transforming the soul wound: A theoretical/clinical approach to American Indian psychology.* Berkeley, CA: Folklore Institute.

Earle, K.A. (2000). *Child abuse and neglect: An examination of American Indian data.* Portland, OR: National Indian Child Welfare Association.

Fischler, R.S. (1985). Child abuse and neglect in American Indian communities. *Child Abuse & Neglect, 9*, 95–106.

Fisher, P.A., Bacon, J.G., & Storck, M. (1998). Teacher, parent and youth report of problem behaviors among rural American Indian and Caucasian adolescents. *American Indian and Alaska Native Mental Health Research: The Journal of the National Center, 8*, 1–27.

Forquera, R. (2001). Challenges in serving the growing population of urban Indians. In M. Dixon & Y. Roubideaux (Eds.), *Promises to keep: Public health policy for American Indians and Alaska Natives in the 21st century* (pp. 121–134). Washington, DC: American Public Health Association.

Gone, J.P. (2004). Mental health services for Native Americans in the 21st century United States. *Professional Psychology—Research and Practice, 35*, 10–18.

Goodluck, C., & Willeto, A.A. (2000). *Native American kids 2000—Indian child well-being indicators.* Portland, OR: National Indian Child Welfare Association.

Grossman, D.C. (2003). Measuring disparity among American Indians and Alaska Natives: Who's counting whom? *Medical care, 41*, 579–581.

Grossman, D.C., Krieger, J.W., Sugarman, J., & Forquera, R. (1994). Health status of urban American Indians and Alaska Natives: A population-based study. *Journal of the American Medical Association, 271*, 845–850.

Harris, C. (2002). Indigenous health: Fulfilling our obligation to future generations. *American Journal of Public Health, 92*, 1390.

Hauswald, L. (1987). External pressure/internal change: Child neglect on the Navajo reservation. In N. Scheper-Hughes (Ed.), *Child survival* (pp. 145–164). Dordrecht, Holland: D. Reidel.

Henry J. Kaiser Family Foundation. (1999). *Sources of financing and the level of health spending for Native Americans.* Menlo Park, CA: Henry J. Kaiser Family Foundation.

Indian Health Service. (1999). *Regional differences in Indian health.* Washington, DC: Indian Health Service.

Ishisaka, H. (1978). American Indians and foster care: Cultural factors and separation. *Child Welfare, 57,* 299–308.

Johnson, J. L., & Cameron, M. C. (2001). Barriers to providing effective mental health services to American Indians. *Mental Health Services Research, 3,* 215–223.

Jones, B. J., Gilette, J. A., Painte, D., & Paulson, S. (2000). *Indian Child Welfare Act: A pilot study of compliance in North Dakota.* Portland, OR: National Indian Child Welfare Association.

Katz, R. J. (2004). Addressing the health care needs of American Indians and Alaska Natives. *American Journal of Public Health, 94,* 13–14.

Kessler, R. C., McGonagle, K. A., Zhao, S., Nelson, C. B., Hughes, M., Eshleman, S., Wittchen, H. U., & Kendler, K. S. (1994). Lifetime and 12-month prevalence of DSM-III-R psychiatric disorders in the United States: Results from the National Comorbidity Survey. *Archives of General Psychiatry, 51*(1), 8–19.

Kunitz, S. J., & Levy, J. E. (2000). *Drinking, conduct disorder, and social change: Navajo experiences.* Oxford: Oxford University Press.

Libby, A. M., Orton, H. D., Barth, R. P., Webb, M. B., Burns, B. J., Wood, P., & Spicer, P. (in press). Alcohol, drug and mental health specialty treatment service by race/ethnicity: A national study of children and families involved with child welfare. *American Journal of Public Health.*

Lujan, C., DeBruyn, L. M., May, P. A., & Bird, M. E. (1989). Profile of abused and neglected American Indian children in the southwest. *Child Abuse & Neglect, 13*(4), 449–461.

Mannes, M. (1995). Factors and events leading to the passage of the Indian Child Welfare Act. *Child Welfare, 74,* 264–282.

Manson, S. M. (2000). Mental health services for American Indian and Alaska Natives: Need, use, and barriers to effective care. *Canadian Journal of Psychiatry, 45,* 617–626.

Manson, S. M. (2001). Behavioral health services for American Indians: Need, use, and barriers to effective care. In M. Dixon & Y. Roubideaux (Eds.), *Promises to keep: Public health policy for American Indians and Alaska Natives in the 21st century* (pp. 167–190). Washington, DC: American Public Health Association.

May, P. A. (1996). Overview of alcohol use epidemiology for American Indian populations. In G. D. Sandefur, R. R. Rindfuss, & B. Cohen (Eds.), *Changing numbers, changing needs: American Indian demography and public health.* Washington, DC: National Academy Press.

National Center for Educational Statistics. (1997). *Characteristics of American Indian and Alaska Native education: Results from the 1990–91 and*

1993–94 Schools and Staffing Surveys. Washington, DC: U.S. Department of Education.

National Child Abuse and Neglect Data System. (2004). *Child maltreatment 2002.* Washington, DC: U.S. Department of Health and Human Services.

Noren, J., Kindig, D., & Sprenger, A. (1998). Challenges to Native American health care. *Public Health Reports, 113,* 22–33.

Norton, I.M., & Manson, S.M. (1996). Research in American Indian and Alaska Native communities: Navigating the cultural universe of values and process. *Journal of Consulting and Clinical Psychology, 64*(5), 856–860.

O'Connell, J., Novins, D.K., Beals, J., Spicer, P., & The AI-SUPERPFP Team. (2005). Disparities in patterns of alcohol use among reservation-based and geographically dispersed American Indian populations. *Alcoholism: Clinical and Experimental Research, 29,* 107–116.

Office of Technology Assessment. (1990). *Indian adolescent mental health.* Washington, DC: Office of Technology Assessment.

Pfefferbaum, R.L., Pfefferbaum, B., Rhoades, E.R., & Strickland, R.J. (1997). Providing for the health care needs of Native Americans: Policy, programs and procedures, and practices. *American Indian Law Review, 21,* 211–258.

Piasecki, J.M., Manson, S.M., Biernoff, M.P., Hiatt, A.B., Taylor, S.S., & Bechtold, D.W. (1989). Abuse and neglect of American Indian children: Findings from a survey of federal providers. *American Indian and Alaska Native Mental Health Research, 3,* 43–62.

Robin, R.W., Chester, B., & Goldman, D. (1996). Cumulative trauma and PTSD in American Indian communities. In A.J. Marsella & M.J. Friedman (Eds.), *Ethnocultural aspects of posttraumatic stress disorder: Issues, research, and clinical applications* (pp. 239–253). Washington, DC: American Psychological Association.

Roubideaux, Y. (2002). Perspectives on American Indian health. *American Journal of Public Health, 92,* 1401–1403.

Simmons, D., & Trope, J. (1999). *PL 105-89 Adoption and Safe Families Act of 1997: Issues for tribes and states serving Indian children.* Portland, OR: National Indian Child Welfare Association.

Simmons, T.M., Novins, D.K., & Allen, J. (2004). Words have power: Re-defining serious emotional disturbance for American Indian and Alaska Native children and their families. *American Indian & Alaska Native Mental Health Research, 11*(2), 59–64.

Spicer, P., Beals, J., Croy, C., Mitchell, C.M., Novins, D.K., Moore, L., Manson, S.M., & the AI-SUPERPFP Team. (2003). The prevalence of DSM-III-R alcohol dependence in two American Indian populations. *Alcoholism: Clinical & Experimental Research, 27,* 1785–1797.

Spicer, P., & Fleming, C. (2000). American Indian children of alcoholics. In H.E. Fitzgerald, B.M. Lester, & B.S. Zuckerman (Eds.), *Children of addiction: Research, health, and policy issues* (pp. 143–164). New York: RoutledgeFalmer.

U.S. Census Bureau. (1990). *United Stated Department of Commerce News: New Census Bureau report provides analysis of fertility of American women.* Retrieved November 1, 2004, from http://www.census.gov/Press-Release/cb96-182.html.

U.S. Census Bureau. (2000). *The American Indian and Alaska Native Population: 2000.* Retrieved November 1, 2004, from http://www.census.gov/prod/2002pubs/c2kbr01-15.pdf.

U.S. Census Bureau. (2001). *Age: 2000.* Retrieved November 1, 2004, from http://www.census.gov/prod/2001pubs/c2kbr01-12.pdf.

U.S. Census Bureau. (2003). *Current population survey, 2001, 2002, and 2003 Annual Social and Economic Supplements.* Retrieved November 1, 2004, from http://www.census.gov/hhes/poverty/poverty02/pov2_and_3-yr_avgs.html.

U.S. Commission on Civil Rights. (2003). *A quiet crisis: Federal funding and unmet needs in Indian country,* from http://www.usccr.gov/pubs/na0703/na0204.pdf.

White, R. B. (1981). Navajo child abuse and neglect study: A comparison group examination of abuse and neglect of Navajo children. *Child Abuse & Neglect, 5,* 9–17.

Wichlacz, C., Lane, J., & Kempe, C. (1978). Indian Child Welfare: A community team approach to protective services. *Child Abuse & Neglect, 2,* 29–35.

Zuckerman, S., Haley, J., Roubideaux, Y., & Lillie-Blanton, M. (2004). Health service access, use, and insurance coverage among American Indians/Alaska Natives and Whites.

Chapter 12

ARE THERE SOCIOECONOMIC DISPARITIES IN CHILDREN'S MENTAL HEALTH?

Nitika Tolani and Jeanne Brooks-Gunn

The authors would like to thank the National Science Foundation, the National Institute of Child Health and Human Development, the Spencer Foundation and the Virginia and Leenard Marx Foundation for their support.

ARE THERE SOCIOECONOMIC DISPARITIES IN CHILDREN'S MENTAL HEALTH?

This chapter will focus on the differential impact of four socioeconomic conditions on externalizing and internalizing problem behaviors: income, parental education, family structure, and neighborhood conditions. In the first section, we explore the methodological difficulties in measuring these four conditions of socioeconomic status (SES). We also explore the prevalence of these SES conditions, contributing factors to such conditions, and the interconnections among them. In the third section, we review findings from extant research that reveal direct associations between these SES conditions and externalizing and internalizing behavior problems. The fourth section of this chapter examines the indirect associations between poverty and child development, or the pathways through which SES may influence the aforementioned aspects of children's well-being. We conclude with implications for policy and future research.

Although estimates of mental health problems in children and adolescents vary, a consistent picture is beginning to emerge. Mental health problems, such as anxiety, depression, and conduct and attentional disorders, are estimated to affect 15 percent to 25 percent of American children and youth within the general population The disparity in prevalence estimates is the result of several factors, such as the source of data used to calculate estimates (i.e., children's self-report, parent report, or teacher report), the age of the child, and other characteristics related to children and their families (Jensen, Brooks-Gunn, & Graber, 1999). Prevalence rates are also dependent upon the type of disorder being examined. For example, the Methodology for Epidemiology of Mental Disorders in Children and Adolescents (MECA) study conducted by the National Institute of Mental Health (NIMH), estimated that 11 percent of youth within the multisite community sample suffered from anxiety disorders, while only 4 percent of youth were found to suffer from depressive disorders. When considering the severity of the mental disorders, prevalence estimates again varied: almost 21 percent of youth aged 9–17 has a diagnosable mental or addictive disorder with at least minimum impairment. When diagnostic criteria included significant functional impairment, estimates dropped to 11 percent, while estimates of youth with extreme impairment were even lower—approximately 5 percent (Shaffer et al., 1996). The incidence of mental health disorders in three- to five-year-old children is consistent with that found in older children. Within such preschool-aged populations, the prevalence of behavior problems in community samples ranges from 21 percent in pediatric populations to 26 percent in low-income populations (Lavigne et al., 1996). Given such prevalence rates, the study of behavioral problems and associated disorders across the life span presents a challenge to many fields, including psychology, psychiatry, and early childhood education.

Extant literature categorizes emotional outcomes into two groups: externalizing behaviors, including aggression, hyperactivity, bullying, defiance, and conduct disorders, and internalizing behaviors, such as anxiety, social withdrawal, and depression (Dearing, McCartney, & Taylor, 2001). In this chapter, we explore linkages between SES and these two aspects of children's mental health. Exploration of the linkages between SES and indicators of children's well-being is critical given the association between poverty and poorer emotional and behavioral outcomes. For example, research has shown that a significant association exists between low-income status and the diagnosis of one or more psychiatric disorders among 4- to 11-year olds, especially boys aged 6 to 11. Children aged 6 to 16 living in families who have received some type of public assistance also had a significantly higher chance of having one or more psychiatric disorders (Lipman & Offord, 1997). In fact, the chances of these children being diagnosed with an emotional disorder are three times greater than for a nonpoor child. A brief review of externalizing and internalizing behaviors is necessary prior to exploring the association between socioeconomic conditions and children's mental health.

Externalizing behavior problems are not unidimensional and range from impulsivity, opposition, and defiance, and verbal, physical, and relational aggression. While such problem behaviors are the most common and persistent forms of childhood maladjustment, externalizing behaviors change dramatically in their expression and frequency throughout development such that studies of them at a specific time point provides very limited information (Bongers, Koot, van der Ende, & Verhulst, 2004). And while it is true that the expression of externalizing behaviors does change over time, analysis of existing longitudinal data sets do also point to the existence of strong, continuous pathways for such behaviors. Internalizing behavior problems, including withdrawal, anxiety, fearfulness, and depression also are subject to developmental trends; that is, as children age, internalizing problems tend to increase and place children at risk for other learning and behavioral disorders. Weak to moderate correlations have been found between internalizing behavioral problems (specifically depression, anxiety, and social withdrawal) and aspects of cognitive functioning, such as intelligence and vigilance (Rapport, Denney, Chung, & Hustace, 2001). Indeed, early difficulties in such aspects of self-regulation are considered precursors to mental health and behavioral problems later in childhood and adolescence.

Measurement of SES

In our discussion of the measurement of SES, we consider four conditions: income, education, family structure, and neighborhood conditions. Earned income is the most common indicator of familial economic hardship and financial strain; that is, measuring if families have the resources necessary to provide their children with high quality education, nutrition, and home environments. The second condition, parental education, is considered an indicator of human capital, or personal attributes that are productive in an economic market, another aspect of a family's SES. Third, family structure serves as an indicator of the adults available within the familial unit to procure necessary resources, to provide human capital, and to spend time engaging in caretaking activities. Finally, neighborhood conditions, such as its affluence or poverty, and safety and crime levels, are another indicator of familial SES. In this section, we discuss the empirical measurement of each condition, as well as its connection to children's emotional and behavioral outcomes.

INCOME

As mentioned earlier, the primary indicator of SES is a household's earned income. This is problematic in that earned income underestimates the utilization of such resources as welfare (e.g., Temporary Assistance to

Needy Families [TANF]), disability (e.g., Supplemental Security Income [SSI]), and child support payments. In addition, earned income excludes the receipt of resources that substitute income (e.g., subsidized health care, child care, and housing), as well as government cash transfers and tax benefits. Earned income also does not represent fully the assets and wealth of families. Assets can include savings accounts, stocks, and real estate, which may be more stable indicators of SES as they are less variable than annual earned income. However, asset measures may be irrelevant for low-income individuals who may not have any assets. Cash transfers and other forms of support supplement yearly income and must be considered in the assessment of families' economic conditions for low-income families.

The most common indicator of the prevalence of poverty, at least in the case of low-income families, is the poverty threshold. The official poverty threshold in the United States was originally developed in 1959 based on expected food expenditures for families of different sizes. Annual adjustments in the poverty thresholds are based on the Consumer Price Index (CPI) cost of living. Issued by the U.S. Census Bureau, these thresholds are the primary version of the federal poverty measure used. In 2003, the poverty threshold for a single parent raising two children was $14,824 and $18,660 for a two-parent, two-child home (U.S. Census Bureau, 2003). Existing federal thresholds also distinguish between deeper levels of poverty. For example, single parents with two children subsisting at 50 percent of the poverty threshold (i.e., deep poverty) would earn approximately $7,400 per year, while two-parent families with two children living at 50 percent of the federal poverty threshold would earn about $9,300. An extension of the federal poverty threshold is the income-to-needs ratio, which also allows researchers to distinguish between various levels of poverty. For example, an income-to-needs ratio of 1.0 means that the family of interest is living exactly at the poverty threshold, while a ratio of 0.5 indicates the family is living at half the poverty threshold. While one benefit of the current threshold is the ability to make annual comparisons, many individuals question whether it accurately reflects consumption patterns and evolving standards of living. Common criticisms of the measure include its underestimation of material hardship and the lack of consideration for cost of living differences across regions of the United States. Many families living at these poverty levels, especially those in metropolitan areas, are not able to fulfill their most basic needs with the income they receive.

In 1995, the National Research Council (NRC) of the National Academy of Sciences (NAS) criticized the existing federal poverty measure for excluding work-related expenses such as child care, health care, and transportation, and supplemental sources of income provided by the government such as in-kind benefits and transfer programs. Clearly, if these expenses were to be integrated into a revised measure of poverty, the "statistical face" of children living in poverty would significantly change and likely increase in accuracy. While the majority of poor children would continue to be those who live with a single parent and who are black, we would likely witness a sizable increase in the proportion of children living in two-parent families who do not receive governmental assistance (and with one parent employed full-time). In sum, the current absolute measure of poverty presents a more positive picture, in terms of the number of children and families living in poverty, than potentially exists.

PARENTAL EDUCATION

Investments in education, vocational training, medical care, and other such resources are often defined as human capital. Education and training are the two most important investments in the development of human capital. Such investments have high likely returns in the form of wage earnings (Brooks-Gunn, Linver, & Fauth, 2005). Many studies have shown that high school and college education directly increases an individual's income, even after adjusting for the fact that those with higher education levels often come from wealthier, highly educated families. Another example of human capital is a parent's cognitive ability, which impacts both familial SES and the welfare of that parent's child. Cognitive abilities are assessed through a variety of standardized tests and include receptive verbal ability, achievement, and comprehensive intelligence tests. The amount of formal education (i.e., years of completed schooling) each parent has obtained is an important indicator of parents' cognitive abilities. In fact, maternal educational attainment is the indicator of child's socioeconomic status that is most widely used. Parents who have higher levels of education are more likely to help their children complete their homework, develop their language skills, and foster high educational aspirations. However, the years of schooling obtained by the parent are itself influenced by other personal attributes of the parent, including motivation and personality. In sum, years of schooling alone do not represent the quality of education received or the actual amount an individual has learned or achieved. As such, social scientists often include measures of parental achievement (i.e., language competency, intelligence) in analytic models to supplement the information provided by educational attainment of parents and to estimate all aspects of human capital.

FAMILY STRUCTURE

Family structure, or the presence or absence of one biological parent in the household, also has a significant impact on the amount and quality of resources parents can provide for their children, and in turn, child well-being (McLanahan, 1997). These categories are not mutually exclusive (e.g., a child who resides in a stepfamily could also have lived within a single-parent family). Domains of child well-being examined in family structure analyses include IQ and intelligence test scores, educational attainment (e.g., grade retention, GPA, college attendance), behavioral and psychological problems (e.g., teen out-of-wedlock childbearing, hyperactivity, and other externalizing and internalizing behaviors), income (e.g., occupational status, poverty status, and wage earnings), and health (e.g., chronic health conditions). The importance of such research lies in the fact that within the past four decades, the proportion of children living in single-parent households has increased dramatically, rising from approximately 12 percent in 1960 to 40 percent in 1995. The association between family structure and poverty is also clear: children living in single-mother households are more likely to be poor than those living in two-parent households (Ginther & Pollak, 2003).

NEIGHBORHOOD CONDITIONS

Current interest in the effects of neighborhood conditions on child and adolescent outcomes is due in part to increased acceptance of contextual frameworks in developmental psychology. Such a perspective mandates the examination of the multiple contexts that influence children and their families (such as communities, schools or child care, and peers), as well as the interrelationships between such contexts. For example, researchers must consider the bidirectionality of influence between individuals and the neighborhoods in which they live—that is, not only do neighborhood conditions influence residents, but individual characteristics of these individuals also shape the conditions in which they live. Aspects of neighborhoods that have an impact on child and adolescent outcomes include: concentration of poverty, absence of middle-class residents, higher proportion of female-headed families, and joblessness (Brooks-Gunn, Duncan, & Britto, 1999; Leventhal & Brooks-Gunn, 2000, 2004).

Several economic and demographic indices are used to define neighborhoods. For example, neighborhoods with poverty rates of 40 percent or higher are defined as high-poverty neighborhoods. Such neighborhoods typically have higher rates of crime and overcrowding, male joblessness, dependence on welfare, and single-parent, female-headed families. U.S. Census data suggest that over 15 million children are living in neighborhoods where 20 percent of residents are poor; of these children, approximately 2.5 million live in areas of extreme poverty, where over 40 percent of residents are classified as poor (U.S. Census Bureau, 2003). As children who live in poor neighborhoods are also more likely to be from poor families, separating the effects of familial poverty from neighborhood poverty is a challenging task. Most empirical findings linking neighborhood quality to children's outcomes are based on U.S. Census data, which provides indicators for sociodemographic characteristics of neighborhoods such as SES, residential instability, unemployment, dominant family structures, and racial composition. Here, neighborhoods are defined as census tracts that contain between 3,000 and 8,000 people; subsumed within census tracts are one to four smaller units containing about 1,100 individuals each (U.S. Census Bureau, 2002). Neighborhood poverty is measured through the median income for a particular tract and the proportion of residents living within various income ranges (Brooks-Gunn, Linver, & Fauth, 2005).

Researchers have criticized neighborhood literature due to its "selection bias," as current studies do not allow us to determine if "poor families in less poor neighborhoods differ in some unobservable ways from poor families in poor neighborhoods" (Leventhal & Brooks-Gunn, 2004, p. 488). In addition, neighborhood residence is not a randomly assigned variable as individuals do choose where they wish to reside. As such, it is possible that omitted variables, such as parental mental health, may in fact account for the observed impact of neighborhoods on children's outcomes. Later in this chapter we discuss a series of studies initiated by the U.S Department of Housing and Urban Development called the Moving to Opportunity for Fair Housing Demonstration (MTO), which controls for much of the selection bias inherent within nonexperimental neighborhood evaluations and allows a more precise examination of the impact of neighborhood conditions on children's behavioral and educational outcomes.

In sum, familial SES is comprised of several factors, and the research reviewed in this section suggests that each exerts an independent effect on children's outcomes. As such, composite measures of SES are not appropriate for accurately and realistically measuring the effect of SES on children. Social scientists often try to statistically isolate the effects of such complex phenomena, but the interrelationships between these factors make this an onerous task. For example, researchers who are interested in the impact of inequality on youth must identify the household member who most impacts the family's economic well-being; in single-parent homes this question becomes more complicated as the importance of qualities related to the absent parent (i.e., educational attainment) arises. Given the difficulties in measuring the independent effects of each of these factors, researchers are obligated to include all potential determinants of child well-being. Studies that include, rather than control for, such important determinants of children's well-being will foster theoretical advances on child development and contribute to an increasingly accurate understanding of the lives of children and their families (Deaton, 2002).

How Many Children Are Living in Poor SES Conditions?

Recent research demonstrates an intensified interest in the deleterious consequences of poverty on children's outcomes across many domains, including mental health, behavioral problems, educational outcomes, and physical health. Examination of the impact of poverty on children is a critical issue for many researchers given the unsettling rates of child poverty in the United States. For families, living in poverty occurs when the household's before-tax income falls at or below the federal poverty level (i.e., $18,850 for a family of four in 2004). Rates of childhood poverty in the United States surpass those of other industrialized countries—for example, in 2001, 16 percent of America's children lived below the poverty line. While the past two decades have witnessed a decline in rates of childhood poverty (i.e., 22% in 1993 to the current rate of 17%), children in the United States are still more likely to live in poverty than any other age group. Research on the role of poverty in shaping children's earliest experiences is especially important as children under age six are more likely to live in low-income families than those older than age six (Koball & Douglas-Hall, 2004). Approximately 40 percent of young children in the United States live in low-income families. Percentages across race provide a clearer picture: 30 percent of black children and 27 percent of Hispanic children live in poverty in comparison to 9 percent of their white counterparts (Child Trends, 2004). Finally, the rate for children who live in female-headed households is even higher with 50 percent of these children living in poverty (Brooks-Gunn et al., 2005). These statistics suggest that many American children lack the financial resources necessary to meet basic needs, which invariably suggests that food, clothing, housing, and health care for these children are also inadequate. Naturally, these conditions severely impact children's health and development.

The examination of childhood poverty is also important as it is during early childhood (defined as birth to age five) that behavioral and emotional trajectories are set. While such trajectories can be changed, as children age this becomes increasingly difficult. The negative consequences of growing up in poverty extend across several domains, including children's school readiness and cognitive outcomes, physical health outcomes, social competence, and psychological adjustment (Brooks-Gunn & Duncan, 1997). The aforementioned studies have also shown that children from economically disadvantaged backgrounds experience greater psychological distress than their more advantaged counterparts. That is, poor children experience greater emotional and behavioral problems than do nonpoor children.

Recent findings published by Child Trends (2004) on early childhood indicators demonstrates the importance of factors such as family income, parental education, family structure, and neighborhood quality in determining children's outcomes. An expert panel reviewed findings on over 30 indicators from several longitudinal, nationally representative studies. With respect to socioemotional development, 72 percent of kindergartners living in two-parent homes in these samples exhibited behavioral self-control, as compared to approximately 60 percent of kindergartners living in single-parent or stepfamilies. The development of good social skills and positive emotional characteristics is quite important as these often predict later intellectual development and educational achievement. An early inability to develop healthy social competence can lead to antisocial behaviors and rejection by peers later in life. The percentage of parents who rate their children as higher in dimensions of social competence increases as income and parental education levels increase. In 1998, 70 percent of kindergartners whose mothers had not graduated high school demonstrated prosocial behaviors, compared to 84 percent of kindergartners whose mothers had obtained a vocational or college degree. In addition, children from the lowest income brackets are least likely to develop behaviors indicative of social competence (as assessed by parent ratings). Approximately 70 percent of kindergartners in the bottom fifth percentile of the income distribution were rated as socially competent by their parents, compared to 86 percent of their wealthier counterparts.

We have briefly discussed the importance of neighborhood quality to child outcomes. Child Trends (2004) has found that neighborhood poverty is associated with problem behaviors, lower levels of school readiness in younger children, and poorer academic achievement in adolescents. Concerns with neighborhood quality vary across type of residence as well; for example, 40 percent of kindergartners living in urban areas had parents who rated their neighborhood as unsafe compared with 18 percent of parents in rural areas and 26 percent in suburban areas. In addition, the percentage of children living in extremely poor neighborhoods varies across states; for example, approximately 8 percent of children live in very poor neighborhoods in New York, while less than one percent of children live in such neighborhoods in Iowa, Vermont, Oregon, and Nevada.

Does SES Influence Mental Health Outcomes in Children?

While the number of studies examining the connections between SES conditions in childhood and children's mental health is large, the precision of many of these studies does not allow researchers to disentangle the complexity of this association (Brooks-Gunn & Duncan, 1997). The best evidence comes from experimental studies in which the impact of SES gradients on children's mental health is measured independent of other familial conditions that are associated with living in a low-income household. Such studies isolate the effect of SES on children's emotional and behavioral well-being by statistically controlling for other family conditions, including maternal ethnicity, education, and marital status (Brooks-Gunn, Duncan, & Britto, 1999). In this section, we review findings demonstrated by current research on the direct effects of income, parental education, family structure, and neighborhood conditions on the emotional and behavioral outcomes of young children and adolescents.

INCOME

Generally, studies have found that income-to-needs ratios are associated with behavioral problems in three- to five-year-olds (Brooks-Gunn, Duncan, & Britto, 1999; Chase-Lansdale, Gordon, Brooks-Gunn, & Klebanov, 1997). Current research has yet to pinpoint the precise magnitude of the association between income and children's emotional wellbeing (Duncan & Brooks-Gunn, 1997; Mayer, 1997). For example, while studies have shown that income has a significant impact on children's ability and achievement, family income did not have equally large effects on mental health, behavior, or physical health measures (Duncan & Brooks-Gunn, 1997). In fact, several studies have found family income to have no effect on anxiety or hyperactivity in middle childhood and depression in adolescence (Pagani, Boulerice, & Tremblay, 1997). Such divergent findings point to a need for additional research on the adequacy of indicators of economic stability and wealth, as well as the association of each on children's mental health. In sum, although there is consensus among social scientists that utilization of permanent income is a more accurate indicator of economic stability than annual, current income, there is disagreement as to which indicator best predicts child outcomes.

Although wealthier children perform better across a variety of domains (i.e., report less behavioral problems, are healthier, achieve higher scores on cognitive tests, obtain higher rates of educational attainment) across the life span, the supposition that children's outcomes improve over time in conjunction with increases in parental income is not supported empirically. The importance of income can be seen in its association with what Mayer (1997) calls "command over resources," suggesting that it is in fact parents' abilities to increase the quality and quantity of resources available to their children and to reduce their own parental stress that impact children's outcomes (p. 66). Beyond the accessibility and availability of resources provided by increasing incomes, the duration and timing of poverty is also quite important, as studies have shown that the effects of long-term poverty on children's mental health outcomes are significantly greater than the effects of short-term poverty. Children in persistently poor families exhibit greater externalizing and internalizing behavioral problems than those children who have never experienced poverty. For example, Pagani et al. (1997) found that children from a family enduring chronic poverty when they were aged 8 to 12 were more likely to exhibit externalizing behaviors, such as aggression, and were 1.7 to 2.0 times more at risk for fighting. Interestingly, data from the 1986 National Longitudinal Survey of Youth (NLSY) illustrated that for children aged 4 to 8, persistent poverty was found to predict internalizing symptoms (i.e., anxiety, dependence), even when such factors as current poverty status, maternal education, age, and marital status were statistically controlled for (McLeod & Shanahan, 1993). Chronic poverty was associated with greater behavioral problems for children aged 3 to 11 as well (Korenman, Miller, & Sjaastad, 1995). Short-term poverty was related to externalizing symptoms, such as hyperactivity and peer conflict (McLeod & Shanahan, 1993). In addition, the negative effects of persistent poverty were also found to be cumulative—that is, these effects increased as children got older. While short-term poverty is also related to behavioral problems, the effect of chronic income poverty on behavioral problems is larger in magnitude. Important to note is that the analyses from which these findings come statistically controlled for the effects of maternal education, child health and nutrition, and family structure variation on children's mental health outcomes, such that researchers were able to more precisely measure the direct impact of poverty on children's mental health (Duncan, Brooks-Gunn, & Klebanov, 1994).

Welfare Reform and Child Outcomes

Prior to 1996, the Aid to Families with Dependent Children (AFDC) program functioned as the principle cash assistance program for low-income families, focusing primarily on single mothers and their children. AFDC was not very effective in providing low-income families with sufficient financial support. In 1996, the passage of the Personal Responsibility and Work Opportunity Reconciliation Act (PRWORA) enacted Temporary Assistance to Needy Families (TANF), which functions as a replacement to AFDC. TANF allows states greater flexibility in determining levels of eligibility and benefits. Unlike AFDC, the TANF program requires recipients to work after receiving two years of cash assistance, eliminating the guarantee of financial aid for poor families. After five years of cash assistance, recipients are no longer able to receive benefits. Research has suggested that work mandates, income supplements, and time limits on benefits are the welfare-reform provisions that may have the greatest impact on preschool aged children and adolescents' cognitive, behavioral, and emotional outcomes, especially among long-term welfare recipients (Duncan & Brooks-Gunn, 2000). In a synthesis of several welfare experiments, Morris (2002) found that welfare programs designed to increase employment and income through earnings supplements had a small but consistently positive impact on elementary school-aged children's cognitive outcomes. Such improvements were seen two to three years after the parent first entered the program. But these effects are not necessarily due to income alone and could be due in part to increases in employment and income together.

Programs such as the New Hope Project (Huston et al., 2003) and the Canadian-based Self-Sufficiency Project (SSP; Foley et al., 2002) illustrate the benefits of income increases on child outcomes and the difficulty in analyzing the exact cause of the effects. Both the New Hope Project and the SSP were designed to evaluate the efficacy of welfare-to-work interventions that also provided wage supplements to raise family income above the poverty threshold. Subsidies for health and child care were also provided for a period of three years. For both programs, it was hoped that these provisions would not only increase parental employment and use of licensed health care services and health insurance, but would subsequently have a positive impact on child well-being. Findings indicate that parents in the New Hope Project did indeed experience more stable employment, lower rates of poverty, and higher wages after five years (Huston et al., 2003) as did parents involved in the SSP (Foley et al., 2002). Parents in both programs also reported lower depressive symptoms and a greater awareness of community resources than parents who did not receive enhanced benefits. The impact of these programs on child outcomes was also positive for the most part. New Hope boys and girls received higher ratings from parents on dimensions of social behavior, such as compliance, self-control, and sensitivity. Conversely, the SSP had adverse effects on young adolescents (aged 13–15) as evidenced at the three-year follow-up. Program children performed worse at school and committed more delinquent acts (i.e., smoking, drinking) than their control group counterparts, suggesting the importance of supervision for children this age; however, these effects did not extend into late adolescence. It may be that failure of parents to provide adequate supervision mediated the association between changes in income level and the number of psychiatric symptoms in boys and girls.

Difficulties in disentangling social causation and social selection are potentially remedied by experimental designs that allow for the manipulation of poverty levels when examining the impacts on mental illness (Costello, Compton, Keeler, & Angold, 2003). The Great Smoky Mountains Study, a longitudinal study of the development of psychiatric disorders in rural and urban youth, is one example. The opening of a gambling casino during the fourth year of this eight-year intervention provided American Indian adults and children living on a reservation a percentage of the profits (totaling $6,000 in 2001). The casino also provided job opportunities for Indians and others living in the area. Costello et al. (2003) found that as measures of family income increased, the frequency of child psychiatric diagnoses for both Indian and non-Indian children decreased across all eight years of the study. Consistent with previous research, children living in poverty were more likely to have a psychiatric disorder than their wealthier counterparts (22 percent versus 15 percent). While income generated from the casino did not lift all Indian families out of poverty, a significantly higher proportion of Indian families moved above the federal poverty line than white families. Children in these families showed a significant decrease in the average number of psychiatric symptoms. These children also exhibited a 40 percent decrease in behavioral symptoms, while children in families who remained poor showed a 21 percent *increase* in behavioral problems, such as diagnoses of conduct and oppositional disorder. Costello et al. (2003) note that there was no significant association between income and emotional symptoms such as depression and anxiety; that is, moving above the poverty line did not lead to a reduction in anxiety and depression in children.

Overall, studies reviewed in the chapter have found that income does have a small impact on children's emotional outcomes. The magnitude of the impacts found increase in size when examining children's behavioral and cognitive outcomes. Further research is needed to disentangle causation and selection issues inherent within much of current research. Later in this chapter, we discuss important mediating pathways through which income may also affect child well-being.

PARENTAL EDUCATION

Research has consistently demonstrated the effect of parental education on children's mental health outcomes. As in analyses of behavioral and cognitive outcomes, the effect of parental education on children's emotional health is larger than the effect of income. Positive associations between maternal education and child well-being are among the most replicated findings in developmental studies. For example, in Dearing et al. (2001), analyses of data from the National Institute of Child Health and Human Development (NICHD) Study of Early Child Care suggest that maternal education is positively associated with prosocial behaviors and negatively associated with behavioral problems. Also, while a positive change in families' income-to-needs ratios proved to be a powerful buffer for behavioral and social outcomes of poor children, such changes had little impact on positive social behaviors in nonpoor families. Indeed, the impact of maternal education on such child outcomes was significantly larger than that of a family's income-to-needs ratio.

A rigorous analysis of data from the National Evaluation of Welfare-to-Work Strategies Child Outcome Study (NEWWS COS) sought to estimate the effect of increases in educational levels for low-income mothers receiving welfare on children's academic and behavioral outcomes (Magnuson, 2003). Previous research has established the importance of maternal education for children's home environments and also for children's resilience. A consistent association between behavioral outcomes and maternal education is less common but also demonstrated in existing research (e.g., Magnuson, 2003). Such studies have found that higher levels of education predict lower rates of behavioral problems in children. Maternal education was not strongly associated with children's behavioral problems or positive social behaviors; in fact, these results suggest increases in maternal education had little to no effect on children's behavioral outcomes. However, Magnuson (2003) is quick to note that measures of behavioral outcomes in NEWWS were based on maternal report and may not have been sensitive enough to accurately capture significant differences. Dependence upon maternal report data could be biased due to the mother's mental health status, past experiences, and reporter bias.

The effects of parental education on children's well-being may be both direct and indirect. For example, mothers may learn skills in school that translate to other aspects of their lives and foster positive parenting practices with their children through the provision of more stimulating home environments. Highly educated mothers are also more likely to marry men with similar levels of education, which in turn will potentially increase household income (Magnuson, 2003). Extensions of such empirical work in an effort to examine the causal nature of this relationship will be helpful in developing interventions that target parental education. Policy implications of research on the association between maternal education and child outcomes are discussed later in this chapter.

FAMILY STRUCTURE

The proportion of children who have grown up with both biological parents has declined dramatically throughout the past four decades

(Brown, 2004; McLanahan, 1997). The presence or absence of both parents impacts the resources parents can provide for their children, and in turn, children's well-being. In fact, children of single-parent families, especially those headed by mothers, are especially vulnerable to poverty and intergenerational dependence on welfare and are less successful than children who grow up with both parents. Current research demonstrates that family structure has a more substantial effect on behavioral problems, such as truancy and teen pregnancy, than on psychosocial outcomes, such as depression and anxiety (Brown, 2004; Ginther & Pollak, 2003). Family disruptions are associated with increases in school behavior problems, social impairment, and fighting and hyperactivity (Hanson, McLanahan, & Thomson, 1997). Children in single-parent families often receive less parental supervision from both parents and are not able to depend on the social capital that intact families have. Parent absence is also associated with increases in psychological problems, such as depression and lower self-esteem, but such increases do not extend to adulthood. Research has shown that the recency of family disruptions has more of a negative, and statistically significant, impact on girls and boys across a variety of domains (McLanahan, 1997).

Children who live with married biological parents have significantly fewer behavior problems when compared to their peers in single-parent homes (Dearing, McCartney, & Taylor, 2001). In fact, children raised by one biological parent are less likely to be successful across a variety of domains. A parent's absence is associated with increased school behavior problems, increased fighting and hyperactivity, and social impairment. While parental absence also exerts a negative influence on psychological problems, this effect diminishes with age. For example, studies of adults from intact and nonintact families showed no remnants of negative psychological consequences, while studies of school-aged children pointed to an increase in psychological problems such as low self-esteem and depression (Pagani, Boulerice, & Tremblay, 1997). Most surprising is the finding that remarriage does not alleviate the negative impact of single parenthood on child outcomes, suggesting that income inequality in and of itself does not account for the deleterious effects of one parent's absence (McLanahan, 1997). Children who live in two-parent cohabiting families and cohabiting stepfamilies display significantly more behavioral and emotional problems than those children whose biological parents are married (Osbourne, McLanahan, & Brooks-Gunn, 2004). Indeed, residing in a stepfamily was more likely to negatively impact children's behavioral problems and psychological adjustment than their educational attainment (Brown, 2004). It appears, then, that the addition of a cohabiting partner does not guarantee improvements in child well-being. Factors such as parental supervision and social capital may help explain the variance in child outcomes above and beyond income poverty.

NEIGHBORHOOD CONDITIONS

Poor children are more likely than nonpoor children to live in unsafe neighborhoods (i.e., high crime rates), which subsequently impacts children's emotional well-being in negative ways (Leventhal & Brooks-Gunn, 2000). Based on estimates from the Panel Study of Income Dynamics (PSID), 1 in 10 children live in a very poor neighborhood, while nearly 2 in 10 children live in a moderately poor neighborhood (Brooks-Gunn, Duncan, & Britto, 1999). Findings for the effects of neighborhood conditions on behavioral and emotional problems are again less consistent. After statistically controlling for family-level characteristics, such as household income, parental education, race/ethnicity, maternal age at birth, and family structure, studies have shown that the presence of low-SES neighbors had the strongest effect on children and adolescents' mental health outcomes (Leventhal & Brooks-Gunn, 2000). This effect was slightly stronger for externalizing behaviors than for internalizing behaviors. Such studies often demonstrate that the family-level variables reviewed earlier may have stronger effects on children's mental health than neighborhood conditions. Most of these studies also identify structural aspects of neighborhoods at the census-tract level to be significantly associated with development more during the school-age years (Chase-Lansdale & Gordon, 1996).

Among younger children, two national studies have utilized maternal-report data to measure internalizing and externalizing behavior problems: the Infant Health and Development Program (IHDP) and the National Longitudinal Study of Youth-Child Supplement (NLSY-CS). Such studies have shown that, for example, the absence of managerial and professional workers in the neighborhood was associated with higher rates of behavioral problems for three-year-old children in the IHDP sample. The presence of low-SES neighbors was also associated with higher externalizing behavior problems in five- and six- year-olds in the same sample. However, studies using NLSY-CS data have shown that neighborhood SES is positively associated with reports of internalizing behavior problems in young children (Chase-Lansdale et al., 1997). NLSY-CS data has also suggested that greater ethnic diversity within the neighborhood is associated with lower rates of internalizing behavior problems for three- to four-year-old African-American children, but not for white children (Chase-Lansdale et al., 1997). Interestingly, such diversity had the opposite effect on reports of internalizing behavior problems of five- to six- year-olds in the same sample.

The effects of neighborhood SES on the behavioral and emotional outcomes of adolescents have also been examined mostly in regional and city-based studies. One such example is the Pittsburgh Youth Study, which found that 13- and 16- year-old males living in low-SES neighborhoods (i.e. those characterized by poverty, unemployment, welfare receipt, high proportion of single-mother families, and nonmarital childbearing) exhibited higher rates of criminal and delinquent behavior. The strength of this association appears to decline with age; that is, residing in a low-SES neighborhood has a stronger effect on the delinquent behaviors of younger adolescents than on older adolescents. An evaluation of the Yonkers Project also suggested that adolescents who continued to reside in low-SES neighborhoods were more likely to engage in problem behaviors, such as drinking and smoking marijuana, than youth who had moved to middle-class residences. Finally, analyses of the New York subsample of the MTO experiment found that mental health program effects were larger for children than for parents; among children, effects were strongest for children aged 8 to 13 years (Leventhal & Brooks-Gunn, 2004). Specifically, moving to a more affluent neighborhood reduced levels of depression and anxiety in boys by 25 percent when compared to boys who remained in low-income neighborhoods. However, effects were not found for older youth (aged 14–18 years), perhaps due to "their ability to travel back to their old high-poverty neighborhoods or from their disruption of peer networks, which are salient during adolescence" (Leventhal & Brooks-Gunn, 2004, p. 1580). Another explanation may lie in the buffering effects of parental mental health, which improved significantly for those parents who moved to low-poverty neighborhoods. Leventhal and Brooks-Gunn (2000) suggest the importance of the family context for younger children in explaining these results; that is, peers often exert more influence on adolescents than parents. As such, superior mental health functioning in parents may not necessarily provide the buffering effects for adolescents as it does for younger children.

Indirect Pathways between SES Conditions and Children's Emotional Wellbeing

The empirical evidence reviewed thus far does point to moderately significant associations between SES conditions and emotional, behavioral, and cognitive child outcomes. Establishment of these associations has allowed researchers to focus on the mediating mechanisms, or pathways, that explain the effects of such conditions on children. Mediating mechanisms are also often termed process, or intervening variables. The pathways reviewed in this chapter will clarify how variables such as income, family structure, and neighborhood conditions predict children's emotional, behavioral, and cognitive outcomes, as well as why these variables might explain such outcomes. Important to note is the distinction between mediating pathways and correlates of poverty, such as maternal education and single parenthood. Examination of such mechanisms is necessary in order to more fully understand the complexities of the association between SES and children's outcomes. Such examinations can also further the development of policies and interventions designed to alleviate the effect of poverty on children.

Extant poverty literature groups potential pathways into two categories. The first theory is grounded within the "family stress model" as formulated by Conger, Conger, and Elder (1997). Briefly, this model posits that parental responses to economic difficulties and other stressful situations mediate the impact of economic stresses on child and adolescent outcomes. The familial stress model posited by these authors proposes that economic hardship creates a host of negative emotions within parents ranging from depression to anxiety to anger. This negativity has detrimental effects on parent–child interactions, which can become increasingly hostile, and can lack the warmth and support necessary for healthy family functioning. Obviously, then, such intrafamilial stresses can prove injurious to the emotional health of children and adolescents.

A second model of pathways demonstrated in current research is the economics-based "investment model," which highlights the role of income in terms of the resources parents invest in to foster their children's emotional and behavioral development (Mayer, 1997). Such resources include safe living conditions and enriching childcare. The investment model is often associated with cognitive outcomes, while the family stress model is often utilized in explanations of emotional and behavioral outcomes. As such, in this chapter we focus exclusively on a discussion of how mechanisms suggested by the family stress model impact children's emotional and behavioral outcomes, often in concert with poverty.

THE FAMILY STRESS MODEL

As explained earlier, one potential pathway is that parental practices, such as inconsistent discipline, harsh punishments, parental responsiveness, and warmth, play a mediating role between economic hardship and children's wellbeing. Economic hardships, or stressors, are not limited to poverty per se and include other conditions that can cause financial strain within a household, such as consistent unemployment or unstable employment. Often, such situations force families to reside in unsafe neighborhoods, obtain public assistance, or reduce their utilization of goods and services. According to the family stress model, financial hardships lead to parents' psychological distress. Such emotional instability can lead to other problems, such as marital conflict, which in turn can lead to negative parenting practices. Parenting practices such as high levels of warmth and cognitive stimulation have been associated with positive emotional and behavioral outcomes in children. More importantly, for those families living in poverty, parents who adopt such positive parenting practices with their children can significantly reduce, or buffer their children against, the risks associated with economic hardship. Conversely, harsher parenting practices have been linked to negative socioemotional outcomes, such as insecure mother-infant attachments, and psychosocial outcomes later in life (e.g., DeKlyen, Brooks-Gunn, & McLanahan, 2004). The studies described shortly illustrate the significance of how parents adapt to financial hardship and the extent to which such hardship impacts young children's developmental trajectories.

The family stress model has also been used to explain the impact of familial disruptions due to financial hardships on adolescent behavior. Note that this model highlights the loss of income and the impact such declines have on intrafamilial relationships rather than the effect of chronic poverty on such interpersonal dynamics. Conger et al. (1997) found that emotional distress caused by extreme financial hardships experienced during the Great Depression often led to increases in marital conflict and harsher parenting practices. As a result, adolescents in this study, most notably boys, were often more poorly adjusted and experienced poorer cognitive outcomes. Conger et al. (1997) conducted an analysis on a more contemporary sample in an economically depressed rural town. For the white teenagers in this sample, the authors found that while economic pressures and financial conflicts did not have a direct impact on adolescents' self-confidence, harsh maternal parenting practices and financial conflicts did have a statistically significant, negative impact on adolescents' self-confidence, sense of self-worth, and self-efficacy. These findings were especially robust for boys. Previous literature indicates that adolescent males are especially vulnerable to such reductions in self-esteem as a result of financial conflicts between parents (Conger et al., 1997). Marital stability is also included in these analyses as it has a tremendous impact on economic strain (i.e., in times of divorce) and on parenting practices, and a variety of adolescent outcomes for boys and girls. Such associations between economic loss, parents' psychosocial functioning, and parenting practices, as well as their impacts on children's emotional outcomes, have also been replicated in urban black samples (e.g. McLeod & Shanahan, 1993).

Consistent evidence for the familial stress theory is based mostly on smaller, community-based samples—analyses using larger, nationally representative samples are generally less uniform. In addition, much of the existing literature focuses on familial stresses on adolescents and older children. In Hanson et al.'s (1997) analysis of National Survey of Families and Households (NSFH) data, the authors explored the possibility that parenting practices functioned as mediators between economic resources and older children's emotional well-being. While harsher parenting practices (i.e., yelling and spanking) were associated with lower income in two-parent households, overall income-to-needs ratios do not have consistently strong, negative effects on effective parenting practices. They found that low income does not impair children's emotional well-being through a reduction in parenting involvement and effectiveness in either two-parent or single-parent households. Parenting practices explained a significant proportion of the effects of income-to-needs ratios on internalizing and externalizing behaviors, sociability, and initiative. Parenting practices also mediated the association between familial debt and internalizing behaviors. Finally, given the strong association between indicators of parental warmth and supportiveness (i.e., praising and hugging) and children's emotional well-being in two-parent homes, Hanson et al. (1997) suggest that high levels of warmth and supportiveness may serve as a buffer for poor children in such families against the deleterious consequences of economic hardship. In one-parent families, parental aspirations for children, as well as the amount of time mothers reported spending with their children, had a stronger impact on the children's emotional wellbeing.

A considerable omission in the poverty literature is the impact of the pathways specified in this model on younger children (Duncan & Brooks-Gunn, 1997, 2000). As reviewed earlier in this chapter, studies have shown that poverty experienced earlier in life is linked to higher internalizing and externalizing outcomes in younger children, as well as other negative emotional outcomes, such as poor adjustment and psychiatric disorders later in life. As such, application of the family stress model to younger children is critical to the understanding of adolescent socioemotional development.

In sum, existing studies have explored the mediating effects of peer support, availability of institutional resources, and employment opportunities on disadvantaged children's externalizing problem behaviors, antisocial behavior, substance use, and school achievement. In the next section, we review the findings presented throughout this chapter on mental health outcomes of children and adolescents, discuss ways in which public policy can shape the emotional and behavioral well-being of children living in poverty, and present directions for future research.

Summary and Policy Implications

Mental health problems are thought to affect between 15 percent and 25 percent of children and youth within the general population. Given the prevalence of emotional and behavioral problems in American children and adolescents today, the examination of the association between SES gradients and children's mental health outcomes is most important. In this chapter, we addressed the need for researchers and policymakers alike to explore the association between poverty and children's development across a variety of domains—specifically, we asked whether socioeconomic disparities exist in children's mental health. The answer is yes! Through our exploration of the linkages between four components of SES—income, parental education, family structure, and neighborhood conditions—on externalizing and internalizing behavior problems in children and adolescents, we see that a moderate proportion of the statistically significant differences in children's mental health functioning are in fact due to variation in familial income, maternal education, family structure, and in some cases neighborhood conditions. In this final section, we provide a brief summary of our findings for each of the four linkages presented earlier, directions for future research, and policy implications based on these findings.

INCOME

The studies reviewed in this chapter have found that, to varying degrees, economic hardship does have a significant, negative, and immediate impact on children's emotional and behavioral health. Family income has been linked with fighting in middle childhood, but not with anxiety and hyperactivity in the same period. Those children living in deep and persistent poverty early in life are more likely to exhibit poor psychosocial and behavioral outcomes later in life as well, such as higher rates of externalizing behavior problems, adjustment issues, and psychiatric disorders. However, the magnitude of the effect of family income on mental health and behavioral functioning is not as large as its effect on children's ability and achievement. Changes in familial income also were not found to reliably predict children's emotional and behavioral outcomes. Research suggests that the effect of income on child outcomes is mediated by the accessibility and availability of resources parents can provide their children, as well as the reductions in parenting stress such resources afford.

PARENTAL EDUCATION

Maternal educational attainment is the indicator of children's SES most often used in extant research. The effects of parental education on children's emotional and behavioral development are larger than the effects of income and are among the most replicated in current developmental research. Increases in maternal education, such as those provided by welfare-to-work programs, are associated with better school readiness and positive social behaviors in school for younger children; however, the duration of such effects are short-lived and do not extend throughout middle childhood into adolescence.

Policy Implications: Family Income and Parental Education

As reviewed earlier, welfare experiments, such as the New Hope Project and the Self-Sufficiency Project, have shown that welfare policies that are designed to increase *both* parental income and education mostly benefit the behavioral outcomes of elementary-aged children living in long-term poverty. The effect is small but significant for such programs and may be explained through increases in parental mental health brought about by the financial stability and increased employment provided by these welfare programs. Those welfare-to-work programs that focus solely on increasing employment but do not seek to increase parental income have fewer positive effects on children's outcomes. Such findings point to the necessity of welfare policies that go beyond supplementing the earnings of low-income parents, given the impact of increases in maternal education on children's school outcomes. Future research should focus on the educational participation patterns of welfare recipients and evaluations of adult education programs, which have been found to increase children's academic achievement and social competence well after the effects of welfare-to-work programs have diminished (Magnuson, 2003). If existing welfare programs cannot immediately or permanently alleviate financial hardships experienced by low-income families, educational programs on the adverse consequences of financial hardship on psychosocial functioning, parenting practices, and adjustment issues, will help foster the healthy functioning of these families.

FAMILY STRUCTURE

Research on family structure and child well-being indicates a negative association between cohabitation and emotional and behavioral outcomes. Family structure exerts a strong, negative influence on children's behavioral outcomes, such as bullying and hyperactivity. The negative effects of family structure on the psychological well-being (i.e., depression and low-self-esteem) of children decreases with age. Studies on the effects of family structure on child well-being tell a cautionary tale: the emotional and behavioral outcomes observed are not due solely to family structure but are mediated by the allocation of resources within families that are thought to ameliorate the negative effects of cohabitation. Future research to unpack the complexities of the association between family structure and child well-being must also seek to evaluate the causal ordering of family structure and economic factors. Such research will facilitate the development of interventions necessary to alleviate the potentially harmful effects of living in low-income cohabiting and single-parent families. Interventions should include factors that facilitate positive psychosocial functioning for low-income single mothers, such as social support. The presence of support can alleviate burdens associated with caregiving, increase positive parenting practices, and improve the quality of mother-child interactions. Public policies supporting early intervention programs and other community-based services that can provide assistance to low-income mothers lacking necessary forms of social support are also a critical piece to improving low-income children's emotional outcomes.

NEIGHBORHOOD CONDITIONS

As reviewed earlier in this chapter, structural aspects of neighborhoods do have a significant impact on children's emotional and behavioral outcomes. Experimental evidence from national and community-based samples suggests that moving out of poverty and into high-SES neighborhoods does have a positive effect on children's emotional and behavioral problems. Neighborhood SES is also associated with internalizing problems in younger children and externalizing behavior problems, lower school achievement, and social competence problems in younger adolescents. Finally, ethnic diversity within a neighborhood is associated with lower rates of internalizing problems for young African American children, but not for white children. Neighborhood effects, particularly those seen from relocation experiments, were especially robust for adolescent boys, a group that is particularly at risk for joblessness and dropping out of school. As such, public policies meant to increase the mobility of low-income families—in conjunction with public health efforts to monitor the mental health of families in high poverty neighborhoods—would benefit low-income families, policymakers, and educators alike.

INDIRECT PATHWAYS

Further research on the indirect linkages, or pathways, between SES and children's mental health will inform the development of successful intervention programs. One such pathway reviewed in this chapter was the family stress model. Given its focus on parenting and intrafamilial relationships, the family stress model has often been associated with emotional and behavioral outcomes. This theory states that economic stress leads to negative parenting practices, which in turn lead to poor child outcomes. Positive parenting practices, such as warmth and supportiveness, can buffer young children against the negative effects of financial hardship. Findings from larger, nationally representative data sets suggest both the importance of parental practices as a mediator between economic resources and child outcomes and the need for further exploration of the association between poverty and parent–child interactions. Replication analyses using multiple informants could provide researchers with critical information on the pathways that exist between poverty, parental mental health, and children's emotional wellbeing.

CONCLUSION

The evidence presented in this chapter clearly shows the detrimental impacts of low SES conditions on children's emotional and behavioral outcomes at any age, particularly if poverty is experienced early in life. Many studies suggest the programs and policies that reduce family poverty and financial hardship will have an immediate impact on children's cognitive outcomes and academic achievement—but the link between poverty and emotional well-being is more tenuous. As such, programs meant to alleviate financial hardship for low-income families may not prove as beneficial in improving mental health outcomes for children and adolescents. Unless changes to familial income are large and permanent, such policies will have minimal impact on children's outcomes. Finally, given that almost one-half of the effect of family income on developmental outcomes is mediated by the home environment, it appears, then, that programs and policies focusing on educating young children and their families will be most successful in ameliorating children's emotional and behavioral outcomes. Through careful crafting of educational programs, developmental interventions, and social policies meant to alleviate financial hardship for low-income families, we can reduce the differences in emotional and behavioral well-being between poor and nonpoor children.

REFERENCES

Bongers, I. L., Koot, H. M., van der Ende, J., & Verhulst, F. C. (2004). Developmental trajectories of externalizing behaviors in childhood and adolescence. *Child Development, 75*(5), 1523–1537.

Brooks-Gunn, J., & Duncan, G. J. (1997). The effects of poverty on children. *The Future of Children, 7*(2), 55–71.

Brooks-Gunn, J., Duncan, G. J., & Britto, P. R. (1999). Are socioeconomic gradients for children similar to those for adults? Achievement and health of children in the United States. In D. P. Keating & C. Hertzman (Eds.), *Developmental health and the wealth of nations: Social, biological and educational dynamics* (pp. 94–124). New York: Guilford Press.

Brooks-Gunn, J., Linver, M., & Fauth, R. C. (2005). Children's competence and SES in the family and neighborhood. In A. Elliot & C. Dweck (Eds.), *Handbook of competence and motivation.* New York: Guilford Press.

Brown, S. L. (2004). Family structure and child wellbeing: The significance of parental cohabitation. *Journal of Marriage and the Family, 66,* 351–367.

Chase-Lansdale, P. L., & Gordon, R. A. (1996). Economic hardship and the development of five- and six-year-olds: Neighborhood and regional perspectives. *Child Development, 67,* 3338–3367.

Chase-Lansdale, P. L., Gordon, R., Brooks-Gunn, J., & Klebanov, P. K. (1997). Neighborhood and family influences on the intellectual and behavioral competence of preschool and early school-age children. In J. Brooks-Gunn, G. J. Duncan, & J. L. Aber (Eds.), *Neighborhood poverty: Context and consequences for children* (Vol. 1, pp. 79–118). New York: Russell Sage Foundation Press.

Child Trends. (2004). *Early child development in social context: A chartbook.* New York: Author.

Conger, R. D., Conger, K. J., & Elder, G. H. (1997). Family economic hardship and adolescent adjustment: Mediating and moderating processes. In G. Duncan & J. Brooks-Gunn (Eds.), *Consequences of growing up poor* (pp. 288–310). New York: Russell Sage Foundation.

Costello, E. J., Compton, S. N., Keeler, G., & Angold, A. (2003). Relationships between poverty and psychopathology: A natural experiment. *Journal of the American Medical Association, 290*(15), 2023–2029.

Dearing, E., McCartney, K., & Taylor, B. A. (2001). Change in family income-to-needs matters more for children with less. *Child Development, 72*(6), 1772–1798.

Deaton, A. (2002). Policy implications of the gradient of health and wealth: An economist asks, would redistributing income improve population health? *Health Affairs, 21*(2), 13–30.

DeKlyen, M., Brooks-Gunn, J., & McLanahan, S. (2004). *The mental health of married and unmarried parents with infants.* Unpublished manuscript.

Duncan, G. J., & Brooks-Gunn, J. (1997). Income effects across the life span: Integration and interpretation. In G. J. Duncan and J. Brooks-Gunn (Eds.), *Consequences of growing up poor* (pp. 596–610). New York: Russell Sage Foundation Press.

Duncan, G. J., & Brooks-Gunn, J. (2000). Family poverty, welfare reform and child development. *Child Development, 71*(1), 188–196.

Duncan, G. J., Brooks-Gunn, J., & Klebanov, P. K. (1994). Economic deprivation and early-childhood development. *Child Development, 65*(2), 296–318.

Foley, K., Ford, R., Gyarmati, D., Michalopoulos, C., Miller, C., Morris, P., Redcross, C., Robins, P., & Attrite, D. T. (2002). *Making work pay: Final report on the Self-Sufficiency Project for long term welfare recipients.* New York: MDRC.

Ginther, D. K., & Pollak, R. A. (2003). *Does family structure affect children's educational outcomes?* National Bureau of Economic Research, Working Paper No. 9628.

Hanson, T., McLanahan, S., & Thomson, E. (1997). Economic resources, parental practices, and child wellbeing. In G. Duncan & J. Brooks-Gunn (Eds.), *Consequences of growing up poor* (pp. 190–238). New York: Russell Sage Foundation.

Huston, A. C., Miller, C., Richburg-Hayes, L., Duncan, G. J., Eldred, C. A., Weisner, T. S., Lowe, E., McLoyd, V. C., Crosby, D. A., Ripke, M. N., & Redcross, C. (2003). *New Hope for families and children: Five-year results of a program to reduce poverty and reform welfare.* New York: MDRC.

Jensen, P., Brooks-Gunn, J., & Graber, J. A. (1999). Introduction—Dimensional scales and diagnostic categories: Constructing crosswalks for child psychopathology assessments. *Journal of the American Academy of Child and Adolescent Psychiatry, 38*(2), 118–120.

Koball, H., & Douglas-Hall, A. (2004, September). *Fact sheet: Geography and of low-income families and children.* New York: National Center for Children in Poverty.

Korenman, S., Miller, J. E., & Sjaastad, J. E. (1995). Long term poverty and child development in the United States: Results from the National Longitudinal Survey of Youth. *Children and Youth Services Review, 17*(1), 127–151.

Lavigne, J. V., Gibbons, R. D., Christoffel, K. K., Arend, R., Rosenbaum, D., Binns. H., Dawson, N., Sobel. H., & Isaacs, C. (1996). Prevalence rates and correlates of psychiatric disorders among preschool children. *Journal of the American Academy of Child and Adolescent Psychiatry, 35,* 204–214.

Leventhal, T., & Brooks-Gunn, J. (2000). The neighborhoods they live in: The effects of neighborhood residence on child and adolescent outcomes. *Psychological Bulletin, 12*(2), 309–337.

Leventhal, T., & Brooks-Gunn, J. (2004). A randomized study of neighborhood effects on low-income children's educational outcomes. *Developmental Psychology, 40*(4), 488–507.

Lipman, E. L., & Offord, D. R. (1997). Psychosocial morbidity among poor children in Ontario. In G. J. Duncan & J. Brooks-Gunn (Eds.), *Consequences of growing up poor* (pp. 239–287). New York: Russell Sage Foundation.

Magnuson, K. (2003). The effect of increases in welfare mothers' education on their young children's academic and behavioral outcomes: Evidence from the National Evaluation of Welfare-to-Work Strategies Child Outcomes Study. Institute for Research on Poverty, Working Paper 1274-03.

Mayer, S. E. (1997). Trends in the economic wellbeing and life chances of America's children. In G. Duncan & J. Brooks-Gunn (Eds.), *Consequences of growing up poor* (pp. 49–69). New York: Russell Sage Foundation.

McLanahan, S. (1997). Parent absence or poverty: Which matters more? In G. J. Duncan & J. Brooks-Gunn (Eds.), *Consequences of growing up poor* (pp. 35–48). New York: Russell Sage Foundation.

McLeod, J. D., & Shanahan, M. J. (1993). Poverty, parenting and children's mental health. *American Sociological Review, 58,* 351–366.

Morris, P. A. (2002). The effects of welfare reform policies on children. *Social Policy Report, 16*(1), 1–20.

Osbourne, C., McLanahan, S., & Brooks-Gunn, J. (2004, June). *Child behavior in married and cohabiting families.* Unpublished manuscript.

Pagani, L., Boulerice, B., & Tremblay, R. E. (1997). The influence of poverty on children's classroom placement and behavior. In G. J. Duncan & J. Brooks-Gunn (Eds.), *Consequences of growing up poor* (pp. 311–339). New York: Russell Sage Foundation.

Rapport, M. D., Denney, C. B., Chung, K. M., & Hustace, K. (2001). Internalizing behavior problems and scholastic achievement in children: Cognitive and behavioral pathways as mediators of outcome. *Journal of Clinical Child Psychology, 30*(4), 536–551.

Shaffer, D., Fisher, P., Dulcan, M. K., Davies, M., Piacentini, J., Schwab-Stone, M. E., Lahey, B. B., Bourdon, K., Jensen, P. S., Bird, H. R., Canino, G., & Regier, D. A. (1996). The NIMH Diagnostic Interview Schedule for Children Version 2.3 (DISC-2.3): Description, acceptability, prevalence rates, and performance in the MECA Study. Methods for the Epidemiology of Child and Adolescent Mental Disorders Study. *Journal of the American Academy of Child and Adolescent Psychiatry, 35,* 865–877.

U.S. Census Bureau. (2002). *Census 2000 basics.* Washington, DC: U.S. Government Printing Office.

U.S. Census Bureau. (2003). *Poverty thresholds for 2003 by size of family and number of related children under 18 years.* Retrieved September 10, 2004, from http://www.census.gov/hhes/poverty/threshld/thresh02.html.

Chapter 13

A STATEWIDE COMMUNITY SYSTEM OF CARE AND EDUCATION: INCREASING SCHOOL READINESS THROUGH PARENT INVOLVEMENT AND EDUCATION

Celeste Sturdevant Reed, Laurie A. Van Egeren, Jacqueline Wood, Laura V. Bates, Betty Tableman, and Hiram E. Fitzgerald

This contract was supported by state school aid grant funds; the All Students Achieve Program-Parent Involvement and Education was legislatively created by Section 32b (6) of Public Act 121 of 2001.

We wish to acknowledge the project participation of our former Project Principal Investigator Marguerite Barratt, Ph.D., Director of the MSU Institute for Children, Youth, & Families (currently on leave with the National Science Foundation, Division of Behavioral and Cognitive Sciences). We also thank the staff of the 23 grantees, especially the program directors and parent educators who provided us with information about their projects. Finally, we appreciate the many efforts of the graduate student members of our evaluation team who interviewed staff, read reports, cleaned data, wrote drafts; in short, who were our partners in the work of the evaluation.

This chapter describes one state department of education's experiences and experiment with a unique school readiness program–a program that simultaneously emphasized

- parents' role as their child's first teacher
- the school's responsibility for programming aimed at children birth to five years of age
- universality of service (i.e., no eligibility requirements for participation)
- the importance of a collaborative community approach to service delivery

Although only school systems could receive funds and some basic service components were required, substantial leeway was allowed for grantees to design service approaches that best responded to their local context. This program tried to combine the best of family supportive services with a comprehensive system of care and education.

The authors were members of the university-based statewide evaluation team and the state department of education consultant who oversaw the program. They shared the responsibility for answering the overarching question, "To what extent did the program accomplish the intended outcomes for families and children?" As became apparent over the life of the initiative, an equally important question was, "What impact did the approach to service delivery (i.e., a collaborative approach) have on these outcomes?"

THE HISTORY OF THE INITIATIVE

During the late 1990s, a variety of conditions converged in Michigan that allowed for the emergence of the All Students Achieve Program–Parent Involvement and Education (ASAP–PIE) Grant Program. The Michigan economy was strong, resulting in a surplus in state revenues and especially in the state school aid fund. The legislature had allocated $100,000 to fund a "Ready to Learn" summit where legislators, state agency leadership, and business leaders gained information on the critical importance of young children's brain development related to the state's future success. A legislative bipartisan caucus on early childhood had been formed with strong leadership from both parties. The leaders of this caucus had been working closely with early childhood advocates, education leaders, and local communities to explore better ways to address the needs of young children and families.

During this time, the legislative majority party was seeking passage of legislation to reduce the legal restrictions for carrying a concealed weapon in Michigan. These two issues converged when a first-grade child shot and killed a six-year-old classmate on a Michigan school playground. The incident aroused public sentiment and the governor and the legislature were called upon to take action on gun control as well as early childhood intervention. As a consequence, those legislators wanting to move the concealed weapons bill forward worked with the Legislative Children's Caucus to add legislation that included wording in the state school aid act directed at parent involvement and education focused on parents of children birth to five years of age.

The enabling legislation made an annual allocation of 45 million dollars available for three years from the state school aid fund. The source of this funding constitutionally required the money to flow to local and intermediate school districts, and a competitive grant process was designed to award the funds. Grantees were mandated to make services available to all parents of children birth to five years of age, and a successful parent involvement and education program operated by an intermediate school district in southwestern Michigan served as the model.

The proposed legislation brought mixed reactions. Some early childhood and education groups supported the legislation, but other groups opposed the ASAP–PIE legislation based on its linkage to other gun legislative bills, and still others were against funds going to school districts rather than family and children's agencies. Nonetheless, the legislation passed, with the support of key education and child advocacy individuals who spoke to legislative committees and state agencies. Grants were made to 23 intermediate school districts in February 2001. The state of Michigan has 83 counties and 57 intermediate/regional educational school districts (ISDs and RESAs). The ISDs/RESAs provide a range of services to the local school districts—such as early childhood education and technical training—that would be prohibitive for the local districts to finance individually. However, an economic downturn resulted in the elimination of funding for the third year of the original three-year initiative. The MSU evaluation team was contracted in May 2002, 15 months after the initiative began and 13 months before it ended. The late beginning and short time period available made new, standardized data collection difficult; in conjunction with the state consultant, the decision was made to collect and aggregate data collected by grantees' local evaluations and request supplementary information to fill data gaps.

WHAT MADE THE ASAP–PIE PROGRAM UNIQUE?

ASAP–PIE was an unusual case of a state legislature coming together to support a community system of care and education across (although not in every area of) the state. The ultimate goal of the program was to improve school readiness among birth to five-year-olds primarily by changing or enhancing the environment provided by parents. This approach was based on the early childhood field's increasing understanding of how early relationships with parents and other caregivers can have an impact on children's development, and of how early intervention can influence those relationships (Shonkoff & Phillips, 2000). ASAP–PIE was modeled after the Parents as Teachers Program (PAT; Parents as Teachers National Center), a widely used model of universal services for parents of young children. With this goal in mind, all of the grantees shared common, legislatively defined outcomes aimed to improve school readiness for children from birth to age five, foster the maintenance of stable families, and reduce the need for special education services by

- encouraging positive parenting skills
- enhancing parent–child interactions
- providing learning opportunities that promote development
- promoting access to needed community services through a home-school-community partnership

In particular, *school readiness* formed the core outcome of the initiative. However, the specific characteristics that constituted school readiness were left to be defined by individual grantees. Research has shown that kindergarten teachers place as high a value on a child's socioemotional development upon school entry as they do upon their mastery of specific academic concepts (National Association for the Education of Young Children, 1990; Kagan, Moore, & Bredekamp, 1995). Moreover, The National Education Goals Panel (Halle, Zaslow, Zaff, & Calkins, 2000), supported by research (e.g., Peth-Pierce, 2000), has identified physical, social, emotional, and cognitive components of school readiness, all of which impact a child's capacity to learn and to function in the school environment. In collaboration with the grantees, we therefore defined school readiness as a multifaceted construct comprised of the development of age-appropriate (a) language and cognitive skills; (b) emotion regulation abilities; and (c) capacity to form and maintain relationships (Schonkoff & Phillips, 2000).

To promote these outcomes, services required by the ASAP–PIE legislation included

1. home visits conducted by home visitors trained in child development to help parents understand each stage of their children's development, encourage learning opportunities, and promote strong parent–child relationships
2. group meetings of participating families
3. periodic screenings for children's development, health, vision, and hearing
4. a community resource network that provided referrals to state, local, and private agencies to assist parents in preparing their children for academic success and to foster stable families
5. connections to quality preschools

These services were to occur as a community collaborative effort with grantee districts working with local community collaborative bodies, local health and welfare agencies, and private nonprofit agencies. Services were not to duplicate or supplant existing services in the community and were to be based on validated research-based methods and curricula.

Although the ASAP–PIE legislation did not mandate the development of a community system of care and education, communities were pointed in that direction by the legislative requirements for a community resource network and a community collaborative effort. This emphasis reflected legislators' recognition that some services for parents and their children ages birth to five were already available in the community and/or not exclusively the responsibility of the education system (i.e., periodic health, vision, and hearing screening). Further, promoting family stability required referral to other community services. In short, this initiative acknowledged the premise that comprehensive, community-based systems of services provide better outcomes for children and families, especially when children are considered to be at increased risk because of poverty or other life circumstances. In her review of successful programs for high-risk children and families, Schorr (1989) identifies a "broad spectrum of services" (p 256) that provide concrete help as well as social and emotional support as one essential component for success. Likewise, studies of the implementation of Early Head Start programs for at-risk families indicate that programs have developed community partnerships to meet families' needs and that these partnerships have evolved over time to meet emerging needs (Kisker, Pausell, Love, & Raikes, 2002).

In addition to these required services, some grantees also provided additional services as part of their recruitment of families with young children into the program and/or comprehensive approach to service delivery. The most common targeted recruitment strategy employed by ASAP–PIE grantees was systematic outreach to families with newborns, including the provision of information and home visiting services. Other special populations targeted included parenting teens, fathers and ethnic families. Some grantees recognized the necessity to respond differentially to those children at greatest risk by providing specialized services. These included hiring speech and language specialists for one-on-one therapy, contracting for expulsion prevention consultants to work with preschool staff and parents, and funding infant mental health (IMH) specialists. Fourteen ASAP–PIE programs had infant mental health specialists available in their community provider network; five specifically built in additional resources to expand the services to their families and children.

WHO WERE THE GRANTEES?

The 23 intermediate school districts receiving ASAP–PIE funds were geographically dispersed throughout the state, covering 35 of the 83 counties (see Figure 13.1), although the two largest urban areas, Detroit and Grand Rapids, did not receive grants. Generally, grantees served a single county. However, since population density is low in the rural northern Lower Peninsula and the Upper Peninsula and service areas of agency partners tended to cover multiple counties, these grantees served more than one county.

The potential population of children ages birth to five available to be served varied considerably among the grantees, ranging from just over 2,500 to more than 60,000, resulting in a total potential population of 274,545 children (Tableman et al., 2003). This represented 31 percent of the state's population of children ages birth to five. Additionally, significant differences were apparent across grantees' service areas in the degree of diversity and poverty. The percent of white children aged birth to five in the local population ranged from 65 percent to 96 percent, and the percent of children whose families were living in poverty ranged from under 10 percent to approximately 30 percent (Van Egeren, Bates, Tableman, Reed, & Kirk, 2002). Thus, not only the size of the potential service population, but the degree of service need varied greatly among the grantees.

Grants to the 23 grantees ranged from a low of $347,400 to the maximum allowable of $4,500,000. With two exceptions, grantees were awarded the amount requested, and most received less than $2,000,000— however, grantees did not use a standard method to estimate the amounts

Figure 13.1 Locations of ASAP–PIE grantees and counties served in the state of Michigan

they requested. Because the size of the grantees' potential service populations varied considerably, the decision by the state to use a dollar rather
than a per capita maximum on funding resulted in substantial discrepancies among the grantees in the amount of funding received per potential
child to be served: Grants ranged from a low of approximately $28 per
child birth to four years of age to a high of approximately $640, with the
median grant equivalent to $238 per child (Van Egeren et al., 2002).

A THEORY OF CHANGE: COMPREHENSIVE
SERVICES TO SCHOOL READINESS

Although the authorizing legislation did not explicitly link the service
components to the desired outcomes for parents and their young children,
these relationships were implied in the legislative requirements. The evaluation team therefore developed a theory of change in order to inform the
evaluation process (Figure 13.2).

This theory of change suggests that *school readiness,* the desired legislative
educational outcome, could be influenced by three factors that contribute to
family stability: (a) the parents' teaching skill; (b) their interactions with their
children, and (c) the extent to which the family's basic needs are met (Caughy,
1996; Radke-Yarrow, Nottleman, Martinez, Fox, & Bellmont, 1992).

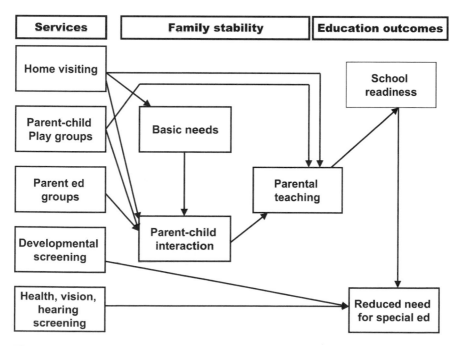

Figure 13.2   ASAP–PIE Theory of change

Services provided through the initiative, in turn, were expected to affect the factors that contribute to family stability. For example, home visiting is a service provided by parent educators to parents and children together in their home. For the ASAP–PIE program, parent educators generally focused on modeling and teaching strategies that improve parent–child interactions and parental teaching skills; consistent with other home visiting programs, parent educators often found it necessary to connect families to services designed to help meet basic needs as well (Fitzgerald, Mann, Cabrera, & Wong, 2003; Tableman, 1999–2000a & b). Parent education groups and parent–child play groups are venues to offer information, emotional support, and modeling of positive parenting behaviors with the goal of enhancing parent–child relationships. Early screening of children's development, health, vision, and hearing can identify children who have health concerns or developmental delays that are amenable to remediation. By providing corrective services early, it was expected that children would have a reduced need for future special education services, a second desired outcome identified in the legislation—however, the evaluation team also noted that increased early screening might actually increase the number of children enrolled in special education as children with previously unidentified developmental delay were found in need of service.

Two other requirements in the legislation also influenced how grantees would target and organize their efforts. The first was a requirement for *universal services*—that is, those services provided without eligibility requirements (e.g., low income, low parent education, teen parenthood). This requirement was consistent with the public school mission (services to all children). In addition, removing eligibility restrictions was anticipated to attract families who might otherwise not reach out for services. Families who could meet eligibility tests for traditional services because of income or diagnostic classification but who were reluctant to be labeled as such, as well as families with serious problems such as substance abuse problems, postpartum depression, isolation, and/or anger management issues, would be able to participate in ASAP–PIE services without stigma. In short, parents from all kinds of backgrounds and all socioeconomic levels could receive and therefore benefit from information and supportive services.

The other mandate that influenced the organization of ASAP–PIE services was the inclusion of specific community partners: minimally, the local multipurpose collaborative body (MPCB), local health and welfare agencies, and private nonprofit agencies involved in programs and services for preschool children and their parents. Multipurpose collaborative bodies formally represent all 83 counties since this designation by the governor in the early 1990s. Prior to that, many of these groups existed to support local families and children. Their duties include working to forge community alliances, creating a shared vision, and mobilizing resources. They have a long history of providing an infrastructure that supports many state and federal program directions.

Taken together, the combination of mandated ASAP–PIE services, plus the additional requirements for universal service to families delivered via a community partnership, laid the groundwork for grantees' development of a comprehensive system of care and education. Local history, resources, and opportunities also influenced the services provided.

WHAT DID UNIVERSAL SERVICES MEAN IN PRACTICE?

By the official end of funding in June 2003, 44,691 children had received some combination of core services (home visits, parent education groups, and parent–child play groups), screening (developmental, hearing, vision), and referrals to other services. On average, grantees served a quarter (24%) of the potential population of children ages birth to five and their families in their service areas. Penetration rates (the degree to which grantees provided services to all children in their area) varied widely among grantees. Almost half (11) of the grantees accessed 20–40 percent of their children, six grantees served less than 20 percent, and three grantees served 60–80 percent. Not surprisingly, the grantees who served the smallest percentage of children in their areas were from the largest communities. However, the reverse was not true; grantees with the smallest populations did not necessarily have the highest penetration rates.

The ASAP–PIE program was required to be offered as a universal service, but demographic data suggest that this initiative also presented an opportunity to reach out to families at risk. Informal conversations with some of these grantees suggest that they viewed themselves as providing *levels of service* to families triaged for risk; for example, families perceived as functioning well (or who were not interested in seeking more intensive services) may have received informative newsletters or a single screening visit; families who would benefit from modeling and coaching may have had regularly scheduled home visits; and families with higher levels of need may have been referred to agencies for additional assistance.

Poverty status was collected for 27,262 children, and nearly half (48%) of these children were available were TANF eligible. Children who were TANF eligible were 1.6 times more likely to receive some type of service compared to all children served. This rate was calculated using an odds ratio, a statistical technique for estimating the likelihood that an occurrence will occur (e.g., improvement or no improvement) given a particular circumstance (e.g., income is low or high; Hopkins, 2002). Penetration rates for children in poverty were even more varied than for all children who received services. Although only three grantees had accessed over 60 percent of *all* children in the service area, seven grantees had served over 80 percent of their children experiencing poverty. Five grantees served 40–60 percent and an equal number served 0–20 percent of their children in poverty. Notably, those grantees who were most successful in accessing children in poverty were serving the communities with the smallest populations of children in poverty. In communities with higher numbers of children in poverty, grantees had lower penetration rates.

Not every child or family who participated in home visits, parent–child play groups, and screening received the same services. Two-thirds of enrolled children received home visits. These children were younger, particularly under 12 months of age, and from families with one or more factors that placed them at risk of not being ready for school. (Risk factors included low family income, low parental education, higher family mobility, and living with a single or adolescent mother.) Almost half (44%) of the enrolled children and their families participated in play groups. Most children who participated in play groups tended to be between 12 and 36 months of age and from families with only one or no risk factors for school readiness. Finally, overall, 30 percent of the enrolled children received a developmental screening, but 40 percent of the children in poverty were screened. Approximately one in five children received hearing and vision screening, but again, children in poverty were almost three times as likely to receive these services.

To summarize, although the legislation mandated universal services, funds were insufficient to provide equal levels of service to every family with birth to five-year-old children; nor did all families want these services. Some grantees met this challenge by developing level systems that targeted service intensity to need, recruited particular populations of at-risk families, spread their services across different children, or concentrated most of their intensive services on one group of children while promoting screening and information services among the rest.

HOW DID CHILDREN BENEFIT FROM ASAP–PIE?

Because of the inconsistency in availability and measurement of outcomes data, the results should be viewed with caution. Nevertheless, trends suggested that some of the service components and combinations were effective in improving developmental outcomes for children:

- Children who had developmental delays when first screened and received home visiting were more likely to show improvement in their development when compared with children who did not receive the service.

- Children with delays specifically in personal-social or problem-solving skills appeared to benefit from parent–child play groups.
- Children who had developmental delays and received home visiting combined with play groups were three times more likely to show no developmental delay at a second assessment.
- Children with developmental delays in communication or problem solving were more likely to improve if they received a hearing screening.

Unfortunately, because 21 of the 23 grantees used the Parents as Teachers curriculum and most also used one or more other curricula as well, it was not possible to assess differential results due to program model used.

It was difficult for the evaluation team to determine grantees' differential success with specific subpopulations because the collection of demographic data was both inconsistent across grantees and also within a single grantee's service programs. Anecdotal reports from grantees suggested that this was due in part to some grantees' reluctance to request personal family information, especially for the less intensive services and/or those programs where a relationship had not been developed between the service provider and the family. In addition, grantees that formed partnerships with other community agencies to deliver required services did not have accompanying agreements to provide data on those families. As a result, an ironic consequence is that the better integrated the community system of care; the less likely data were available on families and children served via that system.

Service Delivery Approaches

Although a number of studies compare the outcomes of different approaches to service delivery (e.g., home-based vs. center-based), few studies specifically examine the impact of developing a collaborative system of care on child and family outcomes. In an early report on family systems reform in Pennsylvania across a broad range of services, research sites reported improved results for children and families in one or more dimensions of child well-being, including school achievement (Bruner, 2000).

Two recent studies did specifically compare the effectiveness of different models of service delivery. One study in the health field examined the impact of developing a coordinated system of health services on health outcomes for low-income pregnant women and their infants compared with delivering health services in a more traditional practice model (Margolis et al., 2001). The intervention focused on community-, (health care) practice-, and individual-level strategies to improve the processes of care delivery. The results indicated there were high levels of participation, systems changed, and preventive health outcomes improved. The investigators concluded that tiered, interrelated interventions directed at an entire population of mothers and children hold promise to improve the outcomes of health care for families and children.

A major longitudinal study of early childhood education in the United Kingdom (Sylva, Melhuish, Sammons, Siraj-Blatchford, & Taggart, 2004) examined type of service delivery model as one factor affecting child outcomes in early elementary school. For children at higher educational risk, the model that integrated preschool with child care and family support services demonstrated better child outcomes when other factors, such as family socioeconomic status, duration of preschool experience, and social mix of children attending the center were controlled. However, these centers were also more likely to have had other characteristics related to higher-quality preschool, such as well-qualified staff and good staff–child relationships.

The same purpose, program components, and outcomes guided every ASAP–PIE grantee's effort, and in all instances the fiscal agent was the intermediate school district. However, these commonalities did not result in standardized organizational configurations, service arrangements, service delivery partners, and/or participating families–nor should they. Differences in community resources and values, family situations, prior experiences with collaboration, and the role played by the intermediate school district in programming for young children are just some of the factors that may have contributed to the varied grantee responses to this challenge.

HOW DID GRANTEES APPROACH SERVICE DELIVERY?

The ASAP–PIE grantees used two basic approaches to organizing and delivering services. Fifteen grantees saw their task as implementing the specified services within the *education system* (Figure 13.3). Four of these education-based grantees saw the intermediate school district as the primary organizer, manager and service provider (the ISD model). For the other seven education-based grantees, the ISD organized and managed the services, but the local school districts delivered the services (the Local School District Model). Education system-based grantees were more likely to

- co-locate (i.e., different agencies provide services in the same location) or co-administer all services for children ages birth to five operated by the ISD
- incorporate birth to five services as part of the district's school improvement plan
- emphasize connecting parents to elementary schools
- promote planning for school transition

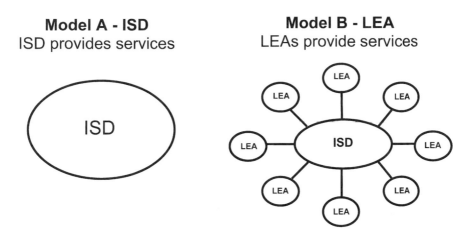

Figure 13.3   Education-based approaches

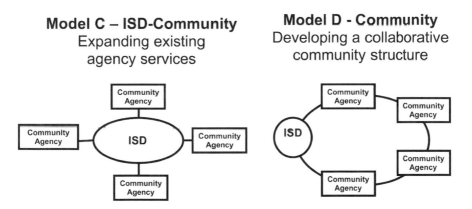

Figure 13.4   Community-based approaches

The other 12 grantees viewed their task as expanding and enhancing *community* services (Figure 13.4). For five of these community-based grantees, the ISD contracted with existing community agencies to provide services by expanding existing services or funding new services (the ISD-Community Model). Seven grantees downplayed the role of the ISD and emphasized the role of community agencies, working toward the development of an interagency community system (the Community Model). Grantees using a community-based approach were more likely to

- consider services provided by the ISD as only one component in an overall system of services for children ages birth to five

- include agencies that were providing services but were not receiving ASAP–PIE subcontracted funds as partners in the system
- co-locate ISD staff and staff of partner agencies

UNDER THE LENS OF SERVICE MODEL, WHAT DID "UNIVERSAL SERVICES" MEAN?

When penetration rates were examined across the four models, the rates were similar (28–38%); however, grantees using different models placed a difference emphasis on the age groups served. If children were served proportionally by age groups (i.e., 20% of the children served were from birth to age one, 40% from ages one to three and 40% from ages three to five years), the grantee would have provided universal services across age groups. Among the four, the Local School

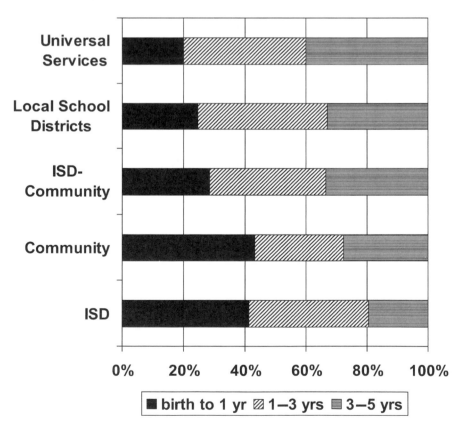

Figure 13.5   Comparisons of children served by age and delivery model

District Model services to children were the closest to the 20 percent–40 percent–40 percent proportional pattern. The ISD-Community Model grantees, in contrast, served children in all three ages groups similarly. Both the Community and the ISD Models focused their services on younger children; twice as many as expected (approximately 40%) of the children receiving services in both models were aged one year or younger (Figure 13.5).

UNDER THE LENS OF SERVICE MODEL, WHAT SERVICE COMPONENTS WERE EMPHASIZED?

Differences in services delivered emerged based on the service delivery model used. Grantees using Community Models were less likely than the other three to do home visiting; this may be due to their smaller per-child grants and the relatively higher cost of home visiting services; or community partners may have delivered these services as part of the community system of care. (Recall that we do not know if fewer families actually received home visits, since no grantee reported data on services delivered by their community partners.) The grantees using ISD Models were less likely to provide group experiences for parents and their children. This may have been a function of their prior experience coordinating early intervention services for infants and toddlers

Table 13.1
Service Component Emphases by Service Approach and Model

Service Components	Education System Approaches		Community-based Approaches	
	ISD	Local School District	ISD-Community	Community
Home Visiting	(No differences among models)			2.6x Less Likely
Parent–child Play Groups	3.5x Less Likely	2.8x More Likely		
Parent Education	5x Less Likely	3.3x More Likely		2.8x Less Likely
Screening	1.5x–2.3x More Likely	2x Less Likely		2.4x More Likely
Referrals			2.1x More Likely	3.1x Less Likely

Each model is compared to the other three combined.

with disabilities, through which ISD staff provided parent education via home visits rather than in group settings. Those employing Local School District Models were more likely to provide parent education and parent–child play groups. Again, comfort working with parents and children in groups may have influenced this ASAP–PIE programming choice. The differences among the models are summarized in Table 13.1. Values in the table range from 1.5 to 5 times more or less likely. An odds ratio of 1.50 (i.e., something is 1.5 times more likely to occur in one condition than in another condition) is considered small, 3.5 is moderate and 9.0 is large (Hopkins, 2002).

USING THE LENS OF SERVICE MODEL, WHAT BENEFITS DID CHILDREN RECEIVE?

There were striking differences in the benefits received by families and children based on the service delivery model used. Children enrolled in services delivered using a Community Model were twice as likely to improve on at least one subscale of the Ages and Stages Questionnaire (ASQ) as children enrolled in other models. Further, children enrolled in a community model were more likely to improve in communication and problem-solving (ASQ subscales) than children enrolled in other models.

It would be tempting to assume that some of the benefits accrued from differences in funding levels (i.e., more funds) or service components (i.e., more home visits) previously mentioned. However, compared to grantees using the other three models, those adopting a Community Model spent the least amount of funds per child and were least likely to do home visits (probably a reflection of their smaller amount of available funds and use of unfunded community partners to deliver services).

Discussion

Our data suggest that community-based models of service delivery may provide better outcomes for children with a lower investment of dollars. Recognizing the limitations in our data and the fact that local community contexts vary widely, we have recommended that the Michigan Department of Education promote a *philosophy* of the ISD as *partner* in the system of care and education for families and children ages birth to five in their future programming. In addition, we have made a suggestion that those communities without a history of or positive experiences with collaboration have the option of planning grants prior to receiving service delivery grants.

HOW DO WE EXPLAIN THE DIFFERENCES
ACHIEVED BY SERVICE DELIVERY APPROACH?

If community-based approaches are to be promoted, then it is important to understand how community approaches can be fostered, especially in different community contexts. An interesting question for us was how these intermediate school districts, presumably with preexisting structures and supports for families and children in place in their communities, came to have such different models for organizing their services. That led us to hypothesize that the four models represent phases or stages along a continuum or developmental pathway.

History/Collaboration

The first developmental pathway, shown below, is characterized by the amount of cross-organization collaboration required:

ISD Model → Local School District Model →
ISD-Community Model → Community Model

In this pathway, the ISD model is assumed to require the least amount of collaboration since grantees organized, managed, and delivered their services entirely in-house. At the opposite end of the continuum is the community model, which requires extensive collaboration so that all organizations operate as equal partners to deliver services to families and young children. Most local schools districts would not have all the services available in-house, but at least they would potentially be working with a smaller number of community partners in a more defined geographic area than that required in the ISD-Community Model. Both the Local School District and the ISD-Community models might also have the advantage of being able to contract for services, rather than develop the collaborative partnership assumed in a true Community model.

There were some data that could be used to test this pathway. As part of the state-wide evaluation, grantees were asked questions about their prior collaborative efforts. These questions focused on prior membership in the local MPCB and the roles that group played in grant development and grant management. We found the following:

- For all grantees the ISD had been a member of the local multipurpose collaborative body (MPCB) prior to the advent of the ASAP–PIE funds.
- Seventeen of the 23 grantees worked through an existing workgroup of the MPCB to develop their proposal; this included all of the ISD

Model grantees, but four of seven for the grantees using a Local School District Model.

- Every grantee was required to establish a collaborative advisory committee to guide its policies and actions. For 19 of the 23 grantees, the MPCB workgroup on birth to age five services was the grantee's collaborative advisory group; there was no pattern among those grantees that developed special advisory groups.

- Grantees using the Local School District Model were the least likely to have common release forms; there were no differences among the other models.

- The ISD-Community Model grantees were the most likely to have common intake forms; there were no differences among the grantees using the other three models.

While it may be the exception that proves the rule, one grantee using an ISD Model offered a home visiting intervention with families of young children that predated the existence of their community's MPCB and were central to their MPCB. Therefore, given the data we had, there were no obvious patterns for the differences among models based on prior history of collaboration.

Old/New Relationships

An alternative pathway might be drawn if the challenge is conceived as one of moving partners from "doing business as usual" to synthesizing new relationships. That progression could be shown as:

ISD Model → ISD-Community Model → Local School District Model → Community Model

Here, the progression is one from the ISD doing what it does well (special services for children and families not regularly provided by local schools) to a contractual relationship with community agencies (partners work together but each is doing its usual job). The Local School District Model represents a more complicated progression, because this configuration stretches elementary schools to perform unusual services for families who are not yet affiliated with the school (at least for the target children). Finally, the Community model is seen as the most complicated, because all partners have a "larger than themselves" interest in families and young children. While this progression presents an intriguing possibility, unfortunately, there were no data that could test the legitimacy of this pathway.

Managing the Territory

When the evaluation team examined the size of the child populations grantees had available to serve, another possible pathway emerged:

ISD-Community Model ↔ ISD Model → Community Model → Local School District Model

In the smallest communities (6,000 or fewer children ages birth to five years), the ISD and ISD-Community Models were generally interchangeable. Grantees with medium-sized populations (more than 6,000 and fewer than 17,000 children) predominantly used the Community Model. When grantees had the most children to serve (21,000–62,000 children), the Local School District Model was most frequently used. There were several exceptions: two Community Models and a Local School District Model were used in the smallest communities; an ISD Model in the medium-sized communities; and an ISD-Community Model in the largest communities.

However, the overall pattern seems to suggest that there may be an optimal size for partnering models. Perhaps in the smallest communities, contractual arrangements between the ISD and community agencies are more easily formed and can be promoted as the minimal level of partnering in which an ISD engages on its progression to the optimal Community Model. Among these grantees in medium-sized communities the Community Model was the clear preference for serving families and young children. In communities this size, there may be enough differentiated services for agency representatives to understand the benefits of working together, but not so many partners that the process becomes cumbersome. Grantees in the largest communities adopted a Local School District Model. Perhaps this choice reflects their attempt to apportion services for their many families in manageable chunks of territory, and for this grant-making program, the obvious territory was the local school district.

WHAT RECOMMENDATIONS EMERGED?

Funds are not currently available in the state budget to mount a comparable initiative; nonetheless, MDE Office of Early Childhood and Family Services is promoting other, less expensive parenting education and school readiness efforts. What lessons have MDE and MSU learned from this venture? The evaluation team made a number of recommendations for improving outcomes-related data in future projects, such as the identification of common definitions (e.g., services, levels of service, dosage, enrollment categories, etc.). Strategies for improving measurement learned here (e.g., common instruments and tools) have already been incorporated into a subsequent contract between MDE and MSU for out-of-school time programming. However, neither of these recommendations will necessarily increase and/or improve ISDs' participation as community partners in the services they provide to families and young children. Four recommendations may have that effect.

1. Improve the collaborative relations among the state level agencies that are expected to partner at the local level.

In some communities, the local school districts, county public health departments, and public welfare agencies, along with their private agency partners and public libraries worked out unique arrangements to the mutual benefit of families as well as agencies. These arrangements, more often than not, depended on the social capital developed among partners rather than any clear super-organization mandate. With the clear gubernatorial interests in families with young children, this would appear to be an optimal time for securing state-level interagency agreements.

2. Set aside funds for planning grants to support the development of local interagency collaborative arrangements prior to the development of intervention services.

Communities with little previous collaborative experience were at a decided disadvantage in the ASAP–PIE grant-making process, and even these experienced communities averaged multiple-months' start-up delays. Unfortunately, communities without previous experiences are likely to be the same ones where families and children can benefit from integrated early childhood opportunities. Planning grants with clear goals could improve start-up times immeasurably.

3. Provide consultation, training, and technical assistance on collaborative approaches to grantees.

Requiring collaborative or shared approaches to service organization and delivery is the first step to instigating these approaches, but it is not sufficient. Partners are likely to benefit from a variety of technical assistance in developing integrated service systems. There are many potential sources of this expertise, not the least of which are some of the ASAP–PIE grantees themselves. In addition, Michigan, through the Department of Community Health, has extensive experience in providing consultation and training to members of local multipurpose collaborative bodies; the Department of Human Services (the state public welfare department) and others have worked on systems reform efforts at the state level for a number of years; and the Department of Education, along with others, is currently a learning partner in the Build Initiative (Building Early Learning Systems in the States). The Build Initiative is a multistate partnership that helps states construct a coordinated system of programs, policies, and services that responds to the needs of young children and their families. It was created by the Early Childhood Funders' Collaborative, a consortium of national and local foundations that have substantial grant-making programs in early childhood care and education.

4. Systematically collect data on the mechanisms for implementing collaborative structures, not solely on family and child outcomes associated with these structures.

The alternative service delivery models, used here as categories to help explain benefits for families and children in this evaluation, show promise. However, the evaluation team's initial attempts to develop a "collaboration index" could not meaningfully distinguish among the grantees. More conceptualization and specification are necessary to transform these into explanatory variables if the phrase "community-based models for systems of early care and education" is to be descriptive rather than motivational.

WHAT IS THE ASAP–PIE LEGACY?

The ASAP–PIE grant program linked directly to two MDE reform initiatives, ensuring early childhood literacy and integrating communities and schools. The State Board of Education recognized the role of parents and the importance of children's early years in fostering each child's readiness for learning and success in a later formalized school environment. The ASAP–PIE program served as a major initiative to educate parents of very young children more fully regarding the development of their children, thus enhancing their children's school readiness.

This effort provided a vehicle to move toward a seamless system of early education and care for families with young children. Early childhood programs offered by the department, such as Early On, and other community agencies were linked to ASAP–PIE. Families of three- and four-year-olds were linked to quality preschool community settings such as MDE's Michigan School Readiness Program, Head Start, and accredited full-day and half-day child-care centers. Individual children also received Early On services, preprimary special education services, infant mental health services, and/or assistance in transitioning to quality preschools and kindergarten. Families were linked to mental health services, local elementary schools, family counseling, Even Start family literacy programs, Zero to Three Secondary Prevention programs (to prevent child abuse and neglect), and other programs in the areas of housing, health, and so on, depending on their needs.

Prior to ASAP–PIE, in many communities there was a disconnection between education institutions and the broader community. Today, these relationships are improving, due in part to the work of ASAP–PIE programs and many individuals at the local and state levels. MDE has also been able to redirect a small amount of existing funding (3.3 million dollars) to every ISD's budget to expand parent education and involvement statewide through the Great Parent/Great Start Program. The MSU evaluation team worked with MDE and the Michigan Association of Intermediate School Administrators to provide insights from the ASAP–PIE experiences for new and experienced grantees. Through this mechanism, there continues to be an opportunity state-wide to bolster community collaborative efforts that include local education institutions as integral partners.

In the foreseeable future, the state of Michigan is unlikely to have the funds to embark on a direct, large-scale application of the lessons learned from ASAP–PIE. However, significant shifts have occurred in cross-department and interagency thinking. The MSU evaluation team and MDE have applied their joint experiences to a subsequent evaluation contract on out-of-school time programs. MDE is applying its experience to other interdepartmental actions. At the local level, individual agency resources are being regarded as part of the community's total set of assets to be used in the most effective way. Discussions are changing from protective discussions of agency needs and limitations to creative problem-solving discussions on how best the community can assist families and children to be successful. As Michigan moves to a system of early education and care across all services, the lessons of ASAP–PIE hold valuable information in that systems redesign.

REFERENCES

Bruner, C. (2000, March). *Family service systems reform in Pennsylvania: An assessment of impact and opportunity*. Des Moines, IA: Child and Family Policy Center.

Caughy, M.O. (1996). Health and environmental effects on academic readiness of school-age children. *Developmental Psychology, 32*, 515–522.

Fitzgerald, H.E., Mann, T., Cabrera, N., & Wong, M.M. (2003). Diversity in caregiving contexts. In R.M. Learner, M.A. Easterbrooks, & J. Mistry (Eds.), *Handbook of psychology*. Vol. 6. *Developmental psychology* (pp 135–170). New York: Wiley.

Halle, T., Zaslow, M. Zaff, J., & Calkins, J. (2000). Background for community-level work on school readiness; A review of definitions, assessments, and investment strategies. Child Trends: Final report of the Knight Foundation.

Hopkins, W. G. (2002). A scale of magnitudes for effect statistics. In: *A new view of statistics. Internet Society for Sport Science.* http://www.sportsci. org/resource/stats/effectmag.html.

Kagan, S. L., Moore, E., & Bredekamp, S. (1995). *Reconsidering children's early development and learning: Toward common views and vocabulary.* Washington, DC: National Goals Panel.

Kisker, E. E., Paulsell, D., Love, J. M., & Raikes, H. (2002, December). *Pathways to quality and full implementation in Early Head Start programs.* Princeton, NJ: Mathematica Policy Research.

Margolis, P. A., Stevens, R., Bordley, W. C., Stuart, J., Harlan, C., Keyes-Elstein, L., & Wisseh, S. (2001). *Pediatrics, 108*(3), 42–52.

National Association for the Education of Young Children. (1990). NAEYC position statement on school readiness. *Young Children, 46,* 21–23.

Peth-Pierce, R. (2000). A Good beginning. Sending America's children to school with the social and emotional competence they need to succeed. Retrieved (9/10/2000), from the National Institute of Mental Health Web site: http://nimh.nih.gov/childhp/fdnconsb.htm.

Radke-Yarrow, M., Nottleman, E., Martinez, P., Fox, M., & Belmont, B. (1992). Young children of affectively ill parents: A longitudinal study of psychological development. *Journal of the American Academy of Child and Adolescent Psychiatry, 31,* 68-76.

Schorr, L. (1989). *Within our reach: Breaking the cycle of disadvantage.* New York: Doubleday.

Shonkoff, J. P., & Phillips, D. A. (Eds.), (2000). *From neurons to neighborhoods: The science of early childhood development.* Washington, DC: National Academy Press.

Sylva, K., Melhuish, E., Sammons, P., Siraj-Blatchford, I., & Taggart, B. (2004, November). *Effective pre-school education.* London: The University of London, Institute for Education.

Tableman, B. (Ed.). (1999–2000a). Effective home visiting for very young children—1 (Outcomes), *Best Practice Brief #17,* E. Lansing, MI: Michigan State University; University Outreach and Engagement. Available online at http://www.outreach.msu.edu/bpbriefs.

Tableman, B. (Ed.). (1999–2000b). Effective home visiting for very young children—2 (Approaches to intervention), *Best Practice Brief #19,* E. Lansing, MI: Michigan State University; University Outreach and Engagement. Available online at http://www.outreach.msu.edu/bpbriefs.

Tableman, B., Bates, L., Reed, C. S., Bohne, B., Kay, J., Mahaffey, M., & Van Egeren, L. (2003, April 3). *The statewide evaluation of the ASAP–PIE Program – Report 2 with an emphasis on grantees' programs.* East Lansing, MI: Michigan State University Institute for Children, Youth & Families and University Outreach and Engagement.

Van Egeren, L. A., Bates, L., Tableman, B., Reed, C. S., & Kirk, R. (2002, September 2). *Statewide evaluation of the ASAP–PIE Program – Year 1 report implementation and program characteristics.* East Lansing, MI: Michigan State University Institute for Children, Youth & Families and University Outreach and Engagement.

Chapter 14

THEORETICAL BASIS FOR EXPECTED EFFECTS OF A FAMILY SUPPORT PROGRAM ON FAMILY AND CHILD OUTCOMES

Jessica V. Barnes and Hiram E. Fitzgerald

This work is supported by University Outreach and Engagement at Michigan State University and by contracts with the community partners. The authors want to recognize Cassandra Joubert, Sc.D., currently at the Southwest Detroit Community Foundation, for her encouragement and support in the development of the initial Passport evaluation plan. We also thank Mott Children's Health Center for the oversight and support of the development of the *"Ready, Set, Grow!" Passport Initiative.*

INTRODUCTION

A number of parent support programs have developed across the United States to ameliorate the effects of poverty, low levels of education, and family stress on children's development. This chapter will briefly describe one such family support program, the *"Ready, Set, Grow!" Passport Initiative,* and provide the theoretical underpinnings of program effects on family and child outcomes.

ASSESSMENT OF COMMUNITY NEED

The *"Ready, Set, Grow!" Passport Initiative* provides support services for families with young children in Genesee County, Michigan. Genesee County, the fourth largest county in Michigan, is located in the southeast portion of the state. The county contains a major metropolitan area, the city of Flint, as well as many suburban and rural areas. It is rich in diversity: 74.1 percent of the population are white (non-Hispanic), 20.4 percent are black or African American, 2.3 percent are of Hispanic or Latino origin, 2.2 percent are multiracial, 0.8 percent are Asian, 0.8 percent are of a race not specified, and 0.6 percent are of Native American origin. Census Bureau data point to a higher percentage of residents living in poverty: 13.1 percent of residents in Genesee County report living below poverty level versus 10.5 percent reported in Michigan overall.

Along with high poverty levels, numerous other challenges facing Genesee County have been clearly identified. High rates of young parents with low educational attainment, high teenage and single-parent birth rates, and a lack of health insurance have led to high rates of poor pregnancy outcomes, high infant death rates, high rates of infant and child morbidity, and high rates of child abuse and neglect (Annie E. Casey Foundation, 2002).

The Genesee County *"Ready, Set, Grow!" Passport Initiative* is a community-wide collaboration that was designed to build a broad-based system of support to connect families with existing services and to teach families the importance of the first five years of life. The goal is to enhance the well-being of children ages birth to six in the county by providing two basic services to participating families: (1) information about child development and (2) linkages with services and programs. The program provides these services to all families of Genesee County. Approximately 9,000 children are currently enrolled in the Passport Program, and of the families enrolled in the program, 49 percent are Caucasian, 42 percent are African American, 6 percent are multiracial, 2 percent are Hispanic, and 1 percent identifies their ethnicity as either Asian, Native American, or other. Further, 25 percent of the participants have not graduated from high school, 46 percent have graduated from high school, 18 percent have completed some college, and 11 percent have completed a Bachelor's degree or graduate school.

RATIONALE OF PROGRAM EFFECTS

The primary goal identified by the community for Passport is to increase positive social development in children by providing parents with knowledge about child development, incentives to participate in activities with their children that promote positive social and cognitive development, and case advocacy to identify family needs and provide connections with community agencies to meet those needs. Based on the services Passport provides to families, it is expected that involvement in Passport will increase parent confidence, knowledge of child development, and positive parent practices. Changes in the parents are expected to influence the children's development, the community-identified outcome.

The Relations among Parent Factors, Prevention Efforts, and Child Outcomes

Parent Knowledge of Child Development

The educational materials on child development, the incentives to participate in particular activities with their children, and the family advocacy services are expected to lead to an increased knowledge of child development.

Knowledge of child development is defined as knowledge of normative development from birth to toddlerhood. Parent knowledge of development is indicative of parents' understanding of how to meet their child's needs (Dichtelmiller et al., 1992). The effects of that understanding on parental expectations and behaviors and on child development have been consistently documented.

Parents who are more knowledgeable about infant development and milestones have more positive and more realistic expectations about their child's behavior (Contreras, Rhodes, & Mangelsdorf, 1995; Larsen & Juhasz, 1985). Additionally, there is evidence that the unrealistic expectations associated with low parental knowledge lead to negative interpretations of the child's behavior and inappropriate use of child management techniques (Rickard, Graziano, & Forehand, 1984). Knowledge of child development, in combination with age and maturity, is predictive of the style with which parents interact with their children (Fry, 1985). Mothers who provide their children with more stimulation and who have more positive interactions with their children tend to have greater knowledge about child development.

Moreover, interventions such as Passport aimed at increasing parent knowledge have been found to influence parent behaviors and expectations. The evaluation of one intervention found that training mothers with a curriculum that focused on improving parental interactions and knowledge of child development led to a decrease in unrealistic expectations and to an increase in appropriate use of discipline (Fewell & Wheeden, 1998). Another intervention utilizing two different teaching methods to increase knowledge of child development found that participation in the intervention, regardless of the method of teaching used, led to decreases in unrealistic expectations of their children and increases in the use of more appropriate discipline (Wint & Brown, 1987).

The effects of parent knowledge of child development on child outcomes have been less frequently documented than have the effects on parent outcomes. Nonetheless, parents with greater knowledge of child development tend to have children with fewer behavior problems, stronger cognitive and motor development, and less risk of injury (Benasich & Brooks-Gunn,

1996; Dichtelmiller et al., 1992; Pomerleau et al., 1998; Rickard et al., 1984; Rivara & Howard, 1982).

Perceived Parental Confidence

By providing parents with information about child development and access to community resources, the Passport program is expected to lead to more realistic appraisals of their parental skills. Thus, the evaluation of Passport included the measurement of parental confidence.

In the literature, parent confidence, or parent perception of competence, has been defined as "an estimation of the degree to which parents perceive themselves as capable of performing the varied tasks associated with this highly demanding role" (Teti, O'Connell, & Reiner, 1996, p. 238). Others have defined parental confidence as "parents' beliefs in their competence and effectiveness in the parental role" (Coleman & Karraker, 2003, p. 127). We define parent confidence as the parents' perception of their parenting skills and ability to care for their child.

Several studies have explored the relationship between parent confidence and parent characteristics. Parent confidence has been related to parent depression, maternal adjustment, and parent attitudes (East, Matthews, & Felice, 1994; Panzarine, Slater, & Sharps, 1995; Williams et al., 1987). Additionally, parent confidence has been identified as a goal for intervention and prevention programs (Miller Heyl, MacPhee, & Fritz, 1998; Pisterman et al., 1992; Thompson, Ruma, Schuchmann, & Burke, 1996).

While some researchers have reported significant and positive relations between parent confidence and quality of parent/child interactions, others have not. How do we explain these discrepancies? One potential explanation is that there is a discrepancy between the confidence parents have in their ability and their true competence. In other words, parents' perceptions of their parenting abilities may be different than their actual parenting skills. In support of this explanation, research has demonstrated that parents' knowledge of child development interacts with parents' confidence to create such group differences (Conrad, Gross, Fogg, & Ruchala, 1992). In this study, the authors found that it was the interaction between the knowledge of child development and parent confidence that led to the significant prediction of the quality of mother/toddler interactions. It may be that parents who do not know the basics of child development may be much less likely to critically evaluate their performance and knowledge as parents, potentially because they do not understand their error.

Parent Activities

The information about specific parent behaviors and activities provided in the educational materials and encouraged by the incentive system are expected to increase the amount of positive parent activities engaged in by Passport families. A number of studies have shown the positive effects of prevention and intervention programs on parent behavior and activities (Gross et al., 2003; Parker, Boak, Griffin, Ripple, & Peay, 1999).

Additionally, many studies have been conducted to examine the relationship between a variety of parent behaviors and child outcomes. The review of how parent activities/behaviors relate to child social competence consists of three aspects of child social competence. The three aspects of child social competence are: social problem-solving skills, emotion and behavior regulation, and emotion identification/understanding.

Parent Behavior and Child Social Problem Solving

The literature concerning the effect of parent behavior on child social problem solving can be grouped into three broad categories. First, child social problem-solving skills have been related to the child's experience of abuse. Second, child social problem-solving skills have been related to the parents' controlling/restrictive versus warm/supportive behaviors. Third, child social problem-solving skills have been related to the parents' conflict resolution behaviors/strategies.

Child Abuse and Social Problem Solving

Research concerning child social problem solving and the experience of abuse has consistently found that children who are abused are more likely to experience difficulty in social problem solving than children who have not been abused. The experience of abuse, especially for children five and younger, is a strong predictor of early expressions of violence, and this early aggressive behavior has been linked to deficiencies in social problem-solving skills (Dodge, Bates, & Pettit, 1990). In this seminal study by Dodge and his colleagues, social processing skills were assessed in 309 children recruited at pre-kindergarten registration. The children watched 24 cartoon vignettes of negative events and were asked a series of questions about each story to assess patterns of social information processing. The interview addressed the children's attribution biases, ability to attend to social cues, identification of solutions, and evaluation of solutions. The children's mothers were interviewed in the home to assess children's experience of physical abuse and family ecological information. Six months later, teacher, peer, and researcher ratings of child aggression were collected. The investigators found that assignment of hostile intentions to others in social conflict and the tendency to generate fewer and less competent solutions were all significantly related to child experience of abuse (Dodge et al., 1990).

More recent research assessing the relations among children's emotion knowledge, social problem-solving skills, behavior problems, social competence, and experience of abuse has also shown that children's experience of abuse is predictive of problem-solving ability (Smith & Walden, 1999).

Parent Discipline/Support and Child Social Problem Solving

Much research has been conducted to clarify the relation between child-rearing behaviors and child social problem solving (Domitrovich & Bierman, 2001; Carlson-Jones, Rickel, & Smith, 1980). A study of child-rearing practices and social problem-solving skills of 72 preschoolers found that maternal nurturance and restrictiveness were related to the quality of solutions children gave in response to hypothetical situations (Domitrovich & Bierman, 2001; Carlson-Jones et al., 1980). Specifically, greater levels of parent warmth positively related to child use of prosocial solutions, and greater levels of maternal restrictiveness were related to higher use of evasive solutions.

This research has been replicated and extended by Domitrovich and Bierman (2001), in which child social behavior, social problem solving, and social distress were related to parent reports of parent practices in 140 fourth-grade children. Child social behavior and social distress information was obtained from sociometric ratings of social behavior (social and aggressive behavior) and peer evaluation of popularity and victimization. Children also answered questions concerning their perceptions of their own experience of victimization and loneliness. Child social problem-solving skills were obtained from the children's proposed solutions to hypothetical problems; responses were coded as aggressive or prosocial. For the parent information, a written interview containing 14 items describing warm behaviors and 9 items describing negativism, harsh punishment, and punitive control was completed by parents. Additional information concerning maternal and child warmth and negative behaviors was gathered from the children; children were asked verbally the same 23 questions concerning parent practices of both parents and peers.

The researchers found that although maternal warmth behaviors were directly related to child social problem solving, maternal harsh discipline and punitive control had an indirect link to social problem solving via child perceptions of peer support (Domitrovich & Bierman, 2001).

Parent Conflict Management and Child Social Problem Solving

Although the information concerning child abuse and caregiver behaviors is informative in predicting child social problem-solving skills, the underlying mechanism behind these relations may be addressed more fully in research examining caregiver conflict resolution style. A number of studies examining the relation between how parents' solve social conflict and child social problem-solving skills have found a strong relationship between them (Dunn & Herrera, 1997; Fagot, 1998; Fagot & Gauvain, 1997; Goodman, Barfoot, Frye, & Belli, 1999; Pakaslahti, Asplund Peltola, & Keltikangas Jaervinen, 1996).

An earlier study in this area examined the social problem-solving strategies of the families of aggressive and nonaggressive boys in Finland. Similar to research previously discussed on the relation between parent discipline and support, parents of aggressive boys were more likely to identify punishment as a solution to the child's presentation of the conflict. Additionally, parents of aggressive boys were more likely to identify diversion strategies (i.e., deny or divert responsibility). One of the more unique findings of the study, however, was that it was the fathers' social problem-solving skills that most strongly predicted child aggression. The fathers of the nonaggressive boys produced a greater number of strategies that focused on assisting the child in finding a solution to the problem. The fathers of aggressive boys failed to identify solutions to the conflicts presented (Pakaslahti et al., 1996).

Other research studies have shown that the mother's conflict resolution style is also predictive of child conflict resolution style (Dunn, Brown, & Beardsall, 1991; Goodman et al., 1999). In a study of families with children aged 10–13 years, the relationship between marital conflict and children's social problem-solving skills was examined (Goodman et al., 1999). The parents' frequency of marital conflict, conflict resolution style (using reasoning versus aggression), and the likelihood of type of outcome as the result of conflict (escalation of conflict versus resolution and intimacy) were assessed via maternal report. The children's perceptions of their parents' conflict were derived using a questionnaire that assesses children's perceptions of conflict properties (intensity, resolution, and frequency), threat (threat and coping efficacy) and self-blame (self-blame and content). Finally, children's social problem-solving skills were assessed by measuring the effectiveness of solutions to hypothetical peer conflict situations.

Negative conflict characteristics of the mother combined with a high frequency of conflict were predictive of less effective problem-solving skills for children. Less frequent positive conflict characteristics for the mother in the context of lower frequency of conflict also predicted less effective problem solving for children. Surprisingly, the children's perceptions of their parents' conflict did not predict the children's social problem-solving skills, despite moderate correlations between parent and child reports of conflict. Goodman et al. (1999) concluded that children learn problem-solving skills from their parents via modeling, and children's perceptions of parental conflict were less important than modeling or emotional arousal.

Children learn social skills through interacting with others, not by merely observing others interact (Bandura, 1997). This view does not discount observational learning; rather, it extends the notion of modeling to include the importance of the interaction. The dynamic process of interacting within the parent–child relationship is the forum for organizing the developing child's social problem-solving skills.

Parent Behavior and Child Emotion Regulation

Children develop ways to regulate and control emotions from maturation of the cognitive system in conjunction with socialization. Research concerning parent socialization and child regulation has been divided into two categories based on the type of child regulation: effortful control and emotion display control.

Parent Behavior and Child Effortful Control

Research has shown that parent emotionality, beliefs about their own emotions, beliefs about child emotions, and parent/child communication about emotions are related to child behavior and regulation. Gottman and his colleagues have provided a philosophy of *parental meta-emotion* that asserts that parents have definitive and consistent beliefs and behavior about emotions that are predictive of child outcomes such as emotion regulation, effortful control, social competence, and health (Gottman, Katz, & Hooven, 1996; Hooven, Gottman, & Katz, 1995).

In a longitudinal study that followed families with children from age five to eight years, parental meta-emotion was assessed via a semistructured interview about the parent's experience of emotion (Hooven et al., 1995). These interviews were coded for the parents' awareness and acceptance of their own negative emotions, and their acceptance of and assistance with their child's negative emotions. Observational data were also collected concerning social problem solving within the marital relationship, emotional affect experienced and displayed within the marital relationship, and marital emotional expressiveness. Indicators of peer/child and parent/child interaction, child emotion display, behavior problems, child health, and the experience of emotions were collected from parent ratings, teacher ratings, and observations. Assessments of child attention regulation, child vagal tone, child emotion display, and child academic achievement were conducted during child interviews.

The authors found that parent social skills exhibited during parent/child interactions and marital conflict were related to meta-emotion (understanding of emotion, beliefs about expression of emotion, emotion display, emotion assistance with child). Additionally, parent meta-emotion had a direct effect on the child's regulation, and child regulation was predictive of later child health (Hooven et al., 1995). In later work on this longitudinal study, the authors identified a relationship between parent meta-emotion and how the parent interacted with the child (Gottman et al., 1996). Parent/child interactions were then related to early childhood regulatory physiology (vagal tone), which was related to later emotion regulation abilities.

With these results from the Gottman study, other researchers further defined and explored the effect of parent meta-emotion on child regulation. Ramsden and Hubbard (2002) conducted a study of meta-emotion, child regulation, and child aggression in 120 families of fourth-grade children. Child effortful control was identified from parent and teacher ratings; child aggression was identified from teacher ratings alone. The mothers' awareness of emotion and emotion acceptance were identified through the meta-emotion interview used in the previously described Gottman studies. The families' frequencies of expression of positive emotions and of negative emotions were assessed via mother ratings. The authors defined three dimensions of emotion coaching (Gottman's meta-emotion): emotion awareness, emotion acceptance, and expression of positive emotions.

Of the three dimensions of emotion coaching, only the mothers' acceptance of the child's negative emotions was related to inhibitory control. Additionally, family expression of negative emotion was negatively related to inhibitory control. Child regulation was, in turn, related to child aggression (Ramsden & Hubbard, 2002). Thus, it seems that it is the parents' actions during conflict involving their child that may have the strongest direct effect on the child's regulation, in addition to the child's experience of negative emotions within the family. This hypothesis has been supported by other research findings as well (Smith & Walden, 2001).

However, Eisenberg and her colleagues have identified strong relations between both negative and positive maternal emotion expression with child regulation (Eisenberg et al., 2001; Eisenberg et al., 2003). In these studies, maternal expressions of negative and positive emotion were assessed from observational measures and self-report, and child inhibitory control was assessed via observations and mother and teacher reports. The researchers found evidence of a significant and positive relationship between maternal positive emotion expression and child regulation, and a significant and negative relationship between maternal negative emotion expression and child regulation (Eisenberg et al., 2001).

Parent Behavior and Emotion Display Control

Research concerning emotion display control in children has identified similar relations for this type of regulation and parent behavior as found for inhibitory control. Relations have been found between emotion display control and the constructs of family expression of emotion (Carlson-Jones, Abbey, & Cumberland, 1998; Garner, 1999), parent control and acceptance of emotion (McDowell & Parke, 2000), and frequency of parent discussion of emotion (Garner, 1999).

Research concerning emotion display regulation and family expression has identified a consistent relationship between family expression of negative emotion and child display rule use and knowledge (Garner, 1999). In a longitudinal study, child display rule knowledge and emotion detection at the age of eight were related to maternal discourse about emotion four years earlier. Data concerning maternal discourse about emotion was collected via observation of a story-reading task in which the mother was instructed to read a particular story to her child. The frequency of mother-initiated discourse concerning emotion causation or explanation of emotions were coded from these observations. Using multiple regression analyses, the authors identified a significant and positive relation between the frequency of maternal discourse of emotions when the child was four and child knowledge of emotion display rules at the age of eight.

Parent Behavior and Child Emotion Identification and Understanding

The literature examining how the constructs comprising emotion knowledge relate to parent behavior is rather limited. Much of the research concerning emotion identification and parent behavior fails to find a direct relation between the two constructs (Garner, 1999; Garner, Carlson-Jones, Gaddy, & Rennie, 1997). The research that has found a connection between parent behavior and emotion identification has focused on children who have been abused or neglected (Camras et al., 1988; Pollak, Cicchetti, Hornung, & Reed, 2000; Sullivan, Kirkpatrick, & MacDonald, 1995).

Conversely, there is a great deal known about the relationship between child emotion knowledge and parent behavior. Much of the research in this area examines parental (usually maternal) discussion of emotion with the child during semistructured tasks. Most reports from research utilizing this method identify a consistent relation between parental communication of emotion and child knowledge of emotion (Brown & Dunn, 1996; Dunn et al., 1991; Kuebli, Butler, & Fivush, 1995).

However, one study found a relationship between caregiver discussion of emotions and one aspect of child emotion knowledge (Garner, 1999). In this study, maternal discussion of emotion during a wordless picture book-reading task was assessed in low-income mothers of preschoolers. The children's knowledge of emotions was assessed during a structured inter-view. Three aspects of child knowledge of emotions were assessed. First, children's ability to identify emotion in facial expressions was assessed via drawings. Second, children's ability to identify the emotion most likely to be elicited by emotionally charged situations was assessed via audiotapes of vignettes and drawings without facial expressions. Third, the child's ability to identify a person's emotion from their facial expression in spite of a context that would normally elicit an opposite emotion was assessed via drawings and audiotapes of vignettes (role-taking).

The authors of this study failed to find a relationship between mater-nal discourse of emotions and child emotion identification from facial expressions or from situation information; they did report finding a sig-nificant relationship between the child's role-taking ability and maternal discourse of emotion. However, this study did not examine how maternal discourse might be related to the child's aggregate score of emotion knowl-edge (Garner, 1999). More importantly, the children assessed were between the ages of 36 and 70 months of age, and the study was not developmentally oriented. Most other studies examining the relations between these con-structs are longitudinal.

For example, an early study by Dunn et al. (1991) examined maternal dis-cussions of emotion with their three-year-old children and an aggregate of child knowledge of emotions at the age of six. Knowledge of emotions was assessed via the ability to accurately identify emotions and changes in emo-tions from photographs and audiotapes of vignettes. A significant relation was found between maternal discussion of emotion at the age of three and the child's knowledge of emotion at the age of six (Dunn et al., 1991). Other studies examining maternal discourse of emotions at an early age and later child emotion knowledge have found similar results (Brown & Dunn, 1996; Denham, Zoller, & Couchoud, 1994).

Kuebli et al. (1995) provides further support for the hypothesis that maternal discourse about emotions does not begin to influence child knowl-edge of emotions until after the age of five in a study that examined both mother and child discourse about emotions in 18 families. In this study, the mother was instructed to discuss with the child three recent events expected to be salient to the child at three time periods: 40 months of age (Time 1), 58 months of age (Time 2), and 70 months of age (Time 3). Both the child's and mother's use of emotion words during the discussion were counted. No stable pattern of maternal discourse of emotions was detected between Time 1 and Time 2. However, between Time 2 and Time 3, maternal discourse of emotions became consistent. Additionally, a stable pattern of the influence of maternal discourse about emotions on child discourse about emotions was not found.

The authors report that their findings provide support for the notion that maternal discourse about emotion influences the child's developing ability to understand and discuss emotion. While this may be true, their findings also point to a potentially unstable relation between maternal discussion about emotion and the child's emotion understanding. However, the instability found here may also be attributed to the study's low sample size.

A recent report of a dual study of young children's emotion knowledge and attachment style seems to bring about a greater understanding of why maternal discourse may have different effects on child emotion understanding at different ages (Ontai & Thompson, 2002). In the first study, maternal discourse of emotions when the child was three years of age was not related to child knowledge of emotion at that age or to attachment style. However, when the children were five years of age, maternal discourse of emotions in combination with attachment style were predictive of child knowledge of emotions.

It appears that the relationship between maternal discussion of emotions and child knowledge of emotions is not a simplistic one. There are most likely other aspects of the relationship and of the home environment that play a part in the child's developing ability to understand emotions, including but not limited to parent reactions to child emotions and parent expression of emotion (Eisenberg, Cumberland, & Spinrad, 1998).

SUMMARY

The literature concerning the parent factors of knowledge of child development, parent confidence, and parent behaviors indicates these factors are related to the child's social functioning. Additionally, research supports the notion that a parent support program such as Passport would positively influence these parent factors. Thus, we expect that parent support programs like Passport influence child factors indirectly. More specifically, because Passport's services include providing families with knowledge of child development and support services, it is expected that Passport use positively relates to the attributes of knowledge of child development and parent confidence, and that these attributes in parents relate to their behaviors and activities as parents. Additionally, it is expected that parents' behaviors are then directly related to the child's social competence. Much more consistency has been found relating parent knowledge of child development and confidence with parent behaviors than with child outcomes. And there is much more support for the notion that parent behaviors and activities influence child outcomes. Figure 14.1 illustrates these relationships as hypothesized.

In order to test these relationships, we are in the process of conducting a study of a sample of Passport families. Preliminary findings from our work

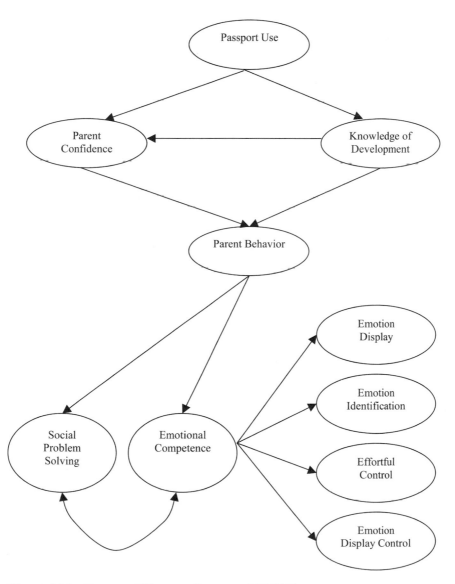

Figure 14.1   Program Effects on Parent and Child Factors

provide evidence that the vast majority of families enrolled in Passport find the services helpful (Figure 14.2).

Furthermore, greater use of these services is related to parenting outcomes (Table 14.1). Specifically, parents who use Passport educational materials are more likely to have higher levels of knowledge of child development, have more confidence in their parenting, and engage more frequently in positive activities with their child. Parents who utilize the program's support services more frequently also engage more frequently in positive activities with their child.

Further work is being conducted to understand how use of the program relates the constructs of parenting and child outcomes. This future work will test the fit of the data collected for the evaluation of Passport with the proposed model of how program use relates to family and child outcomes.

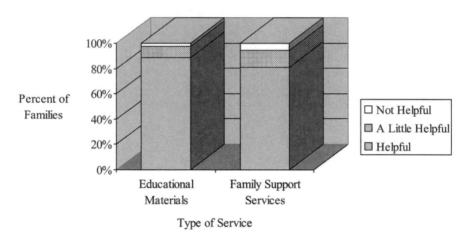

Figure 14.2   Helpfulness of Passport Services

Table 14.1
Correlations among Parent Outcome Variables and Passport Program Use Variables

	Program Use	
Parent Outcomes	*Use of Educational Materials*	*Use of Family Support Services*
Confidence	0.225*	0.188
Knowledge of child development	0.461**	0.179
Parent engagement in activities with child	0.247*	0.285**

** Correlation is significant at the 0.01 level 2-tailed.
* Correlation is significant at the 0.05 level 2-tailed.

By understanding if the proposed theoretical view of how family support programs influence family and child outcomes is accurate, we can provide valuable information to community programs to refine and improve services provided to families.

REFERENCES

Annie E. Casey Foundation. (2002). Kids count in Michigan. *Kids Count data book.* Lansing, MI: Author.

Bandura, A. (1997). Self-efficacy: The exercise of control. New York: Freeman.

Benasich, A.A., & Brooks-Gunn, J. (1996). Maternal attitudes and knowledge of child-rearing: Associations with family and child outcomes. *Child Development, 67,* 1186–1205.

Brown, J.R., & Dunn, J. (1996). Continuities in emotion understanding from three to six years. *Child Development, 67,* 789–802.

Camras, L.A., Ribordy, S., Hill, J., Martino, S., Spacarelli, S., & Stefani, R. (1988). Recognition and posing of emotional expressions by abused children and their mothers. *Developmental Psychology, 24,* 776–781.

Carlson-Jones, D., Abbey, B.B., & Cumberland, A. (1998). The development of display rule knowledge: Linkages with family expressiveness and social competence. *Child Development, 69,* 1209–1222.

Carlson-Jones, D., Rickel, A.U., & Smith, R.L. (1980). Maternal child-rearing practices and social problem-solving strategies among preschoolers. *Developmental Psychology, 16,* 241–242.

Coleman, P.K., & Karraker, K.H. (2003). Maternal self-efficacy beliefs, competence in parenting, and toddlers' behavior and developmental status. *Infant Mental Health Journal, 24,* 126–148.

Conrad, B., Gross, D., Fogg, L., & Ruchala, P. (1992). Maternal confidence, knowledge, and quality of mother/toddler interactions: A preliminary study. *Infant Mental Health Journal, 13,* 353–362.

Contreras, J.M., Rhodes, J.E., & Mangelsdorf, S.C. (1995). Pregnant African American teenagers' expectations of their infants' temperament: Individual and social network influences. *Journal of Applied Developmental Psychology, 16,* 283–295.

Denham, S.A., Zoller, D., & Couchoud, E.A. (1994). Socialization of preschoolers' emotion understanding. *Developmental Psychology, 30,* 928–936.

Dichtelmiller, M., Meisels, S.J., Plunkett, J.W., Bozynski, M.E., Claflin, C., & Mangelsdorf, S.C. (1992). The relationship of parental knowledge to the development of extremely low birth weight infants. *Journal of Early Intervention, 16,* 210–220.

Dodge, K.A., Bates, J.E., & Pettit, G.S. (1990). Mechanisms in the cycle of violence. *Science, 250,* 1678–1683.

Domitrovich, C.E., & Bierman, K.L. (2001). Parenting practices and child social adjustment: Multiple pathways of influence. *Merrill Palmer Quarterly, 47,* 235–263.

Dunn, J., Brown, J., & Beardsall, L. (1991). Family talk about feeling states and children's later understanding of others' emotions. *Developmental Psychology, 27,* 448–455.

Dunn, J., & Herrera, C. (1997). Conflict resolution with friends, siblings, and mothers: A developmental perspective. *Aggressive Behavior, 23,* 343–357.

East, P.L., Matthews, K.L., & Felice, M.E. (1994). Qualities of adolescent mothers' parenting. *Journal of Adolescent Health, 15,* 163–168.

Eisenberg, N., Cumberland, A., & Spinrad, T.L. (1998). Parental socialization of emotion. *Psychological Inquiry, 9,* 241–273.

Eisenberg, N., Gershoff, E.T., Fabes, R.A., Shepard, S.A., Cumberland, A.J., Losoya, S.H., Guthrie, I. K., & Murphy, B. C. (2001). Mothers' emotional expressivity and children's behavior problems and social competence: Mediation through children's regulation. *Developmental Psychology, 37,* 475–490.

Eisenberg, N., Valiente, C., Morris, A.S., Fabes, R.A., Cumberland, A., Reiser, M., Gershoff, E. T., Shepard, S. A., & Losoya, S. (2003). Longitudinal relations among parental emotional expressivity, children's regulation, and quality of socioemotional functioning. *Developmental Psychology, 39,* 3–19.

Fagot, B.I. (1998). Social problem solving: Effect of context and parent sex. *International Journal of Behavioral Development, 22,* 389–401.

Fagot, B.I., & Gauvain, M. (1997). Mother-child problem solving: Continuity through the early childhood years. *Developmental Psychology, 33,* 480–488.

Fewell, R.R., & Wheeden, C.A. (1998). A pilot study of intervention with adolescent mothers and their children: A preliminary examination of child outcomes. *Topics in Early Childhood Special Education, 18,* 18–25.

Fry, P.S. (1985). Relations between teenagers' age, knowledge, expectations and maternal behaviour. *British Journal of Developmental Psychology, 3,* 47–55.

Garner, P.W. (1999). Continuity in emotion knowledge from preschool to middle-childhood and relation to emotion socialization. *Motivation and Emotion, 23,* 247–266.

Garner, P.W., Carlson-Jones, D., Gaddy, G., & Rennie, K.M. (1997). Low-income mothers' conversations about emotions and their children's emotional competence. *Social Development, 6,* 37–52.

Goodman, S.H., Barfoot, B., Frye, A.A., & Belli, A.M. (1999). Dimensions of marital conflict and children's social problem-solving skills. *Journal of Family Psychology, 13,* 33–45.

Gottman, J.M., Katz, L.F., & Hooven, C. (1996). Parental meta-emotion philosophy and the emotional life of families: Theoretical models and preliminary data. *Journal of Family Psychology, 10,* 243–268.

Gross, D., Fogg, L., Webster-Stratton, C., Garvey, C., Julion, W., & Grady, J. (2003). Parent training of toddlers in day care in low-income urban communities. *Journal of Consulting and Clinical Psychology, 71,* 261–278.

Hooven, C., Gottman, J.M., & Katz, L.F. (1995). Parental meta-emotion structure predicts family and child outcomes. *Cognition & Emotion, 9,* 229–264.

Kuebli, J., Butler, S., & Fivush, R. (1995). Mother-child talk about past emotions: Relations of maternal language and child gender over time. *Cognition and Emotion, 9,* 265–283.

Larsen, J.J., & Juhasz, A.M. (1985). The effects of knowledge of child development and social-emotional maturity on adolescent attitudes toward parenting. *Adolescence, 20,* 823–839.

McDowell, D.J., & Parke, R.D. (2000). Differential knowledge of display rules for positive and negative emotions: Influences from parents, influences on peers. *Social Development, 9,* 415–432.

Miller Heyl, J., MacPhee, D., & Fritz, J.J. (1998). DARE to be you: A family-support, early prevention program. *Journal of Primary Prevention, 18,* 257–285.

Ontai, L.L., & Thompson, R.A. (2002). Patterns of attachment and maternal discourse effects on children's emotion understanding from 3 to 5 years of age. *Social Development, 11,* 433–450.

Pakaslahti, L., Asplund Peltola, R.L., & Keltikangas Jaervinen, L. (1996). Parents' social problem-solving strategies in families with aggressive and non-aggressive boys. *Aggressive Behavior, 22,* 345–356.

Panzarine, S., Slater, E., & Sharps, P. (1995). Coping, social support, and depressive symptoms in adolescent mothers. *Journal of Adolescent Health, 17,* 113–119.

Parker, F.L., Boak, A.Y., Griffin, K.W., Ripple, C., & Peay, L. (1999). Parent–child relationship, home learning environment, and school readiness. *School Psychology Review, 28,* 413–425.

Pisterman, S., Firestone, P., McGrath, P., Goodman, J.T., Webster, I., Mallory, R., & Goffin, B. (1992). The effects of parent training on parenting stress and sense of competence. *Canadian Journal of Behavioural Science, 24,* 41–58.

Pollak, S.D., Cicchetti, D., Hornung, K., & Reed, A. (2000). Recognizing emotion in faces: Developmental effects of child abuse and neglect. *Developmental Psychology, 36,* 679–688.

Pomerleau, A., Malcuit, G., Seguin, R., Lamarre, G., Moreau, J., & Jeliu, G. (1998). Adolescent mothers' report of their nine-month-old infants' temperament: Psychosocial variables, infants' neonatal characteristics, and psychomotor development. *Archives de Psychologie, 66,* 67–84.

Ramsden, S.R., & Hubbard, J.A. (2002). Family expressiveness and parental emotion coaching: Their role in children's emotion regulation and aggression. *Journal of Abnormal Child Psychology, 30,* 657–667.

Rickard, K.M., Graziano, W., & Forehand, R. (1984). Parental expectations and childhood deviance in clinic-referred and non-clinic children. *Journal of Clinical Child Psychology, 13,* 179–186.

Rivara, F.P., & Howard, D. (1982). Parental knowledge of child development and injury risks. *Journal of Developmental and Behavioral Pediatrics, 3,* 103–105.

Smith, M., & Walden, T. (1999). Understanding feelings and coping with emotional situations: A comparison of maltreated and nonmaltreated preschoolers. *Social Development, 8,* 93–116.

Smith, M., & Walden, T. (2001). An exploration of African American preschool-aged children's behavioral regulation in emotionally arousing situations. *Child Study Journal, 31,* 13–45.

Sullivan, L.A., Kirkpatrick, S.W., & MacDonald, P.M. (1995). Interpretations of facial expressions of emotion by sexually abused and non-abused girls. *Journal of Child Sexual Abuse, 4,* 45–61.

Teti, D.M., O'Connell, M.A., & Reiner, C.D. (1996). Parenting sensitivity, parental depression and child health: The mediational role of parental self-efficacy. *Early Development and Parenting, 5,* 237–250.

Thompson, R.W., Ruma, P.R., Schuchmann, L.F., & Burke, R.V. (1996). A cost-effectiveness evaluation of parent training. *Journal of Child and Family Studies, 5,* 415–429.

Williams, T.M., Joy, L.A., Travis, L., Gotowiec, A., Blum-Steele, M., Aiken, L. S., Painter, S. L., & Davidson, S. M. (1987). Transition to motherhood: A longitudinal study. *Infant Mental Health Journal, 8,* 251–265.

Wint, E., & Brown, J. (1987). Promoting effective parenting: A study of two methods in Kingston, Jamaica. *Child Welfare, 66,* 507–516.

INDEX

AAI. *See* Adult Attachment Interview

Abecedarian Early Childhood Intervention, 223

ABRs. *See* Auditory brain stem responses

Academic achievement: child-care impact on, 243; earnings supplement programs impact on, 238–39; socioemotional development predictor of, 248; from welfare and employment programs, 242

Adaptive characteristics, individual differences in, 5

Addiction: conflicting views of, 31; criminal act of, 31

ADHD (Attention Deficit Hyperactivity Disorder): aggression from, 162; alertness marker for, 167; among American Indian Children, 262; analysis levels of, 160–63; anterior attention network of, 166; antisociality with, 162; arousal regulation with, 166; behavioral symptoms of, 159; birth weight impact on, 175; brain structure concerning, 163, 165; causes and determinants of, 158, 177; cognitive control with, 168–70; cognitive research on, 164–67; conduct disorder with, 169; cortical arousal in, 171; cost of, 157; cultural and ethnicity effects on, 176; delay-reward gradient of, 168; developmental pathways to, 172, 177; disease entity of, 161; dopamine activity in, 167–68, 170, 175; dysfunctional parenting for, 174; ecological contribution to, 175–75; EEG of, 167; extraversion in, 171; extrinsic causal factors in, 172–73; family and parenting correlates of, 173–74; family and peer context for, 161–62; genetic basis of, 161, 173; genotype-environment correlations to, 162; health problems with, 158; heritability of, 161; hyperactive-impulsive type of, 160; incentive response with, 167; incidence increase of, 174; industrial toxins impact on, 175; inhibition control impact on, 99; medical treatment for, 157;

CONTRIBUTING
AUTHORS AND EDITORS

NATACHA A. AKSHOOMOFF's research and clinical work has been focused on typical and atypical development for over 15 years. She received her Ph.D. in Clinical Psychology from the UCSD/SDSU Joint Doctoral Program, completed her internship at the University of Florida, and received her B.S. in Psychobiology from UCLA. She is currently a faculty member in the Psychiatry Department at the University of California, San Diego and a Research Scientist at the Child and Adolescent Services Research Center at Children's Hospital San Diego. Her current research focuses on evaluation and training of assessment practices in clinical and school settings for children with autistic spectrum disorders.

LYNNE ANDREOZZI, Ph.D., is a psychologist at the Infant Development Center at Women and Infants Hospital in Rhode Island. She holds a doctorate from the University of Rhode Island in Child Development and School Psychology. Her work encompasses the assessment of infants and young children, and behavioral consultation with area professionals and caregivers. Her current research interests include attachment and substance exposed infants. As well as staff faculty at the Infant Development Center, Dr. Andreozzi Fontaine is an Associate Professor of Psychology at the Community College of Rhode Island. Dr. Andreozzi Fontaine has utilized the NNNS for clinical, research, and teaching purposes

LINDSEY APPIAH, J.D., is an attorney in Washington, D.C. She received her Bachelor's Degree from Brown University. While at Brown, she focused her studies on Community Health, and specifically on maternal and child health. Her interest in at risk children and families stems from 20 years of involvement with foster care both as a member of a family who took in foster children and as a clerk for the Massachusetts Probate and Family Court. She received her J.D. from Georgetown University Law Center.

JESSICA V. BARNES, PH.D. is a Research Associate and a Research Fellow for University Outreach and Engagement at Michigan State University. She received her doctoral degree in Developmental Psychology in 2003. She currently serves as chairperson of the Community Based Scholarship Team at Michigan State University. Her major areas of research focus on the development of collaborations with communities to conduct program evaluation, understanding how community and school based prevention and intervention programs influence family and child outcomes, developing methods for sustaining community and school partnerships, and child cognitive and social-emotional development within the contexts of family, neighborhood, and school.

LAURA V. BATES, M.A. is a research associate for University-Community Partnerships & the Institute for Children, Youth, and Families, at Michigan State University. She has extensive experience managing community research projects and developing university-community partnerships, including statewide afterschool programs and programs for families with 0-5 age children. Ms. Bates has published extensively on topics related to the factors associated with successful outcomes among preschool children born to low-income adolescent mothers. Before coming to the university she had 20 years of experience in program development and management in the areas of early childhood and youth development.

JEANNE BROOKS-GUNN is the Virginia and Leonard Marx Professor of Child Development and Education at Teachers College and the College of Physicians and Surgeons at Columbia University and co-director of the National Center for Children and Families. Her research centers on designing and evaluating interventions and policies aimed at enhancing the well-being of children living in poverty. She has received the Urie Bronfenbrenner Award for lifetime contribution to developmental psychology, the Jon B. Hill Award from the Society for Research in Child Development, and the James McKeen Cattell Fellow Award from the American Psychological Society. She was elected Margaret Mead Fellow for 2004 by the American Academy of Political and Social Science.

NANCY EISENBERG, Ph.D. is Regents' Professor of Psychology at Arizona State University. Her research interests pertain to social, emotional, and moral development. Her books include *The Caring Child* (1992), *The Roots of Prosocial Behavior in Children* (with Paul Mussen, 1989), and *How Children Develop* (with Robert Siegler and Judy DeLoach, 2003). She has been a recipient of Research Scientist Development Awards and a Research Scientist Award from the National Institutes of Health (NIH and NIMH). She was President of the Western Psychological Association; associate editor of *Merrill-Palmer Quarterly* and *Personality and Social Psychology Bulletin*; and editor of *Psychological Bulletin*.

ROBERT N. EMDE, M.D., is Emeritus Professor of Psychiatry at the University of Colorado Health Sciences Center. He serves as Scientific Adviser for the World Association of Infant Mental Health and was previously President of that organization. He was President of the Society for Research in Child Development and Editor of the *SRCD Monographs*. He is Scientific Advisor for the Board of Professional Standards of the American Psychoanalytic Association and is Head of the College of Research Fellows of the International Psychoanalytic Association. Dr. Emde's research interests include early social emotional development and the evaluation of early intervention programs. He served as a national coordinator for a follow-up study of a 17-site national randomized trial of first wave Early Head Start programs.

KEVIN EVERHART, Ph.D. is a Clinical Child Psychologist and Community Psychologist with expertise in infant mental health, child development, and early intervention. A graduate of the University of Minnesota, Dr.Everhart completed his doctoral training at the University of South Carolina. Dr. Everhart recently completed a post-doctoral research fellowship in the UCHSC Developmental Psychobiology Research Training Program, during which time he began his work with the Early Head Start National Research Consortium. Dr. Everhart currently holds appointments in the departments of Psychology and Psychiatry at the University of Colorado Denver and Health Sciences Center.

HIRAM E. FITZGERALD received his Ph.D. in developmental psychology in 1967 from the University of Denver. He is a Fellow of the American Psychological Association and the American Psychological Society. Currently, he is Assistant Provost for University Outreach and Engagement and University Distinguished Professor of Psychology at Michigan State University. His research has focused on biobehavioral organization during early infancy, factors regulating father-child relationships, and the impact of community network prevention programs for families with birth to three age children, and the etiology of alcoholism He is Executive Director of the World Association for Infant Mental Health.

JUDITH M. GARDNER received her Ph.D. from City University of New York in Biopsychology. Her research interests focus on studies of brain-behavior relations over early development, specifically how early arousal and attention in high-risk neonates affects subsequent autoregulation and cognitive and motor development. She is a member of numerous professional societies including the Society for Research in Child Development and the International Society for the Study of Behavioral Development. She is a Fellow of the American Psychological Association, and is a Senior Research Scientist and founding member of the Department of Infant Development at the New York State Institute for Basic Research, Staten Island, NY, heads the Infant Neurobehavioral Laboratory and currently is the Acting Chair.

LISA GENNETIAN is a Senior Research Associate at MDRC. Dr. Gennetian's expertise is in the application of experimental and nonexperimental techniques to answer questions about the effects of social programs on the development of low-income children and the well-being of their families. She is a senior researcher in MDRC's children and families' policy area and has written numerous articles in leading academic journals and policy reports. Dr. Gennetian applies instrumental variables techniques to experimental data to examine the effects of welfare, employment and anti-poverty policies on children's outcomes, family structure and relationships, and child care. Dr. Gennetian holds a Ph.D. in Economics from Cornell University, specializing in economics of the family.

BERNARD Z. KARMEL received his Ph.D. from George Washington University in Experimental Psychology. His research uses neurophysiological, psychophysiological, and neurobehavioral techniques to study perception, cognition, and motor development in normal, brain-insulted, and cocaine-exposed infants. He is a member of numerous professional societies including The College on Problems of Drug Dependency and The International Society for Infant Research. He is a Fellow of the American Psychological Association and a Senior Research Scientist and Head of the Infant Neurophysiological Development Laboratory, New York State Institute for Basic Research where he helped found the Department of Infant Development, and holds appointments in the Graduate School, City University of New York.

BARRY M. LESTER, Ph.D., is Professor of Psychiatry & Human Behavior and Pediatrics at Brown Medical School. He is founder and Director of the Infant Development Center at Women & Infants Hospital and Bradley Hospital and Brown Medical School. Dr. Lester received his Ph.D. in Developmental Psychology from Michigan State University. His specialty is developmental processes in infants at risk, including infants with prenatal substance exposure. Dr. Lester is currently a member of the National Advisory Council on Drug Abuse and member of the Expert Panel at the National Institute of Environmental Health Sciences Center for the Evaluation of Risks to Human Reproduction. He is past president of the International Association for Infant Mental Health.

PAMELA A. MORRIS is a Senior Research Associate at MDRC and Deputy Director of MDRC's policy area on family well-being and children's development. An expert on the effects of welfare and antipoverty policies on children, Dr. Morris leads MDRC's effort to examine the effects of social policies on children's development. Her newest work leverages data from an experimental study to examine how changes in parents' depression affect the development of children and adolescents in low-income families. She received a bachelor's degree from Columbia University and a doctorate in Developmental Psychology from Cornell University

JOEL T. NIGG is an associate professor in the Psychology Department at Michigan State University. He obtained an A.B. from Harvard University, a Masters Degree in Social Work from The University of Michigan, and a Ph.D. in Clinical Psychology from the University of California at Berkeley. He conducts research on the neuropsychological, genetic, and family correlates of attention deficit hyperactivity disorder. His scientific work is funded by the National Institutes of Health. Dr. Nigg sits on a National Institute of Mental Health scientific review group and on the editorial boards of several major child psychopathology scientific journals. Dr. Nigg also is a fully licensed clinician who also supervises doctoral trainees in clinical psychology when conducting child evaluations for their clinical practicum.

MICHELLE CHRISTENSEN SARCHE is a clinical psychologist with expertise in early child development in American Indian and Alaska Native communities. She has been on the faculty of the American Indian and Alaska Native Programs since 1998, where she is Assistant Professor of Psychiatry. Her research is funded by the National Institute of Mental Health and focuses on intergenerational attachment and parenting among

Northern Plains American Indian mothers and their young children. Dr. Sarche is a member of the Lac Courte Oreilles Band of Ojibwe.

DANIEL S. SHAW is Professor of Psychology and Psychiatry at the University of Pittsburgh. E received his Ph.D. in child clinical and developmental psychology from the University of Virginia in 1988. His primary research interest involves tracing the developmental precursors of antisocial behavior in at-risk children. His most recent work applies an ecologically- and developmentally-based intervention for low-income toddlers at risk for early conduct problems. He was awarded the Boyd McCandless Young Scientist Award by APA's Division of Developmental Psychology and holds a Research Scientist Award from the National Institute of Mental Health, has served on several editorial review boards of journals and published extensively on risk factors associated with conduct problems in early childhood.

LOU ANNA KIMSEY SIMON, Ph.D., is the 20th President of Michigan State University. Prior to assuming the role of president, she was provost and vice president for academic affairs at Michigan State University, and provost of the Michigan State University College of Law. She is regarded nationally as a powerful advocate of a research-active, student-centered university that is an engaged partner with society, in the land grant tradition. Dr. Simon is deeply committed to the development of effective university-community partnerships that focus on solution-based approaches to the problems of children, youth, and families. Most recently, she co-edited with Maureen Kenny, Karen Kiley-Brabeck and Richard Lerner, *Learning to Serve: Promoting Civil Society Through Service Learning* .

PAUL SPICER is a cultural anthropologist with expertise in substance abuse and child development in American Indian and Alaska Native communities. Since 1995, he has been on the faculty of the American Indian and Alaska Native Programs at the University of Colorado, where he is now Associate Professor of Psychiatry, with primary responsibilities for multimethod research in early childhood development and intervention. His current research, some of which is reported here, is funded by the National Center for Minority Health and Health Disparities, the National Institute for Child Health and Human Development, the National Institute of Mental Health, and the Robert Wood Johnson Foundation.

BRIAN S. STAFFORD. Dr. Stafford is a graduate of the Tulane School of Medicine and the School of Public Health and Tropical Medicine. He completed training in Pediatrics, Adult, and Child and Adolescent Psychiatry at the University of Kentucky, and completed advanced training in cultural psychiatry at the University of Cape Town, South Africa. He is currently a faculty member in the Departments of Pediatrics and Child Psychiatry at Tulane where he is Training Director for Child and Adolescent Psychiatry and the combined Pediatrics/Psychiatry/Child Psychiatry residency program. He is helping the state of Louisiana develop an integrated system of care for infants, toddlers, their parents, and the providers and agencies that serve these families.

AUBYN STAHMER has worked in the area of autism for over 15 years. She trained in applied behavior analysis at the University of California, San Diego. Dr. Stahmer helped to found the Childrens Autism Intervention Center and Childrens Toddler School at Childrens Hospital. Dr. Stahmer is a currently a research scientist at Childrens Hospital and UC San Diego. Her research involves examining the effectiveness of early intervention in young children with autism, individualizing early intervention to meet the specific needs of children and families, and better understanding community early intervention systems.

CELESTE STURDEVANT REED is a research associate at Michigan State University Outreach and Engagement, University-Community Partnerships. She has worked with youth development, community problem-solving, evaluation and professional development efforts. She has participated in early childhood, regional youth development and after-school evaluation projects. Most of her evaluation efforts focus on building the capacity of evaluation partners, carried out through formal training as well as individual consultation. She has published extensively in the area of positive approaches to community development and program evaluation.

BETTY TABLEMAN, M.P.A., is editor and writer of BEST PRACTICE BRIEFS, succinct presentations of concepts, processes, models and tools for human services professionals which can be found on the web at *www. outreach.msu.edu/bpbriefs*. She was previously director of prevention services for the Michigan Department of Mental Health. In that role she developed infant mental health services, community collaboratives and child care expulsion prevention services, among others. She is past president of the Michigan Infant Mental Health Association and has been recognized by professional organizations for her public service, including the World Association for Infant Mental Health (Sonya Bemporad Award, 2002); and the Michigan Association for Evaluation ("Friend of Evaluation" Award, 2003).

NITIKA TOLANI received her M.A. in Applied Psychology from Teachers College, Columbia University in 2000 and is currently a doctoral candidate in Developmental Psychology at Teachers College, Columbia University. She also works as a Graduate Research Fellow at the National Center for Children and Families, a research and policy organization at Teachers College. Her general research interests include the effects of families, peers, and communities on the development of urban at-risk youth and the application of this knowledge to resiliency-focused social policy, prevention and intervention program development.

LAURIE A. VAN EGEREN, Ph.D. is the Assistant Director of University-Community Partnerships, in charge of Research and Evaluation at Michigan State University. She is the Principal Investigator for the state evaluation of the 21st Century Community Learning Centers programs. Dr. Van Egeren has expertise in program evaluation, quantitative data analysis, development from infancy through adolescence, and evaluation capacity building in communities, early childhood programs, and human service organizations. She conducts both basic and applied research in the areas of family relations, school readiness, and socioemotional development. Dr. Van Egeren is an Education Policy Fellowship program Fellow.

ELLEN E. WHIPPLE, Ph.D., A.C.S.W. is an Associate Professor at the School of Social Work at Michigan State University. She earned her M.S.W. from the University of Michigan in 1984, and Ph.D. in Social Welfare at the University of Washington in 1989. Ellen has completed two post-doctoral fellowships, the first with Zero to Three/National Center for Infants, Toddlers and Their Families in 1993, and the second as part of the Child Welfare Fellows Program at the University of California at Berkeley in 1998. Her research and clinical work focus on child abuse and neglect, especially in examining the effectiveness of service delivery systems in addressing the needs of maltreating families through prevention and early intervention.

JACQUELINE WOOD, M.A., Office of Early Childhood Education and Family Services, Michigan Department of Education. Ms. Wood is an early childhood education consultant currently managing two grant programs to intermediate school districts for the development and provision of parent involvement and education programs. Her work in this area has included a focus on strengthening collaborative partnerships between education and other community early childhood partners for the more effective delivery of services to families with young children. She also serves on numerous collaborative bodies at the state level related to child injury and death prevention, early childhood professional development, and early childhood systems design.

BARRY ZUCKERMAN M.D., is Professor of Pediatrics and Public Health at Boston University School of Medicine, and Chief of Pediatrics at the University's teaching hospital. Dr. Zuckerman has developed and implemented programs in Boston and throughout the country, which emphasize prevention and extend beyond traditional medical care, including The Pathways to Success Program (child development and parenting information), The Family Advocacy Program (legal advocacy and policy work), The Women and Infant's Program (addiction counseling in a pediatric setting, and The Boston Training Center for Infants supports doctors, nurses, social workers, educators, graduate students, and others who work with young children and their parents.